NOBEL LECTURES PEACE

NOBEL LECTURES

INCLUDING PRESENTATION SPEECHES
AND LAUREATES' BIOGRAPHIES

PHYSICS

CHEMISTRY

PHYSIOLOGY OR MEDICINE

LITERATURE

PEACE

PUBLISHED FOR THE NOBEL FOUNDATION
BY
ELSEVIER PUBLISHING COMPANY
AMSTERDAM – LONDON – NEW YORK

NOBEL LECTURES

INCLUDING PRESENTATION SPEECHES
AND LAUREATES' BIOGRAPHIES

PEACE

1951-1970

VOLUME 3

Edited by

FREDERICK W. HABERMAN

*Professor of Communication Arts
The University of Wisconsin–Madison,
Madison, Wis., U.S.A.*

PUBLISHED FOR THE NOBEL FOUNDATION
IN 1972 BY
ELSEVIER PUBLISHING COMPANY
AMSTERDAM – LONDON – NEW YORK

ELSEVIER PUBLISHING COMPANY
335 JAN VAN GALENSTRAAT
P.O. BOX 211, AMSTERDAM, THE NETHERLANDS

AMERICAN ELSEVIER PUBLISHING COMPANY, INC.
52 VANDERBILT AVENUE
NEW YORK, N.Y. 10017

LIBRARY OF CONGRESS CARD NUMBER 68–20650
ISBN 0–444–41010–4

PRINTED IN THE NETHERLANDS BY
KONINKLIJKE DRUKKERIJ G. J. THIEME N.V., NIJMEGEN
BOOK DESIGN: HELMUT SALDEN

Foreword

In his foreword to the Nobel Lectures in Physics, Chemistry, and Physiology or Medicine the then President of the Nobel Foundation, Professor Arne Tiselius, wrote:

«The Nobel Foundation has, by agreement, granted the Elsevier Publishing Company of Amsterdam the right to publish in English language the Nobel Lectures for 1901–1962. The lectures in the five Nobel Prize domains: Physics, Chemistry, Physiology or Medicine, Literature, and Peace will appear separately, according to the subject ... Short biographical notes and the presentation speeches will also be included.

The Nobel Foundation has since 1901 each year published *Les Prix Nobel* which contains all Nobel Lectures of that year, always in the language in which they were given, as well as short biographies of the laureates. In addition an account is given of the prize–award ceremonies in Stockholm and in Oslo, including presentation addresses and after-dinner speeches, *etc.*, thus covering the whole field of Nobel Prize events of one rapticular year.

In the Elsevier series the Nobel Lectures, presentation addresses, and biographies will now be more readily accessible to those who wish to follow the development in only certain of the Nobel subjects, as reflected in the prize awards during the years passed. For practical reasons English has been chosen as common language for this series.

It is the hope of the Nobel Foundation that the volumes to be published by Elsevier Publishing Company will supplement *Les Prix Nobel* and that together they will serve to spread knowledge of those landmarks on the road of human progress that have been honoured by Nobel Prizes.»

The publication of the Nobel Lectures in Peace brings the beginning of this series to completion. It is hoped that these lectures may prove to be a stimulating message from the persons and institutions who, during the years since 1901, have been awarded the Peace Prize for their outstanding achievements in promoting the great idea of fraternity among nations.

Aase Lionaes–Chairman, Nobel Committee of the Norwegian Parliament

Permissions

I gratefully acknowledge the permissions given by publishers and others to use or reprint several speeches and other material contained in these volumes:

Nicholas Murray Butler, radio address of December 12, 1931, published December 13, 1931. Copyright © 1931 by The New York Times Company. Reprinted by permission.

Dag Hammarskjöld, four lines of poetry from page 31 of *Markings*. Copyright © 1964 translation by Alfred A.Knopf Inc. and Faber & Faber Ltd. Quoted by permission.

Johannes Irgens, speech of August 24, 1912. French text in the *Annuaire de l'Institut de Droit International, 1912* (Paris: A.Pedone, 1912, Vol.25, pp.539–542) used for translation by permission of the Institut de Droit International.

Fridtjof Nansen, «No More War». Norwegian text in *Eventyrlyst–Ingen krig mere: To taler av Fridtjof Nansen* used for translation by permission of Jacob Dybwads Forlag, Aschehougs Forlag, and the Estate of Fridtjof Nansen.

Elihu Root, Nobel lecture. From *Addresses on International Subjects*, pp.153–174 (edited by Robert Bacon and James B.Scott, Harvard University Press). Reprinted by permission.

Carlos Saavedra Lamas, radio address of November 29, 1936, published November 30, 1936. Copyright © 1936 by The New York Times Company. Reprinted by permission.

F.W.H.

Volume 1 covers the years 1901–1925; Volume 2, the years 1926–1950; Volume 3, the years 1951–1970.
For the Editor's Introduction and Acknowledgments, see Volume 1 pp. VII–XVIII.

Contents

ERRATA

p. 43, last paragraph, 1st line, should read:
        But it was many years before he was able ... *etc.*
p. 65, asterisk footnote, 1st line, should read:
        Mr. Hambro, also at this time president of the Odelsting, a section
        of the Norwegian ... *etc.*
p. 109, footnote 1, 1st line, should read:
        These words in Norwegian, NESTEKJAERLIGHET ER REALPOLITIKK, are
        inscrib-
p. 255, Selected Bibliography, last line, should read:
        Cordier, Andrew W., and Wilder Foote, eds., *The Quest for Peace:
        The Dag Hammarskjöld*

Peace 1951

LÉON JOUHAUX

Presentation

by Gunnar Jahn*, Chairman of the Nobel Committee

Alfred Nobel's Peace Prize is this year awarded to Léon Jouhaux.

Léon Jouhaux can look back upon a long life of work and struggle to elevate the working classes–and first of all to improve their conditions. To fight through the trade unions to raise the standard of living of the working class is an important and noble thing to do. But many others have devoted themselves to such work, and that alone would not have brought him here today to receive the Nobel Peace Prize. He is here because from his earliest years he has time after time thrown himself into the fight for peace and against war, doing so in the International Federation of Trade Unions, in the International Labor Office, the League of Nations, the United Nations, and the European Movement. Cooperation reaching across national frontiers and the removal of social and economic inequalities both within nations and between nations have for him been the most important means of combating war. But he has had an even broader objective: to mold a social environment capable of breeding what he calls the man of tomorrow, the man who will be able to create a society in which war is no longer possible.

Léon Jouhaux was born in 1878[1], the son of a factory worker. He went to work himself at the age of thirteen, eventually becoming a worker in the match factory like his father and soon entering the French trade-union movement. In 1909 he became secretary of the national organization [C.G.T.][2] with which he has been associated throughout his life, remaining loyal to it in bad times as well as in good.

In his book *Le Syndicalisme français*, which was published in 1913 and which naturally bears the stamp of that time, he describes the organization

---

* Mr. Jahn, also at this time director of the Bank of Norway, delivered this speech on December 10, 1951, in the Auditorium of the University of Oslo. At its conclusion he presented the Nobel medal and diploma to the laureate, who accepted with a brief speech of thanks. The translation of Mr. Jahn's speech is based on the Norwegian text in *Les Prix Nobel en 1951*, which also carries a French translation.

1. Most sources agree upon 1879 as the correct date.
2. See Jouhaux's lecture, p. 13, fn. 2

of the French trade-union movement, its aims and methods. What is remarkable in a book dealing mainly with collective action is his emphatic conclusion that, in the final analysis, it is essential to awaken and to educate the individual to prepare himself for the great and arduous task of building the society of the future.

Jouhaux has been in the forefront of the French trade-union movement in a difficult and troubled time. War and economic depression have followed hard upon each other, and the trade-union movement has been split asunder, reunified, and split again. Faithful to his principles, Jouhaux has always done his utmost to prevent disunity, but if a schism could not be avoided, he has given his allegiance to the non-Communist section of the trade unions. He has always firmly believed that a trade union should have room for everyone and that it should build on the solidarity of the working class as such, remaining outside political parties. Consequently, he himself has never been an active politician except in the conflict with antidemocratic forces such as fascism in the period between the two wars and communism after the last war. He served the Popular Front in France between the wars and in recent years has taken part in the fight against communism.

We cannot evaluate Jouhaux's contribution without knowing something of his activity in the French trade-union movement, it is true, but today we are concerned primarily with his intensive work for international cooperation and peace.

Even in his youth–before the earliest signs of the First World War – he was involved in trying to reduce national antagonisms and in fighting against war. The most significant example of this activity was the plan for a meeting in Berlin in 1911 between representatives of French, German, and British trade unions to formulate a protest against war. The background of this meeting was the tense situation between France and Germany resulting from their conflicting interests in Morocco. France had occupied the capital of Morocco, and in July Kaiser Wilhelm[1] had sent a warship to Agadir to protect German interests. In both countries this released a wave of nationalism that could easily have led to war.

The meeting in Berlin did not achieve the importance expected. At Germany's suggestion, only a few delegates from the C.G.T. went to Berlin, ostensibly to study the German trade-union movement, but this so-called

1. William (Wilhelm) II (1859–1941), emperor of Germany and king of Prussia (1888–1918).

study culminated in a large public demonstration against war. Later the same year another meeting was held in Paris, attended by representatives from Germany, Spain, and Great Britain.

Jouhaux speaks of both these meetings in his book *Le Syndicalisme français* in the chapter entitled «Contre le guerre». This chapter is a fiery appeal to the workers to oppose war, an appeal which lays great stress on the fact that private capitalism and competition in heavy industry between different countries constitute the main reason for war. It is not at all surprising that Jouhaux saw the situation in this light, for at that time France was building up her colonial empire, and Germany's industry was expanding apace. His attack was therefore directed as much against his own country's colonial policy as against Germany, and he fearlessly opposed the wave of nationalism which was sweeping through both countries. And even though we have now learned that the danger of war is not lessened by individual states' having control over private capital, his appeal will still stand as one of the major attempts made prior to World War I to mobilize the forces of labor against war. It is also the first serious attempt to establish contact between French and German workers. He emphasizes the importance of this, for, he says, in this way a start could be made to erase the bitterness and hatred which had plagued relations between the peoples of France and Germany for the past forty years. «We are thus creating between the French and German people the ‹entente cordiale› so desirable for the peace of the world.»

There were many people at that time–Jouhaux among them–who believed that through mass action the workers would be able to prevent war. But no appeal–including the last, which was sent by the C.G.T. in July of 1914–was to succeed. As we all know, war broke out in 1914, and Jouhaux took an active part in it, for this war was in defense of all that he himself had worked for throughout his life: democracy and freedom. He declared that a German victory would mean the destruction of democracy and freedom in Europe.

Yet all wars end, and everyone who looks ahead must try to find the way to a lasting peace. This Jouhaux sought to do. Already in the autumn of 1914, the C.G.T. traced the outlines of a peace program which was in essence the same as that proposed by the American Federation of Labor[1], and its general theme was seen again in President Wilson's[2] Fourteen Points.

1. See Jouhaux's lecture, p. 18, fn. 1.
2. (Thomas) Woodrow Wilson (1856–1924), recipient of the Nobel Peace Prize for 1919.

Once the war was over, Jouhaux resumed his position in the C.G.T. Thereafter, however, he was to work in a larger area.

In 1919 he was appointed a member of the committee on labor questions at the Paris Peace Conference, and so had the opportunity of taking part in the founding of the International Labor Organization. In the same year he was elected a member of its Governing Body, a position which he still holds. In 1919 he was also elected vice-president of the International Federation of Trade Unions in Amsterdam.

Let us first of all consider Léon Jouhaux's contribution as a member of the International Labor Office. This organization is the only major international institution linked with the League of Nations which has survived the war. It is also the organization with the widest field of activity. Its objective is to remove one of the great obstacles to the realization of a lasting peace; in the words of its Constitution:

Whereas, The League of Nations has for its object the establishment of universal peace, and such a peace can be established only if it is based upon social justice;

And whereas, Conditions of labor exist involving such injustice, hardship, and privation to large numbers of people as to produce unrest so great that the peace and harmony of the world are imperiled...

Whereas also, The failure of any nation to adopt humane conditions of labor is an obstacle in the way of other nations which desire to improve the conditions in their own countries;

The High Contracting Parties, moved by sentiments of justice and humanity as well as by the desire to secure the permanent peace of the world, agree to the following...

Then follow the articles which define the organization and function of the Labor Organization. This new institution differed in one particularly significant respect from the League of Nations: only governments were represented in the latter, whereas the ILO gathered under its roof the representatives of trade unions and employers' organizations, as well as those of governments. Its operation is therefore based on the collaboration of two parties apt to hold divergent views on many issues affecting labor. These two parties come together to confer at an international forum, and nothing is so conducive to understanding and goodwill as personal meeting and discussion of problems. The work of the ILO during the thirty-two years of its existence has been of very great importance in promoting social justice and in creating equal working conditions in different countries. The organization has been quick to lend an ear to new problems as they occurred, and it has not been timid in tackling them.

The work which has been done is impressive, and we can rightly claim that it is work in the service of peace.

Throughout all these thirty-two years, Léon Jouhaux has been on the Governing Body of the ILO, and there is no other living member whose contribution can compare with his.

As a workers' representative at the International Labor Office, Jouhaux was a member of the League of Nations committee entrusted with the study of disarmament problems. He has described this work in his very interesting book *Désarmement* which, although published in 1927, is well worth reading even today. In this book Jouhaux expresses his faith in the League of Nations as an international body capable of giving individual nations a sense of security. For no nation will feel safe, he says, as long as its neighbor is militarily strong, and under such circumstances it will not itself desire disarmament. But if security is guaranteed by an international body, then the road to disarmament is open. These are the same ideas current today, and if Jouhaux was not the first to voice them, he has championed them more energetically than most people. He demands that the armament industry should not be privately owned and that if it is, it must be brought under the control of the state. He calls for the control of international trade in armaments and for effective control by the League of Nations over disarmament. I believe scarcely anyone today would deny that the manufacture of armaments ought not to be a source of economic profit, or that the international arms trade should be subject to control. But even if this can be brought about–and it has been accomplished in a number of countries–we now realize that state ownership of the armament industry and control of the sale of arms do not in themselves offer a guarantee of peace. Be that as it may, we must judge his ideas in the context of the times in which they were conceived, a period when the vast private empires that ruled the armament industry were at the peak of their power and when the trade in arms was unrestricted. Today these factors are no longer the main obstacles to disarmament. On the other hand, the proposal made by Jouhaux for an effective organ to supervise disarmament is just as valid today as it was then and as such is well worth considering afresh.

As we all know, the League of Nations failed in its attempts to secure disarmament. But the man whose goal is to build for the future does not give up the struggle when he suffers a setback. Neither did Jouhaux.

His work during these years was not confined to the Labor Office and the League of Nations. He took part in every kind of work for peace. He fought for the removal of those articles in the Treaty of Versailles which to him and to many others appeared to stand in the way of international cooperation and understanding. He supported the policy of reconciliation pursued by Briand and Stresemann[1].

The period between the wars was a changing one: from the buoyant optimism of the twenties it passed to the steadily growing pessimism of the thirties. The economy of the world collapsed, crisis followed crisis, and high unemployment plagued every nation. It is not strange then that a man like Jouhaux should in times like these call again and again for steps to prevent the recurrence of crises which provide, as he says, a fertile soil for autarchy and consequently for war.

When Hitler[2] rose to power in Germany, the more farsighted saw the danger of war becoming greater and greater from one year to the next. Jouhaux was one of those who interpreted the situation correctly and, unlike so many of his colleagues, strove hard for the strengthening of French defenses. After Hitler's move in Czechoslovakia in 1938, Jouhaux tried to solidify the international democratic front. In that same year he met Roosevelt[3] and asked him to intervene against Germany, but without success.

And then the war broke out. Jouhaux once again worked from the very first days of the war to bring the labor movement to exert its influence to make the eventual peace a true one. He himself stayed in France during the war until the end of 1942 when he was arrested by the Germans. He remained in German captivity until the war ended.

During the years that followed, Jouhaux experienced many disappointments, first when the non-Communist trade-union leaders in France left the C.G.T. in 1947 to set up their own organization, and again when the new World Federation of Trade Unions was split in 1949. In both events he saw a breach in the solidarity of the working class, that solidarity outside political parties for which he had always toiled so earnestly. He himself joined with the non-Communist trade unionists.

1. Aristide Briand (1862–1932), co-recipient of the Nobel Peace Prize for 1926. Gustav Stresemann (1878–1929), co-recipient of the Nobel Peace Prize for 1926.
2. Adolf Hitler (1889–1945), German chancellor and Führer (1933–1945).
3. Franklin Delano Roosevelt (1882–1945), U.S. president (1933–1945).

In his own country Jouhaux has since 1947 been president of the Conseil économique, an advisory body concerned with all important economic questions, one which he had first proposed forty years earlier and which was finally legally established under the new French Constitution[1] of 1946.

On the international front, he has continued his activity in the ILO, he has been a French delegate at the United Nations Assembly, and he has taken part in the European Movement[2], of which he became president in 1949.

This brief sketch of his life's work gives but the merest impression of Jouhaux's contribution and of its influence on world affairs. These cannot be measured by a list of his activities or of his individual achievements. A life-work is given true substance and value only by the vital individual who puts his life into the struggle.

It is this kind of person that we find in Léon Jouhaux. His whole life reveals a man who has never faltered in the fight to attain the goal which he set himself in his youth: to lay the foundations of a world which could belong to all men alike, a world where peace would prevail. He has realized that such a world can never become a reality unless its society is based on social justice and democracy.

He knew that the first step toward this ideal was to uplift the working class and to improve its conditions, but he has also understood that this is only a means of laying the foundation for a new world.

From all this emerges the man, the warm, impulsive, and inspiring human being who has been able to draw others along with him but who has also shown that in order to reach our ultimate goal we must build on the world of reality in which we live.

He has devoted his life to the work of promoting brotherhood among men and nations, and to the fight against war.

1. The French Constitution of 1946 was that of the Fourth Republic (1946–1958).
2. See Jouhaux's lecture, p.26, fn.1.

LÉON JOUHAUX

Fifty Years of Trade-Union Activity in Behalf of Peace

Nobel Lecture*, December 11, 1951

It will certainly come as no surprise to you when I tell you that one of the most moving, as well as one of the happiest, moments of my life occurred on the evening of Monday, November 5, 1951. A reporter whose initiative I have already commended to the French Broadcasting System, eager to satisfy his professional conscience by extracting a sensational statement from me, came to inform me at a somewhat late hour that the Nobel Peace Prize Committee of the Norwegian Parliament had just bestowed on me one of the most renowned and flattering distinctions that this world can offer.

Perhaps he was disappointed by my reception and by the way in which I immediately identified myself with the working classes and their trade unions when I responded to the award of this prize, which reflects so much honor on its founder, on those whose mission it is to confer it, and on him who receives it. But I can assure you that not for the briefest instant did I believe that it was I alone who was the recipient of this great reward.

I have never ceased to do my utmost to be the faithful interpreter and devoted servant of the ideals of peace and justice upheld by out trade-union organizations, and at such a solemn moment it was natural for me to regard myself simply as their representative. I speak as their representative now as I review for you their constant efforts to hasten the advent of an era of peace for which all men long and in which, to borrow the words of Jean Jaurès[1], «mankind, finally at peace with itself» will pursue its own destiny in joy and harmony.

My emotion was, nonetheless, great. Neither my friends nor my family, who should know me better than anyone else does, have ever doubted the strength of my nerves. They would be more likely to reproach me – and sometimes with less than kindly truculence – for a calmness that some of

* The laureate delivered this lecture in the auditorium of the Nobel Institute. The translation is based on the French text in *Les Prix Nobel en 1951*.
1. Jean Léon Jaurès (1859–1914), prominent French Socialist politician, writer-editor, and pacifist.

them call placidity. True enough, nature has endowed me with a fair measure of patience and composure, yet I should be lying if I told you that, having seen the reporter off on his way to make his deadline, I fell peacefully asleep. That evening, all that night, I waited in vain for a slumber that wouldn't come.

And during those long hours I was assailed by many memories.

I saw again the house where I was born, which disappeared in 1898 with the abattoir of Grenelle. I was not quite two years old when my parents left it and, after a brief stay in the country, made a home in Aubervilliers. This town so near Paris where I spent my youth was the Aubervilliers of the end of the last century. Being at that time more than half agricultural, it scarcely resembled the industrial city of today. It afforded us children wide-open spaces, covered with grain in the summer, and it gave us the clear waters of the Courneuve River flowing nearby where we spent many pleasant hours of bathing and swimming.

This almost rustic life made me a sturdy and stable man, and, despite the unpretentiousness of our family life and its hazards, I look back on those days with considerable pleasure.

However, it was at Aubervilliers that I felt for the first time the hard consequences of the struggle of the workers for improvement of their living conditions. These had a considerable influence on my future.

My father, a veteran of the Commune[1], his convictions and his fighting spirit unbroken by the defeat of the workers in 1871, took an energetic and untiring part in the strikes which set the workmen of the match factory where he worked against the management of the company prior to its becoming nationalized. The courageous efforts of my mother, who resumed her job as a cook, were not enough to compensate us for the loss of my father's wages, and it was during one of these strikes that I had to leave elementary school before I was twelve to work at the Central Melting House in Aubervilliers.

My parents, and especially my mother, encouraged by the director of the local school which I was attending, wanted in spite of everything to send me to a National School of Arts and Crafts so that I could later become an

1. The Commune of Paris (March–May, 1871) was set up at the end of the Franco-Prussian War (1870–1871) by the Parisians who, refusing to accept Prussian peace terms, held the city, with the aid of the French National Guard, against the French provisional government at Versailles; the workers, who had protested the war from the beginning, had a large part in encouraging and implementing the revolt.

engineer. I was keen to study and had some natural mechanical ability, and so I entered the Colbert upper primary school. Less than a year later, because of a reversal of the family fortunes, I was forced to leave and go to work in the Michaux Soap Works. From this time on, except for one more attempt at schooling when I spent a year at the Diderot Vocational School, I was, at the age of fourteen, completely caught up in the hard life of the industrial worker.

When I was sixteen, I became a member of the trade union at the match works where I had rejoined my father. I did so without question. My father's vigorous example and my own experience led me quite naturally to participate in the worker's movement. I had suffered personally from the social order. My school work, my intellectual gifts, my eagerness to study, had all come to nothing. I had been brutally compelled to leave the upper primary school and even the vocational training school and to become a wage earner of the humblest order.

This day has been set aside for all countries to celebrate the anniversary of the adoption by the United Nations General Assembly of the Universal Declaration of Human Rights [1]. And with a passion fired by these memories of an adolescent deprived of the right to realize his full intellectual potential, I wish to express my own conviction that, thanks to the action of true trade unionists and sincere democrats, all the sacred and inalienable rights of man will henceforth be recognized without reservation and that man will be able to exercise these rights without hindrance.

The feeling of having been unjustly treated drove me to spend much time in the library of the Aubervilliers libertarian group, one of the few places where I could escape intellectually from my situation. Reading the books that I found there reinforced my feelings of rebellion against the established order and against social injustice.

I propose now to review the progress of trade-union activity for international peace. To this end I shall disregard all its other aspects, but first, in order to stress by a personal example its positive results with regard to the protection of the workers' health, let me give you the reasons for the first strike in which I took part. I participated in this strike not simply as a member of the trade union but as its administrative secretary; in other words–to give you an exact idea of my functions and responsibilities in this humble office–I drafted the minutes of meetings of the trade-union council,

1. On December 10, 1948. See René Cassin, pp.383-411.

of the general assemblies, and sometimes of delegations. I do not think that I owed this mark of confidence to my worth as a trade unionist; I owed it, more likely, to my having received a less sketchy education than that of my comrades: the great school reforms of the Third Republic had not yet been in existence ten years.

Instigated by the National Federation of Match Factory Workers[1], itself adherent to the C.G.T. which had been established in 1895[2], this strike involved the whole trade corporation and aimed principally at prohibiting in the manufacturing process the use of white phosphorus, which constituted no small danger, particularly to the dental health of the personnel. The strike lasted over a month, but it led directly to the calling of the Bern Conference which prohibited the use of noxious substances[3]. This first success naturally could not fail to encourage me to persevere in trade-union action, which at the same time satisfied both my urge to work against iniquity and my youthful need for tangible achievements.

Another consequence of the same strike was the bringing into use of the «continuous» machine, as it was called, which increased production as it eased the drudgery of the workmen. This led me to understand that trade unionism, the instrument of working-class liberation and of social change could, and indeed should, be also an instrument of industrial progress. Nor did it take me long to see therein one of the most effective means for freeing the world of the always menacing specter of war.

Why should I not state openly, Ladies and Gentlemen, the fact that the first manifestation of the trade-union struggle for peace, and particularly the French trade-union struggle into which I threw myself with all the ardor of my youth, was antimilitaristic in thought and sometimes also in deed? Is not one of the greatest sins against the spirit that of knowingly concealing the truth? And would it not be ridiculous to reproach the trade-union movement with having confused cause and effect? Sociologists worthy of

1. Fédération nationale des Ouvriers et Ouvrières des manufactures d'allumettes.
2. Confédération générale du travail [General Confederation of Labor] known as the C.G.T.; one of the leading French labor organizations, it included, before WWI, almost all of the organized workers in France. Although individually its worker members usually voted for Socialists, the C.G.T. kept itself free of any actual party affiliations until the 1940's when the Communists gained control of the organization.
3. Conferences were held in Bern in 1905 and 1906; France was one of the countries that ratified the resulting convention against use of white (or yellow) phosphorus.

the name never make the mistake of reproaching primitive peoples for their belief that the sun moves round the earth. We too, through lack of knowledge and of sufficiently mature reflection, mistook the visible outward appearance of the phenomenon for the phenomenon itself. I would add that my memory of that period, perhaps because of the mirage which the passage of the years evokes, is that of a great enthusiasm, undoubtedly sparked more by irrational hope than by any constructive will; but that fervor makes me feel all the more bitter about the atmosphere of indifference, fatalism, and resignation that has persisted up to the present time on our continent, a continent which two wars seem to have ravaged morally as well as physically. An orator once exclaimed: «When war breaks out, its principal victims are always the people.» He was more right than he knew. Not only does war kill workers by the thousand, nay, by the million, destroy their homes, lay waste the fields which took them centuries of effort to cultivate, raze to the ground the factories they built with their own hands, and reduce for years the standard of living of the working masses, but it also gives man an increasingly acute feeling of his helplessness before the forces of violence, and consequently severely retards his progress toward an age of peace, justice, and well-being.

Oh yes! we were full of enthusiasm back in 1900. Nothing, no matter what it was, seemed impossible to us then, and we had every reason to believe it. We felt already that after Viktor Adler, Wilbur Wright was going to give us wings[1].

On completion of my military service, I went back to the factory and to the trade union. From here on, however, I am going to take myself out of the story of the movement – not because our paths diverged, indeed they intermingle after 1909 – but because trade unionism, despite its close initial connections with libertarian individualism, is essentially and by definition a collective work.

A moment ago, I mentioned in passing the creation in 1895 of the Confédération générale du travail (C.G.T.). It replaced the National Federation of Trade Unions [Fédération des Syndicats et Groupes corporatifs ouvriers de France], which had been founded in 1886. Actually, unity of the workers under the C.G.T. was not completely achieved until 1902 when, at the Montpellier Congress, the Federation of Labor Exchanges (Fédération

1. Viktor Adler (1852–1918), Austrian politician, leader of the Austrian Social Democratic Party. Wilbur Wright (1867–1912), American inventor (with his brother Orville) of the airplane.

nationale des Bourses du travail) was incorporated in the C.G.T. as the Division of Labor Exchanges. However, during this period in which the unity of the working classes was being consolidated, the C.G.T., in its annual congresses, had already gone beyond questions of organization and corporate claims and as early as 1898 had taken its stand in favor of general disarmament:

«The Congress (the motion stated in a somewhat antiquated style) considering all peoples to be brothers and war to be mankind's greatest calamity, [and]

Holding that armed peace leads all peoples to ruin through the increase in taxation required to meet the enormous expense of standing armies,

Declares that money spent on the perpetration of acts suitable only to barbarians and on the support of young, strong, and vigorous men for a period of years would be better used for work serving humanity, [and]

Expresses the wish [*voeu*] that general disarmament take place as soon as possible.»

In 1900 and in 1901, the C.G.T. progressed from theoretical declarations to practical considerations; it decided that «young workers about to undergo conscription should be put in touch with the secretaries of the Labor Exchanges of the towns in which they are to be garrisoned», and agreed in principle to the setting up of a Serviceman's Fund.

Today these declarations and decisions seem very mild. We must not forget, however, that they were accompanied by a significant antimilitaristic agitation which had found solid support in the impassioned propaganda for a retrial of the Dreyfus case[1]. This was opposed with equal vigor by militarists whose affinity with a discredited Council of War laid open the army and particularly its officers to fatal, if unfair, suspicion as far as democratic opinion was concerned.

All the C.G.T. congresses, which took place biennially after 1902, were deeply concerned with action in support of peace. At the outbreak of the Russo-Japanese War[2], the 1904 Congress, held at Bourges, declared: «At a time when two nations are at each other's throats, reenacting on a wider scale the slaughter of the past for the greater good of the ruling classes and exploiters who enslave the proletariat of the whole world, this Congress... censures the ignoble attitude of the governments of the two nations concerned, which, with the object of finding an outlet for the mounting dis-

1. See 1927 presentation speech, Vol. 2, p. 30, fn. 2.
2. 1904–1905.

content of the proletariat, appeal to chauvinistic passions and unhesitatingly organize the death and assassination of thousands of workers in order to safeguard their own privileged position.»

The international sky was increasingly overcast, and the attitude of the unions stiffened. The 1906 Congress approved «all programs of antimilitaristic propaganda», and that of 1908 contemplated replying to a «declaration of war with a declaration of a revolutionary general strike». The Congresses of 1910 and 1912 confirmed these resolutions and strongly protested against repression, but 1912 was the year of the Balkan War[1] and, in view of the rivalries which began to make themselves felt and which threatened to spread the conflict even farther, a special conference held on the first of October decided to call a congress whose sole objective would be to combat the menace of war. The motion passed was a true indication of the confidence of the trade-union organizations in their growing strength. To stop the governments from being drawn any further down the slope to the yawning chasm of fire and blood, the Congress affirmed its resolution to take revolutionary action in the event of military mobilization.

We would gain a false impression of the importance and effectiveness of labor action if we confined ourselves to the motions passed at its congresses. The trade unions, far from being content with these declarations, established international liaisons and supported every policy based on pacification and understanding. Between 1900 and 1901 the C. G. T. and the English working classes together contributed to bringing about the Entente Cordiale[2]. To gain an idea of the value of this contribution, it is necessary only to reflect upon the tension which followed the Fashoda incident[3] and to thumb through the collections of satirical publications of those days.

At the time of the Agadir incident[4], on July 22, 1911, a delegation from the C. G. T. left for Berlin, and in the following month a trade-union dele-

1. Two brief Balkan Wars (1912–1913) involved Serbia, Bulgaria, Greece, Montenegro, Rumania, and Turkey in a struggle for Turkish territory.
2. An informal understanding between Great Britain and France (1904), settling their colonial differences.
3. A diplomatic crisis in Anglo-French relations (1898), involving rival claims in the upper Nile region, occurred when the French took the town of Fashoda in S. Sudan while the British were putting down a revolt in N. Sudan. A peaceful settlement was effected, with the French giving up their claims.
4. Franco-German relations were strained in 1911 when French troops intervened in a Moroccan uprising and the German warship *Panther* appeared at Agadir; mutual agreements resolved the crisis.

gation from Germany arrived in Paris. The French and the German proletariat were uniting their efforts to try to avert war.

These occasional international contacts were not, however, the only ones
to be established between the various national trade-union organizations.
Several international workers' congresses were held after the abolition of
the workers' International. One met in Zurich in 1895 and one in London in
1896, bringing together delegates of the trade unions and representatives of
socialist-minded political parties. In London, the French delegation included,
among other trade unionists: Fernand Pelloutier, the Guérard brothers, and
Keufer[1]. The results of this cooperation–or confusion, as the more critical
historians would have it–were not outstanding, and the idea of a purely
trade-union international organization first came up at the Congress of
Scandinavian Trade Unions in Copenhagen in 1901, thanks to the direct
contact among fraternal delegations. The proposal came from Legien[2] who
represented the General Committee of German Trade Unions. It was decided to request the various national organizations to attend the Congress of
German Trade Unions at Stuttgart in 1902. The organizations of Germany,
Great Britain, Austria, Belgium, Bohemia, Denmark, Spain, France, The
Netherlands, Italy, Norway, Sweden, and Switzerland responded to the
appeal and approved the proposal to organize international trade-union
congresses which would take place at more or less regular intervals. Their
mandate remained limited, at first extending only to the compilation of
common statistics, the exchange of information on legislation affecting
labor, and eventually to solidarity in the event of important strikes. Nevertheless, the first international link had been forged, and it was later strengthened in Dublin in 1903 by the creation of an International Trade-Union
Secretariat.

Without formally withdrawing from the Secretariat, our French C.G.T.
suspended the payment of its contributions in 1904 after the Secretariat had
refused to include the question of antimilitarism in the agenda for the Conference of Amsterdam. I would not go so far as to say that the French trade

1. Fernand Pelloutier (1867–1901), secretary of the Fédération nationale des Bourses
du travail and manager of the weekly journal *L'Ouvrier des deux mondes*. One of the
Guérard brothers was at one time secretary of the C.G.T. Auguste Keufer (1851–
1924), positivist leader of the French union reform movement; secretary of the Fédération du livre until 1920.
2. Karl Legien (1861–1920), chairman of the General Committee of the German Free
Trade Unions.

unions attached greater importance to the struggle for peace than the others did; but they certainly seemed to take it more to heart.

Relations were renewed following the C.G.T. Congress in Marseilles in 1908 and the Secretariat's acquiescence to the demand that the calling of truly international congresses be included in the agenda of the next conference.

This, the fifth Conference, took place in Paris and included some spirited debates – quite spirited, in fact. Having become its secretary, I was the spokes-man for the C.G.T. I recently referred to this meeting in an article, and I think I can do no better than to quote its opening words, for they pinpoint not only our own position but also that of the representative of the American Federation of Labor.

«I saw Gompers[1] again (I wrote) on the evening of September 1, 1909. It was the second day of the International Conference of Trade-Union Secretariats. All day I had been asking for a true international congress, and I had had to ask with a certain amount of vehemence. At the end of the afternoon session, after we had won the majority over to the argument of the French C.G.T., Gompers, who represented the American labor unions belonging to the A.F. of L.[American Federation of Labor], came over to me to express his deep satisfaction!»

There were two more conferences, the first of which was in 1911 at Budapest where this time the A.F. of L. participated officially and the Industrial Workers of the World[2] unofficially. The second was in Zurich in 1913. An attempt at an expanded conference, leading to the international congresses which we had in mind, was made on the latter occasion by ap-pealing to the International Vocational Secretariats. The resolution adopted in Zurich recommended that the trade-union organizations of all countries study the possibility of setting up an International Federation of Labor, whose aim «would be to protect and extend the rights and interests of the wage earners of all countries and»–I emphasize this last part of the sentence–«to achieve international fraternity and solidarity».

The trade-union movement was emerging from its infancy and beginning to be aware of the magnitude of its future. In Zurich it no longer thought of

1. Samuel Gompers (1850–1924), American labor leader; in 1881 helped to found the Federation of Organized Trades and Labor Unions, which became the American Federation of Labor (A.F. of L.) in 1886; president of A.F. of L. (1886–1924, except 1895).
2. The I.W.W. was a revolutionary industrial union founded in Chicago in 1905 which aimed to overthrow capitalism and to set up a trade-union state.

itself as the expression of a single social class; the international solidarity which it was trying to bring about was already something quite different from the solidarity of workers in time of strike – all that had been envisaged up to that time. The dramatic events which its development precipitated were soon to hasten its maturity.

Men of my generation will never forget the last days of July, 1914, least of all those who tried to build a dike against the onrushing sea of blood. After July 27 our C. G. T. never ceased trying to achieve the impossible. To leaders still adhering in spirit to the old motto of «Ultimate Right», which kings used to engrave on their cannons, it opposed the common sense of the man in the street. «War», it cried, «is no solution to the problems facing us; it is, and always will be, the most terrible of human calamities. Let us do everything to avoid it.» On Friday, July 30, the C. G. T. cabled the supreme appeal to the International Secretariat, beseeching it to intervene by «exerting pressure on the governments.»

Alas! As we all know, these desperate efforts were in vain!

This disaster did not force us to abandon our ideal; on the contrary, from the very first months of the conflict, it led us to define precisely the conditions for its realization.

In fact, at the end of 1914, the A. F. of L. took the initiative of proposing to hold «an International Conference of National Trade-Union Organizations on the same day and in the same place that the Peace Congress would be held, in order to help restore good relations between proletariat organizations and to encourage participation with the Peace Congress in laying the foundations of a definitive and lasting peace». Le Comité confédéral of the C. G. T. accepted this proposal and itself issued a manifesto to all the trade-union organizations. I believe that the major portion of this text has become less dated than all of its predecessors. It concludes by demanding: the suppression of the system of secret treaties; an absolute respect for nationalities; the immediate limitation of armaments on an international scale, a measure which should lead to total disarmament; and finally compulsory arbitration for the settlement of all conflicts between nations.

These ideas were soon well on their way. The milestones were to be the Conference of Leeds in 1916, that of London in September, 1917, and those of Stockholm and Bern in June and October of the same year.

At Leeds the idea of an international labor organization appeared in a trade-union text which also drew attention to the danger to the working classes inherent in the existence of international capitalist competition. In the report made on behalf of the C.G.T. we affirmed that the Peace Treaty should, in accordance with the spirit of workers' organizations, lay the first foundations of the United States of Europe. In London there was strong support for the idea of the League of Nations itself, along with all its corollaries: general disarmament preceded by limitation of armaments, and compulsory arbitration, both of which the C.G.T. had advocated three years previously.

At Stockholm in June, 1917, the representatives of the trade unions in the Central European and Scandinavian countries declared their complete agreement with the decisions taken at Leeds and even expressed their congratulations to the union organizations of the Allied countries and most particularly to the C.G.T. Another International Conference of Trade Unions was called at Bern for the beginning of October, 1917, by the Association of Swiss Trade Unions. The national organizations of Germany, Austria, Bohemia, Bulgaria, Denmark, Hungary, The Netherlands, Norway, Sweden, and Switzerland were represented, and they confirmed the resolutions adopted at Leeds and London.

The Inter-Allied Labor and Socialist Conference which took place in London in February of 1918 was perhaps even more important. Our French organization delivered a memorandum there containing, certainly, many ideas that had already been voiced before, but in it we also demanded the creation of a supranational authority, the «formation of an international legislative assembly» and «the gradual development of an international legislation accepted by all and binding all in a clearly defined way». We were ahead of our time, far ahead in fact, since thirty-three years later these proposals have still not been put into effect. The Conference requested that «at least one representative of socialism and of labor should sit with the official representatives at the official Peace Conference». This request, which was reiterated by the C.G.T. on December 15, 1918, in more or less identical terms, was granted by two governments; in consequence, Gompers and I were attached to the delegations of the U.S.A. and France in the capacity of technical experts. We collaborated in bringing our efforts in behalf of the trade-union movement to bear on the elaboration of the Treaty, particularly insofar as Part XIII[1] was concerned. The working classes were becoming more and more sharply aware of the complex causes of international malaise.

1. Part XIII of the Treaty of Versailles became the constitution of the International Labor Organization.

I shall quote two clauses from that part of the Treaty which gave birth to the International Labor Organization and to its permanent instrument the International Labor Office whose activities and tangible results I need not recall here. The two clauses of the Treaty read as follows:

«Whereas, The League of Nations has for its object the establishment of universal peace, and such a peace can be established only if it is based upon social justice;

And whereas, Conditions of labor exist involving such injustice, hardship, and privation to large numbers of people as to produce unrest so great that the peace and harmony of the world are imperiled; and an improvement of those conditions is urgently required...»

From 1918 on, trade unionists were to express from the platforms of their congresses the workers' desire for peace through a rational organization of the world. The meetings of the International Labor Office and even the general Assemblies of the League of Nations, several of which were to have many sessions, were to excite universal interest in their proposals. The trade-union organizations nevertheless continued their autonomous activity. After the International Conference at Bern in February of 1919 and the Congress of Amsterdam in July of the same year, the International Trade-Union Secretariat was replaced by a true International Federation of Trade Unions[1] which immediately acquired over twenty million members. One of its first acts was an appeal to international solidarity to alleviate the terrible misery prevailing within Austria; and the Austrian workers escaped famine, thanks to the many trainloads of supplies sent by various trade unions and cooperative societies. The second intervention of the F.S.I. was on behalf of the Hungarian trade unions, whose liberty was being threatened.

Some have forgotten–for forgetting is as blissful as ignorance–that the F.S.I. intervened with equal vigor on behalf of the Russian workers; its representatives, O'Grady, Wauters, and later Thomson, actually lived in Russia until 1923 in order to supervise the distribution of food and medicines sent by the Federation. Furthermore, it is not distorting history to say that it was largely through the efforts and propaganda of our International Federation that the government of the U.S.S.R. was recognized by the majority of the great powers.

However, the trade unionists did not confine themselves to mitigating the cruel consequences of war. They sought the means to establish a stable

1. Fédération syndicale internationale, or F.S.I.; dissolved in 1945; succeeded by the World Federation of Trade Unions.

peace, emphasizing that it should be founded on a basis of worldwide economic and social stability. In fact, the majority of the proposals ultimately put before the League of Nations originated in the international congresses of the International Federation of Trade Unions and in the World Peace Congress which the latter convened at The Hague in 1922. We asked for the organization of exchanges, the circulation of manpower, the distribution of raw materials, and the prohibition of private manufacture of arms for international circulation.

It was at about this time that the League of Nations set up a Temporary Mixed Commission for the purpose of studying methods for dealing with international traffic in armaments, munitions, and war matériel [1]. The opinion of the workers now carried such weight that the Commission included three representatives of the workers from the Governing Body of the International Labor Office. A convention was drawn up on June 17, 1925, in which the principle of supervision, as opposed to that of simple propaganda, was recognized, thanks to the efforts of the labor members, of whom I was one. However, not all of our suggestions were followed; we had, for instance, requested internationalized supervision, the auditing of the books of business enterprises, proper measures designed to prevent influencing the press and the setting up of international cartels, together with the standardization of national inspections.

It is curious to note – somewhat bitterly – that the principle of internationalized supervision always meets with strong opposition. Yesterday it came from the private manufacture of arms, today from armament itself. I remain convinced, as do my comrades of the C.I.S.L. [2], that we cannot talk seriously of general, or even of partial, disarmament, without accepting the need for effective international surveillance.

At the Economic Conference of 1927 I was again spokesman for the trade unions. The principal arguments in my statement of May 5, were as follows:

«On behalf of my comrades, representing the workers, I would like at this International Economic Conference to pay tribute to the recognition of the high ideals which the trade-union movement has always defended.

1. The Temporary Mixed Commission for the Reduction of Armaments, constituted in 1921, also studied other aspects of the armament problem.
2. Confédération internationale des syndicats libres, formed in 1949 to counter the World Federation of Trade Unions which had become Communist dominated.

It is the opinion of the labor organizations that economic collaboration between peoples is a necessity. Immediately after the war during the armistice period–in February of 1919–in examining the conditions necessary for peace and exploring the possible bases on which to found the League of Nations which was still on the drawing board, so to speak, the labor and socialist conferences, meeting simultaneously in Bern, emphasized the necessity of giving the League of Nations precisely that economic foundation which our chairman, Monsieur Theunis[1], called for yesterday.

... In 1924, we declared that the organization of a definitive peace requires not only the institution of a law of peace but also that of an economy of peace... No true peace can be established... so long as quasi-military strategy is applied in economic relations. What is needed is a committee for economic cooperation.»

On May 23, the last day of the Conference, I voiced the sentiments of my friends when I said: «We have been bold in criticism, too timid in constructive action.»

Three years later, with the idea of concerted economic action in mind, the Conference sent a questionnaire to the member states of the League of Nations. The French government instructed the National Economic Council to work out the essentials of the French answer. I had been representing the C.G.T. on this council since its foundation in 1925, and I investigated the practical means of assuring the most satisfactory conditions for the distribution and optimum utilization of European raw materials among the various nations. Expressing the thoughts of my comrades, I suggested, among other means, the organization of an international information service on inventories, on production, and on the needs of the various countries for raw materials.

We also took an active part in 1931 on the Unemployment Committee of the Commission of Inquiry for European Union[2], in 1933 at the Monetary and Economic Conference in London, and on the Comité des grands travaux internationaux, through which the International Labor Office and the League of Nations, taking up the proposals of the trade unions, sought to establish healthy collaboration among nations in the struggle against under-

1. Georges Theunis (1873–1966), Belgian statesman and twice prime minister.
2. The Commission of Inquiry for European Union was created in September, 1930, under the auspices of the League of Nations, with Aristide Briand its president. Its Unemployment Committee was authorized by the League Council early in 1931.

employment and toward the creation of new sources of wealth. But all these conferences, all these meetings, succeeded in doing nothing to rid the world of the prevailing economic crisis. The will to organize the world on a rational basis, or at least to modify its most apparent incongruities, had clearly not been strong enough to counteract the combined effects of inertia, egoism, and incomprehension.

Efforts to wrest weapons away from nations bending under the weight of so many instruments of death were equally futile. All the same, I cannot forget the first sessions of the Conference for the Limitation and Reduction of Armaments. Those early days of February, 1932, were days of hope for humanity. Millions confidently awaited the results of the proceedings of this conference, which was presided over by that veteran militant Laborite Henderson[1], and we can claim, with justification, to have had a lot to do with the creation of this enthusiasm. The Socialist Workingmen's International and the International Federation of Trade Unions, zealously vying with each other, had each collected thousands of petitions which the delegations presented to the conference. On February 6, after Vandervelde[2] had spoken on behalf of the members of the Socialist Worker's International, I conveyed to the conference the unqualified support of millions of trade unionists.

That day remains one of the highlights of my life. I was intensely aware that I was expressing not only the unanimous hope of the workers of an entire world, still bruised by the recent holocaust, but also their clear understanding of the real conditions necessary for disarmament. In their name, I assured the members of the conference of the complete readiness of the trade-union organizations to cooperate in making effective and sincere the procedures of national and international supervision, without which partial disarmament would be either illusory or inoperative.

The attempt to bring about disarmament was as fruitless as the efforts in the economic sphere, and a few years later, with empty stomachs as its excuse, Italian fascism launched itself upon Abyssinia. We trade unionists knew very well that peace was indivisible, and we had no doubt that the weakness of the League of Nations would render it powerless and herald a new period of massacre and destruction. We were insistent and even violent

1. Arthur Henderson (1863–1935), recipient of the Nobel Peace Prize for 1934. See Henderson, in Volume 2, for details on this conference.
2. Émile Vandervelde (1866–1938), Belgian Socialist leader and statesman; minister of state (1914–1918), minister of justice (1919), minister of foreign affairs (1925).

in our demands that the Covenant should be applied and that sanctions be put into effect. We were voices crying in the wilderness. The sanctions were not applied; war broke out in Ethiopia[1]; and it was followed fatally, logically, and inexorably by the intervention in Spain[2], the reoccupation of the left bank of the Rhine[3], the Anschluss[4], the Munich agreements[5], and the Second World War[6].

I do not want to enlarge upon our opposition to this policy of weakness whereby the principle of collective security was abandoned. We know only too well what the lack of resolution on the part of the democracies has cost them.

Once more the earth was laid waste by war. Even so, we do not believe that action in the cause of peace is a Sisyphean labor, and that the deadly stone will forever keep on rolling back down to crush mankind. We will yet manage to lodge the stone firmly at the top of the hill.

As soon as the Fascists and Nazis had laid down their arms, the trade unionists began to rethink the problems of peace.

Toward the end of 1947, the C.G.T.-F.O.[7] revived the traditions and spirit of our old C.G.T., and in speeches, articles, and reports we again took up and specified the solutions which the C.G.T., along with the International Federation of Trade Unions, had offered to the world as a way to salvation.

We approved the Marshall Plan[8] because it was a manifestation of inter-

1. In 1935 between Ethiopia and Italy; Italian victory and annexation of Ethiopia followed in 1936.
2. In the Spanish Civil War (1936–1939), Germany and Italy supported one side, Russia the other.
3. Germany violated the Treaty of Versailles (1919) and the Locarno Pact (1925) by reoccupying the Rhineland in 1936.
4. The union of Austria and Germany, which took place, in defiance of the 1919 peace treaties, when Germany annexed Austria in March, 1938.
5. The Munich Pact of September, 1938, signed by Great Britain, France, Germany, and Italy, allowed Germany to occupy the Sudetenland in Czechoslovakia.
6. 1939–1945.
7. Force Ouvrière, a non-Communist labor federation officially known as C.G.T.-F.O., was formed in 1947 by a group (including Jouhaux) that seceded from the C.G.T. because of its Communist control.
8. The European Recovery Program, integrating U.S. aid to Europe (after WWII) with an organized program of recovery and cooperation in Europe itself, was proposed (1947) by George C. Marshall, U.S. secretary of state (1947–1949) and recipient of the Nobel Peace Prize for 1953.

national solidarity, because its benefits could be extended to any nation without discrimination, and because we could not see in it any expression of a policy of prestige or force of arms since it invested the beneficiary states with the right to use the credits as they saw fit.

We approved the propaganda in favor of European Unity and emphasized that we would regard such unification as the first step on the road to World Unity. In my capacity as a trade unionist, I was elected president of the European Movement in February of 1949, and in the following spring I opened the Westminster Economic Conference[1] by expressing our common sentiment as follows:

«It is normal, it is logical, it is in conformity with the very spirit of history that the organized working class should have an active part in the construction of Europe. It has always proclaimed that it would not, could not, and had no wish to disassociate the struggle for its emancipation from the constant battle to maintain peace, because doing so would have set up barriers which international events would have swept away like piles of chaff.»

It is a matter of Europe's consolidation, not of its isolation. This human mass, which has such a vast wealth of natural resources at its disposal and whose intellectual potential is the greatest on earth, is not willing to cut itself off from the rest of the world. It is ready to welcome all who wish to be associated with its efforts: «The Europe we are building will have more doors and windows than walls.»

In July, 1950, in an introduction to the reports on the Social Conference of the European Movement, I stressed again the importance of its objective of international peace and of social justice:

«We want to make Europe simply a peninsula of the vast Eurasian Continent, where for thousands of years war has been the only way to resolve conflicts between peoples. We want Europe to be a peaceable community united, despite and within its diversity, in a constant and ardent struggle against human misery and all the suffering and dangers that it engenders. We have no desire to make Europe into a larger, better entrenched, better armed fortress.»

We approved the Schuman Plan for a European Coal and Steel Commu-

1. The European Movement (for European unity) later in 1949 created the Council of Europe, whose objective is a more closely integrated European community. For an account of the Movement and its Westminster Economic Conference, see *European Movement and the Council of Europe*, with Forewords by Winston S.Churchill and Paul-Henri Spaak, published on behalf of The European Movement by Hutchinson, London, 1950.

nity[1]. A few days after the declaration of May 9, 1950–on May 31 to be exact – in commenting on the Ruhr Statute[2] in a C.I.S.L. Conference journal, I wrote:

«The promoters of the ‹Combinat› can take as their objective... only the progressive unification of Europe. However, this unification cannot be an end in itself.

The final and essential goal, the only valid goal, is to extend the well-being of the worker, to give him a more equitable share of the products of collective work, to make Europe a social democracy, and to ensure the peace desired by men of every race and tongue by proving that the democracies can bring about social justice through the rational organization of production without sacrificing the liberty and the dignity of the individual.

... The pool should be only one stage in a process of continuous creation. The C.I.S.L. has decided to follow its development closely in order to be in a position to give it effective collaboration.»

We recommended the organization of a worldwide market for raw materials and in this connection recalled just what it is that we intend to defend in defending democracy:

«What are we all trying to save? What are we trying to safeguard? Civil liberties: specifically, the right of all citizens to hold their own opinions and to express them freely on the great questions of moral, philosophical, political, and economic import, and the right to form associations. But democracy is not, nor can it be, merely a theoretical respect for these rights. It must give every man effective opportunities to enjoy them, and it must do so under the kind of moral and material conditions that will encourage him to exercise such rights.

One who must be constantly preoccupied with his own subsistence cannot be an alert citizen.

I said recently in a short address to the Economic Council that economic

1. A plan proposed on May 9, 1950, by Robert Schuman (1886–1963), French foreign minister (1948–1953), for a European Coal and Steel Community (ECSC) whose members would pool their coal and steel, providing a unified market for them – this to be done and regulated under a supranational authority; the ECSC was established in 1952, with France, Italy, West Germany, Belgium, The Netherlands, and Luxembourg as members.
2. Adopted in December, 1948, at a conference held in London by the United States, Great Britain, France, and the three Benelux countries, it provided an authority under which West German coal, coke, and steel were apportioned between German domestic consumption and export.

justice is one of the factors in the moral health of nations. There is no economic order in inflationist policies and in underemployment.»

The C. I. S. L. commissioned me to put before the U. N. Assembly at Lake Success a draft resolution whose main paragraph read as follows: «The General Assembly... recommends to the participating nations that they seek above all the means of establishing international regulation of the distribution and cost of raw materials and that, to this end, they contribute to the creation of a common stabilization fund.»

We have constantly defended the two inseparable principles of collective security and general disarmament, effected through the reassessment and international supervision of military strength and of all categories of instruments of war.

A synthesis of our doctrine was attempted on the occasion of the C. I. S. L. Congress at Milan in July, 1951, in the report on the role of the trade-union movement in international crisis.

In this report we have fixed our objectives: first and above all, to spare humanity the colossal ordeal of a third world war.

In it we have stated our principles: to act within the framework and under the aegis of the United Nations Organization, to develop a spirit of community and a spirit of cooperation, and to return to collective economic disciplines.

Finally, we have set forth some of the forms our activity will take: the organization of the distribution of raw materials and the fixing of the prices of basic products; the solution of the housing problem; the fight against restrictive practices in production by national and international cartels; and above all the effective participation of the organized workers in the management of social and economic affairs in every country in the world.

Since this Congress is the most recent of the many manifestations of the desire for peace on the part of the free trade unions, I believe I could give no better conclusion to this survey of fifty years of trade-union activity in behalf of the rational organization of the world and of peace–which are absolutely inseparable–than by giving the final lines of this report practically unaltered.

The free trade-union movement is called on to play an essential part in the fight against international crisis and for the advent of true peace. The scope of the task is enormous, matched only by its urgency. Our movement intends to devote its efforts to this task regardless of the cost. I might add that it was enormously encouraged by the recent interventions of the government delegates on the Third Committee of the present General Assembly of the United Nations. The Cuban delegate Mr. Ichaso, among others, showed that certain official circles had adopted the idea which we have been propagating for years and which we have already succeeded in putting into the Treaty of Versailles: the idea that economic disorder and misery are among the determinative causes of wars.

The decision of the Committee of the Norwegian Parliament, which, in awarding me the Nobel Peace Prize for 1951, has recognized and proclaimed the importance and the steadfastness of the pacifist efforts of the trade unionists, cannot but greatly assist the spread of these ideas and considerably extend their sphere of influence. It strengthens the common will of those who have conceived and submitted these ideas to the consideration of men, and of those who have been convinced by them, to work ceaselessly to develop a society free of injustice and violence.

We know well, alas, that men and their civilizations are mortal. We wish to leave to indifferent nature the responsibility of their demise and to free mankind at last from its remorse for having begotten Cain.

Biography

Dean of the French labor movement for forty-five years, Léon Jouhaux (July 1, 1879–April 28, 1954) was born in Paris, heir to the radical beliefs of his grandfather who had fought in the Revolution of 1848 and of his father who had been a part of the Commune that had controlled Paris for a brief time in the aftermath of the Franco-Prussian War. Seeking higher wages, Léon's father left his low-paying municipal job in 1880 to join the labor force of a match factory in Aubervilliers. Léon attended primary school there until the age of twelve; studied at the Lycée Colbert on a scholarship for nine months before he was taken out of school when his father's earnings were stopped by a strike; spent a year at the Diderot Vocational School, again abandoning his studies to help support himself and the family.

In 1895 at the age of sixteen, he entered the match factory, and even before becoming a full-fledged union member, prepared the minutes of the union meetings. After a period of military service in Algeria, from which he was recalled because his father had gone blind as a result of years of working with volatile white phosphorus, Jouhaux returned to work in the factory. In 1900 he participated in his first strike, a protest against the use of phosphorus, was blacklisted, and dismissed. Unable to find steady employment, he held a succession of jobs in a sugar refinery, a fertilizer plant, and on the docks, meanwhile attending classes at the Sorbonne, and the Université Populaire at Aubervilliers.

Reinstated in the factory through the intervention of the union, he embarked upon his life career as a labor leader, rising rapidly to positions of responsibility because of his intelligence, industriousness, organizing ability, impressive personality, and talent as a speaker. In 1906 his local union elected him as their representative to the Confédération générale du travail (C. G.T.); in 1909 he was named interim treasurer of the C. G.T.; and, a few months later on July 12, 1909, was appointed to the post of secretary-general of the C.G.T., a position he held until 1947 and from which was derived his nickname, «the General».

Although Jouhaux gradually moved from a radical philosophical position to a more moderate one in his four decades of labor leadership, he nonetheless preserved a remarkable consistency in the programs of action he espoused. He first strove to bring to realization the demands of labor commonly proposed during the first third of this century. In 1936 he was a signatory of the Matignon Agreement giving French workers the eight-hour day, paid vacations, the right to organize and to bargain collectively. The larger conception of trade unionism to which Jouhaux devoted his life can be found in the pages of *La Bataille syndicaliste*, the main organ of the C. G.T., which he edited from 1911 to 1921, and in his speeches and extensive publications. It included principles of inclusiveness, solidarity, political independence, democratic procedure, and international concern.

He was himself a confirmed internationalist. Alarmed by the crisis in international relations prior to World War I, Jouhaux spoke in England, Germany, Switzerland, and Belgium, urging labor unions to unite in the cause of peace. With the opening of hostilities, however, he declared his support for the war effort and accepted membership on several governmental committees.

Meanwhile, he led the C. G.T. in developing a peace program calling for arms limitation, international arbitration, an end to secret treaties, and respect for nationalities. In 1916 at the Leeds Conference, Jouhaux presented a report laying the groundwork for what later became the International Labor Organization (ILO); in 1919 at the Paris Peace Conference he was one of those influential in getting the constitutional basis of the ILO incorporated in Article XIII of the Versailles Treaty; in that same year he was chosen as one of the worker-representative members of the ILO's Governing Body.

Jouhaux filled other trade union positions of international significance. He was elected first vice-president of the International Federation of Trade Unions in 1919, retaining that office in 1945 when this organization was reconstituted as the World Federation of Trade Unions. When various of its members later found the World Federation politically repugnant, he joined the heads of trade unions in other nations in forming the International Confederation of Free Trade Unions, becoming one of its vice-presidents.

Active also in international political affairs, Jouhaux was from 1925 to 1928 a member of the French delegation to the League of Nations, where he played a part in drafting proposals on various aspects of the question of arms control, and from 1946 to 1951 to the United Nations, where he sought to obtain, among other things, the universal recognition of the human right to free association. In 1949 he became president of the European

Movement, whose Council of Europe was established as a first step toward a
federated Europe.

For some thirty years Jouhaux struggled to keep the C.G.T. free of
political domination. Under intense attack by the French Communists from
1918 on, Jouhaux maintained the integrity of the C.G.T. by forcing the
Communists to split off in 1921. He reunited the two groups against fascism
in 1936, but after the outbreak of World War II in 1939, once again dissociated himself from the Communists.

After the fall of France, the C.G.T. was dissolved. Jouhaux joined the
Resistance, was arrested in December, 1941, and held in house custody until
April, 1943, when he was sent to the Buchenwald prison camp in Germany.
He was liberated in May of 1945, still a healthy man at the age of sixty-six
despite his imprisonment of twenty-five months.

Upon his return to active leadership in a reconstituted C.G.T., he shared
the office of secretary-general with the Communist Benoit Frachon. Opposing the Communists on both ideological and tactical grounds and dismayed by their unwillingness to support the Marshall Plan, Jouhaux reluctantly withdrew in 1947 from the central organization of the C.G.T.
to form, along with other leaders, the C.G.T.-Force Ouvrière, of which he
became president. The C.G.T.-F.O., advocating freedom from political
control, the establishment of a United States of Europe, the pursuit of unity
among the workers of the world, and action to increase the status of labor,
grew rapidly in membership in the next few years.

One of Jouhaux's most important offices was that of president of the
French National Economic Council to which he was elected in 1947. The
Economic Council, whose objective was to integrate the economic forces
within the structure of France, had long been advocated by Jouhaux.
Speaking of Jouhaux's association with the Council, Paul Pisson, the first
vice-president, described him as «a creative force», a man «full of fervor and
vitality», the possessor of a «store of enthusiastic idealism» who had a
«ringing voice and expressive manner»[1]. It was during a session of the
Council that Jouhaux first sustained the symptoms of the heart trouble that
was to bring his career to a close. Before he died on April 28, 1954, he was
informed that he had been elected to the presidency of the Council for the
seventh consecutive time.

1. Quoted in «Léon Jouhaux», *International Labour Review*, p.250.

Selected Bibliography

Bouvier-Ajam, Maurice, *Histoire du travail en France depuis la Révolution*. Paris, Librairie générale de droit et de jurisprudence, 1969.

Bron, Jean, *Histoire du mouvement ouvrier français*. 2 Tomes. Paris, Les Éditions Ouvrières, 1968.

Dale, Leon A., *Marxism and French Labor*. New York, Vantage, 1956. Contains a long bibliography.

Dictionnaire biographique français contemporain, 2e éd.

Dolléans, Édouard, *Histoire du mouvement ouvrier*, 3e éd. 3 Tomes. Paris, Colin, 1947–1953.

Georges, Bernard, et Denise Tintant, *Léon Jouhaux: Cinquante ans de syndicalisme*. 2 Tomes. Paris, Presses Universitaires de France, 1962.

Godfrey, E. Drexel, Jr., *The Fate of the French Non-Communist Left*. Garden City, N.Y., Doubleday, 1955.

Jouhaux, Léon, *À Jean Jaurès: Discours prononcé aux obsèques de Jean Jaurès*. Paris, La Publication Sociale, 1915.

Jouhaux, Léon, *Le Désarmement*. Paris, Alcan, 1927.

Jouhaux, Léon, *The International Federation of Trade Unions and Economic Reconstruction*. Amsterdam, IFTU, 1922.

Jouhaux, Léon, *Le Mouvement syndical en France*. Berlin, Fédération syndicale internationale, 1931.

Jouhaux, Léon, *Le Syndicalisme: Ce qu'il est, ce qu'il doit être*. Paris, Flammarion, 1937.

Jouhaux, Léon, *Le Syndicalisme et la C.G.T.* Paris, La Sirène, 1920.

Jouhaux, Léon, *Le Syndicalisme français: I, Le Syndicalisme français–Conférence faite à la Maison du Peuple de Bruxelles le 6 décembre 1911; II, Contre la guerre–Conférence faite à Berlin*. Paris, Rivière, 1913.

Jouhaux, Léon, «The Work of the General Conference», *International Labour Review*, 5 (March, 1922) 381–384.

Jouhaux, Léon, avec la collaboration de M. Harmel et J. Duret, *La C.G.T.: Ce qu'elle est, ce qu'elle veut*. Paris, Gallimard, 1937.

«Léon Jouhaux, 1879–1954», in *International Labour Review*, 70 (September–October, 1954) 241–257.

Lorwin, Val R., «France», in Walter Galenson, *Comparative Labor Movements*, pp. 313–410. New York, Prentice-Hall, 1952.

Lorwin, Val R., *The French Labor Movement*. Cambridge, Harvard University Press, 1954.

Lorwin, Val R., «The Struggle for Control of the French Trade-Union Movement, 1945–1949», in *Modern France: Problems of the Third and Fourth Republics*, ed. by E. M. Earle. Princeton, Princeton University Press, 1951.

Louis, Paul, *Histoire du mouvement syndical en France*. 2 Tomes. Paris, Valois, 1947–1948.

Martin-Saint-Léon, Etienne, *Les Deux C.G.T.: Syndicalisme et communisme*. Paris, Plon, 1923.

Millet, Raymond, *Jouhaux et la C.G.T.* Paris, Denoël et Steele, 1937.

Peace 1952

(Prize awarded in 1953)

ALBERT SCHWEITZER

Presentation

by Gunnar Jahn*, Chairman of the Nobel Committee

Albert Schweitzer was born in Alsace in 1875, a few years after this province had become part of the German Empire. He has seen Alsace reincorporated with France, overrun by the Germans during the Second World War, and then once again reunited with France. Having grown up in this border country, Schweitzer has from an early age known three languages: the dialect of Alsace, High German, and French. His upbringing has also given him a deep insight into both French and German cultures.

But Albert Schweitzer will never belong to any one nation. His whole life and all of his work are a message addressed to all men regardless of nationality or race. This is not to say that Schweitzer does not, like most of us, bear the stamp of the home and the country of his childhood and youth.

The son of a pastor, Albert Schweitzer grew up in the presbytery of the little village of Günsbach in a happy and harmonious home. He attended the village school along with the sons of the peasants. These childhood years, which he has himself described, saw the development within the boy of those attributes which were later to characterize the man. He speaks of little incidents which suddenly opened his eyes to traits which had previously lain dormant within him. He tells us, for example, of how an old Jew who occasionally passed through the village became a target for ridicule from the boys and of how he responded to their goading with only a gentle smile. That smile overpowered Albert Schweitzer, who subsequently took care to greet the old man with respect. Elsewhere he says that one day he

---

* Mr. Jahn delivered this speech on December 10, 1953, at the award ceremony in the Auditorium of the University of Oslo. The translation is based on the Norwegian text in *Les Prix Nobel en 1953*, which also carries a French text. Dr. Schweitzer was unable to leave his work in Africa to attend the ceremony at which his prize (the Peace Prize for 1952, which had been reserved in that year) was given. The award was accepted on his behalf by the French ambassador, Mr. de Monicault, who read a message from Dr. Schweitzer expressing his gratitude for being thus honored, his regret at having to be absent, and his intention of visiting Oslo the following year.

threw one of his schoolmates at wrestling and that afterwards the boy said to him, «If I could eat broth every day the way you do, I could be strong too.» Those words made a deep impression on the young Albert; from that moment he not only lost his taste for broth but also began to insist upon dressing like the peasant boys. A final instance: a boy once persuaded him to go bird hunting, but Schweitzer scared off the birds before the other had a chance to shoot.

We all no doubt have such experiences during childhood, but we often forget them in later years or merely smile when we recall them in the «wisdom of maturity». But to Albert Schweitzer they became something more. The feelings evoked by these incidents, far from fading, persisted in him and became the very basis of his later life despite all the experience and knowledge which he subsequently acquired.

After finishing at the village school, he continued his education in Münster and later in Mülhausen where he lived with his uncle and aunt. He admits that he was not a particularly promising pupil. «I was probably too much of a dreamer», he says. Only the teachers with whom he established a personal contact were able to record above-average performance. History and natural science were his favorite subjects. It was during those formative years between childhood and adolescence that he opened his eyes to the world about him and began to ask Why? He says himself: «Between the ages of fourteen and sixteen I had a compelling desire to discuss everything. The joy of seeking the truth and the purpose of things became almost an obsession with me.» [1] Some may say that it was the scientist in him that had awakened. Or was the urge to solve the enigma of existence perhaps already asserting itself subconsciously? During this period he also found time to cultivate and develop the great talent for music which he had shown since childhood, and to make a start on his masterly work on Johann Sebastian Bach.

The qualities dimly discernible in Albert Schweitzer as a boy stood out more clearly in early youth, qualities which were to distinguish his entire life and work: deep compassion for every living thing, and the belief that people who live happy lives owe much to those less fortunate and thus have an obligation to help them. «As far back as I can remember», he says, «the thought of all the misery in the world has been a source of pain to me.» [2]

1. See Albert Schweitzer, *Memoirs of Childhood and Youth*, p. 54.
2. *Ibid.*, pp. 60–61.

Without doubt, the young man's feeling of oneness with unhappy and destitute fellow beings, as well as his compulsion to inquire into the meaning and purpose of existence, was largely the result of innate qualities of his own. But it is no less certain that the environment in which the boy was brought up helped to strengthen them. His home, his father's sermons, the tolerance he found in the Günsbach church, where both Catholic and Protestant services were held under the same roof, must all have influenced the sensitive, religious mind of the young boy. And the family traditions, reaching back to the time of the Enlightenment–his maternal grandfather was a well-known rationalist pastor–also left their mark. This view seems to coincide with Schweitzer's own, for, after telling us of his insatiable curiosity, he concludes: «The spirit of the Enlightenment, inherited from my grandfather Schillinger, was rekindled in me.»[1]

I have dwelt so long on Albert Schweitzer's youth because I believe that it explains all of his later life and work. Already at that time a flame burned within him, a flame which he has kept alight throughout his entire life and which has become the inspirational source for all his activity. Here is what he himself has to say: «The conviction that we must, throughout life, struggle to continue to think and to feel as we did in our youth has accompanied me as a faithful adviser. I have instinctively taken care not to become what most of us understand by the term ‹a man of experience›. The knowledge of life which we adults should pass on to the younger generation is: ‹Grow into your ideals so that life cannot rob you of them.›»[2]

His schooldays over, Albert Schweitzer entered upon his academic career, with its years of study and hard work. The curiosity which he had revealed so early in life had by this time swelled into an insatiable desire to seek an answer to all the questions that crowded in upon him. And if we are to know Albert Schweitzer, we must understand the profound respect and reverence in which he held truth acquired through thought and reason. He had shown this respect at an early age, and we have his own word for it that it has in no way faded over the years: «If I were to renounce any of the enthusiasm I feel for seeking truth, I should be renouncing myself.»[3]

His years of study were rich in work and achievement. In addition to pursuing his theological and philosophical studies, he began his work on the life of Christ and on the Gospels, and started rough outlines for his

1. *Ibid.*, p. 55.
2. *Ibid.*, pp. 73, 77.
3. *Ibid.*, p. 55.

works on philosophy, culture, and ethics. At the same time, he was playing
Bach, was engrossing himself in Bach's works, and was becoming the foremost authority of his time on the composer as well as the outstanding interpreter of his music. In spite of all this activity he found time to take an
interest in the construction of organs, and it is largely thanks to him that
so many old organs have been saved from so-called modernization[1].

But all this time, preoccupied as he was by creative work, he heard a
voice within him which gave him no peace: Did he who had enjoyed such
a happy childhood and youth have the right to accept all this happiness
as a matter of course? The natural right to happiness, and all the suffering
prevailing in the world merged into one in his mind and gave decisive direction to his future life and work. It became steadily clearer to him that
anyone who enjoys many of the good things of life should in his turn repay
to others no less than he has received, and that we should all share the burden of life's suffering. These thoughts did not always return with the same
intensity, but gathered slowly and inexorably. At last «they covered the
whole sky», as he puts it, and led him at the age of twenty-one to the
decision to devote himself to the ministry, to scholarship, and to music until
he was thirty and then, after having realized his aspirations in the fields
of art and learning, to help his fellowmen in a more direct manner.

We gather from what Albert Schweitzer has written about this period
of his life that he had not yet formulated any precise plans. But one day
in 1904, when he was twenty-nine years old, he read an appeal from the
French Protestant Missionary Society in Paris asking for help for the Negroes
in French Equatorial Africa. This appeal provided him with a direct answer
to his question: «How can I help best?» He wanted to contribute his share
to the payment of the debt which the white man owed the black, and he
resolved to prepare himself for this task. To do so he had to become a
doctor.

We must try to grasp the full implications of this decision: to be thirty
years old, to be a well-known scholar in both theology and philosophy,
to have written a book on Bach and to have become a world-renowned
interpreter of Bach's music, and then–to cut all this short! He himself explains why he wanted to go through the arduous toil of medical study first
before setting to work: «I wanted to become a doctor in order to be able

1. See Schweitzer's *Out of My Life and Thought*, pp. 70–84, and his pamphlet *Deutsche
und französische Orgelbaukunst und Orgelkunst*.

to work without words. For years I had used the word. My new occupation would be not to talk about the gospel of love, but to put it into practice.» [1]

The study of medicine claimed seven years of Schweitzer's life, from 1905 to 1913. Of it he says:

«The pursuit of natural sciences gave me more than just the knowledge I sought. It was for me a spiritual experience. I had always felt that the so-called humanities with which I had been concerned present a psychic danger because they rarely reveal self-evident truths, but often present value judgments which masquerade as truth because of the way in which they are clothed...

Now, suddenly, I stood in another world. I was now working with truths based on realities, and I was among men who took it for granted that every statement had to be supported by fact.» [2]

The study of medicine gave him great satisfaction; indeed it was as if he had been initiated into an entirely new world. Nevertheless, while pursuing his intensive medical studies (and paying for them by lecturing and giving organ recitals), he continued his work in philosophy and theology and during this period completed the German edition of his work on Bach, as well as his study on Bach's preludes and fugues.

In 1913 Schweitzer finished his studies and qualified as a doctor of medicine. To obtain the money he needed to purchase equipment for his projected hospital in Africa, he pleaded with his friends and acquaintances to the point of begging. Meanwhile, the Protestant Missionary Society had expressed doubts as to his «orthodoxy», and it was only after Schweitzer had given a formal promise to confine himself to his medical work and not try to influence the faith of the Christian Negroes that the Society accepted him.

And so at long last, on Good Friday in the spring of 1913, Albert Schweitzer set out upon his journey to Lambaréné in West Africa. Lambaréné is a small village on the banks of the River Ogowé close to the equator, some 125 miles from the coast. It was here that Schweitzer began his new life, a life totally different from that of the academic world in which he had moved hitherto and one which demanded very different qualities. There, deep in the primeval forest, he began his work among backward natives who had met the white man and who had become acquainted with what Euro-

1. See *Out of My Life and Thought*, p.94.
2. *Ibid.*, p.104.

pean civilization brings in its wake whenever it breaks new ground: alcohol, disease, disintegration of the existing social systems; in short, all the evils which the white man first brings with him. It soon became evident that Schweitzer not only possessed great organizing ability, but also was adept in practical skills such as the building of the houses–or perhaps we should say huts–which were needed for the treatment and care of the sick.

More important still, Schweitzer understood the mentality of these primitive people. He did not appraise them with the eyes of a European and made no attempt to judge them according to our social customs and moral codes. For instance, he recognized polygamy as a natural consequence of their society and he believed that he would only make the bad worse by trying to abolish it. Nor did he adhere to the view that emphasized the educating of the Negroes in order to produce officials and scholars. He had no desire to destroy their existing social organizations and conventions unless he could replace them with something better. He understood that help had to be given in such a way that it could take effect gradually and without any sudden disruption of existing social systems. He realized that the task ahead would be a long and difficult one and that, if he was to make any headway at all, he would have to use simple methods which the natives could understand.

And so he helps them, heals them, and tries with untiring patience, day after day, year after year, to release them gradually from the powerful and pernicious grasp of superstition; all this in the hope that he will in the end perhaps succeed, after innumerable and bitter disappointments, in sowing a seed which may bring to life faith in the gospel of love. If we choose to judge his achievement in terms of success in fighting sickness and disease, then we should of course give pride of place to his work as a doctor. But let us never lose sight of the fact that the very impact of his personality and the propagation of his gospel of love will in the final instance achieve more, and will, in addition, stimulate the growth of brotherhood among races. If we read Schweitzer's own accounts of his life in Africa, the impression we get is not at all one of a sermonizing missionary, but of a realistic man well-acquainted with every aspect of life in the jungle, and of one whose work is dictated by the need to help and to do so where the suffering is greatest.

Albert Schweitzer's initial stay in Africa was, however, short-lived. When the First World War broke out in 1914, he was placed under surveillance as a German citizen, and in 1917 he and his wife were brought back to an internment camp in France. The leisure he enjoyed there enabled him to continue with his religious, philosophical, and cultural studies which he had in any case never entirely laid aside, even in Africa where he devoted part of his nights to them.

When Schweitzer was released from internment in 1918, he was ill, and he stayed on in Europe until 1924. Since that date he has been living in Africa, leaving only to take an occasional trip to Europe; and during the years between 1939 and 1948 he never left at all. Indeed, he is there now.

His visits to Europe have always been marked by intense activity. It seems that he has no need of rest. He has given recitals, both to offer pleasure to others and to obtain funds for the hospital at Lambaréné, which he has steadily enlarged. He has given talks on religious and cultural topics, all the while still searching for a simple definition of his philosophy, some expression of it able to give others a meaning and direction to their lives. We should never forget that Schweitzer is a man with the deepest respect for thought, and that it is through thought that he seeks to answer the questions he asks himself. «If we renounce thought, we become spiritually bankrupt,» he says, «for anyone who loses faith in man's ability to discover truth through thought drifts into skepticism.» [1]

Schweitzer's faith in the power of reason and his craving for truth are unshaken and unaltered. But he has come to the conclusion that systematic, logical thought can take us to a certain point, and no further. He says: «The only progress that knowledge allows is in enabling us to describe more and more in detail the world we see and its evolution. What matters in a world-view is to grasp the meaning and purpose of everything, and that we cannot do.» [2] He believes that he is the first Western thinker who has dared to admit this shattering conclusion without at the same time renouncing a philosophy and a world-view that enshrine life.

But it was many years before he was enable to crystallize this philosophy into the simple formula: Reverence for life. One day in 1915–he was forty years old at the time–while traveling on a river in Africa, he saw the rays of the sun shimmering on the water, the tropical forest all around, and a herd of hippopotamuses basking on the banks of the river. At that moment there came to him, as if by revelation, the phrase which precisely

1. *Ibid.*, p.222.
2. For statements similar in meaning, see Schweitzer's *Civilization and Ethics* (3rd ed., translated by C.T.Campion, revised by Mrs.Charles E.B.Russell. London: A.&C. Black, 1946), pp.240–242.

expressed his thought: Reverence for life[1]. Once again, as before in youth and childhood, a simple incident opened the door for him.

«But», he says, «one cannot come to this by systematic logical reasoning and knowledge, for neither can furnish an explanation of the world and of the purpose of life.» The explanation is found through what he calls elemental thought. This leads to a reverence for that ineffable thing which is life, to an affirmation of life which is more than the will to live. Schweitzer puts it this way: «I am life that wills to live in the midst of other life that wills to live.»[2] There is an affirmation of life in this which leads one beyond self to a reverence for all will to live, so that everything which maintains, nourishes, and ennobles life is good and positive, and all else is evil and negative. On this thought Schweitzer builds his universal ethic, and through it he believes mankind comes into spiritual communion with the eternal. He calls this philosophy of life «ethical mysticism».

Albert Schweitzer has been called an agnostic. If an agnostic is understood to be a man who admits that we cannot find the answer to essential questions through rational thinking, then the term can justifiably be applied to him. But he takes his reasoning a step further and states that if rational thinking is carried far enough it leads to irrational mysticism.

I would prefer to put it like this: Where thought reaches its limits, there faith begins, and we are then close to religion. Schweitzer himself has expressed it in these words: «The world-view based on reverence for life is, through the religious character of its ethic of active love and through its fervor, essentially akin to that of Christianity... What Christianity needs is to be filled with the spirit of Jesus Christ, to become living, intense, a religion of love which it was meant to be. Since I myself am deeply devoted to Christianity, I seek to serve it with fidelity and truth. I hope that the thought which has resulted in this simple, ethical-religious idea–reverence for life–may help to bring Christianity and thought closer to each other.»[3]

This then is what Albert Schweitzer has to say to us about reverence for life, about the religion of love, and about the concept of brotherhood. Great is the number of those who have in the course of time talked to mankind about this, a greater number in the past than in the present when the concept of brotherhood is being eclipsed by so many of today's slogans.

But even in these troubled and uncertain times men are searching for

1. *Out of My Life and Thought*, p. 156.
2. *Ibid.*, p. 157.
3. *Ibid.*, pp. 235–240.

something which will allow them to believe that mankind will one day enjoy the reign of peace and goodwill.

If altruism, reverence for life, and the idea of brotherhood can become living realities in the hearts of men, we will have laid the very foundations of a lasting peace between individuals, nations, and races.

We all realize that we are still far away from this goal. It is the youth of today who will follow the path indicated by Albert Schweitzer. All through his long life he has been true to his own youth and he has shown us that a man's life and his dream can become one. His work has made the concept of brotherhood a living one, and his words have reached and taken root in the minds of countless men.

ALBERT SCHWEITZER

The Problem of Peace

Nobel Lecture*, November 4, 1954

For the subject of my lecture, a redoubtable honor imposed by the award of the Nobel Peace Prize, I have chosen the problem of peace as it is today. In so doing, I believe that I have acted in the spirit of the founder of this prize who devoted himself to the study of the problem as it existed in his own day and age, and who expected his Foundation to encourage consideration of ways to serve the cause of peace.

I shall begin with an account of the situation at the end of the two wars through which we have recently passed.

The statemen who were responsible for shaping the world of today through the negotiations which followed each of these two wars found the cards stacked against them. Their aim was not so much to create situations which might give rise to widespread and prosperous development as it was to establish the results of victory on a permanent basis. Even if their judgment had been unerring, they could not have used it as a guide. They were obliged to regard themselves as the executors of the will of the conquering peoples. They could not aspire to establishing relations between peoples on a just and proper basis; all their efforts were taken up by the necessity of preventing the most unreasonable of the demands made by the victors from becoming reality; they had, moreover, to convince the conquering nations to compromise with each other whenever their respective views and interests conflicted.

The true source of what is untenable in our present situation–and the victors are beginning to suffer from it as well as the vanquished–lies in the fact that not enough thought was given to the realities of historical fact and, consequently, to what is just and beneficial.

The historical problem of Europe is conditioned by the fact that in past

---

* Dr. Schweitzer delivered this lecture in the Auditorium of Oslo University almost a year after having received the award. The Oslo *Aftenposten* for November 5 reports that he read quietly from a manuscript and that the seriousness and simplicity of his speech moved the audience. This translation is based on the text in French, the language which Dr. Schweitzer used on this occasion, published in *Les Prix Nobel en 1954*.

centuries, particularly in the so-called era of the great invasions, the peoples from the East penetrated farther and farther into the West and Southwest, taking possession of the land[1]. So it came about that the later immigrants intermingled with the earlier already established immigrants.

A partial fusion of these peoples took place during this time, and new relatively homogeneous political societies were formed within the new frontiers. In western and central Europe, this evolution led to a situation which may be said to have crystallized and become definitive in its main features in the course of the nineteenth century.

In the East and Southeast, on the other hand, the evolution did not reach this stage; it stopped with the coexistence of nationalities which failed to merge. Each could lay some claim to rightful ownership of the land. One might claim territorial rights by virtue of longer possession or superiority of numbers, while another might point to its contribution in developing the land. The only practical solution would have been for the two groups to agree to live together in the same territory and in a single political society, in accordance with a compromise acceptable to both. It would have been necessary, however, for this state of affairs to have been reached before the second third of the nineteenth century. For, from then on, there was increasingly vigorous development of national consciousness which brought with it serious consequences. This development no longer allowed peoples to be guided by historical realities and by reason.

The First World War, then, had its origins in the conditions which prevailed in eastern and southeastern Europe. The new order created after both world wars bears in its turn the seeds of a future conflict.

Any new postwar structure is bound to contain the seeds of conflict unless it takes account of historical fact and is designed to provide a just and objective solution to problems in the light of that fact. Only such a solution can be really permanent.

Historical reality is trampled underfoot if, when two peoples have rival historical claims to the same country, the claims of only one are recognized. The titles which two nations hold to disputed parts of Europe never have more than a relative value since the peoples of both are, in effect, immigrants.

Similarly, we are guilty of contempt for history if, in establishing a new order, we fail to take economic realities into consideration when fixing

1. The Huns moved into the Danube valley in the fourth century; the Visigoths moved westward into Italy and Spain early in the fifth century; the Vandals moved into France and Spain somewhat later in the century.

frontiers. Such is the case if we draw a boundary so as to deprive a port of its natural hinterland or raise a barrier between a region rich in raw materials and another particularly suited to exploiting them. By such measures do we create states which cannot survive economically.

The most flagrant violation of historical rights, and indeed of human rights, consists in depriving certain peoples of their right to the land on which they live, thus forcing them to move to other territories. At the end of the Second World War, the victorious powers decided to impose this fate on hundreds of thousands of people, and under the most harsh conditions[1]; from this we can judge how little aware they were of any mission to work toward a reorganization which would be reasonably equitable and which would guarantee a propitious future.

Our situation ever since the Second World War has been characterized essentially by the fact that no peace treaty has yet been signed[2]. It was only through agreements of a truce-like nature that the war came to an end; and it is indeed because of our inability to effect a reorganization, however elemental, that we are obliged to be content with these truces which, dictated by the needs of the moment, can have no foreseeable future.

This then is the present situation. How do we perceive the problem of peace now?

In quite a new light – different to the same extent that modern war is different from war in the past. War now employs weapons of death and destruction incomparably more effective than those of the past and is consequently a worse evil than ever before. Heretofore war could be regarded as an evil to which men must resign themselves because it served progress and was even necessary to it. One could argue that thanks to war the peoples with the strongest virtues survived, thus determining the course of history.

It could be claimed, for example, that the victory of Cyrus over the Babylonians created an empire in the Near East with a civilization higher than that which it supplanted, and that Alexander the Great's victory in its turn opened the way, from the Nile to the Indus, for Greek civilization. The reverse, however, sometimes occurred when war led to the replacement of a superior civilization by an inferior one, as it did, for instance, in the

1. The major example: The Potsdam Conference (1945), attended by the principal World War II Allies, allowed the mass expulsion of the German population from Czechoslovakia and from the territories given over to Russian and Polish administration.
2. Nor has a peace treaty with Germany been signed as of August, 1971.

seventh century and at the beginning of the eighth when the Arabs gained mastery over Persia, Asia Minor, Palestine, North Africa, and Spain, countries that had hitherto flourished under a Greco-Roman civilization.

It would seem then that, in the past, war could operate just as well in favor of progress as against it. It is with much less conviction that we can claim modern war to be an agent of progress. The evil that it embodies weighs more heavily on us than ever before.

It is pertinent to recall that the generation preceding 1914 approved the enormous stockpiling of armaments. The argument was that a military decision would be reached with rapidity and that very brief wars could be expected. This opinion was accepted without contradiction.

Because they anticipated the progressive humanization of the methods of war, people also believed that the evils resulting from future conflicts would be relatively slight. This supposition grew out of the obligations accepted by nations under the terms of the Geneva Convention of 1864, following the efforts of the Red Cross. Mutual guarantees were exchanged concerning care for the wounded, the humane treatment of prisoners of war, and the welfare of the civilian population. This convention did indeed achieve some significant results for which hundreds of thousands of combatants and civilians were to be thankful in the wars to come. But, compared to the miseries of war, which have grown beyond all proportion with the introduction of modern weapons of death and destruction, they are trivial indeed. Truly, it cannot be a question of humanizing war.

The concept of the brief war and that of the humanization of its methods, propounded as they were on the eve of war in 1914, led people to take the war less seriously than they should have. They regarded it as a storm which was to clear the political air and as an event which was to end the arms race that was ruining nations.

While some lightheartedly supported the war on account of the profits they expected to gain from it, others did so from a more noble motive: this war must be the war to end all wars. Many a brave man set out for battle in the belief that he was fighting for a day when war would no longer exist.

In this conflict, just as in that of 1939, these two concepts proved to be completely wrong. Slaughter and destruction continued year after year and were carried on in the most inhumane way. In contrast to the war of 1870[1],

---

1. France versus Germany.

the duel was not between two isolated nations, but between two great groups of nations, so that a large share of mankind became embroiled, thus compounding the tragedy.

Since we now know what a terrible evil war is, we must spare no effort to prevent its recurrence. To this reason must also be added an ethical one: In the course of the last two wars, we have been guilty of acts of inhumanity which make one shudder, and in any future war we would certainly be guilty of even worse. This must not happen!

Let us dare to face the situation. Man has become superman. He is a superman because he not only has at his disposal innate physical forces, but also commands, thanks to scientific and technological advances, the latent forces of nature which he can now put to his own use. To kill at a distance, man used to rely solely on his own physical strength; he used it to bend the bow and to release the arrow. The superman has progressed to the stage where, thanks to a device designed for the purpose, he can use the energy released by the combustion of a given combination of chemical products. This enables him to employ a much more effective projectile and to propel it over far greater distances.

However, the superman suffers from a fatal flaw. He has failed to rise to the level of superhuman reason which should match that of his super-human strength. He requires such reason to put this vast power to solely reasonable and useful ends and not to destructive and murderous ones. Because he lacks it, the conquests of science and technology become a mortal danger to him rather than a blessing.

In this context is it not significant that the first great scientific discovery, the harnessing of the force resulting from the combustion of gunpowder, was seen at first only as a means of killing at a distance?

The conquest of the air, thanks to the internal-combustion engine, mark-ed a decisive advance for humanity. Yet men grasped at once the opportunity it offered to kill and destroy from the skies. This invention underlined a fact which had hitherto been steadfastly denied: the more the superman gains in strength, the poorer he becomes. To avoid exposing himself completely to the destruction unleashed from the skies, he is obliged to seek refuge underground like a hunted animal. At the same time he must resign himself to abetting the unprecedented destruction of cultural values.

A new stage was reached with the discovery and subsequent utilization of the vast forces liberated by the splitting of the atom. After a time, it was found that the destructive potential of a bomb armed with such forces was incalculable, and that even large-scale tests could unleash catastrophies threatening the very existence of the human race. Only now has the full horror of our position become obvious. No longer can we evade the question of the future of mankind.

But the essential fact which we should acknowledge in our conscience, and which we should have acknowledged a long time ago, is that we are becoming inhuman to the extent that we become supermen. We have learned to tolerate the facts of war: that men are killed en masse–some twenty million in the Second World War–that whole cities and their inhabitants are annihilated by the atomic bomb, that men are turned into living torches by incendiary bombs. We learn of these things from the radio or newspapers and we judge them according to whether they signify success for the group of peoples to which we belong, or for our enemies. When we do admit to ourselves that such acts are the results of inhuman conduct, our admission is accompanied by the thought that the very fact of war itself leaves us no option but to accept them. In resigning ourselves to our fate without a struggle, we are guilty of inhumanity.

What really matters is that we should all of us realize that we are guilty of inhumanity. The horror of this realization should shake us out of our lethargy so that we can direct our hopes and our intentions to the coming of an era in which war will have no place.

This hope and this will can have but one aim: to attain, through a change in spirit, that superior reason which will dissuade us from misusing the power at our disposal.

The first to have the courage to advance purely ethical arguments against war and to stress the necessity for reason governed by an ethical will was the great humanist Erasmus of Rotterdam in his *Querela pacis (The Complaint of Peace)* which appeared in 1517[1]. In this book he depicts Peace on stage seeking an audience.

Erasmus found few adherents to his way of thinking. To expect the affirmation of an ethical necessity to point the way to peace was considered a utopian ideal. Kant shared this opinion. In his essay on «Perpetual Peace», which appeared in 1795[2], and in other publications in which he touches

---

1. Desiderius Erasmus (1466?–1536), *Querela pacis undique gentium ejectae profligataeque* (Basel: Joh. Froben, 1517).
2. Immanuel Kant (1724–1804), *Zum ewigen Frieden* (1795). English translation entitled *Perpetual Peace* (New York: Columbia University Press, 1932); the introduction is by Nicholas Murray Butler, Nobel Peace co-laureate for 1931.

upon the problem of peace, he states his belief that peace will come only with the increasing authority of an international code of law, in accordance with which an international court of arbitration would settle disputes between nations. This authority, he maintains, should be based entirely on the increasing respect which in time, and for purely practical motives, men will hold for the law as such. Kant is unremitting in his insistence that the idea of a league of nations cannot be hoped for as the outcome of ethical argument, but only as the result of the perfecting of law. He believes that this process of perfecting will come of itself. In his opinion, «nature, that great artist» will lead men, very gradually, it is true, and over a very long period of time, through the march of history and the misery of wars, to agree on an international code of law which will guarantee perpetual peace.

A plan for a league of nations having powers of arbitration was first formulated with some precision by Sully, the friend and minister of Henry IV. It was given detailed treatment by the Abbé Castel de Saint-Pierre in three works, the most important of which bears the title *Projet de paix perpétuelle entre les souverains chrétiens* [Plan for Perpetual Peace between Christian Sovereigns]. Kant was aware of the views it developed, probably from an extract which Rousseau published in 1761 [1].

Today we can judge the efficacy of international institutions by the experience we have had with the League of Nations in Geneva and with the United Nations. Such institutions can render important services by offering to mediate conflicts at their very inception, by taking the initiative in setting up international projects, and by other actions of a similar nature, depending on the circumstances. One of the League of Nations' most important achievements was the creation in 1922 of an internationally valid passport for the benefit of those who became stateless as a consequence of war [2]. What a position those people would have been in if this travel document had not

1. Maximilien de Béthune, duc de Sully (1560–1641), in scattered passages of his memoirs, *Oechonomies royales* (1638), describes a «Grand Design» for world organization which he attributes to Henry IV. Abbé Castel de Saint-Pierre (1658–1743), *Projet de paix perpétuelle* (1712, 1717); *Discours sur la polysynodie* (1719). Jean Jacques Rousseau (1712–1778), *Extrait du Projet de paix perpétuelle de M. l'Abbé de Saint-Pierre* (Amsterdam, 1761). Two other such pieces by Rousseau, on *Polysynodie* and his *Jugement sur la Paix perpétuelle*, were written in 1756 but published for the first time in the posthumous editions of his works.
2. The «Nansen Passport» (so called for Fridtjof Nansen, recipient of the Nobel Peace Prize for 1922) was an identification certificate, established in July, 1922, for Armenian, Chaldean, Turkish, and Syrian refugees, which could be used as a passport.

been devised through Nansen's initiative! What would have been the fate of displaced persons after 1945 if the United Nations had not existed!

Nevertheless these two institutions have been unable to bring about peace. Their efforts were doomed to fail since they were obliged to undertake them in a world in which there was no prevailing spirit directed toward peace. And being only legal institutions, they were unable to create such a spirit. The ethical spirit alone has the power to generate it. Kant deceived himself in thinking that he could dispense with it in his search for peace. We must follow the road on which he turned his back.

What is more, we just cannot wait the extremely long time he deemed necessary for this movement toward peace to mature. War today means annihilation, a fact that Kant did not foresee. Decisive steps must be taken to ensure peace, and decisive results obtained without delay. Only through the spirit can all this be done.

Is the spirit capable of achieving what we in our distress must expect of it?

Let us not underestimate its power, the evidence of which can be seen throughout the history of mankind. The spirit created this humanitarianism which is the origin of all progress toward some form of higher existence. Inspired by humanitarianism we are true to ourselves and capable of creating. Inspired by a contrary spirit we are unfaithful to ourselves and fall prey to all manner of error.

The height to which the spirit can ascend was revealed in the seventeenth and eighteenth centuries. It led those peoples of Europe who possessed it out of the Middle Ages, putting an end to superstition, witch hunts, torture, and a multitude of other forms of cruelty or traditional folly. It replaced the old with the new in an evolutionary way that never ceases to astonish those who observe it. All that we have ever possessed of true civilization, and indeed all that we still possess, can be traced to a manifestation of this spirit.

Later, its power waned because the spirit failed to find support for its ethical character in a world preoccupied with scientific pursuits. It has been replaced by a spirit less sure of the course humanity should take and more content with lesser ideals. Today if we are to avoid our own downfall, we must commit ourselves to this spirit once again. It must bring forth a new miracle just as it did in the Middle Ages, an even greater miracle than the first.

The spirit is not dead; it lives in isolation. It has overcome the difficulty of having to exist in a world out of harmony with its ethical character. It has come to realize that it can find no home other than in the basic nature of man. The independence acquired through its acceptance of this realization is an additional asset.

It is convinced that compassion, in which ethics takes root, does not assume its true proportions until it embraces not only man but every living being. To the old ethics, which lacked this depth and force of conviction, has been added the ethics of reverence for life, and its validity is steadily gaining in recognition.

Once more we dare to appeal to the whole man, to his capacity to think and feel, exhorting him to know himself and to be true to himself. We reaffirm our trust in the profound qualities of his nature. And our living experiences are proving us right.

In 1950, there appeared a book entitled *Témoignages d'humanité* [*Documents of Humanity*] [1], published by some professors from the University of Göttingen who had been brought together by the frightful mass expulsion of the eastern Germans in 1945. The refugees tell in simple words of the help they received in their distress from men belonging to the enemy nations, men who might well have been moved to hate them. Rarely have I been so gripped by a book as I was by this one. It is a wonderful tonic for anyone who has lost faith in humanity.

Whether peace comes or not depends on the direction in which the mentality of individuals develops and then, in turn, on that of their nations. This truth holds more meaning for us today than it did for the past. Erasmus, Sully, the Abbé Castel de Saint-Pierre, and the others who in their time were engrossed in the problem of peace dealt with princes and not with peoples. Their efforts tended to be concentrated on the establishment of a supranational authority vested with the power of arbitrating any difficulties which might arise between princes. Kant, in his essay on «Perpetual Peace», was the first to foresee an age when peoples would govern themselves and when they, no less than the sovereigns, would be concerned with the problem of peace. He thought of this evolution as progress. In his opinion, peoples would be more inclined than princes to maintain peace because it is they who bear the miseries of war.

The time has come, certainly, when governments must look on themselves

1. *Documents of Humanity during the Mass Expulsions*, compiled by K.O.Kurth, translated by Helen Taubert and Margaret Brooke (Göttingen: Göttingen Research Committee, 1952).

as the executors of the will of the people. But Kant's reliance on the people's innate love for peace has not been justified. Because the will of the people, being the will of the crowd, has not avoided the danger of instability and the risk of emotional distraction from the path of true reason, it has failed to demonstrate a vital sense of responsibility. Nationalism of the worst sort was displayed in the last two wars, and it may be regarded today as the greatest obstacle to mutual understanding between peoples.

Such nationalism can be repulsed only through the rebirth of a humanitarian ideal among men which will make their allegiance to their country a natural one inspired by genuine ideals.

Spurious nationalism is rampant in countries across the seas too, especially among those peoples who formerly lived under white domination and who have recently gained their independence. They are in danger of allowing nationalism to become their one and only ideal. Indeed, peace, which had prevailed until now in many areas, is today in jeopardy.

These peoples, too, can overcome their naive nationalism only by adopting a humanitarian ideal. But how is such a change to be brought about? Only when the spirit becomes a living force within us and leads us to a civilization based on the humanitarian ideal, will it act, through us, upon these peoples. All men, even the semicivilized and the primitive, are, as beings capable of compassion, able to develop a humanitarian spirit. It abides within them like tinder ready to be lit, waiting only for a spark.

The idea that the reign of peace must come one day has been given expression by a number of peoples who have attained a certain level of civilization. In Palestine it appeared for the first time in the words of the prophet Amos in the eighth century B.C.[1], and it continues to live in the Jewish and Christian religions as the belief in the Kingdom of God. It figures in the doctrine taught by the great Chinese thinkers: Confucius and Lao-tse in the sixth century B.C., Mi-tse in the fifth, and Meng-tse in the fourth[2]. It reappears in Tolstoy[3] and in other contemporary European thinkers. People have labeled it a utopia. But the situation today is such that it must become reality in one way or another; otherwise mankind will perish.

1. Amos 9:11-15.
2. Confucius (551-479 B.C.); Lao-tse (600-517 B.C.); Mi-tse [also Mo Ti or Micius] (479-372 B.C.); Meng-tse [also Mencius] (371-289 B.C.).
3. In the *Works* (London: Oxford University Press, 1935), Volume 20 is entitled *The Kingdom of God and Peace Essays*. See, for example, «Address to the Swedish Peace Congress in 1909», pp. 583-591.

I am well aware that what I have had to say on the problem of peace is not essentially new. It is my profound conviction that the solution lies in our rejecting war for an ethical reason; namely, that war makes us guilty of the crime of inhumanity. Erasmus of Rotterdam and several others after him have already proclaimed this as the truth around which we should rally.

The only originality I claim is that for me this truth goes hand in hand with the intellectual certainty that the human spirit is capable of creating in our time a new mentality, an ethical mentality. Inspired by this certainty, I too proclaim this truth in the hope that my testimony may help to prevent its rejection as an admirable sentiment but a practical impossibility. Many a truth has lain unnoticed for a long time, ignored simply because no one perceived its potential for becoming reality.

Only when an ideal of peace is born in the minds of the peoples will the institutions set up to maintain this peace effectively fulfill the function expected of them.

Even today, we live in an age characterized by the absence of peace; even today, nations can feel themselves threatened by other nations; even today, we must concede to each nation the right to stand ready to defend itself with the terrible weapons now at its disposal.

Such is the predicament in which we seek the first sign of the spirit in which we must place our trust. This sign can be none other than an effort on the part of peoples to atone as far as possible for the wrongs they inflicted upon each other during the last war. Hundreds of thousands of prisoners and deportees are waiting to return to their homes; others, unjustly condemned by a foreign power, await their acquittal; innumerable other injustices still await reparation.

In the name of all who toil in the cause of peace, I beg the peoples to take the first step along this new highway. Not one of them will lose a fraction of the power necessary for their own defense.

If we take this step to liquidate the injustices of the war which we have just experienced, we will instill a little confidence in all people. For any enterprise, confidence is the capital without which no effective work can be carried on. It creates in every sphere of activity conditions favoring fruitful growth. In such an atmosphere of confidence thus created we can begin to seek an equitable settlement of the problems caused by the two wars.

I believe that I have expressed the thoughts and hopes of millions of men who, in our part of the world, live in fear of war to come. May my words convey their intended meaning if they penetrate to the other part of the world–the other side of the trench–to those who live there in the same fear.

May the men who hold the destiny of peoples in their hands, studiously avoid anything that might cause the present situation to deteriorate and become even more dangerous. May they take to heart the words of the Apostle Paul: «If it be possible, as much as lieth in you, live peaceably with all men.» [1] These words are valid not only for individuals, but for nations as well. May these nations, in their efforts to maintain peace, do their utmost to give the spirit time to grow and to act.

1. Romans 12:18.

Biography

Albert Schweitzer (January 14, 1875–September 4, 1965) was born into an Alsatian family which for generations had been devoted to religion, music, and education. His father and maternal grandfather were ministers; both of his grandfathers were talented organists; many of his relatives were persons of scholarly attainments.

Schweitzer entered into his intensive theological studies in 1893 at the University of Strasbourg where he obtained a doctorate in philosophy in 1899, with a dissertation on the religious philosophy of Kant, and received his licentiate in theology in 1900. He began preaching at St. Nicholas Church in Strasbourg in 1899; he served in various high ranking administrative posts from 1901 to 1912 in the Theological College of St. Thomas, the college he had attended at the University of Strasbourg. In 1906 he published *The Quest of the Historical Jesus*, a book on which much of his fame as a theological scholar rests.

Meanwhile he continued with a distinguished musical career initiated at an early age with piano and organ lessons. Only nine when he first performed in his father's church, he was, from his young manhood to his middle eighties, recognized as a concert organist, internationally known. From his professional engagements he earned funds for his education, particularly his later medical schooling, and for his African hospital. Musicologist as well as performer, Schweitzer wrote a biography of Bach in 1905 in French, published a book on organ building and playing in 1906, and rewrote the Bach book in German in 1908.

Having decided to go to Africa as a medical missionary rather than as a pastor, Schweitzer in 1905 began the study of medicine at the University of Strasbourg. In 1913, having obtained his M.D. degree, he founded his hospital at Lambaréné in French Equatorial Africa, but in 1917 he and his wife were sent to a French internment camp as prisoners of war. Released in 1918, Schweitzer spent the next six years in Europe, preaching in his old church, giving lectures and concerts, taking medical courses, writing *On the*

Edge of the Primeval Forest, The Decay and Restoration of Civilization, Civiliza-
tion and Ethics, and *Christianity and the Religions of the World.*

Schweitzer returned to Lambaréné in 1924 and except for relatively short periods of time, spent the remainder of his life there. With the funds earned from his own royalties and personal appearance fees and with those donated from all parts of the world, he expanded the hospital to seventy buildings which by the early 1960's could take care of over 500 patients in residence at any one time.

At Lambaréné, Schweitzer was doctor and surgeon in the hospital, pastor of a congregation, administrator of a village, superintendent of buildings and grounds, writer of scholarly books, commentator on contemporary history, musician, host to countless visitors. The honors he received were numerous, including the Goethe Prize of Frankfurt and honorary doctorates from many universities emphasizing one or another of his achievements. The Nobel Peace Prize for 1952, having been withheld in that year, was given to him on December 10, 1953. With the $33,000 prize money, he started the leprosarium at Lambaréné.

Albert Schweitzer died on September 4, 1965, and was buried at Lambaréné.

Selected Bibliography

Anderson, Erica, *The Schweitzer Album.* New York, Harper & Row, 1965.

Jack, H. A., ed., *To Dr. Albert Schweitzer: A Festschrift Commemorating His 80th Birthday.* Evanston, Illinois, Friends of Albert Schweitzer, 1955. Contains an excellent bibliography up to 1955.

Joy, Charles R., *Music in the Life of Albert Schweitzer: Selections from His Writings.* London, A. & C. Black, 1953.

McKnight, Gerald, *Verdict on Schweitzer: The Man behind the Legend of Lambaréné.* New York, John Day, 1964.

Montague, Joseph Franklin, *The Why of Albert Schweitzer.* New York, Hawthorn Books, 1965.

Mozley, E. N., *The Theology of Albert Schweitzer for Christian Inquirers.* New York, Macmillan, 1951.

Picht, Werner, *Albert Schweitzer: The Man and His Work.* London, Allen & Unwin, 1964. Also published under the title *The Life and Thought of Albert Schweitzer.* New York, Harper & Row, 1964.

Schweitzer, Albert, *Christianity and the Religions of the World*. (*Das Christentum und die Weltreligionen*. Bern, Paul Haupt, 1924.) Translated by Joanna Powers. London, Allen & Unwin, 1939.

Schweitzer, Albert, *Cultural Philosophy I: The Decay and the Restoration of Civilization*. (*Kulturphilosophie I: Verfall und Wiederaufbau der Kultur*. Bern, Paul Haupt, 1923.) Translated by C. T. Campion. London, A. & C. Black. 2nd ed., 1932.

Schweitzer, Albert, *Cultural Philosophy II: Civilization and Ethics*. (*Kulturphilosophie II: Kultur und Ethik*. Bern, Paul Haupt, 1923.) Translated by John Naish. London, A. & C. Black, 1929.

Schweitzer, Albert, *Deutsche und französische Orgelbaukunst und Orgelkunst*. Leipzig, Breitkopf & Härtel, 1906.

Schweitzer, Albert, *From My African Notebook*. (*Afrikanische Geschichten*. Leipzig, Felix Meiner, 1938.) Translated by Mrs. C. E. B. Russell. London, Allen & Unwin, 1938.

Schweitzer, Albert, *Goethe: Five Studies*, translated by Charles R. Joy. Boston, Beacon Press, 1961.

Schweitzer, Albert, *Indian Thought and Its Development*. (*Die Weltanschauung der indischen Denker: Mystik und Ethik*. Munich, C. H. Beck, 1935.) Translated by Mrs. C. E. B. Russell. London, Hodder & Stoughton, 1936.

Schweitzer, Albert, *J. S. Bach*, translated [into English] by Ernest Newman. 2 vols. London, A. & C. Black, 1911. (First published in French, *J. S. Bach: Le Musicien-poète*. Avec la collaboration de M. Hubert Gillot. Paris, Costallat, 1905.)

Schweitzer, Albert, *Memoirs of Childhood and Youth*. (*Aus meiner Kindheit und Jugendzeit*. Munich, C. H. Beck, 1924.) Translated by C. T. Campion. London, Allen & Unwin, 1924. New York, Macmillan, 1949.

Schweitzer, Albert, *More from the Primeval Forest*. (*Das Urwaldspital zu Lambaréné*. Munich, C. H. Beck, 1931.) Translated by C. T. Campion. London, A. & C. Black, 1931.

Schweitzer, Albert, *The Mysticism of Paul the Apostle*. (*Die Mystik des Apostels Paulus*. Tübingen, J. C. B. Mohr, 1930.) Translated by W. Montgomery. London, A. & C. Black, 1931.

Schweitzer, Albert, *On the Edge of the Primeval Forest*. (*Zwischen Wasser und Urwald*. Upsala, Lindblad, 1920.) Translated by C. T. Campion. London, A. & C. Black, 1922.

Schweitzer, Albert, *Out of My Life and Thought: An Autobiography*. (*Aus meinem Leben und Denken*. Leipzig, Felix Meiner, 1931.) Translated by C. T. Campion. New York, Henry Holt, 1933; 1949.

Schweitzer, Albert, *Paul and His Interpreters: A Critical History*. (*Geschichte der Paulinischen Forschung von der Reformation bis auf die Gegenwart*. Tübingen, J. C. B. Mohr, 1911.) Translated by W. Montgomery. London, A. & C. Black, 1912.

Schweitzer, Albert, *Peace or Atomic War?* (Three appeals broadcast from Oslo on April 28, 29 and 30, 1958.) London, A. & C. Black, 1958.

Schweitzer, Albert, *The Psychiatric Study of Jesus*. (*Die psychiatrische Beurteilung Jesu: Darstellung und Kritik*. Tübingen, J. C. B. Mohr, 1913.) Translated by Charles R. Joy. Boston, Beacon Press, 1948.

Schweitzer, Albert, *The Quest of the Historical Jesus: A Critical Study of Its Progress from Reimarus to Wrede.* (*Von Reimarus zu Wrede: Eine Geschichte der Leben-Jesu-Forschung.* Tübingen, J.C.B.Mohr, 1906.) Translated by W.Montgomery. London, A. & C.Black, 1910.

Seaver, George, *Albert Schweitzer: Christian Revolutionary.* London, A. & C.Black, 1944. 2nd ed.rev.1955.

Seaver, George, *Albert Schweitzer: The Man and His Mind.* New York, Harper, 1947.

Peace 1953

GEORGE CATLETT MARSHALL

Presentation

by Carl Joachim Hambro*, Member of the Nobel Committee

When Cadet First Captain George Catlett Marshall graduated from the Virginia Military Institute, the Nobel Committee of the Norwegian Parliament was meeting to discuss the awarding of Nobel's Peace Prize for the first time. And on the day when Marshall, who had not yet completed his twenty-first year, received a letter from the Adjutant General of the Army informing him that the examining board had found him eminently suitable for appointment to the Regular Army and that his commission would be issued to him after his twenty-first birthday–on that very day[1] the first Peace Prize was awarded in Oslo. It was given to Henri Dunant, who had founded the Red Cross, and to Frédéric Passy[2], who had organized the first French peace society and was a pioneer in the work for international arbitration agreements.

If anybody at that time had told Lieutenant George Marshall that fifty years later he would not only be president of the American Red Cross, but also that he himself would some day receive the Peace Prize–the prediction would hardly have been believed and still less welcomed. Young George Marshall may have seen himself as a future general; but he had a long way to travel before he arrived at the clear and passionate understanding that the final object to be obtained by war, the only justifiable goal, is to make another war impossible. It was a way that would take him over larger areas of the earth and the oceans and under the skies than any commander has traveled before him, and let him see more battlefields and a greater devasta-

---

* Mr. Hambro, also at this time president of the (Odelsting) a section of the Norwegian Parliament, delivered this speech on December 10, 1953, in the Auditorium of the University of Oslo, following Mr. Jahn's speech in honor of Albert Schweitzer. The translation is based upon the Norwegian text published in *Les Prix Nobel en 1953*. General Marshall was present at the ceremony and, at the conclusion of Mr. Hambro's speech, received his award from Mr. Jahn, chairman of the Nobel Committee. General Marshall gave an impromptu response to the presentation.

1. December 10, 1901.
2. Henri Dunant (1828–1910) and Frédéric Passy (1822–1912), Nobel Peace Prize co-laureates in 1901.

tion than any general has seen before him, and let him plan and direct larger armies and fleets and air forces than history has ever known.

Two things stand out for those trying to follow Marshall's development. On the one hand the insatiable desire to learn, to know, to understand, and on the other hand his keen and wide-awake interest in the individual soldier, his indefatigable work for the welfare of the soldier. Both things have had a far-reaching influence on his work and on the spiritual and social evolution of his mind.

His eagerness to find out everything about the human beings for whom he felt responsible made him a sometimes rather terrifying phenomenon among his contemporaries. Twenty-one years old, he was made commanding officer of some of the small and utterly lonely outposts in the Philippines; he studied the language and customs and mentality of the natives; he realized that the discipline he valued so highly depended first of all on his own self-discipline and his capacity for keeping his men intelligently occupied, for giving them tasks which could awaken their interest. Two words above all others became his guide – as he underlined it years later in an address to the graduating class at his old military school – the words *honor* and *self-sacrifice*.

The young officer demanded much from his men, but still more from himself. When he graduated from V.M.I. after four years, there was not a single demerit beside his name. And so it has continued throughout his life. His record has always been perfectly clean and bright. He was as straight and erect morally as he was physically. Wherever he was sent by his superiors he won the same reputation for eminent ability. Typical of the high esteem in which he was held is what happened in 1916 when he returned to the States from his second long stay in the Philippines. He took over the training program of a camp in Utah; and when the camp closed, the commanding officer was required to make an efficiency report on the officers under his command. One standard question is: «Would you desire to have him under your immediate command in peace and in war?»

The Colonel [1] wrote in reply concerning Marshall: «Yes, but I would prefer to serve *under his command*... In my judgment there are not five officers in the Army so well qualified as he to command a division in the field.»

The Colonel then recommended that he be promoted to brigadier gen-

1. Lt. Colonel Johnson Hagood, commanding officer at Fort Douglas, Utah, 1916. The quotation is from Marshall's Efficiency Report, December 31, 1916. See Forrest C. Pogue, *George C. Marshall: Education of a General*, p. 138 and ch. 8, fn. 22.

eral, notwithstanding regulations, and then added to underscore his statement: «He is my junior by over 1,800 files.»

With this reputation and such military recommendations, Marshall sailed for France in June, 1917, with the first ship in the first convoy of American troops. The incredible want of preparedness, the confusion, the chaos, the lack of arms and munitions which resulted in 25,000 casualties in this first division of 27,000 were destined to be Marshall's nightmare for many years to come. It was made his task to organize both this division and others; he became chief of operations of the division and later the aide to General Pershing[1]. In the American official military records it is stated laconically: «He was assigned to general headquarters at Chaumont and given the task of drafting the plans for the St. Mihiel offensive... As that battle got under way, he was given the task of transferring some 500,000 troops and 2,700 guns to the Argonne front in preparation for that battle.»[2] He was made a temporary major, lieutenant colonel, and colonel; he was recommended for promotion to brigadier general by General Pershing whose right-hand man he had become. Pershing's recommendation, however, was not accepted by higher authority, and after the Armistice Marshall became captain once more; for under American law promotion in times of peace can only be given under the strictest rules of seniority. And Marshall had to wait for fifteen years before he was made a colonel again.

It is not hard to understand why, once made chief of staff, he demanded that the rules of promotion be amended. The amendment was passed in September, 1940, and before the end of the year a certain Major Eisenhower was made colonel and then brigadier general, jumping 366 senior colonels.

During the years between the wars, Marshall was stationed in Tientsin for three years. And just as in the Philippines he had become an authority on the history and ethnography of the islands, so in Tientsin he studied Chinese civilization, history, and language. He was the only American officer who could examine Chinese witnesses that appeared before him without the aid of interpreters. And his few spare hours he utilized to learn to write Chinese.

During the years of depression when he was colonel once again, the soldiers' pay was reduced to such an extent that the married men suffered

1. John J. Pershing (1860–1948), American general, commander in chief of the American armies in World War I.
2. Marshall's handling of the staff work for the St. Mihiel offensive is summarized by Robert Payne in *The Marshall Story*, pp. 75–79; by William Frye in *Marshall: Citizen Soldier*, pp. 154–158; by Pogue, *op. cit.*, ch. 11.

real hardship, and their regimental commander started his first Marshall aid. He taught his troops to raise chickens and hogs; he showed them how to start vegetable gardens. He instituted a lunch-pail system by which, on the payment of fifteen cents, each member of the family was fed; the price was the same, however many members there were in the family. He and Mrs. Marshall ate the same dinner so that it should not smack of condescending charity. Marshall had under his command an ever increasing number of C.C.C. camps[1], that curious attempt to combine some kind of military training with the effort to fight unemployment. For the undernourished, anemic, helpless young men of these camps he had an absorbing interest. He organized schools for them, had them start news-sheets, amateur theatricals; he had their teeth taken care of; he stopped all drunkenness among them. And when Marshall in 1938 became assistant chief of staff and then deputy chief and in 1939 was appointed chief of staff, he took with him to Washington this active sympathy for the private soldier, this strong feeling that the soldier has needs other than the merely physical. The United States at that time had an active army of approximately 174,000 enlisted men scattered over 130 posts, camps, and stations. In Marshall's first biennial report[2] on the state of the armed forces he remarks:

«As an army we were ineffective. Our equipment, modern at the conclusion of the World War, was now, in a large measure, obsolescent. In fact, during the postwar period, continuous paring of appropriations had reduced the Army virtually to the status of that of a third-rate power.»

The United States had no military strength that could prevent war or even an attack on America. And Marshall, who saw the total war approaching and his own country powerless, clearly realized the truth of Alfred Nobel's words: «Good intentions alone can never secure peace.»

It was during these years before America was attacked that the ground had to be laid for the later overwhelming war effort. It was during these years that Mrs. Marshall, who was closest to him, prayed every night: «O, Lord, grant him time.»

The task before Marshall, the burdens he had to shoulder during these

1. The Civilian Conservation Corps, created in 1937, grew out of the Emergency Conservation work established in 1933; reorganized in 1939 and disbanded in 1942, it was intended to provide work and training for unemployed young men and to carry on a program of conservation of natural resources.
2. *Report on the Army, July 1, 1939, to June 30, 1941: Biennial Report of General George C. Marshall,* p. 12.

years of war, seemed beyond the power of man to bear. That he did not break down was probably due to what Senator Russell[1] expressed in the words: «Most men are slaves of their ambition. General Marshall is the slave of his duties.»

This deep-rooted, one might say fanatic, sense of duty imposed upon him an iron self-discipline which came close to having the character of a mystic faith. He made it articulate in the most spontaneous and open speech he had ever made. In June, 1941, he gave an address at Trinity College, an Episcopalian institution in Hartford, Connecticut. He himself belongs to the Episcopalian faith and is an active churchgoer. He said in his opening remarks: «I know that being with you here today is good for my soul.» Then he added: «If I were back in my office, I would not be using the word *soul*.» He goes on to define what he means by discipline; his doing so makes this address important for the understanding of the man and his work.

«We are replacing force of habit of body with force of habit of mind. We are basing the discipline of the individual on respect rather than on fear... It is morale that wins the victory. It is not enough to fight. It is the spirit which we bring to the fight that decides the issue.

The soldier's heart, the soldier's spirit, the soldier's soul, are everything. Unless the soldier's soul sustains him he cannot be relied on and will fail himself and his commander and his country in the end... It is morale that wins the victory... The French never found an adequate ‹ dictionary› definition for the word...

It is more than a word—more than any one word, or several words, can measure.

Morale is a state of mind. It is steadfastness and courage and hope. It is confidence and zeal and loyalty. It is *élan*, *esprit de corps* and determination.

It is staying power, the spirit which endures to the end—the will to win.

With it all things are possible, without it everything else, planning, preparation, production, count for naught.

I have just said it is the spirit which endures to the end. And so it is. »[2]

1. Richard B. Russell (1897–1971), U.S. Senator from Georgia, chairman of the Armed Services Committee.
2. See H. A. de Weerd, *Selected Speeches and Statements of General of the Army George C. Marshall*, pp. 121–125. The order in which these sentences occur in the original text is as follows:
«The soldier's heart, the soldier's spirit, the soldier's soul, are everything. Unless the soldier's soul sustains him he cannot be relied on and will fail himself and his commander and his country in the end» (p. 122).

This remarkable address is at the same time a creed and a program. It is the only speech in which Marshall directly and openly expressed the ideas which occupied him most–outside his daily work.

«We are building that morale–not on supreme confidence in our ability to conquer and subdue other peoples; not in reliance on things of steel and the super-excellence of guns and planes and bombsights.

We are building it on things infinitely more potent. We are building it on *belief,* for it is what men *believe* that makes them invincible. We have sought for something more than enthusiasm, something finer and higher than optimism or self-confidence, something not merely of the intellect or the emotions but rather something in the spirit of the man, something encompassed only by the soul.

This army of ours already possesses a morale based on what we allude to as the noblest aspirations of mankind–on the spiritual forces which rule the world and will continue to do so.

Let me call it the morale of omnipotence. With your endorsement and support this omnipotent morale will be sustained as long as the things of the spirit are stronger than the things of earth.»[1]

But after the Trinity address Marshall retired behind his protective armor. And the passion always smoldering in his mind was not expressed in words until 1945 when he wrote his biennial report on the course of the war; in this his words of sympathy for the common soldier have an almost explosive quality:

«It is impossible for the Nation to compensate for the services of a fighting man. There is no pay scale that is high enough to buy the services of a single soldier during even a few minutes of the agony of combat, the physical miseries of the campaign, or of the extreme personal inconvenience of leaving his home to go out to the most unpleasant and dangerous spots on earth to serve his Nation.»[2]

Nobel's Peace Prize is not given to Marshall for what he accomplished

«It is not enough to fight. It is the spirit which we bring to the fight that decides the issue. It is morale that wins the victory.

The French never found an adequate dictionary definition for the word...» (p.122).

«It is more than a word... And so it is» (p.123). [Same in both texts.]

«We are replacing force of habit of body with force of habit of mind. We are basing the discipline of the individual on respect rather than on fear...» (p.124).

1. *Ibid.,* pp.124–125.

2. *The Winning of the War in Europe and the Pacific: Biennial Report of the Chief of Staff of the United States Army, July 1, 1943, to June 30, 1945, to the Secretary of War,* p.110.

during the war. Nevertheless, what he has done, after the war, for peace is a corollary to this achievement, and it is this great work for the establishment of peace which the Nobel Committee has wanted to honor.

But two documents give some idea of General Marshall's importance to the democratic world during the years of war.

When the victory was won on May 8, 1945, Marshall was summoned to the office of the secretary of war, the venerable Republican Henry Stimson, one time law partner of Elihu Root, who was awarded the Nobel Peace Prize for 1912[1]. Mr. Stimson had invited fourteen generals and high officials to be present. The seventy-eight-year-old statesman then turned to Marshall and said:

«I want to acknowledge my great personal debt to you, Sir, in common with the whole country. No one who is thinking of himself can rise to true heights. You have never thought of yourself... I have never seen a task of such magnitude performed by man.

It is rare in late life to make new friends; at my age it is a slow process, but there is no one for whom I have such deep respect and, I think, greater affection.

I have seen a great many soldiers in my lifetime and you, Sir, are the finest soldier I have ever known.

It is fortunate for this country that we have you in this position!»[2]

And when Marshall at his own request resigned as chief of staff in November, 1945, he received from his British colleagues in the combined chiefs of staff a message which is surely without parallel. It was signed by Chief of the Imperial General Staff Sir Alan Brooke (now Lord Alanbrooke), by Admiral of the Fleet Lord Cunningham of Hyndhope, and by Marshal of the Royal Air Force Lord Portal of Hungerford[3]. It reads:

1. Henry L. Stimson (1867–1950), American statesman; secretary of war (1911–1913; 1940–1945) and secretary of state (1929–1933). Elihu Root (1845–1937), Nobel Peace Prize laureate for 1912.

2. See Henry L. Stimson and McGeorge Bundy, *On Active Service in Peace and War* (New York: Harper, 1948), p.664. First part of quotation is in the Stimson and Bundy book; second part is in a document in the files of the George C. Marshall Research Library; complete text in memorandum by Aide to Secretary of War Kyle to Col. Frank McCarthy, Secretary, General Staff, May 11, 1945.

3. Alan Francis Brooke, Viscount Alanbrooke (1833–1963), British field marshal, chief of the imperial general staff (1941–1946). Andrew Browne Cunningham, Viscount Cunningham of Hyndhope (1833–1963), British first sea lord and chief of naval staff (1943–1946). Charles F. A. Portal, Viscount Portal of Hungerford (1893–   ), British air chief marshal and chief of air staff (1940–1945).

«On your retirement after six years as Chief of Staff of the United States Army, we, your British colleagues in the Combined Chiefs of Staff, send you this message of farewell.

We regret that Field Marshal Sir John Dill and Admiral of the Fleet Sir Dudley Pound, two of your greatest friends and admirers, are not alive today to add their names to ours. As architect and builder of the finest and most powerful Army in American History, your name will be honoured among those of the greatest soldiers of your own or any other country.

Throughout your association with us in the higher direction of the armed forces of America and Britain, your unfailing wisdom, high principles, and breadth of view have commanded the deep respect and admiration of us all. Always you have honoured us by your frankness, charmed us by your courtesy, and inspired us by your singleness of purpose and your selfless devotion to our common cause.

Above all would we record our thankfulness to you for the leading part which you have always taken in forging and strengthening the bond of mutual trust and cooperation between the armed forces of our two countries which has contributed so much to final victory and will, we believe, endure to the benefit of civilization in the years to come.

In bidding farewell to you who have earned our personal affection no less than our professional respect, we would address to you a tribute written more than 200 years ago.

> *... Friend to truth! Of soul sincere,*
> *In action faithful, and in honour clear;*
> *Who broke no promise, served no private end,*
> *Who gained no title, and who lost no friend.*»[1]

Between Mr. Stimson's words of national gratitude and the message from the British chiefs of staff, we have General Marshall's third biennial report which contains both his military testament and an introduction to what later came to be called the Marshall Aid.

It is particularly the last section of the report which is of importance here. Marshall called it «For the Common Defense». He opened with the statement that to fulfill its responsibility for protection of the nation against foreign enemies, the army must project its planning beyond the immediate

1. See Katherine Marshall, *Together: Annals of an Army Wife.* The text of the message is found only in the second edition and is the plate in the front of the book; the original document is on display in the George C. Marshall Library Museum in Lexington, Va.

future. «For years men have been concerned with individual security... But effective insurance against the disasters which have slaughtered millions of people and levelled their homes is long overdue.»[1] He then points to Washington's plans for a national military policy and goes on:

«We must start, I think, with a correction of the tragic misunderstanding that a security policy is a war policy. War has been defined by a people who have thought a lot about it – the Germans. They have started most of the recent ones. The German soldier-philosopher Clausewitz described war as a special violent form of political action. Frederick of Prussia, who left Germany the belligerent legacy which has now destroyed her, viewed war as a device to enforce his will whether he was right or wrong. He held that with an invincible offensive military force he could win any political argument. It is the doctrine Hitler carried to the verge of complete success. This is the doctrine of Japan. It is a criminal doctrine, and like other forms of crime, it has cropped up again and again since man began to live with his neighbors in communities and nations. There has long been an effort to outlaw war for exactly the same reason that man has outlawed murder. But the law prohibiting murder does not of itself prevent murder. It must be enforced. The enforcing power, however, must be maintained on a strictly democratic basis. There must not be a large standing army subject to the behest of a group of schemers. The citizen-soldier is the guarantee against such a misuse of power.»[2]

He concludes by emphasizing:

«If this Nation is to remain great, it must bear in mind now and in the future that war is not the choice of those who wish passionately for peace. It is the choice of those who are willing to resort to violence for political advantage.»[3]

Marshall had hardly had a week's rest after his resignation as chief of staff when President Truman sent him to China as a special ambassador to try to stop the pending civil war between the Communists and the Kuomintang, i.e. Chiang Kai-shek[4]. He did not succeed; for when Marshall was gone,

---

1. *The Winning of the War in Europe and the Pacific*, p. 117.
2. *Ibid.*
3. *Ibid.*, p. 123.
4. Chiang Kai-shek (1886–   ), Chinese statesman and general, leader of the Kuomintang or Nationalist Party; led China during World War II; after his defeat in the civil war that followed between the Kuomintang and the Communists, set up a Nationalist government in Formosa in 1950. Harry S. Truman (1884–   ), U.S. president (1945-1953).

neither of the two parties honored the agreements they had undertaken. But what Marshall had seen and experienced in China strengthened the conviction which the devastations of the war had planted in his mind and which now received initial amplification in his report from China to President Truman:

«It was his [Marshall's] opinion that steps had to be taken to assist China and its people in the increasingly serious economic situation and to facilitate the efforts being made toward peace and unity in China... General Marshall felt that Chinese political and military unity could only be consolidated and made lasting through the rehabilitation of the country and the permanent general improvement of economic conditions.»[1]

It is an opinion which Marshall in another connection has formulated more generally in these words: «The historians have failed in their task; they should have been able to discover and reveal the causes of war and make war impossible.»

And when in 1947 Marshall at the insistent request of President Truman accepted an appointment as secretary of state, it was because he believed that he saw the causes of war and chaos and because he intended to remove those causes insofar as humanly possible, and in this way make war impossible.

His apprehension, his fear of war, his feeling that another war would mean the complete collapse of human civilization is closely akin to the apprehension in Nobel's mind when he was drafting his will. In 1893 he wrote in a letter[2]:

«I should like to dispose of a part of my fortune by founding a prize to be given every five years (say six times; for if we have not succeeded in reforming our present system within thirty years we shall inevitably revert to barbarism).

This prize would be awarded to the man or woman who had achieved most in furthering the idea of a general peace in Europe.»

And he also wrote:

«Une nouvelle tyrannie–celle des bas fonds–s'agite dans les ténèbres, et on croit entendre son grondement lointain.»[3]

1. *United States Relations with China*, Department of State (Washington, D.C., Office of Public Affairs, 1949), p.145.
2. Letter to Baroness Bertha von Suttner (recipient of the Nobel Peace Prize for 1905) dated Paris, January 7, 1893.
3. «A new tyranny, that of the dregs of the population, is lurking in the shadows and one can almost hear its distant rumble.» Translation taken from «The Peace Prize» by

Marshall wanted to prevent what Nobel feared. Less than four months after entering the State Department, he presented his plan for that tremendous aid to Europe which has become inseparably connected with his name. He stated in his famous speech at Harvard University:

«Our policy is directed not against any country or doctrine but against hunger, poverty, desperation, and chaos. Its purpose should be the revival of a working economy in the world so as to permit the emergence of political and social conditions in which free institutions can exist. Such assistance, I am convinced, must not be on a piecemeal basis as various crises develop. Any assistance that this government may render in the future should provide a cure rather than a mere palliative.»[1]

Marshall carried out his plan, fighting for it for two years in public and in Congress. And when the Marshall Plan had become a living reality, with the agencies for its operation established, Marshall stepped back.

But again he was called to service, being made secretary of defense in September, 1950. When he assumed this responsibility, it was only to be in a position to put into effect his idea of building the future defense of the United States on a democratic conscription and not on a standing army. When this had been accomplished, he retired once more, this time to realize at last the dream of his life–to grow a vegetable garden on his small estate in Virginia.

The years that have gone by since he submitted his program have demonstrated its constructive character. And the organs which have grown from the Marshall Aid have, more than anything else in these difficult years, contributed to what Nobel termed «the idea of a general peace in Europe» and to a realistic materialization of the idea Nobel in his testament called brotherhood among nations, although within a more narrow framework than Marshall had desired.

The Nobel Peace Prize, therefore, is awarded to George Catlett Marshall.

August Schou, in *Nobel: The Man and His Prizes* (Amsterdam: Elsevier, 1962), p. 528.
1. «European Initiative Essential to Economic Recovery.» Remarks made by the Secretary of State on the occasion of the commencement exercises at Harvard University, June 5, 1947. Department of State, Publication 2882, European Series, 25, p.4.

GEORGE C. MARSHALL

Essentials to Peace

Nobel Lecture*, December 11, 1953

I

I have been greatly and surprisingly honored in the past twenty-four hours, and in return I have been requested to speak here tonight. While no subject has been suggested, it is quite evident that the cause of peace is preeminent in your minds.

Discussions without end have been devoted to the subject of peace, and the efforts to obtain a general and lasting peace have been frequent through many years of world history. There has been success temporarily, but all have broken down, and with the most tragic consequences since 1914. What I would like to do is point our attention to some directions in which efforts to attain peace seem promising of success.

I will try to phrase my views or suggestions in the simplest possible terms though I lack the magic and artistry of that great orator whom the Nobel Committee in Stockholm so appropriately honored yesterday[1]. In making my statement I will assume your familiarity with the discussions and efforts of the past eight years and also with something of the conditions which have governed each long continued peace in world history.

I would like to make special mention of the years of the Pax Romana[2], which endured through almost all of the first two centuries of the Christian era. I do so because of a personal incident which made a profound impression on me in the spring of 1919. Arriving late at night in Chaumont, the American Headquarters in France, I sought shelter for the night in the house

---

* This lecture was delivered in the Auditorium of the University of Oslo. Lecture text, taken from *Les Prix Nobel en 1953*, is identical to that published in the *New York Times* for December 12, 1953, except for differences in paragraphing, an occasional and minor difference in punctuation, and in one instance, the deletion of three words noted below. The lecture was not given a title by General Marshall; the one used here has been taken from a phrase which occurs in the first sentence of Part II of the speech.
1. Sir Winston Churchill, who received the Nobel Prize in Literature.
2. «The Roman Peace», a period of peace *within* the Roman Empire maintained by the power of the central authority.

of a group of friends. I found they were temporarily absent; so I selected an unoccupied room and looked about for a book to read as I waited for sleep to come. The books available were mostly in French or German. Since I was unable to read them with facility, I looked further and finally found an English textbook on the history of Gaul. Casting about for an interesting portion, I landed on a description of the famous Roman Peace. Included in this description was a statement of the dispositions of the Roman troops during this prolonged period, a legion at Cologne, another at Coblenz, a third at Mayence, and the reserve at Trier. Now those happened to be the identical dispositions of our Allied Forces some eighteen hundred years later, with the Peace Commission sitting in Paris and evolving the policy of the League of Nations.

I would not wish to imply that the military deployment I have just described corresponds to the protective NATO[1] deployment of today. The threat today is quite different, but I do think that this remarkable historical repetition does suggest that we have walked blindly, ignoring the lessons of the past, with, in our century, the tragic consequences of two world wars and the Korean struggle as a result.

In my country my military associates frequently tell me that we Americans have learned our lesson. I completely disagree with this contention and point to the rapid disintegration between 1945 and 1950 of our once vast power for maintaining the peace. As a direct consequence, in my opinion, there resulted the brutal invasion of South Korea, which for a time threatened the complete defeat of our hastily arranged forces in that field. I speak of this with deep feeling because in 1939 and again in the early fall of 1950 it suddenly became my duty, my responsibility, to rebuild our national military strength in the very face of the gravest emergencies.

These opening remarks may lead you to assume that my suggestions for the advancement of world peace will rest largely on military strength. For the moment the maintenance of peace in the present hazardous world situation does depend in very large measure on military power, together with Allied cohesion. But the maintenance of large armies for an indefinite period is not a practical or a promising basis for policy. We must stand together

1. Founded in 1949, the North Atlantic Treaty Organization is a defensive alliance entered into by Belgium, Canada, Denmark, France, Great Britain, Iceland, Italy, Luxembourg, The Netherlands, Norway, Portugal, and the United States; Greece and Turkey joined in 1951, and West Germany in 1955. NATO maintains military forces under an integrated command.

strongly for these present years, that is, in this present situation; but we must, I repeat, we must find another solution, and that is what I wish to discuss this evening.

There has been considerable comment over the awarding of the Nobel Peace Prize to a soldier[1]. I am afraid this does not seem as remarkable to me as it quite evidently appears to others. I know a great deal of the horrors and tragedies of war. Today, as chairman of the American Battle Monuments Commission, it is my duty to supervise the construction and maintenance of military cemeteries in many countries overseas, particularly in Western Europe. The cost of war in human lives is constantly spread before me, written neatly in many ledgers whose columns are gravestones. I am deeply moved to find some means or method of avoiding another calamity of war. Almost daily I hear from the wives, or mothers, or families of the fallen. The tragedy of the aftermath is almost constantly before me.

I share with you an active concern for some practical method for avoiding war. Let me first say that I regard the present highly dangerous situation as a very special one, which naturally dominates our thinking on the subject of peace, but which should not, in my opinion, be made the principal basis for our reasoning towards the manner for securing a condition of long continued peace. A very strong military posture is vitally necessary today. How long it must continue I am not prepared to estimate, but I am sure that it is too narrow a basis on which to build a dependable, long-enduring peace. The guarantee for a long continued peace will depend on other factors in addition to a moderated military strength, and no less important. Perhaps the most important single factor will be a spiritual regeneration to develop goodwill, faith, and understanding among nations. Economic factors will undoubtedly play an important part. Agreements to secure a balance of power, however disagreeable they may seem, must likewise be considered. And with all these there must be wisdom and the will to act on that wisdom.

---

1. See the *New York Times*, October 31, 1953, p. 15. For views on speech, December 22, 1953, p. 30, and December 25, 1953, p. 161. For description of protest at the time of the prize presentation, see December 11, 1953, p. 1. Three Communist newspapermen in the balcony, shouting «We protest» and showering leaflets on the audience, interrupted the ceremony just after Dr. Hambro had completed his speech and while General Marshall was accepting the prize. King Haakon VII jumped to his feet applauding the general; the audience joined in, drowning out the noise of the disturbance.

II

In this brief discussion, I can give only a very limited treatment of these great essentials to peace. However, I would like to select three more specific areas for closer attention.

The *first* relates to the possibilities of better education in the various factors affecting the life of peaceful security, both in terms of its development and of its disruption. Because wisdom in action in our Western democracies rests squarely upon public understanding, I have long believed that our schools have a key role to play. Peace could, I believe, be advanced through careful study of all the factors which have gone into the various incidents now historical that have marked the breakdown of peace in the past. As an initial procedure our schools, at least our colleges but preferably our senior high schools, as we call them, should have courses which not merely instruct our budding citizens in the historical sequence of events of the past, but which treat with almost scientific accuracy the circumstances which have marked the breakdown of peace and have led to the disruption of life and the horrors of war.

There may perhaps have been a «last clear chance» to avoid the tragic conflagrations of our century. In the case of World War II, for example, the challenge may well have come in the early thirties, and passed largely unrecognized until the situation was unlikely to be retrieved. We are familiar with specific events such as the march into the Rhineland or aggression in Ethiopia or Manchuria[1]. Perhaps there was also a last clear chance to begin to build up the strength of the democracies to keep the military situation in equilibrium. There may also have been a last clear chance to penetrate to the spirit of the peoples of the nations threatening the peace, and to find ways of peaceful adjustment in the economic field as well. Certainly, had the outcome of the war, with its devastation and disruption, been foreseen, and had there been an understanding on all sides of the problems that were threatening the peace, I feel sure that many possibilities for accommodation would have been much more thoroughly explored.

It is for this reason that I believe our students must first seek to understand the conditions, as far as possible without national prejudices, which have led to past tragedies and should strive to determine the great fundamentals which must govern a peaceful progression toward a constantly higher level of civ-

1. German march into the Rhineland in March, 1936; Italian attack on Ethiopia in December, 1934; Japanese attack on Manchuria in September, 1931.

ilization. There are innumerable instructive lessons out of the past, but all too frequently their presentation is highly colored or distorted in the effort to present a favorable national point of view. In our school histories at home, certainly in years past, those written in the North present a strikingly different picture of our Civil War from those written in the South. In some portions it is hard to realize they are dealing with the same war. Such reactions are all too common in matters of peace and security. But we are told that we live in a highly scientific age. Now the progress of science depends on facts and not fancies or prejudice. Maybe in this age we can find a way of facing the facts and discounting the distorted records of the past.

I am certain that a solution of the general problem of peace must rest on broad and basic understanding on the part of free peoples. Great single endeavors like a League of Nations, a United Nations, and undertakings of that character, are of great importance and in fact absolutely necessary, but they must be treated as steps toward the desired end.

We must depend in large measure on the impartiality of those who teach. Their approach must be on a scientific basis in order to present the true facts. The scientists, no matter of what nationality, make a common approach to their problems.

For my *second* suggestion, I would like to consider the national attitudes that bear on the great problem of peace. I hope you will not think me amiss if I turn to my own country and certain rather special circumstances found there to illustrate my point. Despite the amazing conquest of the air and its reduction of distances to a matter of hours and not days, or minutes instead of hours, the United States is remote in a general sense from the present turbulent areas of the world. I believe the measure of detachment, limited though it is, has been of help in enabling us on occasion to take an impartial stand on heated international problems.

Also, my country is very specially constituted in terms of population. We have many families of Norwegian ancestry in our population. My country also includes large numbers of former citizens of many of the other countries of Europe, including the present satellite states. I recall that when the first Polar flight[1] was made by the Russians from Moscow over the top of the world to land on the little airfield of the post I commanded at Vancouver on the Columbia River in the state of Washington, my home was surrounded within a few hours by hundreds and hundreds of Russians, all presumably

1. On June 20, 1937.

citizens of the United States. Italians, Turks, Greeks, and many, many others who came to our country now constitute an organic portion of our population.

From this fact we have acquired, I think, a feeling and a concern for the problems of other peoples. There is a deep urge to help the oppressed and to give aid to those upon whom great and sudden hardship has fallen.

We, naturally, cannot see a problem in the exact terms as people like yourselves or the Danes, or the Dutch, or the French, for example–people living in the closest contact with each other, yet widely differing in national heritage. I believe there is, however, a readiness to cooperate which is one of the great and hopeful factors of the world of today. While we are not in close contact with the details of problems, neither are we indifferent to them, and we are not involved in your historical tensions and suspicions.

If I am correct in thinking that these factors have given us as a nation some advantage in the quest for peace, then I would suggest that principles of cooperation based on these factors might contribute to a better understanding amongst all nations.

I realize fully that there is another side to this picture. In America we have not suffered the destruction of our homes, our towns, and our cities. We have not been enslaved for long periods, at the complete mercy of a conqueror. We have enjoyed freedom in its fullest sense. In fact, we have come to think in terms of freedom and the dignity of the individual more or less as a matter of course, and our apparent unconcern until times of acute crisis presents a difficult problem to the citizens of the countries of Western Europe, who have seldom been free from foreign threat to their freedom, their dignity, and their security. I think nevertheless that the people of the United States have fully demonstrated their willingness to fight and die in the terrible struggle for the freedom we all prize, to sacrifice their own men in large numbers for this common cause, and to contribute vast sums for the general benefit of the Western countries.

I recognize that there are bound to be misunderstandings under the conditions of wide separation between your countries and mine. But I believe the attitude of cooperation has been thoroughly proven. I also believe that the participation of millions of our young men and women in the struggle in Western Europe, in the closest contact with your people, will bring as its result less of misunderstanding on our side of the Atlantic than perhaps on yours.

In my own case, for example, I spent two and one half years in France during the First World War. Frequently I was quartered in the households of the French peasantry and spent long evenings by the kitchen fires, talking far into the night. I came to know them well, admired them, and in some cases came to love them. Now, how many do you suppose of the present citizens of Western Europe have had a similar look-in on the homes of people in the farms and small towns of America. A few may know much of New York, Washington, and Chicago, but those great cities do not represent the heart of America.

The *third* area I would like to discuss has to do with the problem of the millions who live under subnormal conditions and who have now come to a realization that they may aspire to a fair share of the God-given rights of human beings. Their aspirations present a challenge to the more favored nations to lend assistance in bettering the lot of the poorer. This is a special problem in the present crisis, but it is of basic importance to any successful effort toward an enduring peace. The question is not merely one of self-interest arising from the fact that these people present a situation which is a seed bed for either one or the other oft wo greatly differing ways of life. Ours is democracy, according to our interpretation of the meaning of that word. If we act with wisdom and magnanimity, we can guide these yearnings of the poor to a richer and better life through democracy.

We must present democracy as a force holding within itself the seeds of unlimited progress by the human race. By our actions we should make it clear that such a democracy is a means to a better way of life, together with a better understanding among nations. Tyranny inevitably must retire before the tremendous moral strength of the gospel of freedom and self-respect for the individual, but we have to recognize that these democratic principles do not flourish on empty stomachs, and that people turn to false promises of dictators because they are hopeless and anything promises something better than the miserable existence that they endure. However, material assistance alone is not sufficient. The most important thing for the world today in my opinion is a spiritual regeneration which would reestablish a feeling of good faith among men generally. Discouraged people are in sore need of the inspiration of great principles. Such leadership can be the rallying point against intolerance, against distrust, against that fatal insecurity that leads to war. It is to be hoped that the democratic nations can provide the necessary leadership.

The points I have just discussed are, of course, no more than a very few suggestions in behalf of the cause of peace. I realize that they hold nothing of glittering or early promise, but there can be no substitute for effort in many fields. There must be effort of the spirit–to be magnanimous, to act in friendship, to strive to help rather than to hinder. There must be effort of analysis to seek out the causes of war and the factors which favor peace, and to study their application to the difficult problems which will beset our international intercourse. There must be material effort–to initiate and sustain those great undertakings, whether military or economic, on which world equilibrium will depend.

If we proceed in this manner, there should develop a dynamic philosophy which knows no restrictions of time or space. In America we have a creed which comes to us from the deep roots of the past. It springs from the convictions of the men and women of many lands who founded the nation and made it great. We share that creed with many of the nations of the Old World and the New with whom we are joined in the cause of peace. We are young in world history, but these ideals of ours we can offer to the world with the certainty that they have the power to inspire and to impel action.

I am not implying in any way that we would attempt to persuade other people to adopt our particular form of government. I refer here specifically to those fundamental values on which our government, like many other democracies, is based. These, I believe, are timeless and have a validity for all mankind. These, I believe, will kindle the imagination and arouse the spirit.

A great proponent of much of what I have just been saying is Dr. Albert Schweitzer, the world humanitarian, who today receives the Nobel Peace Award for 1952. I feel it is a vast compliment to be associated with him in these awards this year[1]. His life has been utterly different from mine, and we should all be happy that his example among the poor and benighted of the earth should have been recognized by the Peace Award of the Nobel Committee.

I must not further complicate this discussion with the wide variety of specific considerations which will enfold the gradual growth of a sound approach toward some method of securing an enduring peace in the world. I fear, in fact I am rather certain, that due to my inability to express myself with the power and penetration of the great Churchill, I have not made clear the points that assume such prominence and importance in my mind. However, I have done my best, and I hope I have sown some seeds which may bring forth good fruit.

1. The text in the *New York Times* does not include the words «in these awards».

Biography

George Catlett Marshall (December 31, 1880–October 16, 1959), America's foremost soldier during World War II, served as chief of staff from 1939 to 1945, building and directing the largest army in history. A diplomat, he acted as secretary of state from 1947 to 1949, formulating the «Marshall Plan», an unprecedented program of economic and military aid to foreign nations.

Marshall's father owned a prosperous coal business in Pennsylvania, but the boy, deciding to become a soldier, enrolled at the Virginia Military Institute from which he was graduated in 1901 as senior first captain of the Corps of Cadets. After serving in posts in the Philippines and the United States, Marshall was graduated with honors from the Infantry-Cavalry School at Fort Leavenworth in 1907 and from the Army Staff College in 1908. The young officer distinguished himself in a variety of posts in the next nine years, earning an appointment to the General Staff in World War I and sailing to France with the First Division. He achieved fame and promotion for his staff work in the battles of Cantigny, Aisne-Marne, St. Mihiel, and Meuse-Argonne. After acting as aide-de-camp to General Pershing from 1919 to 1924, Marshall served in China from 1924 to 1927, and then successively as instructor in the Army War College in 1927, as assistant commandant of the Infantry School from 1927 to 1932, as commander of the Eighth Infantry in 1933, as senior instructor to the Illinois National Guard from 1933 to 1936, and as commander, with the rank of brigadier general, of the Fifth Infantry Brigade from 1936 to 1938. In July, 1938, Marshall accepted a post with the General Staff in Washington, D.C., and in September, 1939, was named chief of staff, with the rank of general, by President Roosevelt. He became general of the army in 1944, the year in which Congress created that five-star rank.

In his position as chief of staff, Marshall urged military readiness prior to the attack on Pearl Harbor in 1941, later became responsible for the building, supplying, and, in part, the deploying of over eight million soldiers. From 1941 he was a member of the policy committee that supervised the atomic studies engaged in by American and British scientists. The war over, Marshall resigned in November, 1945.

But Marshall could not resign from public service; his military career ended, he took up a diplomatic career. He had been associated with diplomatic events while chief of staff, for he participated in the conference on the Atlantic Charter (1941–1942), and in those at Casablanca (1943), Quebec (1943), Cairo-Teheran (1943), Yalta (1945), Potsdam (1945), and in many others of lesser import. In late 1945 and in 1946, he represented President Truman on a special mission to China, then torn by civil war; in January, 1947, he accepted the Cabinet position of secretary of state, holding it for two years. In the spring of 1947 he outlined in a speech at Harvard University the plan of economic aid which history has named the «Marshall Plan».

For one year during the Korean War General Marshall was secretary of defense, a civilian post in the U.S. Cabinet. Having resigned from this post in September, 1951, three months before his seventy-first birthday, he retired from public service, thereafter performing those ceremonial duties the public comes to expect of its famous men.

Selected Bibliography

Acheson, Dean, «General of the Army George Catlett Marshall», in *Sketches from Life of Men I Have Known*, pp. 147–166. New York, Harper, 1961.

Frye, William, *Marshall: Citizen Soldier*. Indianapolis, Bobbs-Merrill, 1947.

Jouvenel, B., *L'Amérique en Europe: Le Plan Marshall et la coopération intercontinentale*. Paris, 1948.

Marshall, George C., *Report on the Army, July 1, 1939, to June 30, 1941: Biennial Report of General George C. Marshall*. Washington, The Infantry Journal, 1941.

Marshall, George C., *Selected Speeches and Statements of General of the Army George C. Marshall*, ed. by H. A. De Weerd. Washington, The Infantry Journal, 1945.

Marshall, George C., *The Winning of the War in Europe and the Pacific: Biennial Report of the Chief of Staff of the United States Army, July 1, 1943, to June 30, 1945, to the Secretary of War*. New York, Simon & Schuster, 1945.

Marshall, Katherine Tupper, *Together: Annals of an Army Wife*. New York, Tupper & Love, 1946.

Payne, Robert, *The Marshall Story*. New York, Prentice-Hall, 1951. Contains a select bibliography.

Pogue, Forrest C., *George C. Marshall: Education of a General*. New York, Viking Press, 1963. Contains an excellent bibliography.

Pogue, Forrest C., *George C. Marshall: Ordeal and Hope*. New York, Viking Press, 1968.

Sherwood, Robert E., *Roosevelt and Hopkins: An Intimate History*. New York, Harper, 1950.

United States Army in the World War 1917–1919: Military Operations of the American Expeditionary Forces. Washington, Historical Division, Department of the Army, 1948. Volumes 8 and 9 describe the battles of St. Mihiel and Meuse-Argonne.

Peace 1954

(Prize awarded in 1955)

THE OFFICE OF THE UNITED NATIONS HIGH COMMISSIONER FOR REFUGEES

Presentation

by Gunnar Jahn*, Chairman of the Nobel Committee

The Nobel Committee of the Norwegian Parliament has this year awarded the Peace Prize for 1954 to the Office of the United Nations High Commissioner for Refugees.

War has existed in all times—war between tribes, war between races, war between nations, civil wars and religious wars. War has always laid waste human dwellings, forcing men to flee to escape its horrors and to find a refuge where they might live in peace.

But it is only during our own century that international work to help refugees has begun to take shape. The first High Commission for Refugees was established after World War I by the League of Nations as a result of the initiative of Fridtjof Nansen[1]. No single man has contributed more to this cause than has Nansen, and the work he started has never paused since.

I do not propose to review in detail the activity of the High Commission nor that of the International Labor Office[2] nor yet the help that has been offered on all sides by private organizations and individuals. The work begun at an international level in 1921 was continued throughout the Second World War, for the refugee problem created by the first war had still not been solved at the outbreak of the next.

During this last war, tens of millions of people lost their homes, either because they became refugees in their own country or because they were forcibly deported to other countries or else because they fled of their own accord. It has been estimated that there were between thirty and fifty million

---

* Mr. Jahn, also at this time director of the Bank of Norway, delivered this speech on December 10, 1955, in the Auditorium of the University of Oslo. At its conclusion he presented the prize for 1954 (reserved in that year) to Dr. van Heuven Goedhart who, in a brief speech, accepted for the High Commissioner's Office. The translation of Mr. Jahn's speech is based on the Norwegian text in *Les Prix Nobel en 1955*, which also carries a French translation.
1. Fridtjof Nansen (1861–1930), recipient of the Nobel Peace Prize for 1922.
2. Secretariat of the ILO, recipient of the Nobel Peace Prize for 1969.

homeless at the end of the war. We can never be completely sure of such figures, but one thing at least is certain: when the firing ceased, there were millions of human beings without shelter, human beings who had to be helped to find a place where they could live in safety.

Already in 1943 the Allies had set up the United Nations Relief and Rehabilitation Administration. The first task of this organization was to assist the countries which had been occupied to revive their economy. But another problem awaiting UNRRA at the end of hostilities was the care of those who had lost their homes as a result of the war and who were now in areas under Allied control. It was necessary to arrange for their repatriation.

UNRRA did splendid work; its magnitude can be judged from the fact that its expenditure amounted to $ 3,900,000,000. The greater part of this sum was contributed by various governments, ninety percent coming from the United States and the United Kingdom alone. With the assistance of the military authorities, UNRRA succeeded in repatriating six million people by the autumn of 1945. But many more remained.

Repatriation was not always easy to arrange. This was partly because of inadequate transport facilities, but also because of the frequently woeful conditions in the native country which made it impossible for the latter to take care of its own people. But there were also many people who did not want to return to their own countries, either because they no longer had ties there or because they feared reprisals from the governments then in power. These have become the real refugees, men for whom a chance of a new life must be found outside their native lands.

After the United Nations had begun its activities, the refugee work was taken over on July 1, 1947, by the International Refugee Organization. IRO assumed responsibility both for the refugees who had previously been looked after by UNRRA and for those who had been rendered homeless in the interwar period, taking under its care a total of 1,700,000 people. Substantial progress was made through direct aid to refugees both inside and outside the camps. Thousands of people were rescued from hardship or even from death. But perhaps the greatest service that IRO rendered was that of helping about one million refugees to emigrate. The cost, however, was immense; during the few years of its existence IRO spent $470,000,000.

In 1949 it was decided to wind up IRO, and its place has now been taken by the Office of the United Nations High Commissioner for Refugees.

The Office began its work on January 1, 1951. It is a nonpolitical body, with social and humanitarian aims, its main purpose being to provide legal and political protection for the refugees. Under the terms of its Statute the mandate of the High Commissioner's Office extends to all refugees, with the exception of the Arab refugees from Palestine and of the Korean refugees. Special organizations have been set up to help these[1].

The terms of reference of the High Commission are carefully defined in its Statute. I will give the essential points.

The High Commissioner shall provide for the protection of refugees falling under the competence of his Office by:

(a) Promoting the conclusion and ratification of international conventions for the protection of refugees, supervising their application and proposing amendments thereto;

(b) Promoting through special agreements with Governments the execution of any measures calculated to improve the situation of refugees and to reduce the number requiring protection;

(c) Assisting governmental and private efforts to promote voluntary repatriation or assimilation within new national communities;

(d) Promoting the admission of refugees, not excluding those in the most destitute categories, to the territories of States;

(e) Endeavoring to obtain permission for refugees to transfer their assets and especially those necessary for their resettlement;

(f) Obtaining from Governments information concerning the number and conditions of refugees in their territories and the laws and regulations concerning them;

(g) Keeping in close touch with Governments and intergovernmental organizations concerned;

(h) Establishing contacts in such a manner as he may think best with private organizations dealing with refugee questions;

(i) Facilitating the coordination of the efforts of private organizations concerned with the welfare of refugees.[2]

The task undertaken by the High Commission was a truly difficult and

1. The UN Relief and Works Agency (UNRWA) for Palestine Refugees in the Near East began operations in May, 1950. The UN Korean Reconstruction Agency (UNKRA) was established early in 1951.
2. The translation of this passage is taken from UN General Assembly Resolution 428 (V) and Annex, December 14, 1950, Statute of the Office of the UN High Commissioner for Refugees.

formidable one. The role it assumed may perhaps be described as that of protector of the refugees, acting as a vigilant conscience to some governments, forging cooperation among all others working for the cause of the refugees. But, unlike IRO, it could not play the role of the rich uncle freely dispensing gifts.

The High Commissioner for Refugees cannot solicit voluntary contributions either from governments or from private charitable organizations without the authorization of the United Nations General Assembly. The consent of the General Assembly is also required before the High Commission can initiate repatriation or emigration of refugees.

It has frequently been asked how the UN could relinquish its financial responsibility for the refugees and place the burden on countries which, because of their geographical location, had given shelter to the greatest number of refugees, and on the private and governmental organizations working for the refugees. The answer probably lies in the huge expenditures made by IRO, for it was said that the United Nations had no mandate to dispense charity. Moreover, the world was growing tired of the refugee problem. But then we have only to read the reports of debates held in the Assembly concerning the refugees, to be sharply reminded of the fact that the United Nations is a political organization where political considerations outweigh considerations concerning unfortunate human beings. One remembers the response Fridtjof Nansen met when he begged the League of Nations for help in the fight against famine in Russia[1].

The Office of the High Commissioner receives the funds for its administrative expenses from the United Nations. Its personnel is strictly limited, and even today, after nearly five years of existence, the administrative staff numbers scarcely more than a hundred. The Office headquarters are in Geneva and it has branch offices in fourteen countries[2] so that its representatives, by being on the spot, can keep in close touch with the refugees, giving them any necessary protection and acting as intermediaries between them and the governments concerned.

It soon became apparent that little effective work could be done for the refugees unless the Office itself had funds at its disposal. In 1952, therefore, the High Commissioner, Dr. van Heuven Goedhart, applied to the General Assembly for permission to raise three million dollars to provide the necessary funds. The General Assembly granted its consent, but it did so without

1. Nansen's pleas were refused.
2. In his Nobel lecture, the laureate makes a reference to thirteen branch offices.

enthusiasm even though no burden on the budget of the United Nations was involved.

Dr. van Heuven Goedhart's appeals to governments and private organizations raised the sum of $ 1,300,000 which has made it possible to relieve the most crying needs of the refugees. The expenditure connected with European refugees in Shanghai alone amounts to approximately $ 34,000 a month.

The original intention was that the High Commissioner's Office should operate for only three years. However, it has now been decided that its activities should continue until January 1, 1959[1], and the organization be authorized to raise $ 16,000,000 by voluntary contributions from governmental sources. Of this sum, only $ 4,200,000 is assured as of now.

As I have mentioned, the basic task of the High Commissioner is to provide help and protection to the refugees.

And so the Office has sought, by dint of untiring and sometimes thankless effort, to bring assistance to the refugees and to help the authorities understand their problems. This kind of work cannot be described in terms of figures. But think of what it means to the individual refugee to feel and to know that he has not been forgotten, that in spite of everything there is someone willing to help him, even if the help cannot be brought immediately. In addition, the provision of legal protection gives him some sense of security and so helps to maintain his morale and to encourage him to begin a new life.

Nonetheless, such measures alone are not enough to solve the problem of the refugee. What then is the solution?

The answer appears to be easy. It is simply to give each refugee a social, economic, and legal foundation on which he can rebuild his life. Yet it is in reality as difficult as it appears to be easy.

The High Commissioner has himself indicated three principal ways to solve the problem. The first is to enable those refugees who so wish to return to their own country. But very few of today's refugees wish to go back. Another way is to enable them to emigrate overseas. As already mentioned, IRO succeeded in helping a large number of refugees to resettle in other countries. But it was easier then than it is now, and IRO also had the funds to finance such emigration.

There are yet other factors which now make it more difficult to solve the refugee problem with the aid of emigration. With the years that have

1. The Office is still in existence.

passed, many refugees are approaching or have reached old age, and most countries who accept immigrants give precedence to those who are able to work and who can thus become useful citizens. For example, it frequently happens that a male refugee is granted an immigrant's visa but that his family is rejected. It may be that certain members of the family are unwanted in the new country because of their poor health or old age. In such cases the man usually chooses to remain with them, for his family generally means more to him than his own future.

But despite all the obstacles, the High Commission has done much to stimulate emigration. By appealing to other refugee organizations it has succeeded in promoting emigration to a considerable extent. I might mention by way of example the emigration of 33,000 refugees in 1953, arranged through the Intergovernmental Committee in Geneva[1].

A third possible way to solve the problem is to allow the refugees to remain permanently in the country of asylum and to give them citizenship status. But once again this has proved to be difficult to achieve. It might appear that such a plan could be more easily implemented than before in view of the improvement in the economic situation and the resulting high level of employment enjoyed by some countries harboring large numbers of refugees. Nevertheless, however willing a government may be in principle to grant foreigners work and residence permits, it must first look after the economic interests of its own citizens. We must look reality in the eye. The inhabitants of a country are seldom very anxious to admit foreigners, and government policy is all too often decided by lack of willingness on the part of the budgetary authorities. The economic resources have not always been plentiful either, and there are always many demands today which have higher priority. Nor should we forget that many refugees are living in countries which themselves have considerable unemployment.

The High Commissioner has encountered all these difficulties and many others besides. But he has worked tirelessly to overcome them. When Dr. van Heuven Goedhart has submitted plans only to have them rejected, he has promptly submitted fresh ones. He has often been forced to reduce his demands, but he has never willingly given up until he has secured at least something. And many are the measures which the High Commissioner has

1. Presumably the Intergovernmental Committee for European Migration (the name adopted in November, 1952) which started operations in February, 1952, under the name of Provisional Intergovernmental Committee for the Movement of Migrants from Europe.

succeeded in pushing through. One example of these is the project he sub-mitted to the Austrian government with the object of finding employment in agriculture for refugees. In its final form this plan was not as comprehen-sive as Dr. van Heuven Goedhart would have wished, but it was carried through and proved highly successful. We must not forget that many of the refugees are capable people. Experience shows that they are hard-work-ing and better at economizing than other men; after all, starting with only their bare hands, they strive to create a future for themselves and their fam-ilies. What they need is to be helped to help themselves; and it has been observed that, if given loans, they are more conscientious about repaying them than many of those who receive assistance in all countries but accept it as a gift without ever thinking of paying it back.

But we still have a long way to go before all refugees have been given such an opportunity. Some 300,000 refugees remain in Europe, 70,000 of them in camps. There are about 13,000 refugees of European origin in China, particularly in Shanghai, who have no hope of making a life for themselves there. The refugees both inside and outside Europe who come under the protection of the High Commissioner's Office number some 2,200,000 in all.

Ten years have passed since the war ended and the refugee camps still remain. Here we find the old and infirm and those whose occupations are such that they find it difficult to obtain work in a foreign country. The majority are professional men, among them many intellectuals. They are people who feel that they have nothing to look forward to, and many have given up all hope of a better future. But the camps also house children and young people who have never known any other home, and none of them, neither the old nor the young, have a native country which could give them help or protection. Until the camps are cleared, until the sick and old have been cared for, until the young people and the children have been educa-ted and trained for a profession or trade, the refugee problem is not solved.

Earlier organizations have done much for the refugees living in the camps, and the High Commissioner's Office has carried on the good work. It has also managed to persuade some countries to accept and to look after the old and the ailing. Those who have been taken in by other countries include the blind and the old and even those struck down by tuberculosis. The aim is to bring all these unfortunate people back to a normal life.

But it seems we will be a long time in reaching the goal. I recently heard a description of life in a refugee camp. To be sure, the refugees get enough food to keep them alive. But what else? Dreary hopelessness day after day, bad accommodations, worse than bad clothing and sanitation. Nothing to do but to sit there and wait and wait. For what? For something they no longer have any hope of realizing. Of what use is it to take a few children on a summer holiday in some country, only to send them back again to their camps?

This is the Europe of today, where one nation after another prides itself on having achieved the welfare state.

The Office of the High Commissioner does not have funds to change the situation, and the funds of private organizations do not stretch far enough. The High Commissioner has had the courage to state that deliverance can come only through common action and through financial support supplied by all in a united effort.

There may perhaps be some who do not believe that work for the refugees is work in the cause of peace – although I have never actually heard this view expressed. But it *is* work for peace, if to heal the wounds of war is to work for peace, if to promote brotherhood among men is to work for peace. For this work shows us that the unfortunate foreigner is one of us; it teaches us to understand that sympathy with other human beings, even if they are separated from us by national frontiers, is the foundation upon which a lasting peace must be built.

Today there are many who are active in the refugee cause. And it is the Office of the United Nations High Commissioner for Refugees which is the focus for the work. It is an institution, an organization that has statutes as do all other institutions. But statutes are lifeless; it is people who infuse life. And it is Dr. van Heuven Goedhart and his colleagues who have shaped the High Commission and given it life, for in their constant, intense search for new solutions they have felt and shown sympathy and understanding for the refugees as human beings.

The High Commissioner, Dr. van Heuven Goedhart, has never tired of proclaiming what he believes is right. It is good to know that there are people who dare to make a stand against soulless and bureaucratic authority. He and his colleagues represent the watchful conscience of our world.

For these reasons, then, the Nobel Committee of the Norwegian Parliament, in testimony of its profound gratitude and admiration for you, Dr. van Heuven Goedhart, and for your colleagues, has decided to award the Nobel Peace Prize to the Office of the United Nations High Commissioner for Refugees.

G. J. VAN HEUVEN GOEDHART

Refugee Problems and Their Solutions

Nobel Lecture*, December 12, 1955

On the tenth of December, fifty-nine years ago, Alfred Bernhard Nobel died in his villa at San Remo in Italy, sixty-three years old. The villa bore the name of «Mio Nido», and I do not know whether he himself thus christened his house. Perhaps he acquired it with name and all. Anyway, there is a lot to that name, «Mio Nido», «My Nest». For Alfred Nobel– I use the words of Professor Henrik Schück–was «a lonely man and with his sensitive nature he suffered keenly from the misfortune of being without a home»[1]. He spent his youth in different countries, and most of his later life he was traveling and living in hotel rooms, ships, and night trains. His interests were spread over many lands. Combining the best qualities of an inventor and a business man–a rare phenomenon–fighting most of his life against increasingly failing health, Alfred Nobel became more and more aware of a painful lack of a sense of belonging, and of man's need for roots in a family and in a community. Ragnar Sohlman, who, during the latter years of Nobel's life knew him better than most of his contemporaries, in a sketch of Nobel's closing years, quotes a letter of his saying: «For the past nine days I have been ill and have had to stay indoors with no other company than a paid valet; no one inquires about me... When at the age of fifty-four one is left so alone in the world, and a paid servant is the only person who has so far shown one the most kindness, then come heavy thoughts, heavier than most people can imagine. I can see in my valet's

---

* Dr. Gerrit Jan van Heuven Goedhart (1901–1956), Dutch newspaper editor and writer, former member of the Netherlands Senate and former Dutch delegate to the UN where he was chairman of the Third Committee of the UN General Assembly in 1950, had been the UN High Commissioner for Refugees since the inception of the office late in 1950. Speaking for the UN High Commissioner's Office, he delivered this lecture in the auditorium of the Nobel Institute in Oslo. The text is taken from *Les Prix Nobel en 1955*.

1. Henrik Schück (1855–1947), Swedish literary historian and at one time chairman of the Board of Directors of the Nobel Foundation, in «Alfred Nobel: A Biographical Sketch» in *Nobel: The Man and His Prizes* (Amsterdam: Elsevier, 1962), p. 8.

eyes how much he pities me, but I cannot, of course, let him notice that.»[1]

Alfred Nobel was a lonely man, or, in a sense, a «displaced person», a «homeless foreigner». He was by birth and passport a Swede, but in his later days he spoke not so much his mother tongue, of which he had an unusual command, but mostly English, a language in which he wrote remarkably beautiful poetry. Whereas we may be inclined to combine Nobel's name with the image of a hardboiled businessman, an extremely successful money-maker, Alfred Nobel was in reality a poet, a dreamer, an adventurer in science, an idealist at heart, a philosopher in essence–he did, in fact, leave a sketch for a novel in which he advocated a form of government along Platonic lines. Even in his most striking inventions, of which dynamite is only one, he saw not ends, but means. When Countess Bertha von Kinsky von Chinic und Tettau, later Bertha von Suttner[2]–Nobel Prize winner and world-famous through her *Die Waffen nieder!*–tried to interest him in her peace actions (for a short time, in fact for one week only, she had been secretary and housekeeper of the dynamite-maker Alfred Nobel, who was living in Paris), this was his reply: «My factories may make an end of war sooner than your congresses. The day when two army corps can annihilate each other in one second, all civilized nations, it is to be hoped, will recoil from war and discharge their troops.» And in 1876 he added, again in conversation with Bertha von Suttner, «I want to invent a material or an engine of such horribly destructive effect that it will make wars impossible.»

It is as though those prophetic words are slowly coming true more than seventy years after they were written. Could one not argue that in this atomic age we seem to be near the point where «in one second» two armies, two peoples can indeed annihilate each other? Is it not as if that frightening reality is more behind the «easing of tension» than any real desire for understanding and coexistence? Alfred Nobel, fortunately for his peace of mind, did not foresee the two humiliating wars which mankind was to fight in this century. He firmly believed that his work was a contribution to peace, which in his private life he had never known. And beyond his death he went on, by his will, to foster peace as no one had done before him. It

1. Ragnar Sohlman (1870–1948), Nobel's private assistant during the last three years of his life and one of the executors of his will, quotes the letter, written in October, 1887, in «Alfred Nobel and the Nobel Foundation» in *Nobel: The Man and His Prizes*, p.21.

2. Bertha von Suttner (1843–1914), recipient of the Nobel Peace Prize for 1905.

is in his memory and in his honor that this meeting is held, fifty-nine years after his death.

On the thirteenth of May, twenty-five years ago, Fridtjof Nansen[1] died at his home at Lysaker at the age of sixty-eight. Although his life had been heavily loaded with traveling, although he spent many, many years far from his beloved Norway as an explorer, as minister of Norway to England, as Norwegian delegate to the League of Nations, and as League of Nations High Commissioner for Refugees, he was nevertheless deeply rooted in his country and his people. No «displaced person», no «homeless foreigner», he! A man as great as Nobel and as much of an idealist, but with a completely different approach to life and its problems. Where Nobel followed the inspirations of his inventive mind – he had indeed a poor scholarly background – Nansen was the conscientious scientific adventurer with the great vision and the warm human heart. Perhaps it is true to say that he too, as any great man, was somewhat torn apart, feeling unable to realize all his projects and equally unable to abandon the hope of realizing them all. International missions and duties kept him far from developing new Polar projects, upon which, however, he continued to work up to the last days of his life. Like Alfred Nobel, he had a keen sense of the significance of «belonging», but whereas for Nobel that feeling became almost an obsession because he had no home, Nansen cherished it because he had one. And, having one, he fought to provide homes for hundreds of thousands of his fellowmen. When in 1922 the Nobel Prize – richly deserved – was given to him and in 1938 – again richly deserved – to the Nansen Office for Refugees, it would have been appropriate to recall that those distinctions were awarded in memory of a man who himself was painfully aware of having no home.

In my office in Geneva I have hanging on the wall, written by a hand quite unaccustomed to writing, a short German poem which my father found in a caravan of gypsies whom he visited when they passed our little Dutch village many years ago:

> *Der Mensch braucht ein Plätzchen*
> *Und wär's noch so klein*
> *Von dem er kann sagen:*

1. Fridtjof Nansen (1861–1930), recipient of the Nobel Peace Prize for 1922.

Siehe hier das ist mein,
Hier lebe ich, hier liebe ich,
Hier ruhe ich aus,
Hier ist meine Heimat,
Hier bin ich zu Haus.

How wholeheartedly would the lonely man, at the villa «Mio Nido», have agreed to that! A man needs a little place, small as it may be, of which he can say: «This is mine. Here I live, here I love, here I find my rest. This is my fatherland, this is my home!» Nobel was poor, although wealthy; Nansen was rich, although not primarily in earthly possessions. Nobel never really had a home; Nansen not only had one, but found deep satisfaction in trying to find one for others. Both these great Scandinavians must of necessity be remembered on this day, when the Nobel Prize has just been awarded to an office for refugees. For the essence of the refugee problem is very, very simple. It is: to find «ein Plätzchen», to find a «Mio Nido» for people who for reasons of persecution have been obliged to leave their native country and who have therefore become «uprooted» and homeless.

I hope I may be forgiven for this introduction to some remarks about the problem with which the Office of the United Nations High Commissioner for Refugees has to deal. I even feel that the introduction may be relevant. «Mio Nido» is not just a roof over one's head, not just a place to live in. It is the all-embracing term for a series of elements which together constitute a man's independence, and therefore his freedom and his dignity. The refugee problem has nothing to do with charity. It is not the problem of people to be pitied, but far more the problem of people to be admired. It is the problem of people who somewhere, somehow, sometime, had the courage to give up the feeling of belonging, which they possessed, rather than abandon the human freedom which they valued more highly. It is the problem of rebuilding their existences. It is therefore a legal, an economic, a financial problem, complicated in its aspects, yet simple in its essentials. «Der Mensch braucht ein Plätzchen.» Nobel never really found his «Mio Nido»; Nansen would not have been who he was without his home. And the refugee can solve his problem only by striking new roots.

Under the mandate of the Office of the UNHCR come about 2,200,000 refugees, of whom more than fifty percent are in Europe. Of these, some 300,000 had at the beginning of this year not been able to solve the problem of their independent existence; 70,000 of them are still living in some 200 camps in Germany, Austria, Italy and Greece; and some 15,000 of them are unfit for economic integration anywhere, as they are too old or for some other reason disabled. Outside Europe there are still unsolved problems – in the Middle East, scattered groups of refugees in the Lebanon, Syria, the Kingdom of Jordan, Egypt, and Iran – and in the Far East, particularly on the Chinese mainland where some 13,000 refugees of European origin are endeavoring to leave China in order to resettle elsewhere. The mandate given to the Office by the General Assembly in 1950 is not, however, geographically limited, neither has it a dateline. In principle every victim of racial, political, or religious persecution who is or will be at some time during the lifetime of the Office – that is until the end of 1958 – outside his own country, and who no longer wishes to avail himself of the protection of the authorities of that country, is or will be a refugee under the United Nations mandate. Within the time-limit of the existence of the Office the continuing character of the refugee problem and the worldwide scope of the activities of the United Nations have thus been recognized in the mandate. Still, hundreds of thousands of refugees – in the wider sense of the term – do not come under it. In particular, those for whom a special organization has been established – such as the Arab refugees for whom the United Nations Relief and Works Agency for Palestine Refugees in the Near East is competent – are not within the mandate of the Office. Neither are those refugees who, although they left their homes, are considered to have the rights and privileges of citizens of their countries of present residence, such as the refugees from Eastern Germany now living in the Federal Republic, the Moslem refugees who fled from India to Pakistan, or the Hindu refugees who fled from Pakistan to India. Theoretically it could be regretted that these latter groups are excluded from the United Nations mandate, but practically it must be admitted that a wider definition would include so many millions of uprooted people as to paralyze the Office and make it quite impossible to work out any program. Moreover, it should be remembered that these groups of refugees are essentially different from the ones which come under the mandate of the Office in that they consist of people who in principle have a country to live in and a government ready to protect them and even to treat them as full citizens. For the Federal Republic of Germany, for India and Pakistan, for Turkey – a country which a few years ago generously received some 150,000 Bulgarians of Turkish ethnic origin – the problem of their «national refugees» is certainly a pressing one and one which is hard to solve. Nonetheless, it is more a problem of increasing the economic absorption capacity of these countries through capital investment and industrial development than a refugee problem in the proper sense of the word. The political refugee under the mandate of the United Nations is an alien, and being an alien is his fundamental disability. He does not have the rights of a citizen in his country of asylum, he is not regarded by the population as «one of us», but rather as a «Fremd-körper» [an outsider; a strange character]. In addition to his economic difficulties, which are in themselves far from easy to overcome, he suffers from disadvantages of a legal nature. It is on this front that the first attack on the problem must be made.

Protection of refugees covers a wide field of activities. It begins, or rather should begin, immediately after the refugee has crossed the border of his country into a country of asylum. Is he within the mandate of the United Nations and «eligible» for the benefits of the Convention on the Status of Refugees written in 1951 and now ratified by fifteen parliaments? It is easy to see that in a decision on this vital point the United Nations Office for Refugees should already play a part. Otherwise, the newly arriving refugee will see his fate unilaterally decided by the authorities of the country in which he seeks asylum. In the course of the years, different procedures for establishing the «eligibility» of a refugee have been worked out between governments and our Office. They vary from leaving the decision in principle to our representation in the country concerned – as is the case in Belgium – to our having an observer on the national committee in charge of ruling on the eligibility of a refugee. Ever since the 1951 Convention came into force in April, 1954, the importance of cooperation between governments and our Office in matters of eligibility has increased. For the refugee a favorable decision means obtaining a reasonable «status», whereas an unfavorable decision would mean lasting uncertainty and perhaps an «illegal» existence, even expulsion. Moreover, a fair trial of the newly arriving refugee has become increasingly important, because «integration» into the economy of the country of asylum is possible only when the refugee has a legal status upon which to base his efforts to establish himself.

However, international protection covers many other activities. In saying that at present a quarter of a million refugees have not yet solved their problems, I do not wish to imply that all the other refugees under the mandate, wherever they may be, are only theoretically covered by it. Refugee status comes to an end through the acquisition of citizenship of another country. As long as that process has not been completed, the refugee, even if well on his way to firm establishment in a country of immigration, may run into difficulties arising from his defective legal status, and if that happens, he will appeal to the Office for international protection. Clearly international protection is something basically different from general legal assistance. Much as the refugee may be in need of such assistance, it would be virtually impossible for the Office to provide it in hundreds of thousands of individual cases. As a matter of principle, the United Nations does not and should not go beyond assistance, the need for which arises from the status of the refugee who asks for it.

There are in the realm of international protection of refugees certain problems of particular concern to our Office. To mention only one of them, there is a group of refugee seamen, unknown in numbers but probably a few thousands, which constitutes a problem *sui generis*. These refugees have either no papers at all or inadequate papers to establish their «status». Inasmuch as they have no right of residence in any country, they can never leave the ships on which they are serving. Cases have come to our knowledge of people who for two, three, or four years have spent day and night aboard ships without ever feeling solid earth under their feet. We also know of cases where a refugee seaman could not bear that kind of life any longer and decided to take the risk of going ashore. Often he would end up in jail, as in our complicated world a man without identity papers and without a right of residence in any country is hardly considered as a human being. We have in the past few years registered hundreds of cases of this kind and are greatly encouraged by the fact that a conference of governmental experts coming from seven countries, and convened on the initiative of the Dutch government, has recently tackled this problem in a way which promises much for the refugees concerned.

Refugee problems can only be solved in three different ways – through voluntary repatriation, through resettlement overseas, and through integration either in the country of present residence or in combination with intra-European migration. Of these solutions, voluntary repatriation is no longer of great importance. Immediately after the war the vast majority of the «displaced persons» had the desire to return to their countries, from which they had been forcibly recruited by national-socialist Germany. Those who refused to return – and there were a few millions of them – became refugees instead of «displaced persons», a term which, in the service of clarity, we should now altogether abolish. Whereas some seven million «displaced persons» were repatriated by the United Nations Relief and Re-habilitation Agency between 1945 and 1947, the International Refugee Or-ganization between 1947 and 1951 repatriated only a further 70,000, and since then repatriation has become sporadic, as the refugees simply do not wish to go back to their countries of origin. When a refugee expresses the desire to return to his home country–and any refugee is at any time per-fectly free to do so–he «re-avails» himself of the protection of his national authorities and is therefore no longer a refugee. The task of our Office can only consist of establishing contact between such a refugee and his authori-ties; thereafter, it is for the latter to repatriate him. The United Nations is not called upon to influence the decision of any refugee. Freedom of de-cision is the inalienable right of the refugee himself. It is his wish that counts, and the United Nations, within the limits of the Statute, tries to fulfil that wish, no matter what it is–repatriation, resettlement, or integration.

Whereas repatriation does not play a significant role in the solution of the refugee problems of today, resettlement overseas, particularly in the United States, Canada, and Australia, is the dream of most refugees. «Mio Nido» is, for hundreds of thousands of them, a house and a job in one of the new countries. The International Refugee Organization specialized in resettling refugees overseas, whereas the United Nations Relief and Re-habilitation Administration specialized in the repatriation of displaced per-sons. During the lifetime of the IRO no less than a million refugees crossed the oceans by sea and air. That highly commendable operation had, as we all know, the character of a selective process. It is often forgotten that there is national sovereignty over every square meter of our globe, and that ad-mitting a refugee is therefore always done by the sovereign decision of a sovereign state entitled to put up whatever conditions for admission it sees fit. Demographically, any organized migration is therefore a sort of reversed Darwinistic process: not the «survival», but the «exodus» of the fittest. Those refugees or members of their families who suffer from some disability and therefore cannot meet the rigid requirements of the admission legislation of the country to which they would like to emigrate have to remain behind. Clearly, refugee emigration must gradually decrease. Refugees who seek asylum do not arrive in select categories, as regards health, skills, and age. Many times whole families come over, including aged and sick members. It is only when it comes to transfer from the asylum country to the country of immigration that the principle of selection is applied in all its rigidity. If, in addition, one takes into account the fact that the immigration countries have a wide choice of nationals from overpopulated states, and also that the capital market in theoretically underpopulated areas, particularly in Latin America, does not allow for the investment of the sums required to create the general conditions for mass immigration, it will be clear that integration of refugees into the economy of their countries of present residence becomes more and more–whether one likes it or not–the major answer to refugee problems.

Integration is not assimilation, which covers a much wider field. The United Nations cannot do more than assist in establishing basic conditions for assimilation–a status, a resettlement opportunity, a house, the chance of a job. Thereafter, the difficult process of assimilation has to begin. It is a process in which anyone who lives near a refugee can participate. Only when the refugee has friends around him, when he feels that he is a member of his new community, will he consider his house as «Mio Nido», as his real home.

There are encouraging signs that at least part of the integration solution can be effected in combination with intra-European migration. There is a growing awareness in governmental and private circles in Europe of the existence of a still very tragic and real refugee problem. That awareness has found expression in many ways–admission to the territories of European states of a considerable number of old and disabled refugees, generous contributions to the United Nations Refugee Fund by a number of governments in Europe, successful fund raising in the private sector of some countries. But a particularly welcome demonstration of European interest in the prevailing refugee situation has been the development, by a few European governments, of schemes for the admission to their territories of limited numbers of refugees under criteria far more liberal than those of the average overseas country. It is the ardent hope of my colleagues and myself that during the period of economic prosperity and consequent shortage of manpower which now prevails in Europe, many new opportunities for refugees can be created.

As far as we can predict, voluntary repatriation will in the years to come account for not more than one percent of the solutions to refugee problems still to be solved, and it should be remembered that the effect of repatriation may be offset by the arrival of an equal number of refugees. On the other hand, not more than twenty percent of the refugees today in difficulties may find a solution to their problems through resettlement overseas. Consequently, it is reasonable to suppose that approximately eighty percent will have to look towards integration into the economy of their countries of present residence.

Clearly, the problems of a quarter of a million uprooted people cannot possibly be solved by one method alone. On the contrary, the richer the choice of method, the greater the chance of finally reaching a solution for all concerned. We in our Office are equally in favor of all existing methods for the solution of refugee problems, and in addition we try to use our imagination in order to devise new variations. An office trying to deal efficiently with refugee problems should not be afraid of a bold experiment. It is better to develop one new method through a number of failures than at all times to follow the beaten track.

Five years ago, when the General Assembly of the United Nations decided to set up a High Commissioner's Office for Refugees, a far-reaching principle was agreed upon, of which I am, on the whole, in favor–that is, that the Office was to be «non-operational». It was to be a relatively small unit, mainly charged with providing international protection and assisting governments to find solutions for refugee problems. For its activities it was to rely heavily on the many excellent voluntary agencies working in this field. Moreover, the United Nations were not to pay more from their regular budget than the administrative expenses involved in the running of a head office in Geneva and branch offices wherever they might be established. For these reasons, our budget has never been higher than $650,000 and our total staff at Headquarters, together with our thirteen branch offices, numbers not more than 123 people. Originally I had no right even to appeal for funds. There was a general overoptimistic assumption that the refugee problem, to all practical intents and purposes, had been solved and that the governments of the countries of residence of the refugees, to which the responsibility for the administration of the camps had already been transferred, would bear the burden of providing such material assistance as was still needed.

During the five years of its existence our Office has had to fight many battles, of which the most difficult has been to persuade governments that there was still a tremendous, tragic, and increasingly difficult problem to be solved. I should like to pay a heartfelt tribute to the Third Committee of the General Assembly of the United Nations for its understanding of the difficulties and for the appropriate action which it has taken in three stages. The first stage came in 1952 when it decided to authorize me to establish the United Nations Refugee Emergency Fund, designed to give emergency aid to the most needy groups amongst the refugees. The second stage came in 1953. As the High Commissioner had been elected by the General Assembly for a period of three years, a decision as to the prolongation or discontinuation of his Office had to be taken at the end of 1953. By that time the Office itself was firmly convinced of two things. First of all, it had been given most generous support by the Ford Foundation in the United States, which made nearly $3,000,000 available for experiments in the field of integration. A long series of projects had been carried out through voluntary agencies, and it had become clear that integration could really work. On the other hand, it was also clear that our Office, limited to another term of only three years, could not adequately plan ahead. Therefore, if there were to be any prolongation, it should, we felt, be for at least five years. We had no doubt that such a prolongation was necessary. Both the Economic and Social Council and the General Assembly concurred with these views, and by the end of 1953 we had the certainty that we could work out a plan on a longer-term basis. The decisive action – and this was the third stage – was then taken by the Ninth Session of the General Assembly in 1954, when it approved a four years' program for permanent solutions and emergency aid, to be financed from voluntary governmental contributions to the extent of $16,000,000 over a period of four years. An Executive Committee, consisting of the representatives of twenty states, members and nonmembers of the United Nations, was established to direct the program.

Rightly the emphasis of this new program is on the dissolution of the still existing refugee camps, in which 70,000 refugees–not to speak of some 30,000 to 50,000 others in the so-called «unofficial» camps–are living, many of them for as long as ten years. These camps are black spots on the map of Europe and should burn holes in the consciences of those who are privileged to live in better conditions. Everything possible must be done to close them. But dissolution of camps is a process which is much more complicated than appears at first sight. The building of houses is by no means enough. The refugee, in order to solve his problem, must be able to maintain his family and himself. He must, if he has lost his skill, be retrained in a trade for which there is a demand, and his house must be within a reasonable distance from his work. If he intends to set himself up in a small business, he may need a loan at a moderate interest. If he is not sure how he can solve his problem, he will need counseling. If he hopes to emigrate, his papers must be put in order before he can leave. Clearly, a program for permanent solutions of refugee problems must be broken down into a series of concrete projects, all coordinated with the appropriate governmental authorities in the countries of implementation. Those countries are called upon to support such projects with their own governmental contributions. They almost double the amount of the international funds put into the program. In addition, money disbursed on a loan basis can be used more than once; in other words, the greatest economic use will be made of available funds. If in the years 1955–1958 the $16,000,000 should be forthcoming from governmental sources, it would be fairly safe to assume that altogether some $40,000,000 would benefit the refugees who are at present faced with an unsolved problem.

Unfortunately, there is still a difficult battle to be won. For 1955 the governments, so far, have not made available more than just over fifty-five percent of a target of $4,200,000. An Office which has just been awarded the Nobel Prize for Peace has perhaps no right to be discouraged, but should it be necessary for the United Nations High Commissioner for Refugees to spend such a considerable part of his time on fund raising? In a world where there are so many insoluble problems we can ill afford to neglect one which is soluble. And there can be no doubt that by a combination of efforts, the present refugee problem – *rebus sic stantibus* [things being as they are] – can be solved.

But there is a grave *periculum in mora* [danger in delay]. Everyone who knows the conditions in which tens of thousands of refugees still live must feel ashamed on their behalf. He must also feel admiration for the fact that most of them are still law-abiding, decent people, ready to make their own last effort to liberate themselves from their miserable plight. But above all he must feel the urgency of actions when he realizes that there are amongst «the waiting people» so many who have lost hope to get back to a normal life again because they are too old and too sick. To be a refugee is distressing enough–to be an old or sick refugee, however, is the most tragic fate imaginable.

When people get older, they develop a nostalgia for «Mio Nido»; this was true both for Alfred Nobel and for Fridtjof Nansen. But whereas Nobel and Nansen were free to go back to their fatherlands whenever they wished, the aged refugee knows that he will not see his own country again. For him the only hope is for a quiet room in an old people's home, or, if he is sick, a bed in a decent hospital. Nothing is more deeply moving than to see old and sick refugees for whom warmhearted people have undertaken to provide some comforts in their last years. On their walls they hang photographs showing themselves in beautiful uniforms from the days when they proudly served in the armies of their countries, and pictures of the landscapes of their fatherlands. Sitting on a bench in a garden, they revive memories of old times. Sometimes one can even see them with a bundle of shares in some Imperial Russian company, unable and unwilling to believe that they are just printed paper now. For them the past is glory, the present is at its best bearable, but no longer is there any future. No wonder that my colleagues and I feel that something must be done, and done quickly, to give these old and sick refugees a place, even if it is only a substitute for a real home.

There can be no real peace in this world as long as hundreds of thousands of men, women, and children, through no fault of their own, but only because they sacrificed all they possessed for the sake of what they believed, still remain in camps and live in misery and in the greatest uncertainty of their future. Eventually, if we wait too long, the uprooted are bound to become easy prey for political adventurers, from whom the world has suffered too much already. Before anything of that sort happens, let us join our hands in an all-out effort to solve their problem.

Many years ago I participated in a discussion on the problem of international education. After many experts had presented their complicated theories, an old headmaster of a certain school got up and quietly said: «There is only one system of education, through love and one's own example.» He was right. What is true for education is true also for the refugee problem of today. With love and our own example–example in the sense of sacrifice–it can be solved. And if in the cynical times in which we live someone might be inclined to laugh at «love» and «example» as factors in politics, he would do well to be reminded of Nansen's hardhitting, direct, and courageous words, based on a life full of sacrifice and devotion: «Love of man is practical policy.»[1]

1. These words in Norwegian, NESTEKJAERLIGHETER REALPOLITIKK, are inscribed on the Nansen Medal, honoring Fridtjof Nansen, which van Heuven Goedhart instituted as an annual award in recognition of outstanding services rendered in the refugee cause.

History*

The Office of the United Nations High Commissioner for Refugees (UN-HCR) was originally established by the General Assembly of the United Nations for a three-year period from January 1, 1951, to December 31, 1953, but it has since been voted successive five-year extensions through 1958, 1963, 1968, and 1973. Within the framework of the United Nations, the UNHCR superseded the International Refugee Organization (IRO), 1947–1952, which had in its turn taken over the refugee work of the United Nations Relief and Rehabilitation Administration (UNRRA), 1943–1947.

In the mandate of the UNHCR, the term «refugee» is carefully defined: in general, the refugee is a person who, because of fear of persecution arising from his race, creed, or political philosophy, is living outside his former home country and is unable or unwilling to avail himself of that country's protection. UNHCR provides him international protection in accordance with the provisions of the Convention Relating to the Status of Refugees adopted in 1951, which has been operative since April, 1954, and has now been ratified by sixty countries. The 1967 Protocol broadens the provisions of the 1951 Convention to include new groups of refugees, and the UN Declaration on Territorial Asylum of 1967 extends the effectiveness of international protection. Protection is broadly aimed at promoting international legal instruments for the benefit of refugees and ensuring that they are treated in accordance with such instruments, in particular as regards right to work, social security, and access to travel facilities.

With headquarters in Geneva and at present some thirty branch offices situated in strategic spots throughout the world in addition to special representatives and correspondents, UNHCR is not a specialized agency but an integral part of the UN, its High Commissioner being nominated by the Secretary-General and elected by the General Assembly.

In function, UNHCR, unlike IRO, is promotional rather than operational. It coordinates international action for refugees, establishing liaisons

* The editor gratefully acknowledges permission to use freely material kindly supplied by the UNHCR for this history.

with governments, with UN specialized agencies, with intergovernmental organizations, and with nongovernmental organizations. It seeks permanent solutions to the problem of refugees through voluntary repatriation, a preferred solution; through emigration, a solution applied in conjunction with the Intergovernmental Committee for European Migration; and through integration in the country of residence, a solution that has proved workable for vast numbers of refugees. The aim of UNHCR is to promote action which will help the refugees to become self-supporting, and eventually, through naturalization to cease being refugees. Assistance given in achieving this aim may include emergency aid and rural settlement projects in Africa and to some extent in Asia; mainly housing and establishment assistance in European countries; and counseling, education, and training of one sort or another in most areas.

The UN provides administrative expenses and extends to the High Commissioner permission to obtain appropriations for current programs from individual governments and to accept contributions from private sources. The funding target for any given year is determined by the Executive Committee upon recommendation of the High Commissioner whose budget varies in response to the needs of the time. Special programs are specially financed. For example, early in the 1950's the Ford Foundation provided a grant of about $3,000,000 (increased to about $8,000,000 with matching funds from other sources) to carry out pilot projects in the economic integration of refugees in Austria, Germany, France, and Trieste, and on the resettlement of refugees in Latin America, Canada, and Australia.

From 1955 to 1958 there was an UNHCR material assistance program known as the UNREF Program which was budgeted at $16,000,000. Since 1959 there have been annual programs varying in size between $3,000,000 and $7,000,000. In 1960, World Refugee Year, the annual program was unusually large, amounting to about $12,000,000.

Within these programs special allocations were made for various purposes, such as Camp Clearance (that is, the finding of permanent solutions for refugees in European camps), and assistance to refugees in the Far East. Since 1963, a part of each program has been devoted to projects for refugees of longer standing and part to projects for new refugees.

From 1957, while the work in Europe continued, the Office, acting on the basis of resolutions of the General Assembly requesting the High Commissioner to extend his good offices to refugees not covered by the original Statute of 1950, provided assistance to various groups of refugees in other parts of the world. In 1957 and again in 1962 the High Commissioner was asked to use his good offices to encourage arrangements for contributions to assist Chinese refugees in Hong Kong whose numbers are estimated at over one million. In 1957–1958 UNHCR took action in cooperation with the League of Red Cross Societies to alleviate the plight of Algerian refugees in Tunisia and Morocco, and in 1962 participated in their voluntary repatriation.

Since 1962, and again on the basis of the good offices resolutions, the epicenter of UNHCR material assistance has moved from Europe to Africa and to some extent to Asia, where world events have caused a steady increase in the number of refugees requiring assistance. By 1969 there were in Africa about one million refugees within the competence of UNHCR, of whom 250,000 received material assistance during that year. UNHCR assistance was given also to needy refugees among the Chinese refugees in Macao and the Tibetan refugees in India and Nepal. In Africa, and to some degree in Asia, the main solution for the refugee problem has been rural settlement, in which the Office has cooperated extensively with governments and with agencies, members of the United Nations system. In some cases these settlement projects have led to development programs for refugees and the local population alike.

In the twenty-year history of the Office, there have been four high commissioners: G.J. van Heuven Goedhart (1951–1956), The Netherlands; Auguste R. Lindt (1956–1960), Switzerland; Felix Schnyder (1961–1965), Switzerland; Prince Sadruddin Aga Khan (1965–   ), Iran.

Selected Bibliography

Convention Relating to the Status of Refugees. United Nations Document A/Conf. 2/108, August, 1951.

The Displaced Persons Analytical Bibliography. House of Representatives Report No. 1687. Washington, D.C., Superintendent of Public Documents, 1950.

Edding, Friedrich, *The Refugee as a Burden, a Stimulus and a Challenge to the West Germany Economy.* The Hague, Nijhoff, 1951.

Elbadrawy, B.M.F., *The Refugee: A Problem of International Social Welfare.* New York, Columbia University Press, 1951. Contains a bibliography.

Frings, Paul, *Das internationale Flüchtlingsproblem.* Frankfurt am Main, Verlag der Frankfurter Hefte, 1951.

Heuven Goedhart, G. J. van, «The Problem of Refugees.» Five lectures. Académie de droit international: *Recueil des cours*, 82 (1953) 265–369. Leyden, Sijthoff, 1954.

Holborn, Louise, *The International Refugee Organization*. London, Oxford University Press, 1956.

Proudfoot, Malcolm J., *European Refugees, 1939–1952: A Study in Forced Population Movement*. London, Faber & Faber, 1957. Contains a bibliography.

Stoessinger, John George, *The Refugee and the World Community*. Minneapolis, University of Minnesota Press, 1956. Contains a bibliography.

United Nations High Commissioner for Refugees. *Reports*. See UN General Assembly, *Official Record*, Sixth Session and sessions thereafter. Or see *United Nations Documents Index: United Nations and Specialized Agencies Documents and Publications*, Vols. 1–13 (1950–1962), and its successor, *United Nations Documents Index: Cumulative Index and Cumulative Checklist*, Vol. 14–   (1963–   ).

Vernant, Jacques, *The Refugee in the Post-War World*. London, Allen and Unwin, 1953. Contains a bibliography.

Woodbridge, George, *The History of the United Nations Relief and Rehabilitation Administration*. 3 vols. New York, Columbia University Press, 1950.

See also selected bibliography for the Nansen International Office for Refugees, Vol. 2, p.284.

Peace 1955-1956

Prizes not awarded

Peace 1957

LESTER BOWLES PEARSON

Presentation

by Gunnar Jahn*, Chairman of the Nobel Committee

The Nobel Committee of the Norwegian Parliament has awarded Alfred Nobel's Peace Prize for 1957 to the Canadian Lester Bowles Pearson.

As we all know, Lester Pearson was Canada's foreign minister from 1948 to 1957 when, as a result of the election, the Liberal government resigned.

The winner of the Peace Prize for this year is, then, a politician, and he is still a Liberal member of the Canadian Parliament.

It can perhaps be said that what Lester Pearson has done to prevent or to stop war would not have been possible had he not been an active politician. That, of course, may be disputed. What I want to emphasize is that the Peace Prize has not been awarded to the politician or to the secretary of state as such, but to the man Lester Pearson because of his personal qualities – the powerful initiative, strength, and perseverance he has displayed in attempting to prevent or limit war operations and to restore peace in situations where quick, tactful, and wise action has been necessary to prevent unrest from spreading and developing into a worldwide conflagration.

Lester Bowles Pearson was born in Toronto, Canada, in 1897. His father and grandfather enjoyed high reputations as Methodist preachers, and the boy grew up in a religious but broad-minded environment in which even athletics played an important part in his training. His father saw to it that he received a good education. He enrolled as a history student at the University of Toronto, but his studies were interrupted during the First World War when, at the age of eighteen, he joined the University Medical Corps as a volunteer. At the end of the war in which he eventually became an actual participant, he resumed his studies and obtained his Bachelor of Arts

* Gunnar Jahn delivered this speech on December 10, 1957, in the Auditorium of the University of Oslo. At its conclusion, he presented the prize to the laureate, who responded with a brief speech of acceptance. The English translation of Mr. Jahn's speech used here is basically that appearing in *Les Prix Nobel en 1957*, with certain editorial changes, as well as some emendations made after collation with the Norwegian text, which also appears in *Les Prix Nobel*.

degree in 1919. After an interval in his uncle's meat processing plant, he won a scholarship for studies at Oxford. In 1923 he took his Master of Arts degree. He taught for some time, becoming an assistant professor of modern history at the University of Toronto.

In 1928, when he was thirty-one years old, Lester Pearson entered the service of the Canadian Department of External Affairs. This step marked the end of his academic career and the beginning of his life as a civil servant. He was first secretary at the Department of External Affairs in Ottawa until 1935, when he was appointed counselor at the Office of the High Commissioner for Canada in London. He returned to Ottawa in 1941 as assistant undersecretary of state at the Department of External Affairs, and in the following year he was appointed Canadian minister in Washington, where he stayed until 1946, for the last two years as ambassador. Then followed two years as undersecretary of state at home until—at the age of fifty-one—he became secretary of state for External Affairs in the Canadian government in 1948.

Such is the brief, prosaic data on Mr. Pearson's career, a career which, indeed, bears witness to great proficiency and intelligence; but it reveals nothing concerning what he has accomplished, how he has tackled the tasks with which he has been confronted, or why he has solved problems in the manner he has.

Naturally, during the period when Lester Pearson was a civil servant at the Department of External Affairs, he could express his views and opinions only to the Canadian government. It was, however, during those years, which to him were largely an apprenticeship, that he gathered his wide experience and broadened his outlook. It was during that period that his views on international problems took shape. He participated in the World Disarmament Conference[1] in Geneva in 1933–1934, in the London Naval Conference[2] in 1935, and during that same year in the work of the Canadian delegation to the Sixteenth Assembly of the League of Nations. These con-

1. Convened in February, 1932, under the aegis of the League of Nations, the Conference was deadlocked several times in 1932 and 1933 on the issue of German equality and, with Germany's withdrawal from the Conference and the League in October, 1933, came to a virtual halt despite some later meetings.
2. The Conference resulted in agreement among England, France, and the U.S. on certain naval limitations, but not until after Japan and Italy had withdrawn from the Conference.

ferences cannot have been very encouraging to Lester Pearson. All of us who had to do with the League of Nations in those years felt that we were going from one defeat to another. For the young Lester Pearson, however, just taking part in all this, observing it at first hand, has no doubt proved a valuable experience and contributed infinitely to what he has later been able to accomplish.

The years in London from 1935 to 1941 at the Canadian High Commissioner's Office were very important and instructive for Lester Pearson, in close and permanent contact as he was with what was going on in Europe at that time.

He has given an appraisal of conditions in the Western European democracies after the middle of the 1930's. It is a violent criticism of their domestic policy, as well as of their foreign policy; at home, of their inability to master the economic problems; abroad, of their hesitation and indulgence, their yielding to Hitler again and again in the belief that peace could thus be preserved – bringing them finally to the Munich crisis of 1938. Lester Pearson is said to have been one of the first Canadians who recognized at an early stage that the way which had been chosen would not lead to the desired end. War would have to come.

From 1942 to 1946 Lester Pearson was in Washington, as I said, as Canadian minister and ambassador. During that time he had more and more opportunity to bring himself to the world's attention; he participated in the efforts to build the structure of peace, efforts which started in 1943 long before the war was over.

His first remarkable contribution was made at the 1943 Conference in Hot Springs[1], which was concerned with finding out how the world's food and capital goods were to be distributed in peacetime. Lester Pearson's effective part in this work was obvious. Gove Hambidge gives the following description of him in his book *The Story of FAO:* «‹Mike› Pearson, young, modest, responsive, intelligent, and possessed of a quick sense of humor and a flair for working out effective compromises between opposing viewpoints, had made an excellent impression at the Hot Springs Conference.»

He was elected chairman of the Interim Commission for Food and Agriculture, which was appointed to prepare the plans for the permanent organization FAO. Hambidge makes the following comment on his work

[1]. Meeting in Hot Springs, Va., in 1943, this UN Conference set up the Interim Commission which eventually drafted the constitution for the Food and Agriculture Organization (FAO), formally established in 1945 and affiliated with the UN in 1946.

on that Commission: «More than any other person he was responsible for steering the Interim Commission through two years of successful work.»

At a meeting in Quebec in 1945, when FAO was established, the work of the Commission came to an end. I would like to quote what Lester Pearson himself said on that occasion because it shows so clearly that he was already aware, at that early stage, that international cooperation was threatened by the new progress of science in the field of nuclear research. But his words also show that he holds a vision of a better world for mankind, a world without fear and without want.

This is what he said: «We at this Conference know, and we have shown, what science could do if harnessed to the chariot of construction. Man's fears have, however, harnessed it also to another chariot – that of atomic obliteration. On that chariot race, with science driven by both contestants, all our hopes and fears and agonies and ecstasies are concentrated. If we lose in that contest, anything that we have done here or may do elsewhere in London, or Washington, or San Francisco, or Moscow will have as much consequence as a pebble thrown into the Gulf of St. Lawrence. But if we should acquire some trace of sanity and bring social progress in line with scientific development by subjecting the annihilating forces of science to some sort of social control, which in the last analysis means some sort of international control, then the work we have done at Quebec will have made a worthy and permanent contribution to man's long effort to move upward from the jungle of hatred, suspicion, and death where so many powerful, selfish, and frightening influences even today are working to keep him mired.»

This was said in 1945. Twelve years have passed since then, and we have been witnessing just such a race, menacing and fatal because, if it continues, there can be scarcely a doubt about the outcome: the extermination or decay of a large part, if not the whole, of mankind.

The fact that this is a reality must have contributed greatly to Mr. Pearson's views on the international conflicts of our time and must, more than anything else, have influenced his convictions about the way in which such conflicts ought to be resolved.

At about the same time the plans for FAO were being made, Lester Pearson took part in organizing UNRRA[1], which was set up mainly for the purpose of reestablishing the economy of the war-ravaged countries after the

1. United Nations Relief and Rehabilitation Administration.

war was over. The organization was also to take care of the displaced persons who had lost their homes as a result of war and persecution. UNRRA was founded in 1943, and Lester Pearson became the chairman of its Supply Committee. In 1946 he was made chairman of the Subcommittee for Displaced Persons.

Lester Pearson's efforts in UNRRA bear the mark of the same personal qualities which he displayed during the organization of FAO. He undertook the work because he believed in a better world for mankind. He carried it out by approaching the problems in a matter-of-fact way. After a meeting of the Council of UNRRA in 1944, he said: «So UNRRA must not merely do its job well; it must do it so well that it will give heart and courage to the governments who, slowly but steadily, are building up the international structure of peace; so well that it will, by its example, bring hope to men and women, who, if that structure falls, will again be crushed beneath its ruins.»

In 1946 Lester Pearson returned to Ottawa where he became secretary of state for External Affairs in 1948. He held that position for nine years.

During this period Mr. Pearson has had a part in most of the important conferences which have been held for the solution of international problems. His chief contribution to international politics, however, has been made within the framework of the United Nations Organization.

As early as 1945 at the San Francisco Conference, where the United Nations Charter was formulated, he had been an adviser to the Canadian delegation. He was the one who argued on behalf of Canada against the veto of the great powers–an argument he continued in the meetings of the General Assembly of the United Nations. I would mention that he strongly supported the «Uniting for Peace» Resolution of 1950. That resolution offers the following possibility: when a war of aggression comes up for consideration and the Security Council is prevented from operating by the veto of one of the great powers, the General Assembly can be convened at forty-eight hours' notice. In other words, this resolution reduces the effect of the veto of a great power.

As far as he has been able to do so, Lester Pearson has endeavored to improve the efficiency of the United Nations, to enable that organization to operate as quickly and effectively as possible.

During the time in which the United Nations has been in existence, one international conflict after another has arisen, and the moral strength of the organization has been put to a severe test.

The first really important conflict which the UN had to deal with was the question of Palestine. This matter was considered in a special session in 1947. Mr. Pearson was elected chairman of the Political Committee, and the Special Committee on Palestine recommended that the British mandate over Palestine should be discontinued and that the country should be divided into a Jewish and an Arab state. The recommendation of the committee was considered at the Second General Assembly. The question of division was then dealt with by an *ad hoc* committee in which Mr. Pearson participated very actively. And indeed the recommendation had a positive result. The Palestine problem was actually put to rest for some time[1].

Since then Mr. Pearson has taken part in all the meetings of the General Assembly, except in 1955, and he was its president in 1952. Every time he has made significant contributions–although I cannot here refer to all the different matters which have come up for consideration. I would only call attention to his attitude during the fighting in Korea, when he was in favor of limiting hostilities as soon as the aggressors[2] had been forced back. He dissociated himself entirely from those who wanted to proceed with the war until–as it was said–«final victory had been won».

This is what Pearson himself has said about the fighting in Korea: «The action of free nations against aggression in Korea has been limited and has had as its purpose not the destruction of the North Korean and Chinese peoples, but the localizing of hostilities, repelling the attack, and then negotiating cease-fire arrangements as a prelude to peace.»

These words reflect his realistic and positive attitude, an attitude he has maintained consistently–not just in the Korean conflict. If it is not possible to stop an aggression without using arms, then call off the fighting as soon as the immediate aim has been achieved, he advises; do not go further, but try to create a situation in which it is possible to work for the ultimate goal, which is peace.

The next time the world was threatened by a conflagration of unforeseeable extent was in 1956. It all seems so close to us, and we all remember the course of events.

At the end of July, 1956, Nasser suddenly proceeded to nationalize the

1. The long-standing dispute between the Arab and Jewish peoples involved in this question has yet (as of October, 1971) to be satisfactorily settled.
2. North Korea's attack on South Korea in June, 1950, initiated the Korean War (1950–1953) between North Korea and (after November, 1950) Communist China on the one hand and South Korea and UN forces on the other.

Suez Canal. The Suez conflict was brought before the Security Council in September, and it seemed that it might be possible to find a solution.

Then, on October 29, Israel marched into Egyptian territory. On the 30th the French-British ultimatum was handed to Egypt, and the next day both these countries proceeded to the attack.

The Security Council, which immediately called on the aggressors to cease hostilities, was made inoperative by the veto of Great Britain and France.

The matter then came up before the General Assembly, and on November 2, a resolution was put to the vote which required the aggressors to stop fighting immediately.

Before this resolution was submitted, Lester Pearson had been working unceasingly night and day, through conferences and informal talks, to give the resolution a wider scope, sufficiently comprehensive to form a real basis for a solution of the conflict and for creating peace. With his rich experience, his positive attitude, and his determined vigor, he pointed out that the resolution lacked any provision for solving the problem itself. He felt that this was a matter of decisive importance in that critical phase of the developments when the world was at the very edge of disaster.

But Lester Pearson did not give up his efforts even though the Resolution of November 2 did not contain what he had wanted. In the acutely dangerous situation other ways out would have to be found. On November 4 he submitted to the General Assembly a resolution in which the Secretary-General was requested to put before the General Assembly within forty-eight hours a plan for an international United Nations force to be employed in the area of fighting to secure and supervise the cessation of hostilities. As we all know, this was done.

Never, since the end of the last war, has the world situation been darker than during the Suez crisis, and never has the United Nations had a more difficult case to deal with. However, what actually happened has shown that moral force can be a bulwark against aggression and that it is possible to make aggressive forces yield without resorting to power. Therefore, it may well be said that the Suez crisis was a victory for the United Nations and for the man who contributed more than anyone else to save the world at that time. That man was Lester Pearson.

During the Hungarian Revolution [1] Lester Pearson spoke at the emer-

1. This uprising of the Hungarian people against the Communist controlled government began October 23, 1956, and by November 8 had been effectively suppressed by the Russian army.

gency special session of the General Assembly. He strongly advocated that
an independent international authority should «enable all the Hungarian
people, without fear of reprisal, to establish a free and democratic government of their own choice». «Why», he asked, «should we not now establish
a suitable United Nations mission for Hungary when it has been agreed
to form a United Nations authority in the Middle East?»

During the Hungarian Revolution, however, the United Nations remained powerless.

Mr. Pearson has frequently been mentioned as one of the most enthusiastic
supporters of NATO[1]. In this organization for defense of countries whose
life pattern is based on democracy and personal freedom, he finds a guarantee for the maintenance of peace and human rights in the world. He has
made great efforts to extend the cooperation among NATO countries to
include the political, economic, and cultural fields.

Lester Pearson would be the last to believe that military force can secure
peace in the long run. This is what he said in 1955:

«No person, no nation, no group of nations can view with comfort,
however, the prospects for a world where peace rests primarily on the deterrent effect of collective military strength and regional political unity. That
discomfort becomes deep anxiety in the face of the fantastic development
of nuclear weapons and their inclusion in the armament of a few big powers
now, and of many other powers soon. This makes it more than ever necessary, while maintaining military strength, to put forth any possible effort
to reduce the danger of war and gradually make such strength unnecessary.

In all the long story of mankind, arms alone, however powerful, have
never been sufficient to guarantee security for any length of time. Your
strength for defense becomes the weakness of those against whom you feel
you must be ready to defend yourself. Your security becomes their insecurity; so they in turn seek safety in increased arms. A vicious circle com-
mences which in the past has cost untold misery and destruction and might
now, if we cannot cut through it, cause mankind's extinction. Even adequate
collective force for defense, then, is no final solution. It is merely a means
to an end–peace based on something more enduring than force.»

Lester Pearson's vision is not that of a dreamer. He looks at life and the
conditions of the world as they are, basing his conclusions on realities. One

1. The North Atlantic Treaty Organization, defensive alliance established in 1949.

may say that his visionary ideal has been constructed of the materials of experience.

I have had to confine myself to some of the main features of Lester Bowles Pearson's activities to prevent or to stop war, and I am quite aware that I have given only an account of the result of his efforts, and not a living picture of the man himself. That, however, is not easy to do in the case of a man like Lester Pearson, whose work has been carried out largely on the diplomatic level–in commissions, at meetings, and during discussions of an informal character.

Only those who have taken part in conferences together with Lester Pearson have been able to witness his never tiring determination and his exceptional ability to put forward constructive ideas for the solution of a problem. If his proposal was rejected, he optimistically proceeded to engage his resourcefulness in finding another solution for which–thanks to the experience just gained–he might perhaps more readily win acceptance. For him the main thing was never to give up, but always to try to advance at least one step toward the goal.

Lester Pearson is far from being a compromising man when a vital point is at issue. However, he feels that the basis of any negotiations on international problems must be an attempt to understand the other party and to meet him halfway in order to establish a basis of confidence. It is only when confidence has been built up that it is possible to proceed with the negotiations with any hope of reconciliation.

However, in this work one must never betray the principles on which the United Nations Charter is based. In other words, one must work toward economic and social progress and away from poverty; toward full and free self-government and away from dictatorial regimes imposed from inside or from outside; toward a progressive realization of human rights and the dignity and worth of the individual person.

Lester Pearson believes that the time will come when it is possible, through the United Nations, to realize the dream of a worldwide community of all nations and races, and he feels that just acknowledging such an ideal in some form serves to remind us of our ultimate and underlying kinship even with our opponents. There is a value to this which, if we retain any humility, we will not underestimate.

Lester Pearson's work has been carried on during a period of tension and open conflict, not only among nations but between races and different civilizations. At the same time, technical development has brought countries closer together and made them more mutually dependent upon one another. Any conflict that breaks out anywhere today will involve practically the whole world.

«We are now emerging into an age», Lester Pearson says, «when different civilizations will have to learn to live side by side in peaceful interchange, learning from each other, studying each other's history and ideals, art and culture, mutually enriching each other's lives. The only alternative in this overcrowded little world is misunderstanding, tension, clash, and–catastrophe.»

The fact that the world may have to face the choice between to be and not to be and the fact that it has been left to us ourselves to decide whether life or death shall prevail, make it more necessary than ever before that we choose the right way; we must not let any conceivable method remain untried in our efforts to solve international conflicts in a peaceful way. Here, the goal will not be reached unless the people whose task it is to resolve the conflicts show no sign of failing in their will for peace and in their efforts to attain it.

As Lester Pearson has expressed it, «In our day the penalty for failure–or for serious blundering–is far greater than ever before. Mankind can no longer afford error.»

And still, no matter how dark the outlook for the world may be, Lester Pearson is no pessimist. Had he been pessimistic, he could not have found the endurance and strength which he has displayed in his work. His efforts would not have been possible had he not been supported by a strong faith in the final victory of the good forces of life.

In conclusion, I quote from a lecture which Lester Pearson gave at Princeton University in 1955:

«The fact is, that to every challenge given by the threat of death and destruction, there has always been the response from free men: ‹It shall not be.› By these responses man has not only saved himself, but has ensured his future.

May it be so again this time, as we face the awful and the glorious possibilities of the nuclear age.»

The Four Faces of Peace

Nobel Lecture*, December 11, 1957

I cannot think of anything more difficult than to say something which would be worthy of this impressive and, for me, memorable occasion, and of the ideals and purposes which inspired the Nobel Peace Award.

I would like, at the very beginning, to pay my tribute to the memory of a great man, Alfred Nobel, who made this award – and others – possible. Seldom in history has any man combined so well the qualities of idealism and realism as he did – those of the poet and the practical man of business.

We know all about his dynamite and his explosives and how he lamented the use to which they would be put. Yet ideas can also be explosive, and he had many that were good and were deeply concerned with peace and war. He liked to write and talk about the «rights of man and universal brotherhood», and no one worked harder or more unselfishly to realize those ideals, still so far away.

At this moment I am particularly conscious of the wisdom of one of his observations that «long speeches will not ensure peace».

May I also express my great pleasure at being again in Norway, a country to which my own is so closely bound by ties of friendship, freedom, and understanding. I have worked in a very close and cordial way with Norwegian representatives at many international meetings, and the pleasure I felt at those associations was equaled only by the profit I always secured from them.

Perhaps I may be pardoned for putting any words I may have to say about peace within the framework of my own personal experience. During my lifetime greater and more spectacular progress has been made in the physical sciences than in many centuries that preceded it. As a result, the man who lived in 1507 would have felt more at home in 1907 than one who died fifty years ago if he came back to life today.

A great gulf, however, has been opened between man's material advance and his social and moral progress, a gulf in which he may one day be lost

* This lecture was delivered by the laureate in the Auditorium of the University of Oslo. The text is taken from *Les Prix Nobel en 1957*.

if it is not closed or narrowed. Man has conquered outer space. He has not conquered himself. If he had, we would not be worrying today as much as we are about the destructive possibilities of scientific achievements. In short, moral sense and physical power are out of proportion.

This imbalance may well be the basic source of the conflicts of our time, of the dislocations of this «terrible twentieth century».

All of my adult life has been spent amidst these dislocations, in an atmosphere of international conflict, of fear and insecurity. As a soldier, I survived World War I when most of my comrades did not. As a civilian during the Second War, I was exposed to danger in circumstances which removed any distinction between the man in and the man out of uniform. And I have lived since–as you have–in a period of cold war, during which we have ensured by our achievements in the science and technology of destruction that a third act in this tragedy of war will result in the peace of extinction.

I have, therefore, had compelling reason, and some opportunity, to think about peace, to ponder over our failures since 1914 to establish it, and to shudder at the possible consequences if we continue to fail.

I remember particularly one poignant illustration of the futility and tragedy of war. It was concerned, not with the blood and sacrifice of battles from 1914–1918, but with civilian destruction in London in 1941 during its ordeal by bombing.

It was a quiet Sunday morning after a shattering night of fire and death. I was walking past the smoking ruins of houses that had been bombed and burned during the night. The day before they had been a neat row of humble, red brick, workmen's dwellings. They were now rubble except for the front wall of one building, which may have been some kind of community club, and on which there was a plaque that read «Sacred to the memory of the men of Alice Street who died for peace during the Great War, 1914–1918». The children and grandchildren of those men of Alice Street had now in their turn been sacrificed in the Greater War, 1939–1945. For peace? There are times when it does not seem so.

True there has been more talk of peace since 1945 than, I should think, at any other time in history. At least we hear more and read more about it because man's words, for good or ill, can now so easily reach the millions.

Very often the words are good and even inspiring, the embodiment of our hopes and our prayers for peace. But while we all pray for peace, we do not always, as free citizens, support the policies that make for peace or reject those which do not. We want our own kind of peace, brought about in our own way.

The choice, however, is as clear now for nations as it was once for the individual: peace or extinction. The life of states cannot, any more than the life of individuals, be conditioned by the force and the will of a unit, however powerful, but by the concensus of a group, which must one day include all states. Today the predatory state, or the predatory group of states, with power of total destruction, is no more to be tolerated than the predatory individual.

Our problem, then, so easy to state, so hard to solve, is how to bring about a creative peace and a security which will have a strong foundation. There have been thousands of volumes written by the greatest thinkers of the ages on this subject; so you will not expect too much from me in a few sketchy and limited observations. I cannot, I fear, provide you, in the words of Alfred Nobel, with «some lofty thoughts to lift us to the spheres».

My aim this evening is a more modest one. I wish to look at the problem in four of its aspects–my «four faces of peace». There is peace and prosperity or trade, peace and power, peace and policy or diplomacy, peace and people.

Peace and Prosperity

One face of peace is reflected in the prosperity of nations. This is a subject on which thought has changed greatly within the memories of most of us and is now, I submit, in process of rapid further change.

Not so long ago prominence was always given to economic factors as causes of war. That was at a time when people sought more assiduously than we now do for rational causation in human behavior. To the philosophers of the nineteenth century it seemed that there must be a motive of real self-interest, of personal gain, that led nations into conflict. To some extent there was. But in this century we have at least learned to understand more fully the complexity of motives that impel us both as individuals and as nations. We would be unwise to take any credit for that. The cynic might well remark that never has irrationality been so visible as in our times, and especially in relation to war.

We know now that in modern warfare, fought on any considerable scale, there can be no possible economic gain for any side. Win or lose, there is nothing but waste and destruction. Whatever it is that leads men to fight and suffer, to face mutilation and death, the motive is not now self-interest in any material sense.

If, however, we no longer stress so much economic factors as the direct cause of war, that does not lessen their importance in the maintenance of a creative and enduring peace. Men may not now go to war for trade, but lack of trade may help to breed the conditions in which men do go to war. The connection is not simple. Rich nations are not necessarily more peace-loving than poorer nations. You do not have to have poverty and economic instability; people do not have to be fearful about their crops or their jobs in order to create the fears and frustrations and tensions through which wars are made. But poverty and distress–especially with the awakening of the submerged millions of Asia and Africa–make the risks of war greater.

It is already difficult to realize that a mere twenty years ago poverty was taken almost for granted over most of the earth's surface. There were always, of course, a few visionaries, but before 1939 there was little practical consideration given to the possibility of raising the living standards of Asia and Africa in the way that we now regard as indispensable. Perhaps only in North America every man feels entitled to a motor car, but in Asia hundreds of millions of people do now expect to eat and be free. They no longer will accept colonialism, destitution, and distress as preordained. That may be the most significant of all the revolutionary changes in the international social fabric of our times.

Until the last great war, a general expectation of material improvement was an idea peculiar to Western man. Now war and its aftermath have made economic and social progress a political imperative in every quarter of the globe. If we ignore this, there will be no peace. There has been a widening of horizons to which in the West we have been perhaps too insensitive. Yet it is as important as the extension of our vision into outer space.

Today continuing poverty and distress are a deeper and more important cause of international tensions, of the conditions that can produce war, than previously. On the other hand, if the new and constructive forces which are at work among areas and people, stagnant and subdued only a few years ago, can be directed along the channels of cooperation and peaceful progress, it should strengthen mankind's resistance to fear, to irrational impulse, to resentment, to war.

Arnold Toynbee[1] voiced this hope and this ideal when he said: «The twentieth century will be chiefly remembered by future generations not as an era of political conflicts or technical inventions, but as an age in which human society dared to think of the welfare of the whole human race as a practical objective.»

I hope he was not too optimistic.

It is against this background that we should, I suggest, reassess our attitude to some ideas about which we have of late been too indifferent. It has been fashionable to look on many of our nineteenth-century economic thinkers as shallow materialists. We have, for instance, made light of the moral fervor and high political purpose that lay behind such an idea as free trade. Yet the ideals to which Richard Cobden[2] gave the most articulate expression, at least in the English-speaking world, were not ideals about commerce alone. They visualized a free and friendly society of nations, for whom free trade was at once a result and a cause of good relations. It is a bitter commentary on our twentieth-century society that the very phrase «free trade» has come to have a hopelessly old-fashioned and unrealistic ring to it.

We all recognize that in the depressed and disturbed economic conditions between the wars an upsurge of economic nationalism was inevitable. But why should so many be so ready to go on thinking in the same terms when the conditions that produced them are now different?

We are too inclined to assume that man's today is more like his yesterday than like the day before yesterday. In some respects, I submit, the economics of our day are less different from those of nineteenth-century expansionism than they are from the abnormal period of depression and restrictionism that, just because it is nearer in time, still dominates much of our economic thinking.

The scientific and technological discoveries that have made war so infinitely more terrible for us are part of the same process that has knit us all so much more closely together. Our modern phrase for this is interdependence. In essence, it is exactly what the nineteenth-century economist

1. Arnold J. Toynbee (1889–   ), English historian, well known for his 10-volume *A Study of History*.
2. Richard Cobden (1804–1865), English statesman and economist, known as the «Apostle of Free Trade», who, with John Bright, was primarily responsible for the repeal of England's Corn Laws (1846); actively supported international arbitration and disarmament.

talked about as the advantages of international specialization and the division of labor. The main difference is that excessive economic nationalism, erecting its reactionary barriers to the international division of labor, is far more anomalous and irrational now than it was when the enlightened minds of the nineteenth century preached against it and for a time succeeded in having practiced what they preached.

The higher the common man sets his economic goals in this age of mass democracy, the more essential it is to political stability and peace that we trade as freely as possible together, that we reap those great benefits from the division of labor, of each man and each region doing what he and it can do with greatest relative efficiency, which were the economic basis of nineteenth-century thought and policy. In no country is this more clearly understood than in Norway and in no country is the impulse to peace deeper or more widespread.

In this sphere, our postwar record is better than it is fashionable to recognize. Under the General Agreement on Tariffs and Trade[1] there has been real progress in reducing trade barriers and in civilizing the commercial policies of national governments. The achievement so far has its limits, of course, and there have been setbacks, but there has been more progress, and over a wider area, than any of us would have dared to predict with confidence twelve years ago.

Now the European nations are launching themselves, through the Common Market and its associated free trade area[2], on an adventure in the economic unification of peoples that a few years ago would have seemed completely visionary. Is it any more visionary to foresee a further extension of this cooperative economic pattern? Is it not time to begin to think in terms of an economic interdependence that would bridge the Atlantic, that would at least break down the barrier between dollar and non-dollar countries which, next only to Iron Curtains, has hitherto most sharply divided our postwar One World?

1. Drawn up by an international Conference on Trade and Employment in 1947, it included commitments on over 40,000 different tariff rates and a comprehensive commercial policy code aimed at elimination of discriminating treatment in international commerce.
2. The Common Market (officially the European Economic Community), organized in 1957 by the Benelux countries, France, Italy, and West Germany (Greece became an associate member in 1962), aims at the establishment of an area within which commodities, capital, services, and labor can move freely.

You will say that this is far too unrealistic. I can only reply that in the past decade we have already seen even more profound revolutions in men's political and social attitudes. It would be especially tragic if the people who most cherish ideals of peace, who are most anxious for political cooperation on a wider than national scale, made the mistake of underestimating the pace of economic change in our modern world.

Just as we cannot in this day have a stable national democracy without progress in living standards and a sense that the community as a whole participates in those standards, without too great extremes of wealth and poverty, likewise we cannot have one world at peace without a general social and economic progress in the same direction. We must have rising living standards in which all nations are participating to such a degree that existing inequalities in the international division of wealth are, at least, not increased. For substantial progress on those lines we need the degree of efficiency that comes only with the freest possible movement of commerce through the world, binding people together, providing the basis of international investment and expansion, and thereby, I hope, making for peace.

Peace and Power

I now come to peace and power.

Every state has not only the right but the duty to make adequate provision for its own defense in the way it thinks best, providing it does not do so at the expense of any other state. Every state denies and rejects any suggestion that it acquires military power for any other purpose than defense. Indeed, in a period of world tension, fear, and insecurity, it is easy for any state to make such denial sound reasonable, even if the ultimate aims and policies of its leaders are other than pacific.

No state, furthermore, unless it has aggressive military designs such as those which consumed Nazi leaders in the thirties, is likely to divert to defense any more of its resources and wealth and energy than seems necessary. The economic burden of armaments is now almost overpowering, and where public opinion can bring itself effectively to bear on government, the pressure is nearly always for the greatest possible amount of butter and the fewest possible number of guns.

Nevertheless, defense by power as a first obligation on a state has to be considered in relation to things other than economics. For one thing—and this is certainly true of smaller countries—such power, unless it is combined with the defense forces of other friendly countries, is likely to be futile, both for protection and for prevention, or for deterrence, as we call it. This in its turn leads to coalitions and associations of states. These may be necessary in the world in which we live, but they do extend the area of a possible war in the hope that greater and united power will prevent any war. When they are purely defensive in character, such coalitions can make for peace by removing the temptation of easy victory. But they can never be more than a second-best substitute for the great coalition of the whole United Nations established to preserve the peace, but now too often merely the battleground of the cold war.

Furthermore, the force which you and your allies collect for your own security can, in a bad international climate, increase, or seem to increase, someone else's insecurity. A vicious chain reaction begins. In the past, the end result has always been, not peace, but the explosion of war. Arms, produced by fear out of international tension, have never maintained peace and security except for limited periods. I am not arguing against their short-run necessity. I am arguing against their long–run effectiveness. At best they give us a breathing space during which we can search for a better foundation for the kind of security which would itself bring about arms reduction.

These coalitions for collective defense are limited in area and exclusive in character. And they provoke counter-coalitions. Today, for instance, we have now reached the point where two–and only two–great agglomerations of power face each other in fear and hostility, and the world wonders what will happen.

If the United Nations were effective as a security agency–which it is not–these more limited arrangements would be unnecessary and, therefore, undesirable. But pending that day, can we not put some force behind the United Nations which–under the authorization of the Assembly–might be useful at least for dealing with some small conflicts and preventing them from becoming great ones?

Certainly the idea of an international police force effective against a big disturber of the peace seems today unrealizable to the point of absurdity. We did, however, take at least a step in the direction of putting international force behind an international decision a year ago in the Suez crisis. The birth of this force was sudden and it was surgical. The arrangements for the reception of the infant were rudimentary, and the midwives–one of the most important of whom was Norway–had no precedents or experience to guide them. Nevertheless, UNEF[1], the first genuinely international police force of its kind, came into being and into action.

It was organized with great speed and efficiency even though its functions were limited and its authority unclear. And the credit for that must go first of all to the Secretary-General of the United Nations[2] and his assistants.

Composed of the men of nine United Nations countries from four continents, UNEF moved with high morale and higher purpose between national military forces in conflict. Under the peaceful blue emblem of the United Nations, it brought, and has maintained, at least relative quiet on an explosive border. It has supervised and secured a cease-fire.

I do not exaggerate the significance of what has been done. There is no peace in the area. There is no unanimity at the United Nations about the functions and future of this force. It would be futile in a quarrel between, or in opposition to, big powers. But it may have prevented a brush fire becoming an all-consuming blaze at the Suez last year, and it could do so again in similar circumstances in the future.

We made at least a beginning then. If, on that foundation, we do not build something more permanent and stronger, we will once again have ignored realities, rejected opportunities, and betrayed our trust. Will we never learn?

Today, less than ever can we defend ourselves by force, for there is no effective defense against the all-destroying effect of nuclear missile weapons. Indeed, their very power has made their use intolerable, even unthinkable, because of the annihilative retaliation in kind that such use would invoke. So peace remains, as the phrase goes, balanced uneasily on terror, and the use of maximum force is frustrated by the certainty that it will be used in reply with a totally devastating effect. Peace, however, must surely be more than this trembling rejection of universal suicide.

The stark and inescapable fact is that today we cannot defend our society by war since total war is total destruction, and if war is used as an instrument of policy, eventually we will have total war. Therefore, the best defense of peace is not power, but the removal of the causes of war, and

1. United Nations Emergency Force, proposed by Pearson and created by the UN in November, 1956. See Jahn's presentation speech, pp.124-125.
2. Dag Hammarskjöld (1905–1961), recipient, posthumously, of the Nobel Peace Prize for 1961.

international agreements which will put peace on a stronger foundation than the terror of destruction.

Peace and Policy

The third face of peace, therefore, is policy and diplomacy. If we could, internationally, display on this front some of the imagination and initiative, determination and sacrifice, that we show in respect of defense planning and development, the outlook would be more hopeful than it is. The grim fact, however, is that we prepare for war like precocious giants and for peace like retarded pygmies.

Our policy and diplomacy–as the two sides in the cold war face each other–are becoming as rigid and defensive as the trench warfare of forty years ago, when two sides dug in, dug deeper, and lived in their ditches. Military moves that had been made previously had resulted in slaughter without gain; so, for a time, all movement was avoided. Occasionally there was almost a semblance of peace.

It is essential that we avoid this kind of dangerous stalemate in international policy today. The main responsibility for this purpose rests with the two great world powers, the United States and the U. S. S. R. No progress will be made if one side merely shouts «coexistence»–a sterile and negative concept–and «parleys at the summit», while the other replies «no appeasement», «no negotiation without proof of good faith».

What is needed is a new and vigorous determination to use every technique of discussion and negotiation that may be available, or, more important, that can be made available, for the solution of the tangled, frightening problems that divide today, in fear and hostility, the two power-blocs and thereby endanger peace. We must keep on trying to solve problems, one by one, stage by stage, if not on the basis of confidence and cooperation, at least on that of mutual toleration and self-interest.

What I plead for is no spectacular meeting of a Big Two or a Big Three or a Big Four at the summit, where the footing is precarious and the winds blow hard, but for frank, serious, and complete exchanges of views–especially between Moscow and Washington–through diplomatic and political channels.

Essential to the success of any such exchanges is the recognition by the West that there are certain issues such as the unification of Germany and the stabilization of the Middle East which are not likely to be settled in any satisfactory way without the participation of the U.S.S.R. Where that country has a legitimate security interest in an area or in a problem, that must be taken into account.

It is also essential that the Soviet Union, in its turn, recognize the right of people to choose their own form of government without interference from outside forces or subversive domestic forces encouraged and assisted from outside.

A diplomatic approach of this kind involves, as I well know, baffling complexities, difficulties, and even risks. Nevertheless, the greater these are, the stronger should be the resolve and the effort, by both sides and in direct discussions, to identify and expose them as the first step in their possible removal.

Perhaps a diplomatic effort of this kind would not succeed. I have no illusions about its complexity or even its risks. Speaking as a North American, I merely state that we should be sure that the responsibility for any such failure is not ours. The first failure would be to refuse to make the attempt.

The time has come for us to make a move, not only from strength, but from wisdom and from confidence in ourselves; to concentrate on the possibilities of agreement, rather than on the disagreements and failures, the evils and wrongs, of the past.

It would be folly to expect quick, easy, or total solutions. It would be folly also to expect hostility and fears suddenly to vanish. But it is equal or even greater folly to do nothing: to sit back, answer missile with missile, insult with insult, ban with ban.

That would be the complete bankruptcy of policy and diplomacy, and it would not make for peace.

Peace and People

In this final phase of the subject, I am not thinking of people in what ultimately will be their most important relationship to peace: the fact that more than thirty millions of them are added to our crowded planet each year. Nor am I going to dwell at any length on the essential truth that peace, after all, is merely the aggregate of feelings and emotions in the hearts and minds of individual people.

Spinoza[1] said that «Peace is the vigor born of the virtue of the soul.» He meant, of course, creative peace, the sum of individual virtue and vigor. In the past, however, man has unhappily often expressed this peace in ways which were more vigorous than virtuous.

It has too often been too easy for rulers and governments to incite man to war. Indeed, when people have been free to express their views, they have as often condemned their governments for being too peaceful as for being too belligerent.

This may perhaps have been due to the fact that in the past men were more attracted by the excitements of conflict and the rewards of expected victory than they were frightened by the possibility of injury, pain, and death.

Furthermore, in earlier days, the drama of war was the more compelling and colorful because it seemed to have a romantic separation from the drabness of ordinary life. Many men have seemed to like war – each time – before it began.

As a Canadian psychiatrist, Dr. G. H. Stevenson, put it once: «People are so easily led into quarrelsome attitudes by some national leaders. A fight of any kind has a hypnotic influence on most men. We men like war. We like the excitement of it, its thrill and glamor, its freedom from restraint. We like its opportunities for socially approved violence. We like its economic security and its relief from the monotony of civilian toil. We like its reward for bravery, its opportunities for travel, its companionship of men in a man's world, its intoxicating novelty. And we like taking chances with death. This psychological weakness is a constant menace to peaceful behavior. We need to be protected against this weakness, and against the leaders who capitalize on this weakness.»

Perhaps this has all changed now. Surely the glamor has gone out of war. The thin but heroic red line of the nineteenth century is now the production line. The warrior is the man with a test tube or the one who pushes the nuclear button. This should have a salutary effect on man's emotions. A realization of the consequences that must follow if and when he does push the button should have a salutary effect also on his reason.

People and peace have another meaning. How can there be peace without people understanding each other, and how can this be if they don't know each other? How can there be cooperative coexistence, which is the only

1. Baruch, or Benedict, Spinoza (1632–1677), Dutch philosopher.

kind that means anything, if men are cut off from each other, if they are not allowed to learn more about each other? So let's throw aside the curtains against contacts and communication.

I realize that contact can mean friction as well as friendship, that ignorance can be benevolent and isolation pacific. But I can find nothing to say for keeping one people malevolently misinformed about others. More contact and freer communication can help to correct this situation. To encourage it–or at least to permit it–is an acid test for the sincerity of protestations for better relations between peoples.

I believe myself that the Russian people–to cite one example–wish for peace. I believe also that many of them think that the Americans are threatening them with war, that they are in danger of attack. So might I, if I had as little chance to get objective and balanced information about what is going on in the United States. Similarly, our Western fears of the Soviet Union have been partly based on a lack of understanding or of information about the people of that country.

Misunderstanding of this kind arising from ignorance breeds fear, and fear remains the greatest enemy of peace.

A common fear, however, which usually means a common foe, is also, regrettably, the strongest force bringing people together, but in opposition to something or someone. Perhaps there is a hopeful possibility here in the conquest of outer space. Interplanetary activity may give us planetary peace. Once we discover Martian space ships hovering over earth's airspace, we will all come together. «How dare they threaten us like this!» we shall shout, as one, at a really United Nations!

At the moment, however, I am more conscious of the unhappy fact that people are more apt to be united for war than for peace, in fear rather than in hope. Where that unity is based on popular will, it means that war is total in far more than a military sense. The nation at war now means literally all the people at war, and it can add new difficulties to the making or even the maintenance of peace.

When everybody is directly involved in war, it is harder to make a peace which does not bear the seeds of future wars. It was easier, for instance, to make peace with France under a Napoleon who had been kept apart in the minds of his foes from the mass of Frenchmen, than with a Germany under Hitler, when every citizen was felt to be an enemy in the popular passions of the time.

May I express one final thought. There can be no enduring and creative peace if people are unfree. The instinct for personal and national freedom cannot be destroyed, and the attempt to do so by totalitarian and despotic governments will ultimately make not only for internal trouble but for international conflict. Authority under law must, I know, be respected as the foundation of society and as the protection of peace. The extension of state power, however, into every phase of man's life and thought is the abuse of authority, the destroyer of freedom, and the enemy of real peace.

In the end, the whole problem always returns to people; yes, to one person and his own individual response to the challenges that confront him.

In his response to the situations he has to meet as a person, the individual accepts the fact that his own single will cannot prevail against that of his group or his society. If he tries to make it prevail against the general will, he will be in trouble. So he compromises and agrees and tolerates. As a result, men normally live together in their own national society without war or chaos. So it must be one day in international society. If there is to be peace, there must be compromise, tolerance, agreement.

We are so far from that ideal that it is easy to give way to despair and defeatism. But there is no cause for such a course or for the opposite one that leads to rash and ill-judged action.

May I quote a very great American, Judge Learned Hand, on this point: «Most of the issues that mankind sets out to settle, it never does settle. They are not solved because... they are incapable of solution, properly speaking, being concerned with incommensurables. At any rate... the opposing parties seldom do agree upon a solution; and the dispute fades into the past unsolved, though perhaps it may be renewed as history and fought over again. It disappears because it is replaced by some compromise that, although not wholly acceptable to either side, offers a tolerable substitute for victory; and he who would find the substitute needs an endowment as rich as possible in experience, an experience which makes the heart generous and provides his mind with an understanding of the hearts of others.»[1]

Yet even people with generous and understanding hearts, and peaceful instincts in their normal individual behavior, can become fighting and even savage national animals under the incitements of collective emotion. Why this happens is the core of our problem of peace and war.

That problem, why men fight who aren't necessarily fighting men, was

1. Learned Hand (1872–1961), American jurist, in «A Plea for the Open Mind and Free Discussion», in *The Spirit of Liberty: Papers and Addresses of Learned Hand* (New York: Knopf, 1952), p.281.

posed for me in a new and dramatic way one Christmas Eve in London during World War II. The air raid sirens had given their grim and accustomed warning. Almost before the last dismal moan had ended, the anti-aircraft guns began to crash. In between their bursts I could hear the deeper, more menacing sound of bombs. It wasn't much of a raid, really, but one or two of the bombs seemed to fall too close to my room. I was reading in bed and, to drown out or at least to take my mind off the bombs, I reached out and turned on the radio. I was fumbling aimlessly with the dial when the room was flooded with the beauty and peace of Christmas carol music. Glorious waves of it wiped out the sound of war and conjured up visions of happier peacetime Christmases. Then the announcer spoke–in German. For it was a German station and they were Germans who were singing those carols. Nazi bombs screaming through the air with their message of war and death; German music drifting through the air with its message of peace and salvation. When we resolve the paradox of those two sounds from a single national source, we will, at last, be in a good position to understand and solve the problem of peace and war.

Biography

For four decades Lester Bowles Pearson (April 23, 1897–   ) has been noted for his diplomatic sensitivity, his political acumen, and his personal popularity. He is affectionately called «Mike», a nickname given to him by his flying instructor in World War I, who discarded «Lester» as being insufficiently bellicose.

Born in Toronto of Irish stock on both sides of his family, he received a balanced education in politics, learning the conservative position from his father, a Methodist minister, and the liberal from his mother. Pearson entered Victoria College at the University of Toronto in 1913 at the age of sixteen. Too young to enlist as a private when Canada declared war in 1914, he volunteered to serve with a hospital unit sponsored by the University. After two years in England, Egypt, and Greece, he was commissioned and transferred eventually to the Royal Flying Corps, but, sustaining some injuries from two accidents, one of them a plane crash, he was invalided home. He served as a training instructor for the rest of the war, meanwhile continuing his studies at the University. He received his degree in 1919 and then worked for two years for Armour and Company, a meat processing firm; years later he said, with the wit for which he is renowned, that the Russians were claiming he had once worked for an armament manufacturer.

Returning to academic life, Pearson won a two-year fellowship and enrolled at Oxford University. There he excelled not only in his chosen field of history where he received the bachelor and master degrees, but also in athletics where he won his blues in lacrosse and ice hockey and even played on the British ice hockey team in the 1922 Olympics.

In 1924 Pearson joined the staff of the History Department of the University of Toronto, leaving it and academic life in 1928 to accept a position as first secretary in the Canadian Department of External Affairs. In this post until 1935, Pearson received an education in domestic economic affairs while «on loan» in 1931 as secretary to a commission on wheat futures and during 1934–1935 as secretary of a commission investigating commodity prices; the same post provided him with an apprenticeship in international diplomacy when he participated in the Hague Conference on Codification of International Law (1930), the London Naval Conference (1930), the Geneva World Disarmament Conference (1933–1934), another London Naval Conference (1935), and in sessions of the League of Nations (1935).

Pearson moved forward rapidly. From 1935 to 1941 he served in the office of the High Commissioner for Canada in London; in May, 1941, he was appointed assistant undersecretary of state for External Affairs at Ottawa; in June, 1942, named minister-counselor at the Canadian Legation in Washington; in July, 1944, promoted to the rank of minister plenipotentiary and in January, 1945, to the rank of ambassador. During his Washington stay, Pearson participated in the establishment of the United Nations Relief and Rehabilitation Administration (UNRRA) in 1943 and the United Nations Food and Agriculture Organization (FAO) 1943–1945; in the Dumbarton Oaks Conference on preliminary discussion for an organization of united nations (1944); and in the San Francisco Conference on the establishment of the UN (1945).

Pearson took over the post of undersecretary of state for External Affairs in the fall of 1946, but gave it up two years later for the possibility of action in a larger arena. In that year, Louis S. St. Laurent, the secretary of state, became prime minister of a Liberal government, replacing his retiring leader, Mackenzie King. Pearson, having conducted a successful campaign for a seat in the Commons to represent the Algoma East riding of Ontario, was given the External Affairs portfolio, holding it for nine years until the advent of John Diefenbaker's Conservative government.

Pearson drafted the speech in which Prime Minister St. Laurent proposed the establishment of the North Atlantic Treaty Organization (NATO), signed the enabling treaty in 1949, headed the Canadian delegation to NATO until 1957, and functioned as chairman of the NATO Council in 1951–1952. Pearson also headed the Canadian delegation to the UN from 1946 to 1956, being elected to the presidency of the Seventh Session of the General Assembly in 1952–1953. As chairman of the General Assembly's Special Committee on Palestine, he laid the groundwork for the creation of the state of Israel in 1947. In the Suez crisis of 1956, when the United Kingdom, France, and Israel invaded Egyptian territory, Pearson proposed and sponsored the resolution which created a United Nations Emergency Force to police that area, thus permitting the invading nations to withdraw with a minimum loss of face.

When the Liberals were defeated in the elections of 1957, Pearson relinquished his cabinet post but, accepting that of leader of the Opposition, began to rebuild the party. Six years later, when the Conservative government lost the confidence of the electorate, especially on the issues raised by the Cuban confrontations between the United States and Russia, and when Pearson, after a careful review of his philosophical position on national defense, announced his willingness to accept nuclear warheads from the United States, the Liberal Party was voted enough strength to establish a government with Pearson as prime minister.

In control for five years, Pearson pursued a bipartisan foreign policy based on a philosophy of internationalism. In domestic policy he implemented programs long discussed but never adopted; among them, in the field of social legislation: provisions for old age pensions, medical care, and a generalized «war on poverty»; in education: governmental assistance for higher education and technical and vocational education; in governmental operations: redistribution of electoral districts and reformation of legislative procedures. The most acrimonious debate of his half-decade in office centered on legislation to create a new flag for Canada. This legislation became the battlefield of the Conservatives, who wanted some portion of the design to recognize the traditions of the past, *versus* the Liberals, who wanted to eliminate historical symbols. The Liberals won and the new flag was raised on February 15, 1965.

Pearson retired from the leadership of his party in the spring of 1968.

Selected Bibliography

Ayre, W.Burton, *Mr.Pearson and Canada's Revolution by Diplomacy*. Montreal, Wallace Press, 1962.

Beal, John R., *Pearson of Canada*. New York, Duell, Sloan & Pearce, 1964.

Newman, Peter C., *Renegade in Power: The Diefenbaker Years*. Toronto, McClelland & Stewart, 1963.

Nicholson, Patrick, *Vision and Indecision*. Ottawa, Longmans Canada, 1968.

Pearson, Lester Bowles, *The Crisis of Development*. New York, Praeger, 1970.

Pearson, Lester Bowles, *Democracy in World Politics*. Princeton, N.J., Princeton University Press, 1955.

Pearson, Lester Bowles, *Diplomacy in the Nuclear Age*. Cambridge, Mass., Harvard University Press, 1959.

Pearson, Lester Bowles, *The Four Faces of Peace and the International Outlook*, ed. by Sherleigh G. Pierson. New York, Dodd, Mead, 1964.

Pearson, Lester Bowles, *Peace in the Family of Man*. London, British Broadcasting Corporation, 1969.

Pearson, Lester Bowles, «The United Nations and Peace», in *A Critical Evaluation of the United Nations*, pp.9–24. Vancouver, University of British Columbia, 1961.

Poliquin, Jean-Marc, and John R. Beal, *Les Trois Vies de Pearson*. Première partie par Poliquin, pp.7–70. Deuxième partie par Beal, pp.71–265, is a translation by Poliquin from the English of Beal's *Pearson of Canada*, *q.v.* Ottawa, Longmans Canada, 1968.

Peace 1958

GEORGES PIRE

Presentation

by Gunnar Jahn*, Chairman of the Nobel Committee

The Nobel Committee of the Norwegian Parliament has this year awarded the Nobel Peace Prize to the Belgian Dominican, Father Georges Pire, for his efforts to help refugees to leave their camps and return to a life of freedom and dignity.

Father Pire's work is known to all of us in Western Europe. We have read in the newspapers of this man who, on his own initiative, has set himself the task of rescuing the handicapped refugees, the «Hard Core», or the residue. These are the old and infirm who remained in the camps, doomed to stay there without hope of a brighter future, men for whom our hard, ruthless world, which has taken Efficiency and Working Capacity as its idols, has had no further use.

Just seven weeks ago, we in Oslo had the pleasure of hearing Father Pire speak of his work for these refugees[1]. His talk in the Great Hall of the University was reported in the national press; so most of us in Norway are acquainted with both the practical ventures he has launched and the difficulties which he has encountered. Father Pire told us then that his aim was not merely to rescue individuals from material want, but also to restore to each of these unfortunate human beings the self-confidence dulled by the many years languished away in refugee camps.

As everyone must know, the refugee problem in the form and magnitude which we know today is a legacy of the two world wars. It is one of the blackest stains on the twentieth century. But a great deal has also been done for the refugees.

When the last war ended in 1945, the United Nations Relief and Reha-

* Mr. Jahn delivered this speech on December 10, 1958, in the Auditorium of the University of Oslo. He then gave the insignia of the prize to the laureate who responded with a speech of acceptance. The translation of Mr. Jahn's speech is based upon the Norwegian text published in *Les Prix Nobel en 1958*, which also carries a translation in French.
1. The laureate was then in Oslo to speak at a meeting of the Norwegian chapter of the European Movement.

bilitation Administration was charged with the care of the homeless. Later on, its duties were taken over by the International Refugee Organization. Both of these organizations have since been dissolved and the mission was in turn entrusted to the Office of the United Nations High Commissioner for Refugees, whose achievements have been and still are vitally important. It was in recognition of these that this institution was awarded the Nobel Peace Prize in 1955 [for 1954].

In my speech on that occasion, I tried to describe the work which was being done to secure a legal position for the refugees, to help them to find work in the countries in which they had settled or, as the High Commissioner, Dr. van Heuven Goedhart, expressed it then, to give every single refugee an economic, legal, and social foundation that would enable him to build up a new life by his own efforts. But even in 1955, ten years after the end of the war, there were still 300,000 refugees in Europe, 70,000 of these living in camps. The High Commissioner told me at the time that he was driven to despair by the many obstacles he encountered in his work. And most difficult of all was to overcome the extreme reluctance to accept the refugees, regarded simply as unwelcome foreigners.

A great deal has been done since then to ease their lot, not least by the numerous private refugee organizations existing in various countries of the Western world. But the most difficult problem of all still remains: that of rescuing all those who can be saved only by the help which one human being can give to another, by creating the personal contact necessary to restore to the refugee the faith and confidence that he will again be able to live as a human being among others.

It is to this labor that Father Pire has devoted himself and it is here that his great contribution lies.

Father Pire himself tells us that it was on February 27, 1949, when he was thirty-nine years old, that he suddenly became poignantly aware of the refugee problem. Until that day he had, as a Dominican priest, been actively engaged in helping the suffering, and especially the children. But a conversation with a colonel in UNRRA awakened him to the plight of the refugees, and he began to ask himself what he could personally do to save some of the displaced persons who were still detained in the camps and who were in the majority old and infirm, with little hope of building up a new existence for themselves and their families by their own endeavor.

It is obvious that effective help for this category of refugee must be very difficult because it is to all intents and purposes impossible to think in terms of loans, the arrangement frequently adopted in the case of the young emigrant refugees, who were fit and trained for work. Help for the old people must, at least to begin with, be built entirely on men's unselfish desire to help their fellowmen, on their will to give practical proof of compassion and love.

Father Pire began with an attempt to establish a sponsorship scheme; that is to say, he tried to place refugee families living in the camps in contact with private individuals, or «godparents», who were willing to write to them, send parcels and perhaps money. Today 15,000 «godparents» from twenty countries correspond with 15,000 refugees. In other words, refugees have been put in touch with people outside the camps who, they know, have a kind thought for them. Just imagine what joy the arrival of letters and parcels must bring to them! They have in this way a tangible proof of someone's willingness to reach out a helping hand.

But, and this is a big *but*, their own place is still in the camps and only in the camps. By visiting the refugees, Father Pire has learned to know what this means.

And so, in 1950, he began his work to help the refugees to leave the camps. In the first place, there was the problem of the old people. Within four years he had succeeded in founding four homes for the old people, all in Belgium, where they, to use Father Pire's own words, «are left in peace to dream of their lost homeland». Here they are provided with shelter, clothing, food, medicine, and here they will be cared for until they die.

It can be seen, then, that Father Pire's faith in the goodness of men, his confidence in their capacity to show compassion for their fellows, have proved to be well founded, for all these homes for the aged are the result of voluntary work and of donations of money from private individuals. But at the back of it all stands the personality of Georges Pire, who has managed to awaken in others the urge to help those in need.

That was the beginning. But most of us know how Father Pire's work expanded, how he, both by his own efforts and with the help of others like him, has in the past three years founded his five European Villages for refugees, the first in Aachen, one in Bregenz in Austria, a third in Augsburg. The fourth, near Brussels, is named after Fridtjof Nansen, and on September 21 of this year in the Saar was laid the foundation stone for the latest village, which is to bear the name of Albert Schweitzer.

Father Pire had in 1950 formed a society named Aid to Displaced Persons (L'Aide aux personnes déplacées). This was a Belgian organization and had its headquarters in Georges Pire's home village of Huy. The society became an international organization in 1957 and, after Father Pire had embarked on his scheme for European Villages, rapidly broadened its scope of activity. Article III of its statutes provides as follows:

«The Society has as its aim to provide stateless refugees, regardless of their nationality or religion, with material or moral support in every form and especially through assistance by sponsorship, nursing homes, and European Villages, and to forge a chain of forces for good around the refugees who are without country, in the form of ‹Europe of the Heart›.»

The Society is run by an administrative council composed of seven members, at present two Belgians, one German, one Austrian, one Frenchman, one Swiss, and one from Luxembourg. The president of the society and chairman of the council is Georges Pire. At the present time the organization has branches in Belgium, Austria, Germany, France, Luxembourg, and Switzerland, and national secretariats in Denmark and Italy.

As I have said, Father Pire's homes for the old owe their existence to voluntary work and to donations from individuals. In fact, when building these homes, Georges Pire had to give an undertaking to the Belgian government that he would not ask for help from official sources. The same conditions were imposed on his subsequent work which has been financed solely from private contributions. Is it then surprising that Father Pire spends a large part of his time in raising money for his projects? For Father Pire never begs, and we must remember that the vast proportion of the cash received is donated in small sums from people of average income.

Shortly before the Belgian society was transformed into an international organization, Father Pire and his closest collaborators had founded another society whose aim was the relief of every form of distress in whatever part of the world it might arise. This organization took the name Europe of the Heart in the Service of the World (L'Europe du coeur au service du monde) and invited all countries to become members without regard to any division, whether of frontier or religion, language or culture. In this way it has progressed far beyond the refugee work in Europe, for now Father Pire appeals to all that is best in the West European, exhorting him to promote the feeling of brotherhood among men and asking him to face his responsibilities to the inhabitants of the rest of the world.

I have tried to give a brief outline of Father Pire's work: his sponsorship scheme for refugees, his homes for the old, and his European Villages. I have described his intentions in creating Europe of the Heart in the Service of the World. If his achievement is judged solely on the number of refugees he has rescued, then some might say that it is not great. But, as is so often the case, it would be dangerous to judge on the basis of numbers alone. Of far greater importance are the spirit which has animated Georges Pire in his mission and the seed he has sown in the hearts of men, for they give us the hope of a harvest to come: man's selfless work for his needy fellow-man.

At the age of eighteen, Georges Pire entered the Dominican monastery of La Sarte in Belgium. His training consisted of one year's novitiate, three years of philosophical studies, and four years of theological studies. His interest in social problems directed him to the study of sociology and, having taken his doctorate in 1936, he studied moral philosophy and sociology at Louvain University.

Thus far Georges Pire had followed the path trodden by so many other Dominicans. The Dominican Order, according to one of its members, has always been very intellectual in character and is marked by the pursuit of study and learning, especially in the fields of philosophy and theology. The order has therefore always had close connections with university life.

His studies, reading, and work at the University seem to have meant a great deal to Father Pire. University life should give a person a wider horizon and make him less bound by dogma. But intellectualism can often become sterile and turn a man into an onlooker remote from the world of reality.

Father Pire, however, did not withdraw into the shell of the intellectual. His university life seems to have left him free from narrow dogmatism in his attitude to men. But apart from this, it is assuredly something much deeper, something quite unconnected with learning, which has inspired Father Pire in his work. Might this not be his profound desire to give practical expression to his love for his fellowmen?

In his speech here in Oslo, Father Pire said that each human being is of infinite value, that love is our greatest asset on this earth and that we give it concrete form by practicing it in our relations with each individual. He sees it in this way: Try by loving your neighbor to reach the individual person. This is what he has tried to achieve by his method of helping the refugees through sponsors, homes for the old, and the Villages.

There may perhaps be some who find it difficult to understand that the best way to help the refugees can be to build villages. I have heard it said that to collect refugees in villages is to isolate them from the society into which their children must one day grow up. It may appear so. But then we must remember that the refugees whom Father Pire wishes to rescue are not the healthy and the young ones. His refugee friends, isolated and alone as they are, cannot be thrown suddenly into new and foreign surroundings to make their own way. Here in Oslo Father Pire said of his refugees: «They have been sitting on their luggage and waiting twelve or fourteen years for a train that never comes.» It is for them that Father Pire's villages are intended, so that carefully, little by little, they may be blended into the new society while still feeling secure and protected against the prejudice and ill will with which foreigners are often received.

Father Pire has named two of his villages after Fridtjof Nansen[1] and Albert Schweitzer[2]. He frequently refers to Nansen, a man who was never a member of any particular church but who, in his great work for refugees, for prisoners of war, for the victims of the famine in Russia, followed the precept of brotherly love.

Albert Schweitzer too has lived his whole life by the same principle, applying it to everything he has done, although he has never been a believer in dogmas. In the eyes of Father Pire, all are in the service of good who, without regard for religion, color, or nationality, carry out their work in this troubled world of ours in the spirit of brotherly love.

Father Pire's work for the refugees was undertaken to heal the wounds of war. But he looks much further ahead for, as he has said himself, our aim must be «to erect a bridge of light and love high above the waves of colonialism, anti-colonialism, and racial strife». Indeed, we must do more than that, we must by our actions spread the gospel of brotherhood among men, nations, and races. This is the ideal expressed by Alfred Nobel in his testament when he decreed that the Peace Prize should be awarded to the one who has done the most or the best work for the cause of brotherhood among nations.

For this reason the Nobel Committee of the Norwegian Parliament is today pleased and honored to present the Peace Prize for 1958 to Father Georges Pire.

1. Fridtjof Nansen (1861–1930), recipient of the Nobel Peace Prize for 1922.
2. Albert Schweitzer (1875–1965), recipient of the Nobel Peace Prize for 1952.

GEORGES PIRE

Brotherly Love: Foundation of Peace

Nobel Lecture*, December 11, 1958

«Men build too many walls and not enough bridges.» (Newton) [1]

Please understand that this is not a formal address, but simply a message, a message from the heart, to continue a talk begun here in this very city on October 21, 1958[2]. On that day I said to you: «What my heart seeks this evening is to make contact with yours.» On the tenth and fifteenth of November came the response from the heart of Norway like the bolt from the blue in a classic romance. On November 10, at 3:15 in the afternoon, a telegram arrived from the Chairman of the Nobel Committee of the Norwegian Parliament. On November 15 it was followed by a note from His Majesty King Olav V[3] who wrote:

«My dear Father Pire,

I was very glad to learn of the affection that you have expressed for Norway following your stay here, and I am all the more pleased that the Nobel Peace Prize has now been awarded to you in recognition of your great philanthropic work on behalf of displaced persons.

I congratulate you most sincerely and tender my warmest wishes that your activities in the interest of humanity may continue.»

* The Reverend Father Pire delivered this Nobel lecture in French in the auditorium of the Nobel Institute. The translation is based on the French text in *Les Prix Nobel en 1958*. Collation of the French text with a tape recording of the lecture shows certain differences between the two other than the usual minor verbal ones incidental to delivery. The first involves opening remarks not in the prepared text: in actual delivery the laureate begins with a salutation to the honored guests and expresses his gratitude for the honor done him and his hope that he may be worthy of it. Other differences in the lecture, as printed and as delivered, are noted as they occur.

1. In delivery, the laureate incorporates this quotation and the lecture's title in the lecture itself by saying: «I have entitled my lesson ‹Brotherly Love: Foundation of Peace› and I have taken as introductory text the words of Newton: ‹Men build too many walls and not enough bridges.›» He then continues with the lecture as printed.

2. At the invitation of the Norwegian chapter of the European Movement, the laureate had spoken in the Aula or Auditorium of the University of Oslo, giving an account of his work.

3. Olav V (1903–   ), king of Norway (1957–   ).

Of what good would another account of my life be? I covered the essentials on October 21. An American journalist once said to me: «Your life is a paradox.» I refer him to the poet Charles Péguy[1] who said: «It would take me a day to write the history of a single second. It would take me a year to write the history of one minute. It would take me a lifetime to write the history of one hour. It would take me an eternity to write the history of one day. One can write anything save the history of what one has done.»

Of what good would another lecture on peace be? Peace is not something to lecture about, but something to put into practice. My friend, Doctor Schweitzer, in this very same place, on November 4, 1954, said in his Nobel lecture: «The essential fact which we should acknowledge in our conscience and which we should have acknowledged a long time ago, is that we are becoming inhuman to the extent that we become supermen.» On the same occasion he went on to claim «the intellectual certainty that the human spirit is capable of creating in our time a new mentality, an ethical mentality. Inspired by this certainty», continued our friend from Lambaréné, «I too proclaim this truth in the hope that my testimony may help to prevent its rejection as an admirable sentiment but a practical impossibility. Many a truth has lain unnoticed for a long time, ignored simply because no one perceived its potential for becoming reality.»[2]

What better way is there of making peace a reality than to tackle the problem of human suffering?

I. Help All Men

Whether or not one has won the Nobel Prize, each of us living in contact with our fellowmen feels a joint responsibility for all forms of suffering, both physical and moral. But no one feels capable of discharging the entire responsibility. Common sense and a desire to be practical soon force us, albeit reluctantly, to limit our activities to a particular aspect of the task or to a particular affliction, without ignoring, misunderstanding, or under-estimating the others. From the messages, many and diverse, that have found their way to my desk since November 10, I should like to read you two which highlight the problem precisely. Both are written by people who have suffered much, who have at some time believed all to be lost, and

1. Charles Pierre Péguy (1873-1914), French poet and Catholic writer.
2. See Albert Schweitzer (1875-1965), recipient of the Nobel Peace Prize for 1952, pp. 51 and 56 of this volume.

who therefore possess the insight and detachment needed in order to speak with dignity of suffering. The first writes:

«While visiting the Canadian pavilion at the Brussels International Exhibition, I was impressed by an inscription in bold lettering in the section on social service. The gist of its message was this: ‹No way of helping is more important or more rewarding than that of personal initiative.› In this respect, the Aid to Displaced Persons [1] is a splendid medium and an original one. For us who have so little influence on the great decisions taken at the UN and elsewhere, this is as effective a means as any of working for peace, albeit within Europe alone. Whereas the man in the street despairs of having a say in major political questions, he has every say and every opportunity to put his words into practice on the Displaced Persons problem.

I am unmoved by the pessimists who say that the Nobel Peace Prize has failed to avert violence. I believe that the world is making progress spiritually, slowly no doubt but still making progress. We proceed, as it were, at the rate of three steps forward and two steps back. The important thing is to take that extra third step [2]. In this lies mankind's only chance, and you are among those who make it possible, who are persistently on the attack, who close ranks and charge again, pressing forward and persevering so that, often in spite of ourselves, the rest of us are swept along by the tide of your enthusiasm. You launch your attack with tact, with practical common sense, often with humor–and always with love and a deep respect for man, always with an acute concern for justice.»

As you can see, the suffering of refugees is a problem which has succeeded, as could many other problems of human suffering, in bringing home to many people a part that they can play in the struggle for peace.

This concept is even more sharply underlined in the second letter, which reads as follows:

«At first, I said to myself: What he is doing is admirable, but even if he succeeds in setting up some ten or twenty homes for the aged, he will still have saved only a fraction of the Hard Core [3]... You have stuck to your

1. See biography.
2. In *Europe of the Heart* (p.211) Hugues Véhenne excerpts the lecture in a way which would seem to attribute the first four sentences of the paragraph to Father Pire himself rather than to the letter writer. The punctuation of the text in *Les Prix Nobel* and the context itself suggest that these sentences are in fact part of the letter.
3. «Hard Core» was the term used for refugees left in the D.P. camps who, because of age, physical infirmities, lack of relatives, etc., had little hope of clearance for emigration and resettlement.

task, however, and your success has followed a geometrical progression. The time *had* to come, and has indeed arrived, when you would be in a position to solve the entire problem, or at least to make a start on the greater part of it.

You are the living proof that the true solution results from this and this only: setting your whole heart and soul to the one task, however modest, that Providence suggests, and never letting go.

This initial act of love, which at first seems to benefit only a few unknown people, eventually affects the whole world, becoming a bond of international solidarity. This is truly magnificent.»

The «initial act of love» to which my correspondent refers, helps you not only to become a man of single purpose (in itself a powerful attribute), but further and above all, to maintain contact with mankind itself. Such contact is rewarding both to yourself and to those you meet. No longer do you run the risk of allowing humanity to become a mere concept, increasingly abstract and theoretical until it disappears altogether. It becomes once again what it really is: the individual man, the personal crisis, the single destiny, the specific needs. The heart resumes its role as the source of the noblest virtues that initiate pacific action: Love, Initiative, Tenacity, Realism, Patience.

Love. Through love we come close to the hearts of our brothers–at the beginning, throughout the course of, and right up to the end of our lives. Recently, a refugee wrote to his godmother: «I always look forward to receiving your letters; the warmth that radiates from them is a great comfort to me. Yes, I feel that spiritual values are the most important things in our earthly lives and that without them life itself is so full of sadness that it is scarcely worth living. Often, when I was alone, I used to think of you beside me, taking my hand and stroking my forehead. I would have liked to put my head between your hands and to feel your warmth and affection flowing through me. I always had to remind myself that we can be together only in spirit. This thought consoled me, for spiritual bonds are by far the most rewarding. They never deceive us and they go with us to our graves, and even beyond. Thank you for comforting me and for having made the last years of my life the best. I face the end of this life with serenity, even though I know that my wish to be buried in Hungary can never be fulfilled.»

Initiative. I have frequently said and written: «A loving heart is an inventive one.» It finds a thousand ways to help and comfort others. It stays fresh and full of life; one might say it stays *green*. The editor of a leading Norwegian newspaper was aware of this when he wrote: «There is an old saying that a person who can make plants and flowers grow has a ‹green thumb›. Father Pire, then, has a ‹green thumb›. Whenever his heart comes in contact with other hearts, something immediately starts to grow.»

Tenacity. In thanking me on October 21 at the aula, Mr. Finn Moe[1] said: «You have explained something which strikes me as both essential to and characteristic of the work about which you have spoken tonight. That essential is an individual who decides to devote all his energy, faith, and enthusiasm to this task of restoring self-respect and faith in humanity to those who have been forced to flee, leaving everything behind.»

Realism. Man-to-man contact teaches us not to expect others to be as we would have them be, but to accept them for what they are. This, of course, calls for enormous *patience*. A woman refugee from one of the Baltic countries wrote in a well-known Belgian[2] newspaper: «Few people fully appreciate how much love and patience are needed in dealing with refugees. When these people leave their countries, their only possessions are their characters and their bitterness. What intrigue one must unravel, what caprice one must deal with every day in these homes for the aged, in these villages of Europe of the Heart[3].»

Let us be wary of mass solutions, let us be wary of statistics. We must love our neighbors as ourselves. To be sure, helping men individually naturally implies that one cannot help them all, at least not directly. After all, who in one lifetime can give himself completely to everyone? But what one man cannot do alone, the will of many may yet achieve. There is perhaps no surer road to peace than the one that starts from little islands and oases of genuine kindness, islands and oases constantly growing in number and being continually joined together until eventually they ring the world.

II. Let No Man Be Forgotten

How mistaken are those who think that I reduce all problems of suffering in the world to the sole dramatic one of Displaced Persons. My friends, all the time that I am helping those who are but a fraction of the number of refugees in Europe alone, I keep seeing behind them all the other refugees,

1. Finn Moe (1902–   ), Norwegian diplomat.
2. The word «Belgian» is omitted in the tape recording of the lecture.
3. See biography.

not only in Europe but in every corner of the world, whom I cannot help. Recently, I read an article entitled «The Seven Sorrows of the World», in which the author listed the seven great refugee centers of the world.

Behind this multitude of refugees, however, I see so much other suffering: the starving, the homeless, the imprisoned, and legions of others. My colleague Follereau, champion of the leper cause[1], wrote to me on November 11 from Tokyo:

«May I say how happy and proud I am to be counted among your friends. All who combat social injustice and human misery, all who wish to see peace reign on earth between men of goodwill, will be honored by this distinction. I am at present visiting the leper colonies of Japan. I shall then go on to Korea and Formosa. Barring unforeseen complications on my trip, I expect to return to Paris around Christmas. Shall I at last have the pleasure of seeing you? But I realize, as you wrote and told me, that we do not have to see each other to know one another. I have not forgotten my plans for the village offered me by Africa. I hope that events will allow us to carry them out soon.

Once again, my heartfelt congratulations.

Yours with devoted affection.»

And so it is that each of us can remain exactly and humbly what he is, doing whatever task God has set before him; this in my case is to continue with love, initiative, tenacity, realism, and patience, to plow my little furrow in the interests of Displaced Persons. We not only can, but should, stay each in his own place, not cutting ourselves off from the rest of the world, but *working for peace wherever we may be*. An architect wrote me: «The struggle goes on, and there are still millions who must be made to realize that all men are brothers, that each one of them is bound to the others by ties of brotherhood.»

III. *The Sacred Union*

Speaking at Augsburg on May 5, 1957, at the laying of the foundation stone of our third European Village, I said to my listeners:

«Deep-rooted as our differences may be, they nevertheless remain superficial. And that which divides us is of less significance than that which we

1. Raoul Follereau (1903–   ), French philanthropist and man of letters, nicknamed the «Vagabond of Charity».

have in common. The best way to live in peace, with mutual love and respect, is to recognize our common denominator. This common denominator carries a truly splendid name: Man. Let us learn, then, once and for all, to see a human brother in each person, no matter now greatly he differs from us in his ideas, his social position, his mentality, or his beliefs. Let us learn, also, once and for all, to assess a man at his true value, a value which is always infinite.»

He who dedicates himself with all his heart to saving just one of his brothers and who persuades just one other brother to do likewise will become immediately aware of a wonderful phenomenon: «the common denominator».

A Norwegian whom I met here in Oslo in October wrote to me two days after my departure: «From the very first moment, you appear not as a stranger, but as a brother whom we have known all our lives and in whose veins flows the same blood as our own.» An important official who had grasped my message wrote on November 14: «In giving aid, you begin by treating every man, whoever he is, as a man... The arc of the bow bent by spiritual force takes on greater significance than the trajectory of a lunar rocket. We can and we should differ on points of religion, philosophy, and science, but we should always let man be what he is: a human being, who is neither better nor worse than any other human being and who therefore deserves the same attention as any other.» A lady wrote to me from Berlin: «I enclose an article from a Berlin newspaper which has impressed me very much and made me think. Many people would do well to read this article and take it to heart; the world would be a better place. We should not be satisfied merely with saying that people today are evil. That is easy to say. We should, instead, be doing our utmost to persuade them to embrace good, for dispute and rivalry lead only to war, and today war means the end of the world. Never can we emphasize too often the fact that, in the final reckoning, good always triumphs over evil.»

My friends, at such a point denominational disputes and national vainglory might well seem contemptible. So let me read to you some wonderful messages of fraternity.

The message from the French Rabbi Azra comes in the form of a prayer[1]: «Lord,

Inspired by the precepts of Your Law, we are gathered here for the build-

1. The tape includes the words: «at Augsburg».

ing of a new ‹European Village›. We are here to implement a work of fraternity and love, and to ask You to bless the laying of the foundation stone of this village.

Oh Lord, who hast brought us into this world to live in peace and harmony, You who hast endowed us with reason in order that we might tame the forces of nature and not that we might conceive of new means of desecrating the lives we owe to You, hasten the happy age of universal brotherhood. May this ceremony, Lord, which is a symbol of this brotherhood, herald the day, which shall be blessed a thousandfold, when the entire human race shall belong to one and the same family and when its members, Your children, shall at last be delivered from the suffering, the miseries, and the scourges which yet afflict them. Purified and ennobled by their ordeals, they will from then on, live together in peace and harmony. God of mercy, Master of our destinies, bless all those who work for good, all those who inspire; bless that greathearted man Father Dominique Pire [1] and crown with success the work he has undertaken; bless all men, our brothers, inspire them with reason and wisdom and fill them with the spirit of peace, love, and concord.»

Here now, is a message from a German burgomaster: «One is forced, in spite of oneself, to go along with you, to follow your example. This is what has happened to me since our meeting. I write to you thus, in simple terms, about my impressions both of our first meeting and of the later one on the occasion of the laying of the foundation stone, and I ask you to take all that I write in the truest sense of the words.»

A message from an American reads: «I am a Jewess, yet feel fellowship for all Catholics... all good people, regardless of their denomination.»

A married couple writes: «The magnificent example of your great work on behalf of humanity revives the eternal hope and belief that we all cherish, that a ‹good life› can help the world toward recovery. In these days of gloomy cynicism, you symbolize the action and morality that can give new heart and new life to those who have lost faith as a result of man's inhumanity. One a Catholic, the other a Jew, both of us have experienced a reawakening of our hopes and ideas, our faith, and our love toward our fellow human beings, thanks to the way, worthy of Christ Himself, in which you approach men of any class or creed.»

1. The tape omits «Father Dominique Pire».

This message comes from a woman whose husband was lost[1] in the Belgian concentration camp at Breendonck, whose only son died at the age of twenty in an extermination camp, and who herself was near death when she returned from the camp at Ravensbrück. She writes:

«On the social level, I try to give aid–to the best of my ability–to all who seek it from me, regardless of their opinions. I deserve no special credit for this; it is simply my nature. Tolerance, kindness, and charity–that is my code; and God is good to me, for in this way He permits me to alleviate my utter loneliness.»[2]

Here also is a message from an important French official: «Our Norwegian friends could not have made a better choice since they once again recognize in this way that love and charity are the real sources of peace.»

A message from a Catholic priest: «Your providential success is good for all since, in applauding you, we proclaim the very evangelic truth and charity which give life and salvation their being.»

A message from a Protestant pastor: «Please accept my warmest congratulations on your being chosen to receive the Nobel Peace Prize, to the great joy of *all* your friends. Personally, I am more than happy: I am, in fact, delighted.»

And this from the wife of a great industrialist: «It is your Christian faith, animated by true tolerance, which has won you so many followers.»

And a Norwegian woman: «This award is like a star shining in the dark firmament of today's world. Let me thank you for this ray of light which your work represents.»

The voice of a Protestant: «I am a Protestant, and it was through one of our religious publications that I came to hear of, to admire, and to respect your work, in which I have since taken the greatest interest. I think that you and your colleagues are endeavoring to live the beautiful prayer of St. Francis of Assisi[3] and that in effect, wherever there is despair, there also do you appear, with God's help, to bring hope.»

An item from a Corsican journalist: «Nothing gives me greater joy than this evidence that the spirit of Peace is not yet lost.»

1. The text reads «perdu» (lost); the tape records «pendu» (hanged).
2. The tape records that at the end of this sentence the laureate inserted a second letter (or quotation therefrom) from the same woman, a letter which he had just received and which, of course, is not in the text; in it the writer condemns hatred and despair, praises Father Pire's work, urges fraternal love throughout the world, and sends her greetings to those Norwegian women who had been at Ravensbrück with her.
3. St. Francis of Assisi (1182–1226), founder of the Franciscan order.

And finally this testimony from a fellow countryman: «It is comforting still to be able to find, in this world ravaged by materialism and by its inevitable companion egotism, minds perspicacious enough and fearless enough to pay a solemn tribute to Charity.»[1]

The sacred union existing between two brother human beings who rediscover themselves as men of true dignity while working together to save a third, rids us of many of the barriers of prejudice, narrow-mindedness, and discrimination that poison human love and sap its strength. We must now have faith in the power of love and set it to work. Let me point out right away that a gesture of brotherly love extended jointly requires no compromise of principle, but on the contrary is justified and indeed welcomed by the right-minded. Let us not speak of *tolerance*. This negative word implies grudging concessions by smug consciences. Rather, let us speak of mutual understanding and mutual respect. Every man is obliged to act in accordance with his conscience. If my neighbor holds an opinion different from mine, do I have any right to consider him dishonest or evil? Should I not rather believe as a matter of course that he is good and expect him to adhere faithfully to the dictates of his conscience? St. Thomas Aquinas[2], the prince of all theologians, wrote in connection with the differences in religious beliefs: «If a man truly believes it wrong to serve Christ, he commits a sin if he serves Him.»

For ten years now, we have always acted in accordance with these principles, both in our work on behalf of Displaced Persons and for the sake of the Europe of brotherly love which we are endeavoring to create around the refugees. The award of the Nobel Peace Prize has obliged me, contrary to habit and against my better judgment, to look back, in spite of St. Paul's words: «No man, having put his hand to the plough, and looking back, is fit for the kingdom of God.»[3]

I received each journalist individually and calmly, as a human being ought to be received. But the paths of introspection and of delving into the past along which each one of them wanted to lead me, have given me a chance to see that, basically, what the last ten years have brought about is simply the forging of individualized human links into a solid chain of love, origi-

1. The tape records that at this point the laureate inserted some transitional words not in the text: «Dear friends, you have appreciated these wonderful messages just as I have. They show that the sacred union existing...»
2. St. Thomas Aquinas (1225-1274), Italian philosopher and theologian.
3. See Luke 9:62.

nating from the small group of friends who met in Brussels on February 27, 1949 [1], spreading to the friends of those friends and again to their friends in turn, and reuniting us here this evening as true brothers, and not as an anonymous mass. Let us hope that this chain of friends and many others like it will soon constitute the Europe of the Heart and perhaps one day, the World of the Heart [2]. Since November 10 I would have found complete joy and hope in the unanimous support of those who adjudge and pronounce the decision of the Nobel Committee of the Norwegian Parliament, were it not for the «curtain» behind which live other brothers like ourselves, with the same right to live but in even greater need of brotherly love than we are. What more appropriate message could we send them all this evening, to their leaders as well as to the humblest of them, than this: Brothers of the East, Brothers of Asia, I love you and I am willing to give my life for each one of you.

IV. Responsibility

The 1958 Nobel Peace Prize is not the end of a career, but a beginning, a fresh start, the continuation with renewed zeal, of all that has been done in the last ten years. The responsibility involved is enormous. A man who once watched me at work wrote to me:

«To the many congratulations showered on you on the occasion of your winning the Nobel Prize, I should like to add my own. I do so, even though I am sure that this distinction holds little significance for you personally and that you attribute the honor involved only to the spiritual principles which you stand for. All the same, you must surely admit, even if only to yourself, the joy it has brought you. The idea and the man go together. You personify your idea to such an extent that you are its chief bearer. You inspire faith, and in describing your principles, you describe yourself.»

And what can one reply to this writer who sums it up in these words: «At present, you are part of everyone's dream of peace.»

1. On this date Father Pire and a group of Girl Guides in Brussels listened to a talk on the plight of those in the refugee camps and decided to write letters to some refugees whose names the speaker supplied. This action initiated what eventually became Aid to Displaced Persons. (*Europe of the Heart*, pp. 94–96.)
2. See biography.

Whether you are believers or not, dear friends, give me your affection, your support, and help me to further the cause of true friendship. In concluding, I leave you with four simple, yet glorious, lines of verse, recently written by an old Russian refugee whom I restored to a decent life. He entitles these lines: «The Work of the Reverend Father Dominique Pire». Here they are:

> *A kiss of Peace, a ray of light on earth...*
> *A Solace to a lonely heart...*
> *A noble Promise...*
> *A Caress like that of God's own Hand...*

Biography

Georges Charles Clement Ghislain Pire (February 10, 1910–January 30, 1969), born in Dinant, Belgium, the first child of Georges and Berthe (Ravet) Pire, assigned his life to action in striving to achieve understanding among peoples of the world, to eliminate poverty and hopelessness in the emerging nations, to alleviate the lot of the refugees of the post-World War II period. His refugee work may well have stirred memories of his own childhood, for when he was four and a half, he and his family fled from Belgium before the advancing German troops in 1914, spending four years in France and returning to find their home a charred ruin.

In Dinant where his father was a civic official, Georges Pire studied classics and philosophy at the Collège de Bellevue and at eighteen entered the Dominican monastery of La Sarte in Huy, Belgium, where he took the name Henri Dominique and said his final vows on September 23, 1932.

He continued his studies at the Collegio Angelico, the Dominican university in Rome, was ordained in 1934, and granted the doctorate in theology in 1936. After a year of study in the social sciences at the University of Louvain in Belgium, he returned to the monastery at Huy to teach sociology and moral philosophy.

In 1938, the Reverend Father Pire began his long service of organizational work for the unfortunate by founding the Service d'entr'aide familiale [Mutual Family Aid] and Stations de plein air de Huy [Open Air Camps] for children. During and after World War II the stations were more than camps; they were missions that fed thousands of Belgian and French children.

Father Pire himself during World War II was chaplain to the resistance movement, agent for the intelligence service, and participant in the underground escape system that returned downed Allied flyers to their own forces. For his services, this man of peace was awarded the Military Cross with Palms, the Resistance Medal with Crossed Swords, the War Medal, and the National Recognition Medal.

Constantly supplementing his duties as curé of La Sarte, Father Pire decided early in 1949 to study the refugee problem. He visited the camps for refugees in Austria, wrote a book, *Du Rhin au Danube avec 60,000 D.P.*, and founded an organization, Aid to Displaced Persons.

There were three levels of action in Father Pire's work for the refugees. There was, first, his «sponsoring» movement in which interested people could «sponsor» a family of refugees, sending parcels and letters of encouragement; by 1960 there were some 18,000 sponsors. On a second level there were his homes for the aged, four of them, all situated in Belgium: at Huy (1950), Esneux (1951), Aertslaer (1953), and Braine-le-Comte (1954).

It was evident, however, that the refugees needed to have the opportunity to put down roots, to gain economic independence, to achieve psychological wholeness. Consequently, Father Pire conceived the idea of building small villages for them, to be located on the outskirts of a city where these communities would be free to grow, not in the center of a city where they might degenerate into ghettoes. Using private contributions from the «hearts of men», he constructed seven «European Villages», each for about 150 people: at Aix-la-Chapelle, Germany (1956); Bregenz, Austria (1956); Augsburg, Germany (1957); Berchem-Sainte-Agathe, Belgium, (the Fridtjof Nansen Village, 1958); Spiesen in the Saar (the Albert Schweitzer Village, 1958); Wuppertal, Germany (the Anne Frank Village, 1959); Euskirchen, Germany (1962). All seven of these villages still exist, each now housing about twenty D.P. families.

In 1957, Aid to Displaced Persons, the organization charged with executive authority in carrying out activities on behalf of the refugees, became Aid to Displaced Persons and European Villages, an international charitable association, with self-governing sections in ten European states. The funds spent by this organization on activities for the relief of refugees in 1958 and in later years were raised by a continuous crusade called Europe of the Heart, a crusade aimed at the hearts of all men regardless of religious, national, racial, and linguistic barriers.

After winning the Nobel Peace Prize, Father Pire pursued more aggressively a worldwide application of effort. Beginning June 5, 1959, the crusade was henceforth carried on by an official organization known as The Heart Open to the World. Its program is both abstract and concrete, welding human attitudes and specific actions. The objective is international fraternity; the technique is that of «fraternal dialogue»; the agencies are the University of Peace, World Friendships, World Sponsorships, and Islands of Peace.

Father Pire founded the University of Peace at Huy in 1960 and by 1965 had completed a major building, with dormitory space for fifty, a large

---

conference room and several small ones, kitchen and dining facilities. The University is open to anyone who wishes to devote himself to constructive work for peace. He may enroll in «long sessions» of two weeks held in the summer or in «short sessions» of two days scheduled throughout the year, or even in individual sessions to hear lectures given in four languages– French, English, German, and Dutch–and to participate in face-to-face fraternal dialogue. About 4,000 people from forty countries have taken part in the sessions of the University.

World Friendships is an agency that encourages fraternal dialogue carried on at a distance by correspondence between people of different heritages. About 6,500 are enrolled in this program. World Sponsorships enables people to sponsor, with material help, refugee families in Africa or in Asia. This program, emphasizing education of children and adolescents, now has about 400 enrolled sponsors or «godparents».

After a Pakistan visit in 1960, Father Pire inaugurated a new venture that would combine local self-help with private international aid in order to increase food production, improve medical services, and develop educational and recreational programs. His idea was to select a rural area made up of several villages, to encourage the people of the area to form organizations that would require intervillage collaboration for specified purposes, to provide these organizations with outside technical experts and some material aid, to devise plans of action with targets to be reached in five or six years, and finally, at the end of the specified period, to turn over the entire program to the initiative of the local inhabitants. The first of these ventures, running from 1962 to 1967, was at Gohira in East Pakistan; the second, begun in 1969, is a six-year program at Kalakkad, near the southern point of the Indian land mass. Father Pire called these programs Islands of Peace.

Throughout his thirty-two years of work for peace and human dignity, Father Henri Dominique Pire lived simply in the monastery at Huy, discharging his religious duties and continuing to lecture. He died at fifty-eight at Louvain Roman Catholic Hospital on January 30, 1969, of complications following surgery.

Selected Bibliography

Bartlett, R.M., «Heart Open to the World», *Christian Century*, 78 (August 9, 1961) 955–956.

Current Biography, 20 (1959) 362–364.

Houart, Victor, *The Open Heart: The Inspiring Story of Father Pire and the Europe of the Heart*. London, Souvenir Press, 1959.

Northcott, Cecil, «Profile: Father Dominique Pire», *Contemporary Review*, 1160 (1962) 130–131.

«Père Pire's Peace Corps», *America*, 109 (October 5, 1963) 373.

Pire, Dominique Georges, *Building Peace*, in collaboration with Dr.Charles Dricot. Preface by Prof.Robert Oppenheimer. Translated from the French by Graeme M. Ogg. London, Transworld, 1967. (*Bâtir la paix*. Verviers, Belgium, Gérard, 1966.)

Pire, Dominique Georges, *Europe of the Heart: The Autobiography of Father Dominique Pire*, as told to Hugues Véhenne. Translated from the French by John L. Skeffington. London, Hutchinson, 1960. (*Souvenirs et entretiens du R.P. Dominique Pire*. Bruxelles, 1959.)

Pire, Dominique Georges, *Vivre ou mourir ensemble*. Avant-propos, introduction... de Raymond Vander Elst. Bruxelles, Presses Académiques Européennes, 1969.

Weyergans, Franz, *Le Père Pire et l'Europe du Coeur*. Paris, Éditions Universitaires, 1958.

Peace 1959

PHILIP JOHN NOEL-BAKER

Presentation

by Gunnar Jahn*, Chairman of the Nobel Committee

Frequently when the storm clouds gather – perhaps for that very reason – the world is made aware of the forces of good, rallying to meet the threatened danger. The dark years of this century in Europe started in 1914 and are still with us. Throughout this span of time, for forty-five years, Philip John Noel-Baker has dedicated his efforts to the service of suffering humanity, whether in time of war or in the intervals between wars. But above all else, his efforts to prevent war breaking out have been tireless and ceaseless.

We saw Philip Noel-Baker as a young man serving in the Quaker Ambulance Unit in France and Italy during the First World War; we saw him, standing at Fridtjof Nansen's side during the latter's great work of relief in Russia and Greece [1]. He continued after the Second World War to try to solve the refugee problem that the war had created. And throughout this time, ever since the armistice of 1918, we have heard him proclaiming the cause of disarmament and peace. What disappointments we have suffered since then; and yet, not for a moment did it occur to Noel-Baker to abandon hope that in the future it would be possible to find a solution to political conflicts, not by arms, but through negotiation.

Philip Noel-Baker is probably today the man who possesses the greatest store of knowledge on the subject of disarmament and who best knows the difficulties involved. In his latest book, published in 1958, *The Arms Race*, which he has called *A Programme for World Disarmament*, he has pointed out the way we should go.

We detect in Philip Noel-Baker scarcely a trace of ambition for himself.

---

* Mr. Jahn delivered this speech on December 10, 1959, in the Auditorium of the University of Oslo just before presenting the prize to the laureate, who responded with a brief speech of acceptance. The English translation of Mr. Jahn's speech used here is, with certain editorial changes and some emendations made after collation with the Norwegian text, that published in *Les Prix Nobel en 1959*, which also carries the original Norwegian text.

1. Fridtjof Nansen (1861–1930), recipient of the Nobel Peace Prize for 1922, whose League of Nations assistant and adviser was Noel-Baker.

For him the cause, and it alone, matters. If that can be furthered, it is a matter of indifference to him who gets the credit.

So marked is this selfless and idealistic attitude that it is difficult to explain unless one knows something about the milieu in which he was brought up.

For generations his family has belonged to the Society of Friends, or Quakers. His father, Joseph Allen Baker, was born in Canada, where the family had emigrated from Ireland in 1819. In the late 1870's Allen Baker was sent by his father to England to take charge of a newly established branch of the family business. There he married the deeply religious Elizabeth Balmer Moscrip. Their son, Philip John, was born in 1889. Allen Baker's life in England helps to explain the milieu which must have been largely responsible for shaping his son's character and selfless, constructive attitude to life.

Inspired by the Quakers' feeling of responsibility for brothers in need and by their eagerness to help, Allen Baker devoted his time to a wide range of welfare activities in the London familiar to us after the end of the nineteenth century. He came into close contact with the London slums, establishing schools and even teaching personally those who could not read and write, as well as working for improved housing, temperance, and better traffic conditions. In the course of time this work led to his becoming a member of the London County Council. From 1900 to 1918 he was a member of Parliament where he was to be found in the radical wing of the Liberal Party. As a politician he devoted most of his time to work for peace. As the fatal year of 1914 loomed ominously near, he was indefatigable in his work to forge links between peace lovers in all countries. With his religious background and approach, he considered it essential that Christians in different countries should unite to oppose war, especially those in Germany and England. Allen Baker's efforts proved in vain, and 1914 arrived. Instead of giving way to doubts and dismay, he was inspired anew by Woodrow Wilson's idea of a League of Nations.

There is little doubt that the influence and inspiration of a cultured and harmonious family life, with father and mother working selflessly to help those in need, inevitably left their mark on the son's attitude to life.

Philip Noel-Baker had the advantage of an academic education, something his father had lacked all his life. His schooling commenced at a Quaker school in York. In 1906, at the age of seventeen, he studied at Haverford College in Pennsylvania, and from 1908 to 1912 he was an undergraduate at Cambridge University. His major subject was international law, in which he has a degree. He also studied at the Sorbonne and in Munich during the year preceding the First World War. He was Cassel Professor of International Relations at London University from 1924 to 1929.

I have mentioned his education because his academic schooling was to have considerable influence on his later work. In all he has said and written he has never succumbed to the temptation of making a statement that was not well founded on meticulous documentation. He never brushes the arguments of his opponents aside, but submits them to an unbiased examination and criticism. He endeavors to understand those who do not agree with him; he does not censure their views; and only after he has proved that their position is untenable does he deliver judgment.

Noel-Baker was twenty-six years old when the First World War began. As a Quaker he was against taking an active part in the war. He formed the Quakers' Ambulance Unit and served in it himself behind the front lines in France. In Italy he served with the British Ambulance Unit under Trevelyan[1].

Noel-Baker's entire bent of mind, his upbringing, his experience of war— all these things must inevitably have drawn him, as soon as the war was over, to the work directed at righting some of the wrongs created by the war. Above all he must have felt himself called upon to do everything in his power to prevent any new wars. It was therefore natural that he should seek association with the new international organization, the League of Nations.

Those who never knew the years after the First World War will find it hard to realize how many hopes were pinned to the League of Nations. For the first time an association of states had been formed, an institution whose aim was the prevention of war and the promotion of international cooperation in every possible sphere, especially in welfare, in health, and in the economic area. Many people saw in the League an instrument for creating a new age, even though such countries as Russia, Germany, and the United States were not members. The League, they believed, would realize a hope which most people at that time cherished, the hope that this had been the war to end war.

Soon after the cessation of hostilities, Noel-Baker was posted to the section of the Foreign Office dealing with plans for the League of Nations. In 1919 he accompanied Sir Robert Cecil as his secretary to the peace negotiations in Paris. He assisted in drafting the Covenant of the League of Nations and of

1. George Macaulay Trevelyan (1876–1962), well-known English historian and Cambridge professor, commanded a British ambulance unit in Italy (1915–1918).

the International Labor Organization. Shortly afterwards he was appointed head of the Mandate Section of the League of Nations.

In 1920 an important era in Noel-Baker's life began. This was the year his work with Fridtjof Nansen started, work which was to last as long as Nansen lived. There is no need for me to mention Nansen's tremendous humanitarian work in Russia, in Greece, and in Asia Minor. This is known to all of us. But I should like to emphasize that in all this work Noel-Baker participated, not only as a helper, but as Nansen's friend. I have had the opportunity of going through some of the correspondence between these two men during this period, and it sheds a great deal of light on the contribution made by Noel-Baker. He worked unobtrusively, away from the glare of publicity, continuing to act as Nansen's adviser during the years the latter represented Norway in the League of Nations. Writing to him in 1927, Nansen says:

My dear Baker,

I feel ashamed. I should have written to you long ago to thank you with all my heart for your coming to Geneva and for the splendid help you gave me. You know well enough what it means for me, but it was always like that. I do not know how I could have got on without you. Of course, all I have done in the League has been done with you, and could not have been done without you, at least not in the manner it was achieved. And so it has been from the very beginning and till now. Oh dear friend, how much you have done for me and for the League during many years and how much time you have given to it.

I only wish this work for others could give you more personal satisfaction. It is well enough to work unselfishly for high ideals, but still, as we live in this world, it would be gratifying, at least to others, to see the workers get their due.

Here in Norway we are too apt to think of Noel-Baker only as Nansen's assistant and friend. But this part of his life is only one of many chapters. From the time the letter I have quoted was written and up to the present, more than three decades have passed, years which for Noel-Baker have been filled with unflagging work for disarmament.

Although Noel-Baker spent a comparatively short time as an official of the League of Nations, he continued actively in the work of the League, first as Sir Robert Cecil's personal adviser at the meetings of the Council and in the Assembly, later in disarmament work as adviser to Arthur Henderson, and finally in the Disarmament Commission from 1931 to 1933. He also followed the work of the League of Nations in other fields.

He has recorded his experiences and his personal views on the major questions under discussion at that time, in his books *The Geneva Protocol* (1925), *Disarmament* (1926), *The Coolidge Conference* (1927), and *The Private Manufacture of Armaments* (1936).

Which of us today remembers the Geneva Protocol[1] and the discussions it aroused? Then, as now, it was the fear of handing over any part of one's national sovereignty, as well as the misgivings of the experts, that killed the Protocol. The situation at that time was such that the Protocol might have laid the basis for arbitration and confidence, which in turn would have facilitated disarmament. As Noel-Baker himself writes: «Our generation must get rid of the militarization of the world, and above all of Europe, which the preceding generation thrust upon it. It is a deep-rooted and malignant disease for which palliatives do not suffice, and of which civilized society may die if it be not ended.»[2]

But the Protocol, which was truly a step in the right direction, was quietly shelved and left to molder with other documents, for, then as now, Noel-Baker's words applied: «Those who believe that international institutions can be made and have been made to work, want now to go forward. Those who doubt it, hesitate.»[3] It was the latter who triumphed on this occasion.

In his book *Disarmament*, Noel-Baker discusses all the aspects of the question and expresses the view that international disarmament lies within the bounds of possibility. Being the realist that he is, however, he devotes considerable space to the difficulties which disarmament will encounter, chief among them being the acceptance of reciprocal control. He says: «It will no doubt be thought by many that such a scheme will never, in fact, be generally accepted, because it would involve a sacrifice of military liberty to which no Government in present-day conditions, can be expected to agree.»[4]

1. The Geneva Protocol (1924), condemning aggressive war and providing for security as well as for arbitration in disputes, was dropped by the League of Nations after its rejection by Great Britain in 1925.
2. Noel-Baker, *The Geneva Protocol*, p. 193.
3. *Ibid.*
4. *Disarmament*, p. 322.

To those who hold this opinion he replies: «And are there not new over-riding interests, which, for all Governments, now that a great new international policy is by their common consent to be adopted, should come before the old shibboleths of freedom and secrecy in military preparation - shibboleths which, so far, be it noted, have failed to bring us security from war?»[1]

In his book *The Private Manufacture of Armaments*, Noel-Baker has collected a wealth of material to reveal the role this industry has played. At that time a great many people believed that private ownership of the armaments industry was a material factor in provoking rearmament. They maintained that, once private ownership could be abolished and the armaments industry run by the state, one of the most important reasons for the armaments race would be removed. Developments have shown that the situation has hardly improved with the state as owner. But Noel-Baker's book points out that the reason the private armaments industry played as important a role as it did, was that it worked hand in glove with the government of the country. Then, as now, it was the policy of the state that proved decisive.

All that Noel-Baker has written reflects his tremendous depth of knowledge, and the soundness, shrewdness, and eminent common sense of his views give his books a value far beyond the age in which they were written.

And yet, it is not through his writing but in his personal activities that Noel-Baker has made his greatest contribution. I do not think it an exaggeration to say that he has had some share in practically all the work that has been carried out to promote international understanding in its widest sense, and this is true of him both as a private individual and as a representative of his country. It would be impossible to do full justice to his manifold activities in this connection without recapitulating in detail important sections of the history of the League of Nations and of international politics during the interwar years, a task that would make my speech interminable.

In 1929 Noel-Baker was elected to the House of Commons as a Labor member, and in the 1930's he was one of the Labor Party's foremost spokesmen in advancing the view that England, in her foreign policy, should follow the lines laid down by the League of Nations. This attitude was reflected, as on other occasions, in his bitter resistance to the suggestion that England should abandon her sanctions against Italy after Mussolini's in-

1. *Ibid.*, p. 323.

vasion of Ethiopia[1]. He was against England's policy of nonintervention in the Spanish Civil War[2], and he criticized the vacillating attitude of the British government toward nazism. He was himself a member of a group, led by Churchill[3], which tried to organize resistance against Fascist and Nazi encroachment. In order to give moral support to threatened nations, he visited Czechoslovakia as a representative of the Labor Party, and subsequently Finland. In his own country, Noel-Baker helped to found the League of Nations Union and was one of the most active members of the peace movement, which enjoyed tremendous support in the 1930's.

But in the 1920's and 1930's, Noel-Baker's work was still focused in and around the League of Nations. Few, if any, have done so much to make the League of Nations known, and to get people to understand its significance and to support it. In his excellent little book *The League of Nations at Work*, published in 1926, he has provided a clear account of the idea behind the League of Nations, its organization and its work, and what it had achieved up to that time. He long sustained a hopeful faith in the League's importance for the future. He says: «It is fair to hope, then, that in the institutions of the League there is a sound foundation for whatever more complicated system of international government the future may require.»[4] But he does not ignore the possibility that such hope may come to nothing: «But there is one doubt about the future of the League which may give pause even to the most hopeful of observers. It is this: Will its institutions be given a real chance to build up their strength before the catastrophe of a new world war sweeps them all away? Will the forces of international cooperation and of mutual confidence which the League is bringing into life be strong enough to hold in check the forces of militarism, hatred, suspicion, and revenge?»[5]

As we all know, the League of Nations was swept away by nazism and Hitler. There are many today who have forgotten the work of the League of Nations, and there are those who reproach the League for failing to hold in check the storm that was brewing in the 1930's. This has made them pessimistic and has robbed them of faith in the future. What's the use? they ask.

Noel-Baker has refused to give way to pessimism and despondency.

1. In 1935.
2. 1936–1939.
3. Winston S. Churchill (1874–1965), British statesman and recipient of the Nobel Prize in Literature for 1953; prime minister (1940–1945).
4. *The League of Nations at Work*, p. 128.
5. *Ibid.*, p. 129.

Although he was forced to watch so much that he had worked hard for during most of his adult years crumble away before his eyes, he has, since 1945, set out once again to do battle for the selfsame ideals that the League of Nations represented.

In 1942 he had been made a member of Churchill's government, and in 1945 he served under Attlee[1]. He was named British representative on the Preparatory Commission of the United Nations Organization. With his wealth of experience from the League of Nations, he exercised considerable influence on the form given to the recommendations which laid the ground-work for the organization of the United Nations and its various sections and of the separate organizations affiliated with it, such as the Food and Agri-culture Organization. He also promoted the establishment of the Internation-al Refugee Organization (IRO), and submitted proposals for setting up a separate economic commission for Europe[2]–to mention some of his more outstanding achievements.

During this period he acted as a member of the British government, but there is no doubt that he was personally responsible to a large extent for the wording and form of many of the proposals, and he must be credited with the fact that they were taken up by the British side.

His work as a member of the British government covers a great deal more than this. It was Noel-Baker who directed negotiations with India, Ireland, and Newfoundland, and it is widely accepted that he was largely responsible for the successful issue of negotiations with India, which probably consti-tuted the most important of these problems.

It would be impossible to go into all the international missions Noel-Baker has had. Let me merely mention that he participated actively in the work of the relief organization UNRRA[3], and that he represented the United Kingdom in work in the World Health Organization and in the UN Economic and Social Council.

When Attlee's government went out of office, Noel-Baker's work as a

1. Clement R. Attlee (1883–1967), British statesman and Labor Party leader; prime minister (1945–1951).
2. The Economic Commission for Europe (which includes all European members of the UN plus the U.S.), was established in 1947 by the UN Economic and Social Council as one of four regional economic commissions, the others being for Asia and the Far East, Latin America, and Africa.
3. United Nations Relief and Rehabilitation Administration (1943–1947 [until 1949 in China]) whose work was taken over by FAO and IRO.

representative of his country's government was at an end. But as a member of the Labor «shadow cabinet» he has played an important role, proving to be one of the leading Opposition speakers on questions of foreign policy. We vividly recall his speech during the debate on the Suez action of 1956, which he strongly condemned, chiefly because the British government had acted on its own without having recourse to the United Nations[1].

In 1958 appeared what I think we are justified in calling Noel-Baker's most important work, *The Arms Race*. In it he deals with every aspect of the disarmament problem. With its sound and expert reasoning and its carefully supported appraisals of the difficulties to be encountered in any attempt to solve the problem of disarmament, this book makes a profound impression. It is impossible in a few words to give an adequate idea of this work, of the author's vivid description of the arms race and of the arms of modern times, not only of those which go by the common name of nuclear weapons, but also of chemical and biological weapons.

He traces all the attempts that have been made to reach an agreement on disarmament since the First World War and describes the repeated efforts to find an effective system of control acceptable to all parties. He shows how all these attempts failed because of lack of trust and because no one was willing to accept outside supervision within his own country.

While Noel-Baker is of the opinion that up to 1955 the Soviet attitude was responsible for this failure, he is inclined to think that the West has subsequently proved too adamant in its demands. We should, he maintains, believe that the Soviet Union today is in earnest when it states that it is prepared to disarm.

Disarmament must be complete and must include all kinds of weapons if it is to be effective. In his book Noel-Baker deals with the possibilities that exist for carrying out effective control, and makes a number of definite and concrete proposals, not only for disarmament, but also for mutual control. Instead of dismissing the objections that are made, he counters them with pertinent facts. Above all he believes that we must accept the risk that a control system may not prove to be completely watertight, since this risk is a small one compared to that involved in merely drifting aimlessly along as we are doing today. Noel-Baker emphasizes the importance of developing any

1. Following Egypt's nationalization of the Suez Canal and an Israeli invasion of Egypt in 1956, troops were sent by Great Britain and France to guarantee free passage through the Canal which, it was claimed, was threatened by the Arab-Israeli hostilities; the troops were removed shortly thereafter when the UN took action.

system of collective security through the United Nations. Nowhere in this book, or in explaining his views, does he fail to back up his statements with well-founded facts.

Noel-Baker repeatedly emphasizes that the arms race in itself is one of the main causes of war. If one country arms, the confidence of other countries is undermined, and their feeling of being in danger is increased. As a result, they, in their turn, proceed to arm, for no government dare jeopardize its country's safety by failing to take the necessary precautions which are a direct consequence of its neighbors' arming to the teeth. In this way the arms race is kept going in every country. Insofar as possible, he uses statistics to show how the tempo of this race has accelerated in recent years.

In view of the tremendous fund of experience he has gained from working with these very problems in the interwar years, it would be naive to believe that Noel-Baker is convinced that the problem of disarmament is easily solved. The main point is that he considers it *within the realm of possibility*.

As we all know, disarmament today depends primarily on whether West and East can agree to a control system. Noel-Baker believes that the possibility of this coming about is greater today than at any time since 1945. His optimism has been strengthened by conversations he had in 1958 in Moscow with Khrushchev and Mikoyan[1]. From them he received the impression that they are in earnest when they speak of disarmament. But he says: «Their sincerity can only be tested by offering them the detailed text of a controlled disarmament system that would translate into reality the measures which they say they will accept.»[2]

Some people have accused Noel-Baker of being too starry-eyed in his attitude to the disarmament problem. To such critics he says: «No one who has closely followed disarmament negotiations since 1919 is likely to be guilty of facile optimism about the prospect of success. But no one who understands the present arms race should be guilty of facile pessimism, which is by far the graver fault. Defeatism about the feasibility of plans for disarmament and ordered peace has been the most calamitous of all the errors made by democratic governments in modern times.»[3]

There will always be pessimists among us, people filled with misgivings.

1. Nikita Sergeyevich Khrushchev (1894–1971) and Anastas Ivanovich Mikoyan (1895–   ), Russian Communist leaders, were respectively Soviet premier and first deputy premier in 1958.
2. *The Arms Race*, p. 562.
3. *Ibid.*

These are seldom the people who improve the world. This can be done only if hope and faith stimulate men to new attempts when old attempts fail, and to new ways and means when old ways and means do not succeed.

Philip Noel-Baker is a man cast in this mold. Throughout his life he has been true to the high ideal of the Quakers–to help his fellowmen, without regard to race or creed; he has striven to build a world in which violence and arms are no longer necessary in the struggle for existence, either among men or among nations.

Throughout the years, despite disappointments and setbacks, Philip John Noel-Baker has never admitted defeat, but has looked steadfastly to the future, toward a new and better world.

PHILIP NOEL-BAKER

Peace and the Arms Race

Nobel Lecture*, December 11, 1959

Yesterday I tried to express my gratitude for the honor which I have received.

Why has it come? [Mr. Gunnar Jahn, in his presentation speech, gave part of the answer. I have been of all men the most fortunate of all. I was my father's son. I was close friends with Norman Angell. I spoke with him as a student at Cambridge in the Cambridge Union when he made his first and very brilliant public speech. On August 4, 1914, I was with him in his chambers in the Temple and listened to Big Ben strike midnight as the Horse Artillery thundered along the Embankment to Victoria to entrain for France. And we knew that the guns were already firing, that the First World War had come. When that war was over, fate decreed that I should work] for Robert Cecil, for Arthur Henderson, for Fridtjof Nansen[1].

I could tell a thousand stories of how Cecil and Henderson helped to create and shape the League of Nations, build up the International Court, develop world cooperation in many spheres; of how they turned the policy of all-round armament reduction from general phrases into practical proposals on which a treaty could be made; of how they built up and led the world-wide body of informed opinion which the major governments could have used in 1932 to carry through a plan of drastic disarmament, if they had had the vision and the nerve that were required; of how, when this great opportunity – the greatest in history – had been wasted, they still battled on for the cause for which they stood.

* This lecture was delivered by the laureate in the auditorium of the Nobel Institute. The text is taken from *Les Prix Nobel en 1959*. Collation with the tape recording of the lecture shows that in delivery the speaker departed from the text at various points, making certain deletions, revisions, and additions. The more important additions have been inserted in brackets within the text itself, and the more significant revisions and deletions noted as they occur. The lecture was given no title; the one supplied here embodies the theme of the lecture.
1. This paragraph in the text reads: «Why has it come? Because I worked for Robert Cecil, for Arthur Henderson, for Fridtjof Nansen.» Angell, Cecil, Henderson, and Nansen were peace laureates for 1933, 1937, 1934, and 1922, respectively.

It was for these great achievements, for their unfaltering courage, that you honored them in days gone by, and I like to think that you are still honoring them today.

And Fridtjof Nansen? To all his friends and colleagues, Nansen was the most gifted and, in all true elements of human greatness, the greatest of great men. He was as great an international statesman as he was a great explorer of the frozen North. Indeed, the best way to understand his international work is to recall how he first won his immense, unprecedented fame.

The whole world still remembers how he crossed the Greenland ice cap when all others had failed; he decided, against the advice of other experts, to force his party through the dangerous drifting ice floes and to land them on the savage, uninhabited eastern coast; once they were ashore, there could be no turning back.

When he set out to reach the Pole, again with every expert voice against him, he called his ship *Fram* because once he had jammed her in the ice field of the Arctic Ocean, there was only one way which she could travel: Forward; again there could be no possibility of turning back.

When the *Fram* had accomplished half its journey, it was already farther North than men had ever been; it was certain that in another eighteen months, it would emerge victorious on the other side, with Nansen's theories proved.

But it would miss the Pole; so Nansen, with Johansen[1]–only one companion–set out with dogs and sledges to try to reach it, to return by kayak to Franz Josef Land, and to winter there. He had no wireless; he could never find the *Fram* again; it was a journey of 1,100 miles, with dangers of many kinds in every mile. Was there ever such courage and such resolution as Nansen showed when he said good-by to Sverdrup[2], standing in the moonlight on the glittering ice field beside the *Fram*?

The Nansen who stormed the diplomatic fortress of Geneva was the Nansen who stormed the barriers of the Polar Sea.

When the Nobel Committee gave him the Nobel Peace Prize in 1922, it was for the «humanitarian» work he did as High Commissioner of the League of Nations. How richly he had earned it! By what he did to help in cleaning up the wreckage left in Europe by the storms of war, he brought the League

1. Frederik Hjalmar Johansen (1867–1923), Norwegian explorer who shipped as fireman on the *Fram*.
2. Otto Neumann Sverdrup (1855–1930), Norwegian seaman and Arctic explorer; captain of the *Fram*.

of Nations a new authority, made it an instrument of reconciliation, a symbol of hope and reconstruction to the peoples of the world.

And his success had long-term results when the United Nations replaced the League: UNRRA, the UN Refugee Organization, which spent hundreds of millions of dollars on the work he had begun; the High Commissioner for Refugees, World Refugee Year, the UN Children's Fund (UNICEF), UN Technical Assistance and Economic Aid–it is not fantastic to suggest that they all stemmed from his achievements of long ago.

And yet–all of this pales into insignificance beside the historical importance of what he did in the strictly political and diplomatic developments of his day.

Nansen believed with passion that the world needed a new international system based not on force but law; he knew, all too intimately, and he hated the inner workings of the power politics and the secret old diplomacy of the past; he threw all his strength and all his courage into battling for the new.

He went to the First Assembly of the League as leader of the Norwegian delegation, his Prime Minister as Number Two sitting by his side. An early episode showed what kind of delegate he was going to be.

He was a member, with Lord Cecil, of a small committee which examined the claim of Albania for admission to the League. Italy, for reasons of power politics which later years made plain, opposed admission; Britain and France gave Italy their support.

But Nansen and Cecil were convinced that Albania was a nation and should come in. They were defeated in the small committee; and Cecil asked Nansen if they should fight the question in the full Assembly.

«Certainly we should», was Nansen's quick reply.

«But we shall have all the great powers against us», Cecil warned him.

«Of course we shall», said Nansen, as if that were of no account at all.

To *him*, it was of no account, because he believed their case was right. As spokesman of one of the smallest members of the League, he was more than ready to challenge the powers that had just won the war, when they sought to introduce power politics in the League. And his contemptuous scorn was justified by the event. In the open debate in the full Assembly, Nansen and Cecil, Norway and South Africa, were victors. The great powers were routed, and Albania became a member of the League.

How often was that episode repeated!

Nansen and Cecil secured publicity for the Committees of the Assembly, and later for the Council and Commissions of the League. «Publicity», said

Cecil, «is the lifeblood of the League.» A maxim worth remembering today.

Motta of Switzerland urged that Germany should be invited to join the League; he called down upon his head a Gallic torrent of Ciceronian eloquence from Viviani, the ex-prime minister and the greatest orator of France. It was Nansen who followed Viviani and said that Motta had been right. Years later it was Nansen who persuaded Stresemann and Luther that they must come in[1].

In 1923, Mussolini[2] used a frontier incident as an excuse to seize the island of Corfu. Greece, in a panic, appealed both to the League and to the Allied Council of Ambassadors in Paris; Cecil, with his own government half against him, upheld the competence of the League; it was Nansen who rallied the Assembly in his support, who organized the smaller nations, answered Mussolini's threats, spoke up in the Assembly and destroyed the specious arguments of the Fascist delegate[3].

«Nansen», said Cecil, «was a pillar round whom the whole of the representatives assembled gathered in order to enforce what they believed to be right and just.»

Nansen, at that grim Corfu Assembly, beyond all question saved the League, he may well have stopped a war; he rescued Corfu from an unscrupulous aggressor bent on empire building; Venizelos[4] told me it was the League's greatest triumph and that without Nansen it could never have been done.

The mandates, slavery, forced labor, the compulsory jurisdiction of the International Court, collective security, the admission of Russia, the constitutional development of the League–on all these things he was a leader; on all, in Cecil's phrase «he gave to others something of his courage and determination»; in all, in Cecil's metaphor, «his ship was still the *Fram*».

1. Giuseppe Motta (1871–1940), president of the Swiss Confederation (1915, 1920, 1927, 1932, 1937), opened the First Assembly of the League. René Raphaël Viviani (1863–1925), French premier (1914–1915), French delegate to the Assembly (1920–1922), to the Council (1919, 1923). Gustav Stresemann (1878–1929), German foreign minister (1923–1929) and co-recipient of the Nobel Peace Prize for 1926. Hans Luther (1879–1962), German chancellor (1925–1926).
2. Benito Mussolini (1883–1945), Italian Fascist premier (1922–1945).
3. The Italian delegate, Antonio Salandra, raised the question of whether the League should deal with the question while it was also under consideration by the Council of Ambassadors. The incident itself ended when Italy evacuated its troops and Greece apologized.
4. Eleutherios Venizelos (1864–1936), several times Greek premier.

But one issue, above all others, seemed to him most urgently important—disarmament.

Let me end this brief and halting panegyric of Norway's modern Viking hero with a quotation from what he said in a Nobel speech in 1926[1].

«The problem of how to get rid of war is the first of all questions, not only in international, but in national politics as well...

If we do not get rid of war, if we do not end it altogether, if we do not reduce and limit armaments, then... we may be very sure that in the future, as in the past, armaments will breed counterarmaments; they will breed alliances and counteralliances, suspicion and distrust; ...they will produce international crises, they will lead at first, perhaps, to small local wars, but in the long run, and inevitably, to a great world war like that we have seen in our own day and generation.

If we retain our armaments, if we do not carry through the work of disarmament which the League of Nations has so successfully begun, war will certainly ensue.»

In 1926 these words were spoken; in 1933, when Nansen spoke no more in Geneva for Norway and for mankind, there came the failure of the Disarmament Conference, the abandonment of the Covenant system, the return to stark power politics, the melancholy sequence of Manchuria, the Chaco, Abyssinia, Spain, Austria, Munich, and the Second World War which Nansen had foreseen[2].

And today, thirty-three years later, where do we stand about the arms

1. See Vol. 1, pp. 389–390.
2. The Disarmament Conference, convened under the auspices of the League of Nations in February, 1932, never fully recovered from Germany's withdrawal in October, 1933. The League of Nations Covenant included recognition of the need for disarmament, enforcement of international obligations by common action, and settlement of international disputes by peaceable means. Japan attacked China in Manchuria in September, 1931. Bolivia and Paraguay fought the Chaco War (1932–1935) over disputed boundaries in the Chaco region. Italy invaded Abyssinia (Ethiopia) in 1935. The Spanish Civil War (1936–1939), although a domestic struggle, became in effect a battleground for Russia on one side and Germany and Italy on the other. Hitler's Germany announced the union of Austria and Germany (the Anschluss) in 1938. The Munich Pact of September, 1938, signed by Germany, England, France, and Italy, ceded territory from Czechoslovakia to Germany and destroyed Czech military power. Second World War (1939–1945).

race, which Nansen thought the supreme issue of the age? The arms race still goes on; but now far more ferocious, far more costly, far more full of perils, than it was then.

What are the perils of the arms race? I take an old and inoffensive illustration–the facts are well–established and the men are gone.

In 1905 the British Admiralty decided to produce a great deterrent, to make it plain that Germany could never win a war and had better drop her challenge to the British fleet. They laid down the Dreadnought, a battleship so powerful that it could sink the whole German Navy without peril to itself. [Even before the Dreadnought was commissioned, a prime minister newly come to power and Lord Balfour, the prime minister of the government which had agreed to its construction, admitted in the House of Commons that the Dreadnought might have been a grave mistake. And so it proved.]

It had made obsolete overnight twenty-eight German battleships and armored cruisers. But the Germans built Dreadnoughts in reply; and they made obsolete not twenty-eight but eighty-three British battleships and cruisers that could have taken on even the most powerful vessel in the German fleet. [In 1906 we had an immense margin of thirty-four ships of the line over the German, Austrian, and Italian fleets combined.]

In other words, the Dreadnought was not needed for national defense[1]. But ten years later, in the Battle of Jutland[2], where only Dreadnoughts counted, our margin was only two to one; if our commanders had made mistakes which fortunately they avoided, we might have lost the battle and the war.

Strategically, the Dreadnought was an error of the gravest kind; politically, it was an absolute disaster. It gave enormous power to Tirpitz[3] and the elements in Germany who wanted war; year by year, the race in Dreadnoughts led to panics and to counterpanics in Germany and Britain; by 1909 our foreign minister, Lord Grey[4], said it had become the most important single factor in increasing European tension and the risk of war.

1. In delivery this sentence was omitted.
2. The major naval battle of WWI (May, 1915), fought between the British and the Germans.
3. Alfred von Tirpitz (1849–1930), German admiral and state secretary of the navy (1897–1916).
4. Sir Edward Grey, Viscount Grey of Fallodon (1862–1933), British foreign minister (1905–1916).

In 1912 Sir Winston Churchill, then at the Admiralty, and Bethmann-Hollweg, the German chancellor[1], both warned their governments that if it were not stopped, it would bring war within two years. Their prediction was fulfilled, almost to the very day.

When the war was over, Lord Grey wrote his famous verdict[2]: «The enormous growth of armaments in Europe, the sense of insecurity and fear caused by them – it was these that made war inevitable. This is the truest reading of history, the lesson that the present should be learning from the past.»

[It was because they, like all the statesmen who had fought the war, agreed with Lord Grey's verdict, that Lloyd George and Balfour helped Hughes of the United States[3] to make the Washington Naval Treaty of 1922, a treaty that ended an angry and feverish naval race between the U.S., Britain, and Japan by making large reductions in their battleships and aircraft carriers and by establishing the famous ratio 15:15:9. This treaty provided a splendid prelude to the general disarmament agreement which, under the Covenant, the League of Nations was to make.] But, alas, no general disarmament treaty was ever made. When after lengthy preparations, the Disarmament Conference met in 1932, President Hoover[4] put forward a proposal for a further cut in navies, with a ratio of 10:10:6; a drastic cut in armies, with the abolition of all tanks and heavy mobile guns; the abolition of all aircraft that could carry bombs – a first-stage plan, designed to lead at later stages to the level of armaments imposed on Germany by the Treaty of Versailles.

That plan was enthusiastically welcomed by Germany, Russia, Italy, and all the middle and smaller powers. I well remember the joy of Dr. Christian Lange[5] and his Norwegian colleagues when it was proposed. It might have led the Conference to full success, if Britain had agreed.

1. Winston L.S. Churchill (1874–1965), first lord of the Admiralty (1911–1915). Theobald von Bethmann-Hollweg (1856–1921), German chancellor (1909–1917).
2. Viscount Grey of Fallodon, *Twenty-Five Years, 1892–1916* (New York: Stokes, 1925), Vol. I, p. 90.
3. David Lloyd George (1863–1945), British prime minister (1916–1922). Arthur James Balfour, Earl of Balfour (1848–1930), British prime minister (1902–1905); leading British delegate to Washington Conference (1921–1922). Charles Evans Hughes (1862–1948), U.S. secretary of state (1921–1925).
4. Herbert Clark Hoover (1874–1964), U.S. president (1929–1933).
5. Christian L. Lange (1869–1938), co-recipient of the Nobel Peace Prize for 1921 and member of the Norwegian Nobel Committee (1934–1938); Norwegian delegate to the League (1920–1938).

Many people in Britain wanted to agree, among them Mr. Baldwin, the deputy prime minister[1] and leader of the Conservative Party. Indeed, he wanted to go much further, and to abolish all battleships of over 10,000 tons displacement, all aircraft carriers, and all military aircraft of every kind. This would have meant as well the abolition of the submarine, and with such a lead from the leading naval power, the Conference could not have failed. But there was a conflict in the British Cabinet; Mr. Baldwin was defeated by a narrow margin; a British admiral was allowed to say in the Conference[2] that «battleships are more precious than rubies to those who possess them»; by those words he killed the Hoover Plan.

After having been so near success, the Conference failed; the arms race swiftly gained a new momentum; the major governments went back to the sordid principles of power politics; Abyssinia and the Covenant were betrayed; the Second World War came by precisely the process which Nansen and Cecil and Henderson had predicted.

And what happened in the war? What part was played by the battleships for which such great hopes had been destroyed? They were almost useless; while, as Norwegian sailors know as well as we do, the submarines, for the second time in thirty years, almost brought us to our knees.

And today? The arms race has gone on; aircraft have become a deadly menace to surface shipping; the nuclear-powered submarine, the nuclear missile have sealed the doom in any future war of the merchant convoys without which Britain cannot live.

Not only so: in 1906, before the Dreadnought was commissioned, Admiral Lord Fisher, its inventor, could say that it was «absurd to talk of anything endangering our naval supremacy».

After a half-century of the arms race, in which battleships have played so regrettable a part, we are only third in naval power; we have learnt how a new weapon of great offensive power, introduced by one nation, spreads to other nations and undermines the national defense of the nation which introduced it first; how it stimulates the general arms race and brings new weapons which, in naval warfare, now threaten the very life of nations which depend upon the sea; how, even on the plane of naval armaments alone, at every stage, 1906, 1932, 1955, a treaty of armament reduction and limitation would have been an incomparably better measure of national

1. Stanley Baldwin (1867–1947) was later prime minister three times.
2. In delivery, the words «in the Conference» were changed to «in Geneva».

defense than the launching or maintenance of more powerful vessels for naval war.

But all this is still more true of the other, «modern» means of war. Look at the facts of our present arms race.

Lord Grey thought the competition before 1914 was frenzied madness; before 1939 the pace was hotter still; since 1945 it has been far beyond what anyone could have dreamed of in 1939.

In 1914 the nations had something over five million men in their standing peacetime forces; today they have more than sixteen million. In 1914 they were spending about £ 500 million a year on preparing for war; today they are spending £ 40,000 million.

The most significant figure is what we spend on military research; on using scientists of genius to «improve» existing weapons and to develop new ones that are cheaper, more destructive, swifter in delivery than those we have today.

In 1938[1] Britain spent less than £ 6 million on military research; in 1953, £ 100 million; in 1959, £ 210 million–by official figures, and allowing for the change of prices, more than twenty times what we were spending twenty years ago.

The United States in 1940 spent £ 5 million on military research–even less than us. In 1958, they spent £ 1,900 million–nine times our figure; and no doubt the Soviet Union spent even more. The results, in every class of armament, have been revolutionary; Britain is now equipping her land forces with new weapons, from the rifle to tanks that will be transportable by air; France is making bombing aircraft with twice the speed of sound.

But the great changes since 1945 are in the so-called «modern» weapons. The bloodcurdling history of the nuclear bomb is familiar to us all. In 1945 the Hiroshima weapon multiplied by 2,000 the explosive power of the ten-ton «blockbuster» which our pilots had dropped on Berlin; it is the yardstick of nuclear armament, so we must remember what it did.

It killed 100,000 people in an instant of time; it crippled, burnt, blinded, riddled with radiation sickness 100,000 more; in 1959 scores of people have died a lingering, hideous death as the result of a bomb dropped fourteen years ago. A city as large as Oslo was utterly destroyed: houses, factories, offices, barracks, docks–nothing remained.

1. In delivery, the words «In 1936, on the eve of Hitler's war» were substituted for «In 1938».

In 1954 the so-called H-bomb–the first primitive, unliftable thermo-nuclear device–multiplied by almost a thousand the power of the Hiroshima bomb. A British Home Office Manual on Civil Defense rells us that a ten-megaton bomb–ten million tons of Nobel's high explosive–much smaller than the weapon of 1954–would wipe out London: total annihilation of the center, and around it an unbroken circle of roaring flame, from which it would be a miracle if anything escaped.

And the pace of the advance in weapons is still increasing. In four years, since the government ceased discussing «comprehensive» disarmament and started seeking for «partial» measures instead, we have seen: the production of the supersonic bomber; the development of the «intermediate» missile, to have a range of 1,200 or 1,500 miles; the intercontinental missile, which may be «operational» by 1961, with the Soviet Union then producing fifteen a month; the adaptation of the H-bomb into weapons which can be carried by a fighter-bomber, and into warheads for the intercontinental missile.

We have seen the introduction of the nuclear-powered submarine, with all its menace, and the Polaris nuclear missile, which may soon be fired from underwater. We have seen the great development of chemical and biological methods of conducting war.

The Pugwash Scientists, so generously helped by Mr. Cyrus Eaton of the United States[1], have shown this year that poison gas and «biologicals» may well become weapons for the mass elimination of human life. Goering[2] tried a nerve gas, which he called «Tabun», on a herd of goats; they went mad and massacred each other, before the few survivors died, after hours of agonizing pain.

An American general has told us that our nerve gas is ten times as potent now; others say even more. «Biologicals» may be just as potent, and, if they start a large-scale epidemic, more horrifying still.

No doubt with the best of motives [–I say nothing against the General Staffs–no doubt] the major military governments have kept secret the facts about their chemical and biological work; General Staffs have used euphemistic phrases like the «tactical atomic bomb» or the «low-yield thermo-

1. The Pugwash Conference on Science and World Affairs, so called because it first met (1957) at Mr. Eaton's Pugwash estate in Nova Scotia, was financially aided in holding several of its early meetings by Cyrus S. Eaton, a Cleveland industrialist.
2. Hermann Wilhelm Goering (1893–1946), German Nazi leader; president of council for war economy (1940–1945); founded the Gestapo (secret police) in 1933, heading it until 1936.

nuclear device»–phrases against which the scientists who made these weapons openly revolt.

But it is vital that the citizens of every country should realize the true nature of the present arms race. What are the salient facts?

First, it is by far the most potent factor in the conduct of our international affairs.

Second, it is the strangest paradox in history; every new weapon is produced for national defense; but all experts are agreed that the modern, mass-destruction, instantaneous delivery weapons have destroyed defense.

Third, it is a patent error to speak as though, for an indefinite future, there will be two military «giants», and no more. If the arms race goes on, in ten years there may be six or even more, and who knows which nation will be the greatest giant.

Fourth, the advance in weapons has already brought us within measurable distance of the sudden, decisive, irreparable knockout blow.

Dr. Ellis Johnson, the head of the Johns Hopkins Operations Analysis Office, which does tactical and strategic studies for the American army, believes that such a crushing attack by Russia on the United States is possible today. Others believe that the United States, with 10,000 megaton bombs and a vast delivery system from land bases and from the sea, will soon be able to knock out Russia, without the danger of reply.

Fifth, military research is not standing still: the highest authorities tell us that weapon «progress» will be as great in the next fifteen years as in the past. The dangers of the weapons will continually increase.

Sixth, we are continually being «conditioned» to their use. Fifty years ago the Hague Conventions codified the laws of war, forbidding gas or other poison, the use of fire bombing from the air, attacks on open towns and civilians, either on land or sea.

Within ten years all these rules had been violated in the First World War. But the Second World War was incomparably more degraded and degrading than the First.

In the First War, we had poison gas–I was at Ypres when the chlorine cloud was first released–a gas wall a hundred feet high and two miles long; I saw the French Colonial Troops flying in terror and throwing away their weapons as they ran; I saw the Canadian soldiers choking to death, with an evil yellow froth oozing from their mouths; we had poison gas, but no gas chambers; we knew the ferocious cruelty that sometimes goes with dare-all heroism, but not the organized sadism of the concentration camp. We had spying and treason and executions, but not the Gestapo's torture chambers, with the thumbscrew and the rack.

And what is happening to us now, as we prepare for the Third Great War?

When Hitler was exterminating seven million Jews in Poland, we had millions of German prisoners in our hands; we did not kill them; we took no reprisals of any kind. But now governments are constantly asserting that if they or their allies are attacked, they will instantly reply with weapons that will wipe out tens of millions of men and women and little children, who may bear no shadow of personal responsibility for what their government has done.

What is left of the morality on which our Western civilization has been built?

How can we end the arms race?

I start with a forthright proposition: it makes no sense to talk about disarming unless you believe that war, *all* war, can be abolished. The Western governments declared precisely that in the UN Commission in 1952. «The goal of disarmament», they said, «is not to regulate, but to prevent war, by making war inherently, as it is constitutionally under the Charter, impossible as a means of settling disputes between nations. To achieve this goal, all states must cooperate to establish an open and substantially disarmed world, in which armed forces and armaments will be reduced to such a point... that no state will be in a condition of armed preparedness to start a war.»[1]

That was the objective declared by the Western governments eight years ago; it is the objective which Mr. Khruschev declared in the General Assembly in September last[2].

Unless there is an iron resolution to make it the supreme object of international policy and to realize it now, I believe all talks about disarmament will fail.

This[3] rules out attempts to «limit» war by new laws or understandings about how weapons will be used. I fear we should not get far with the kind

---

1. From «Essential Principles for a Disarmament Programme» (as quoted by Noel-Baker in *The Arms Race*, pp. 12–13), submitted by the U.S. to the new UN Disarmament Commission in April, 1952.

2. Nikita Sergeyevich Khrushchev (1894–1971), Russian Communist premier (1958–1964). His speech is reported verbatim in *UN General Assembly Records*, 14th Session: Plenary Meetings, Sept. 15–Dec. 13, 1959, pp. 31–38.

3. In delivery, the words «If that is true, it» were substituted for «This».

of «partial» measures which have been debated for the last four years. Everyone would favor «partial» measures, if they were real, if they created confidence, if nothing better could be done.

Some people honestly believe that small steps will be much easier to take than large ones. They quote proverbs to support their point–the crude English: «Don't bite off more than you can chew»; the elegant French: «The better is the enemy of the good»; the Russian: «The slower you ride, the further you go». Well, in Russia I should have thought it would depend on whether you had a pack of wolves howling hungrily at your horse's heels. We have a pack of wolves, the modern weapons, howling at our heels.

I prefer the words of our great economist and political thinker, John Stuart Mill: «Against a great evil, a small remedy does not produce a small result; it produces no result at all.» Or the saying of Lloyd George: «The most dangerous thing in the world is to try to leap a chasm in two jumps.» There is a great chasm, a great gulf, between the armed world of today and the disarmed world which we must have on some near tomorrow.

I will not discuss the «partial» measures which have been debated in recent years: the «cut-off» of new nuclear weapons; measures against surprise attack; exchange of budgetary information; and the rest – in my view, except as part of a general disarmament treaty, they were almost bound to fail.

I rejoice that, for the present, they have been set aside, that the new Committee of Ten will meet to discuss a «comprehensive» plan for general and complete disarmament, and that its mandate is to prepare detailed proposals within the shortest practicable time [1].

Some people say the Committee should work on Mr. Khruschev's proposals made in the Assembly the other day. Others seem to think that it would be dangerous to start on a Kremlin basis, to appear to let the Kremlin have the lead. They remind me of a Scottish minister of the Kirk, who, after a period of draught, when the crops were withering in the corn fields, was asked by the farmers of his parish to pray to the Almighty to send some rain. «No, no», he replied, «I cannot do that while the wind is in the East!»

---

1. A four-power communiqué of September 7, 1959, addressed to the Secretary-General, stated that agreement had been reached on the creation of a ten-nation disarmament committee composed of France, U.S.S.R., U.S., U.K., Bulgaria, Canada, Czechoslovakia, Italy, Poland, and Rumania. (DC/144, 8 September 1959). The mandate is contained in General Assembly Resolution 1378 (xiv; 20 November 1959, item 70).

Can we really not negotiate on proposals that come to us from the East? I should have thought that that might be the very moment when we had the greatest prospect of success; that, perhaps, Dr. Christian Lange's «golden hour of opportunity» had come again. But first, they say, we *must* know: Is Mr. Khruschev genuinely sincere?

I answer the doubters' question in three ways. First, perhaps no one knows if Mr. Khruschev is sincere, and we shall never know unless we start a serious negotiation with him without delay. Second, if we do negotiate, we shall know within a week if he is sincere or not; that is certain. Third, if we do *not* soon start a serious negotiation on the basis of the mandate which the General Assembly has defined, then *he* may say, and others will believe, that it is we who are not sincere.

The words «general and complete disarmament» are Mr. Khruschev's; he proposed the elimination of all armaments and all armed forces within four years, leaving nations with militias bearing small arms to maintain order within their states. He proposed as well a general and complete inspection and control, with no reservations or limitations of any kind. In other words, he proposed an ultimate objective, and a timetable of the stages by which it should be reached.

His objective, I repeat, is simply that declared by the Western governments in 1952; and, unless I misread the speeches in the Assembly, there is no one who rejects this as the final purpose now.

Is the timetable too ambitious? Of course, there are dangers in avoidable delay; but four years is very short for so vast and revolutionary a change; in all good faith, it might take six, or eight, or ten; I hope Mr. Khruschev will be elastic about the point, provided real disarmament is being pursued.

In any case, I hope the new Committee of Ten will remember what was said by an American delegate some years ago: that the further you carry disarmament, the easier it becomes; the technical problems grow simpler, the inspection more certain to succeed.

Of course, there must be a first-stage treaty, by which the initial reductions will be made.

In our British United Nations Association Statement we set out what we believe would be a wise first-stage agreement: reductions of manpower–army, navy, air force all together–to one or at most 1.5 million men for Russia, China, and America, with lower «ceilings» for other nations; a corresponding reduction of conventional weapons; agreement to abolish, by prescribed measures, all the weapons of mass destruction, including the existing stocks; budgetary reduction and limitation; and of course the appropriate measures of inspection and control.

We believe the first-stage treaty should also make quite clear, at least in principle, the further reductions to be made in stages two and three; the whole negotiation will be far easier if the steps to the ultimate objective are made plain in everybody's mind.

How practical is this program? Are there vast, unsolved technical problems to be faced? Well, a treaty of general disarmament will be a long and complex document. But, broadly, Salvador de Madariaga's[1] words [spoken in 1932] are true [today]: «Technical difficulties are political objections in uniform».

And, in fact, nearly all the technical problems of reducing armies, navies, and air forces, of reducing or abolishing conventional armaments, of reducing and limiting military budgets, were already solved long years ago. The London and Washington Naval Treaties[2], the Reports of the Disarmament Conference of 1932, Sir Anthony Eden's Draft Disarmament Convention[3] of March, 1933 – these provide model [treaty] clauses from which the Committee of Ten might well begin.

But there is one new technical difficulty to be faced – the clandestine nuclear stock. Suppose the nuclear powers agree to abolish all their A- and H-bombs, how could they be certain a disloyal government, planning to conquer or blackmail the world, would not keep a part – ten percent, twenty percent – of their existing stocks in a lead and concrete hideout that no one could ever find?

«It is now a fact», said Sir Winston Churchill in the House of Commons, «that a quantity of plutonium, perhaps less than would fill this Box on the table…would suffice to produce weapons which would give indisputable world domination to any great power which was the only one to have it.»[4]

This has been the crux of the deadlock of recent years. Some governments

1. Salvador de Madariaga (1886–   ), Spanish diplomat and writer, known especially for his studies on national and international psychology; in the 1920's held posts in the League of Nations, including that of director of the Disarmament Section.
2. Treaties limiting naval armaments, signed by France, Great Britain, Italy, Japan, and the U.S. in Washington (1922) and by Japan, Great Britain, and the U.S. in London (1930).
3. Robert Anthony Eden (1897–   ), British foreign undersecretary (1931–1933). The British Draft Convention was based on the principle of qualitative disarmament.
4. Hansard, March 1, 1955, col. 1899 – as cited by Noel-Baker in *The Arms Race*, p. 107.

have argued that the only safeguard is for the nuclear powers to retain a great part of their stocks to act as a deterrent to aggression, that total abolition will only be safe when there is some new Geiger counter, some miraculous new instrument or method that will detect the faintly radioactive H-bomb behind its concrete shield.

But if we wait for this Geiger counter, we may wait for decades, as Mr. Stassen[1] said in 1957; or we may wait forever. What happens while we are waiting?

Will France stop making nuclear weapons? Will China, with its vast potential power? If France and China, then surely Japan, India, Pakistan, Germany, Italy, and others will join the nuclear club – there are now a dozen countries which, within a decade, could mobilize the necessary materials and skills. Simply waiting for a Geiger counter means the gravest risk of all. Is there nothing else that we can do?

Of course there is. We could abolish the «means of delivery», the military aircraft and the missiles by which nuclear weapons can be used. That is quite easy; Mr. Khruschev has proposed it; there is no problem of control – bombers and missiles could not be made or tested without UN inspectors finding out, nor could troops be given training in their use.

Second, we can agree, as in principle I understand we have agreed, to abolish the land, sea, and air forces without which no government could embark upon aggressive war.

Third, we could set up general and complete control of all the means, including nuclear plants, by which war can be prepared; I discussed this in great detail with Mr. Khruschev and his colleagues, and I am sure that, for real disarmament, they will agree.

These three measures are the real safeguards, far better than any Geiger counter; they would remove the whole temptation to keep a secret nuclear stock. The risk of accepting such a system would be incomparably less than the risk of allowing the arms race to go on.

Disarmament is not a policy by itself; it is part of the general policy of the UN. But it is a vital part of that policy; without it, the UN institutions can never function as they should.

For every nation, it is the safest and most practicable system of defense. Defeatism about the past is a grievous error; the Disarmament Conference of

1. Harold Edward Stassen (1907–   ), U.S. statesman; special assistant to President Eisenhower on disarmament questions and U.S. representative on the UN Disarmament Commission (1955–1958).

1932 was not inevitably bound to fail; failure was due to human errors we can plainly see.

Sir Winston Churchill called the Second War «the most unnecessary war in history». [Defeatism about the past is a grievous error;] defeatism about the future is a crime. The danger is not in trying to do too much, but in trying to do too little. Nansen said here in 1926 that «in the big things of life, it is vitally important to leave no line of retreat...We must destroy the bridges behind us which lead back to the old policy and the old system, both of which are such utter failures.»[1]

In the age when the atom has been split, the moon encircled, diseases conquered, is disarmament so difficult a matter that it must remain a distant dream? To answer «Yes» is to despair of the future of mankind.

«Politics», it is said, «is the art of the possible.» How often that weary cliché provides excuse for defeatist surrender, before the real difficulties of a problem have been faced! [Democracy is the art of mobilizing popular opinion in support of reforms that are technically possible and that the people want. Disarmament is technically—I repeat it—far simpler than any other method of national defense. Who doubts that all the peoples want it?]

Nansen was the first to say what others have repeated, that «the difficult is what takes a little while; the impossible is what takes a little longer». If politics is the art of the possible, statesmanship is the art, in Nansen's sense, of the impossible; and it is statesmanship that our perplexed and tortured humanity requires today.

But even with statesmanship of that high order, we may have a long and dangerous voyage still before us, full of hazards and, it may be, storms; if at last we are to reach our destination, our ship must be the *Fram*.

---

1. See Vol. 1, p.392.

Biography

The Right Honorable Philip John Noel-Baker (November 1, 1889–) is a man of strong and steadfast convictions. To a reporter who interviewed him after the Norwegian Nobel Committee announced that he had been awarded the Peace Prize, he said, «War is a damnable, filthy thing and has destroyed civilization after civilization – that is the essence of my belief.»[1]

Noel-Baker, who formally joined his wife's surname with his own in 1943, was reared in an atmosphere of affluence, religious observance, and political activism. He was one of seven children of a Canadian-born Quaker, Joseph Allen Baker, who moved to England to establish what became a profitable machine manufacturing firm. The elder Baker was a pacifist and humanitarian who held a seat on the London County Council from 1895 to 1907 and in the House of Commons from 1905 to 1918.

Noel-Baker excelled in school. After attending Bootham School in York and Haverford College in Pennsylvania – both of them Quaker-affiliated institutions – he took honors in the history tripos in 1910 and in the economics tripos in 1912 at King's College, Cambridge, and in both 1911 and 1913 was named the Whewell scholar in international law. Before the First World War he also studied for a brief time in Paris and Munich. At Cambridge in 1912, Noel-Baker was president of the debating society and from 1910 to 1912 president of the Cambridge University Athletic Club. A stellar performer in the middle distances, he ran in the Olympic Games held in Stockholm in 1912 and captained the British track team at the 1920 Olympics in Antwerp and at the 1924 Games in Paris.

From 1914 until the present day, Noel-Baker has three times accepted academic posts but has left them to pursue a career in public service. Having completed his M.A., he accepted the post of vice-principal of Ruskin College at Oxford in 1914, but with the onset of the war, he organized and became the commandant of the Friends' Ambulance Unit attached to the fighting front in France (1914–1915) and subsequently became adjutant of the First British Ambulance Unit for Italy (1915–1918). In France he won

1. *New York Times* (November 6, 1959), p. 4.

the Mons Star (1915); in Italy, the Silver Medal for Military Valor (1917) and the Croce di Guerra (1918). In 1915 he met and married a field hospital nurse, Irene Noel, the daughter of a British landowner in Achmetaga, Greece.

Noel-Baker participated in the formation, the administration, and the legislative deliberations of the two great international political organizations of the twentieth century–the League of Nations and the United Nations. In 1918–1919, during the Peace Conference in Paris, he was principal assistant to Lord Robert Cecil on the committee which drafted the League of Nations Covenant; from 1920 to 1922 a member of the Secretariat of the League, being principal assistant to Sir Eric Drummond, first secretary-general of the League; from 1922 to 1924 the private secretary to the British representative on the League's Council and Assembly. Meanwhile, he also was acting as a valued adviser to Fridtjof Nansen in his prisoner-of-war and refugee work. From 1929 to 1931 he was a member of the British delegation to the Assembly of the League and then for a year an assistant to Arthur Henderson, the chairman of the Disarmament Conference.

For a brief period notable for its scholarly productivity, he returned to academic pursuits. He accepted the invitation issued by the University of London to become the first Sir Ernest Cassell Professor of International Law, occupying this chair from 1924 to 1929. Out of his League experience and further research, he wrote and published *The Geneva Protocol for the Pacific Settlement of International Disputes* (1925), *The League of Nations at Work* (1926), *Disarmament* (1926), *Disarmament and the Coolidge Conference* (1927). From his research for a course of lectures in the summer of 1927 at the Academy of International Law at The Hague, came *Le Statut juridique actuel des dominions britanniques dans le domaine du droit international* (1928). Except for a year spent as Dodge Lecturer in 1933–1934 at Yale University, Noel-Baker henceforth devoted his life to politics and international affairs.

For four decades Noel-Baker was prominent in the Labor Party. He was unsuccessful in a 1924 contest for a seat in the House of Commons, but from 1929 to 1931 he sat as a member from Coventry, from 1936 to 1950 as a member from Derby, and from 1950 to 1970 from Derby South. He was elected to the National Executive Committee of the Labor Party in 1937 and in 1946 succeeded Harold Laski as chairman of the party.

From 1936 to 1942, Noel-Baker was in the Opposition in the Commons, but accepted the office of Joint Parliamentary Secretary to the Minister of War Transport proffered by Winston Churchill in 1942. In the Attlee government elected in 1945, he was, successively, Minister of State in the Foreign Office (1945–1946), Secretary of State for Air (1946–1947), Secretary of State for Commonwealth Relations (1947–1950), and Minister of Fuel and Power (1950–1951). When the Labor Party lost power, Noel-Baker became a member of the «shadow cabinet», was named vice-chairman of the foreign affairs group of the Parliamentary Labor Party in 1961 and its chairman in 1964.

At the close of World War II, the functions which Noel-Baker discharged in connection with the United Nations were analogous to those he performed for the League of Nations a generation earlier. Having been in charge of British preparatory work for the United Nations beginning in 1944, he helped to draft the Charter of the UN at San Francisco the next year and in 1946 was appointed to membership on the British delegation.

In the formative days of the UN, Noel-Baker was concerned with the selection of a site for UN headquarters (he favored Geneva)and with outlining privileges, restrictions, and responsibilities of members of the UN staff–the ground rules, in a sense, of a world civil service. A delegate to the Food and Agriculture Organization at Quebec in 1945, he helped give viability to that imperiled organization by delineating a compromise between pure research programs on the one hand and relief operations on the other. As the United Kingdom delegate to the Economic and Social Council, he called for an action program to abolish poverty in an affluent world. In the General Assembly, he supported regulation of arms traffic, plans for atomic controls, economic aid for refugees and re-institution of the «Nansen passport», the economic unification of the Allied zones in Germany, and wide-ranging plans for economic development and organization in Europe.

In the decade of the fifties, Noel-Baker returned to his studies on disarmament. He had published a long book in 1936, *The Private Manufacture of Armaments*. In *The Arms Race: A Programme for World Disarmament*, published in 1958, he summarizes the results of extensive research combined with «personal experiences which began at the Peace Conference in Paris in 1919». This comprehensive, historical, and analytical study won the Albert Schweitzer Book Prize in 1961.

Although his days of active participation in track have long since passed, Noel-Baker retains the lean look of the athlete and an absorption in athletics. He was commandant of the 1952 British Olympic team and in 1960 became president of the International Council of Sport and Physical Recreation of UNESCO.

Noel Baker has continued to reside in London since the death of his wife in 1956. For about twenty years he had the pleasure of serving in the House of Commons as a colleague of his only child, Francis Noel-Baker.

Selected Bibliography

Baker, Elizabeth B., and Philip John Noel-Baker, *J. Allen Baker, Member of Parliament: A Memoir*. London, Swarthmore, 1927.

Current Biography, 7 (1946).

The *New York Times* (November 6, 1959). Announcement of Prize, pp. 1 and 4. «An Athletic Pacifist», p. 4.

Noel-Baker, Philip John, *The Arms Race: A Programme for World Disarmament*. London, Stevens, 1958.

Noel-Baker, Philip John, *Disarmament*. London, Hogarth, 1926.

Noel-Baker, Philip John, *Disarmament and the Coolidge Conference*. London, Leonard and Virginia Woolf, 1927.

Noel-Baker, Philip John, *The Geneva Protocol for the Pacific Settlement of International Disputes*. London, King, 1925.

Noel-Baker, Philip John, *Hawkers of Death: The Private Manufacture and Trade in Arms*. London, Labour Party, 1934.

Noel-Baker, Philip John, *The League of Nations at Work*. London, Nisbet, 1926.

Noel-Baker, Philip John, «A National Air Force No Defence» and «The International Air Police Force», in *Challenge to Death*, ed. by Storm Jameson. London, Constable, 1934.

Noel-Baker, Philip John, «The Obligatory Jurisdiction of the Permanent Court of International Justice», in *The British Year Book of International Law* (1925), pp. 68–102.

Noel-Baker, Philip John, «Peace and the Official Mind», in *Challenge to Death*, ed. by Storm Jameson. London, Constable, 1934.

Noel-Baker, Philip John, *The Present Juridical Status of the British Dominions in International Law*. London, Longmans, Green, 1929. English version of «Le Statut juridique actuel des dominions britanniques dans le domaine du droit international», in Académie de droit international: *Recueil des cours*, Tome 4 en 1927, pp. 247–491. Tome 19 de la Collection. Paris, Hachette, 1928.

Noel-Baker, Philip John, *The Private Manufacture of Armaments*. London, Gollancz, 1936.

Noel-Baker, Philip John, «UN, the Atom, the Veto.» Speech at the Plenary Assembly of the United Nations: 25 October, 1946. London, Labour Party, 1946.

Noel-Baker, Philip John, *The Way to World Disarmament–Now!* London, Union of Democratic Control, 1963.

Russell, Bertrand, «Philip Noel-Baker: A Tribute», in *International Relations*, 2 (1960) 1–2.

Peace 1960

(Prize awarded in 1961)

ALBERT JOHN LUTULI

Presentation

by Gunnar Jahn*, Chairman of the Nobel Committee

This year the Nobel Committee of the Norwegian Parliament has awarded two Peace Prizes. The prize for 1960 goes to Albert John Lutuli, and the prize for 1961 is awarded posthumously to Dag Hammarskjöld.

In many respects these two recipients differ widely. Albert John Lutuli's life and work have been molded by the pattern of the African tribal community and by the influence of Christianity, while Dag Hammarskjöld's were a product of Western culture. Lutuli's activities have been, and are, confined to his own country, while Dag Hammarskjöld worked in the international sphere. Yet despite these differences, they had one thing in common: both fought to implant the idea of justice in the individual, in the nation, and among the nations; or we might put it like this: they fought for the ideals expressed in the declaration of human rights embodied in the Charter of the United Nations.

Albert John Lutuli was born in 1898. He comes from a long line of Zulu chiefs, but he was influenced by Christianity in his school days and in his later education, first in the American mission school he attended and afterwards during his training as a teacher. After passing his examination at Adams College in Natal, he became a faculty member of the college, where he taught, among other subjects, the history of the Zulu people. During his seventeen years as a teacher, he took no part in the political life of South Africa.

In 1935 a great change took place in Lutuli's life when he was called to assume the functions of tribal chief. The choice of a chief must be approved by the state, which pays his salary. It was on the basis of this authority that the government was able to remove him in 1952. His seventeen years

---

* Mr. Jahn delivered this speech on December 10, 1961, in the Auditorium of the University of Oslo. At its conclusion he presented the Peace Prize for 1960 (reserved in that year) to Mr. Lutuli, who accepted in a brief speech. The English translation of Mr. Jahn's speech is, with certain editorial changes and emendations made after collation with the Norwegian text, that carried in *Les Prix Nobel en 1961*, which also includes the original Norwegian text.

as a chief brought him daily contact with the individual members of the tribal community, as well as an active part in the work of the Christian church in South Africa, in India, and in the United States.

Both as a teacher and later as a chief, Lutuli did outstanding work. He took his duties as chief very seriously and in doing so won the affection of his tribe. He endeavored to blend its ancient culture with the precepts of Christianity and to promote its economic welfare in various ways–for example, by introducing new methods of sugar production.

Describing this period of his life, he tells us: «Previous to being a chief I was a school teacher for about seventeen years. In these past thirty years or so, I have striven with tremendous zeal and patience to work for the progress and welfare of my people and for their harmonious relations with other sections of our multiracial society in the Union of South Africa. In this effort I always pursued... the path of moderation. Over this great length of time I have, year after year, gladly spent hours of my time with such organizations as the church and its various agencies, such as the Christian Council of South Africa, the Joint Council of Europeans and Africans, and the now defunct Native Representative Council.» [1]

But it was neither as a teacher, nor as a chief, nor as an active member of various Christian organizations that he took a focal position in what was to be his great effort in the postwar years.

The forces that induced Albert John Lutuli to abandon his tranquil educational activities and enter politics were unleashed by the increasing pressure which the ruling white race exerted on members of other races in South Africa. In 1944 he became a member of the African National Congress, an organization founded in 1912. In 1952 he was elected its president, an office he held until the Congress was banned in 1960. It is first and foremost for the work he carried on during these years–from the 1940's to the present –that we honor him today.

To get some idea of Lutuli's achievements, we must know something of the society in which he worked. The white population of South Africa settled there in the latter half of the seventeenth century. The first settlers were French Huguenots, followed later by Dutch farmers. They cleared the land, and their descendants–the Boers–have lived there ever since. They look upon the country as their fatherland; they have no other. The English settlers, who arrived on the scene at the end of the eighteenth century,

1. Lutuli, «The Road to Freedom Is via the Cross» (statement made in November, 1952, after his dismissal as chief), in *Let My People Go*, p.235.

maintained close contact with their mother country. The first natives whom the Dutch pioneers met were Hottentots and Bushmen. The Hottentots have now virtually disappeared as a separate racial entity; but through inter-marriage with European and other races they have contributed in large measure to the racial characteristics of those called «the colored people». When the Boers moved into the interior, they encountered other native tribes, among them the Zulus, whom they fought and conquered. These tribes constitute the largest part of the population of South Africa today. In the course of time other racial elements were added: the Dutch imported a number of Malays from the East Indies as slaves, while the British intro-duced Indian labor to the sugar plantations. In the nineteenth century two communities took shape: the Boer republics of Transvaal and the Orange Free State, and the British colony of South Africa, both ruled by whites. At the turn of the century these two communities fought the Boer War of 1899–1902, from which Britain finally emerged victorious. The ultimate result was that the Union of South Africa was set up as an independent British Dominion in 1910[1]. At that time the outside world heard little about relations between whites and nonwhites.

During the fifty years that have since elapsed, South Africa, in common with so many other countries, has developed from an agricultural com-munity into one in which mining, industry, trade, and other such operations now predominate. As in other such countries, the urban population has increased rapidly.

The present-day population of South Africa is some 14.7 million, of whom only some 3.3 million are white. Of the remainder, 9.6 million are Africans, some 0.4 million Asian (mainly Indians) and 1.4 million of mixed race (the so-called «colored people»). Of the 9.6 million Africans, some 3.3 million live in the agricultural districts of the whites, a large proportion of them as agricultural workers on white farms; 3.7 million live in the African reservations; and 2.6 million live in the towns.

Although some of these figures are only approximate, they still present

---

1. Transvaal was set up as a Boer state in 1837; recognized by the British in 1852; organized as the South African Republic in 1856; annexed by the British in 1877; and restored to independence in 1881 under British suzerainty. The Orange Free State, settled by the Boers 1835–1848, was created a free republic in 1854. After the Boer War, both became British crown colonies, with the promise of eventual self-govern-ment, which they attained 1905–1907; and both became part of the Union of South Africa when it was organized in 1910.

a picture of a community whose economy and therefore future are dependent on cooperation between all races. The figures testify to the fact
that people of all races have helped to build this community. The whites
could never have done it alone. This is an incontestable fact. But what is
the position of the nonwhite population?

In this community, nonwhites are denied all right to participate in the
government of the state. They are discriminated against legally, economically, and socially. And this discrimination between whites and nonwhites
has grown steadily during the postwar years. The aim of those now ruling
the country is to draw a line between the two communities[1]–between
whites and nonwhites–despite the fact that the march of events has clearly
shown that the whole community has been developed by the efforts of all
races. I cannot here go into the network of laws and regulations passed
in order to maintain the barrier between whites and nonwhites. The purpose
of these laws is to restrict and regulate every facet of the life of the nonwhite. He has no vote, he has no part in determining his own status; under
the pass system, he is deprived not only of the right to live where he likes
but also of the right to choose his employer; he has virtually no redress
against police tyranny; he is not entitled to the same schooling or education
as the white; and any sexual relation between white and nonwhite entails
punishment for both parties. An African Christian is frequently not allowed
to worship God under the same roof as a white Christian. In short, nonwhites are treated as a subject race.

Is it surprising then that the nonwhites have protested against such treatment? What is surprising is that the protest has not been accompanied by
acts of violence on their part. Their patience is remarkable, their moral
strength in the struggle boundless.

It was the discrimination between white and nonwhite that prompted
nonwhite Africans in 1912 to establish the African National Congress. Its
founders were nonwhite Africans who had obtained a higher education,
either abroad or at home, in the days when they still had the opportunity
to do so. At first the African National Congress tried to influence political
development by means of petitions and deputations to the authorities, but
when the attempt proved fruitless and new laws restricting the rights of
nonwhites were passed, the African National Congress adopted a more active line, especially after 1949. It was in the mid-1940's that Lutuli began

1. The segregation policy known as «apartheid», promoted by the Nationalists, the
party in power since 1948.

to participate in this work of the African National Congress, of which he became a member in 1944. He was elected to the Committee of the Natal Section in 1945 and in 1951 became president of the Natal Section. In December, 1952, he was elected president of the entire African National Congress, a position he retained until the organization was banned by the government in 1960.

It was during these transitional years of adopting stronger action, based on boycotts, defiance campaigns, and strikes, that Lutuli came to influence so profoundly the African National Congress. He says himself that the Congress never passed any specific resolution to the effect that its struggle was to be pursued by nonviolent means. Actually, however, it has been waged with peaceful means, a policy at all times supported by the Congress administration. Lutuli himself has always been categorically opposed to the use of violence. Within the organization he has had to overcome opposition from two different quarters: from the older members, who supported the more passive approach, and from those members–mainly the younger ones –who wanted to make South Africa an entirely nonwhite state.

As a result of Lutuli's participation in the more active struggle of the African National Congress, the government presented him with an ulti-matum: he must either renounce his position as a chief or give up his seat in the Congress. He refused to comply with either of these alternatives and was immediately deposed as chief, whereupon he issued his significant dec-laration entitled «The Chief Speaks», which concludes with the words: «The Road to Freedom Is via the Cross.» In his declaration, he says:

«What have been the fruits of my many years of moderation? Has there been any reciprocal tolerance or moderation from the Government, be it Nationalist or United Party? No! On the contrary, the past thirty years have seen the greatest number of Laws restricting our rights and progress until today we have reached a stage where we have almost no rights at all: no adequate land for our occupation, our only asset, cattle, dwindling, no security of homes, no decent and remunerative employment, more restrictions to freedom of movement through passes, curfew regulations, influx control measures; in short, we have witnessed in these years an in-tensification of our subjection to ensure and protect white supremacy.

It is with this background and with a full sense of responsibility that, under the auspices of the African National Congress (Natal), I have joined my people in the new spirit that moves them today, the spirit that revolts openly and boldly against injustice and expresses itself in a determined and nonviolent manner...

The African National Congress, its nonviolent Passive Resistance Campaign, may be of nuisance value to the Government, but it is not subversive since it does not seek to overthrow the form and machinery of the State but only urges for the inclusion of all sections of the community in a partnership in the Government of the country on the basis of equality.

Laws and conditions that tend to debase human personality–a God-given force–be they brought about by the State or other individuals, must be relentlessly opposed in the spirit of defiance shown by St. Peter when he said to the rulers of his day: ‹Shall we obey God or man?› No one can deny that insofar as nonwhites are concerned in the Union of South Africa, laws and conditions that debase human personality abound. Any chief worthy of his position must fight fearlessly against such debasing conditions and laws...

It is inevitable that in working for Freedom some individuals and some families must take the lead and suffer: the Road to Freedom Is via the Cross. [1]»

In 1952, after he had been dismissed from his position as chief and had been elected president of the African National Congress, he was forbidden to leave his home district for two years[2]. In 1954 he went to Johannesburg to address a meeting which had been called to protest the forced evacuation of colored people from Sophiatown to Meadowsland. He was refused permission to speak and was banned for another period of two years from leaving his home district. In 1956, together with 155 other persons, he was arrested and charged with high treason. In 1957 the charge against him and sixty-four others was withdrawn; the rest were all acquitted in 1961. In 1959 Lutuli took part in several mass meetings, but was again subjected to a travel ban, this time for a period of five years. In 1960 there was a large mass demonstration against the pass regulations which led to the events in Sharpeville, where police fired on the crowd, killing and wounding many. A state of emergency was declared and wholesale arrests were made. Lutuli, who had been summoned as a witness in the treason trial, which

1. Lutuli, op. cit., pp. 236–238.
2. Actually, he was banned from the larger centers of the Union and from all public gatherings, but was not restricted to one area. Lutuli, op. cit., p. 145; Benson, Chief Albert Lutuli of South Africa, p. 25.

had dragged on ever since 1956, was among those arrested but was allowed to give evidence in the trial. During the last year, he has lived at home, debarred from leaving his village and from taking part in any meetings. Moreover, he is now no longer president of the African National Congress, for this organization–as already mentioned–was dissolved by order of the government in April, 1960.

He now lives in his village, deprived of freedom of movement and of the right to speak in open debate, but he still maintains his avowed policy, expressing his views in articles published in the newspaper *Post*[1]. Just before the travel ban was imposed on him in December, 1959–the year before the Union of South Africa was to celebrate the fiftieth anniversary of its foundation–he wrote a long article entitled «Fifty Years of Union–Political Review» which he sent to the South Africa Institute of Race Relations.[2] This presents, as far as I know, the clearest and the most complete statement of his position concerning the policy pursued by the government of South Africa.

In this article, his attack on the policies of the South African government is stronger and more detailed than before. This discussion and attack on the policy of apartheid and its plan that the nonwhite community should develop along its own lines is new. He asks: Who has drawn the lines? The answer is: Not those who are to follow them, the nonwhites, but the whites in power. The nonwhites have no rights. There is therefore no reason, he says, for them to rejoice or to participate in the Fiftieth Anniversary celebration. The only thing for the nonwhites to do is to work, each and everyone, with courage and patience, to achieve freedom and democracy for all.

Since he wrote this, South Africa has become a republic and is no longer a member of the British Commonwealth. But this has not improved relations between whites and nonwhites, nor has it altered Lutuli's attitude in any way. He gives a most concise expression of the view he has always maintained in a letter to Prime Minister Strijdom[3], in which he says:

«We believe in a community where the white and the nonwhite in South

---

1. Perhaps a reference to the *Golden City Post* of Johannesburg.
2. The rest of this paragraph and the four paragraphs that follow it are omitted in the English translation in *Les Prix Nobel en 1961*.
3. Johannes Gerhardus Strijdom (1893–1958), Nationalist Party leader; prime minister of the Union of South Africa (1954–1958); advocate of apartheid and of the Union's withdrawal from the British Commonwealth.

Africa can live in harmony and work for our common fatherland, sharing equally the good things of life which our country can give us in abundance.

We believe in the brotherhood of peoples and in respect for the value of the individual. My congress has never given expression to hatred for any race in South Africa.»

Time and again he has reiterated this, right up to the very present.

His activity has been characterized by a firm and unswerving approach. Never has he succumbed to the temptation to use violent means in the struggle for his people. Nothing has shaken him from this firm resolve, so firmly rooted is his conviction that violence and terror must not be employed. Nor has he ever felt or incited hatred of the white man.

Albert John Lutuli's fight has been waged within the borders of his own country; but the issues raised go far beyond them. He brings a message to all who work and strive to establish respect for human rights both within nations and between nations.

Well might we ask: will the nonwhites of South Africa, by their suffering, their humiliation, and their patience, show the other nations of the world that human rights can be won without violence, by following a road to which we Europeans are committed both intellectually and emotionally, but which we have all too often abandoned?

If the nonwhite people of South Africa ever lift themselves from their humiliation without resorting to violence and terror, then it will be above all because of the work of Lutuli, their fearless and incorruptible leader who, thanks to his own high ethical standards, has rallied his people in support of this policy, and who throughout his adult life has staked everything and suffered everything without bitterness and without allowing hatred and aggression to replace his abiding love of his fellowmen.

But if the day should come when the struggle of the nonwhites in South Africa to win their freedom degenerates into bloody slaughter, then Lutuli's voice will be heard no more. But let us remember him then and never forget that his way was unwavering and clear. He would not have had it so.

Let us all rise in silent and respectful tribute to Albert John Lutuli.

ALBERT JOHN LUTULI

Africa and Freedom

Nobel Lecture*, December 11, 1961

In years gone by, some of the greatest men of our century have stood here to receive this award, men whose names and deeds have enriched the pages of human history, men whom future generations will regard as having shaped the world of our time. No one could be left unmoved at being plucked from the village of Groutville[1], a name many of you have never heard before and which does not even feature on many maps – to be plucked from banishment in a rural backwater, to be lifted out of the narrow confines of South Africa's internal politics and placed here in the shadow of these great figures. It is a great honor to me to stand on this rostrum where many of the great men of our times have stood before.

The Nobel Peace Award that has brought me here has for me a threefold significance. On the one hand, it is a tribute to my humble contribution to efforts by democrats on both sides of the color line to find a peaceful solution to the race problem. This contribution is not in any way unique. I did not initiate the struggle to extend the area of human freedom in South Africa; other African patriots – devoted men – did so before me. I also, as a Christian and patriot, could not look on while systematic attempts were made, almost in every department of life, to debase the God-factor in man

---

* The laureate delivered this lecture in the Auditorium of the University of Oslo. The occasion saw some «firsts» in Nobel ceremonies: Lutuli was asked to bring his wife to the platform – never before done – and, after much applause at the end of his lecture, he himself sang (in Zulu) the African anthem, «Nkosi Sikelel iAfrika», being joined by the Africans present and by others in the audience. The text of his lecture, which he gave in English, is taken from *Les Prix Nobel en 1961*. A tape of it records many extemporaneous additions made in delivery. In an informal and often humorous opening paragraph not in the prepared text, he thanked the Nobel Committee and Oslo – its people and its mayor – and paid tribute to the «human» King of Norway (Olaf V). His other additions were for the most part repetitions or amplifications of points already made.

1. Groutville, Lutuli's home village of some 500 population on the Natal coast about fifty miles north of Durban, is the center of the Umvoti Mission Reserve that supports about 5,000 Zulus.

or to set a limit beyond which the human being in his black form might not strive to serve his Creator to the best of his ability. To remain neutral in a situation where the laws of the land virtually critized God for having created men of color was the sort of thing I could not, as a Christian, tolerate.

On the other hand, the award is a democratic declaration of solidarity with those who fight to widen the area of liberty in my part of the world. As such, it is the sort of gesture which gives me and millions who think as I do, tremendous encouragement. There are still people in the world today who regard South Africa's race problem as a simple clash between black and white. Our government has carefully projected this image of the problem before the eyes of the world. This has had two effects. It has confused the real issues at stake in the race crisis. It has given some form of force to the government's contention that the race problem is a domestic matter for South Africa. This, in turn, has tended to narrow down the area over which our case could be better understood in the world[1].

From yet another angle, it is welcome recognition of the role played by the African people during the last fifty years to establish, peacefully, a society in which merit and not race would fix the position of the individual in the life of the nation.

This award could not be for me alone, nor for just South Africa, but for Africa as a whole. Africa presently is most deeply torn with strife and most bitterly stricken with racial conflict. How strange then it is that a man of Africa should be here to receive an award given for service to the cause of peace and brotherhood between men. There has been little peace in Africa in our time. From the northernmost end of our continent, where war has raged for seven years, to the center and to the south there are battles being fought out, some with arms, some without. In my own country, in the year 1960, for which this award is given, there was a state of emergency for many months. At Sharpeville, a small village, in a single afternoon sixty-nine people were shot dead and 180 wounded by small arms fire[2]; and

---

1. In one of his extemporaneous insertions, Lutuli here points out that the race issue in South Africa is not just a «clash of color», but a «clash of ideas»: oppression versus democratic rights for all.

2. The result of police reaction to anti-pass tactics used by the Pan-Africanist Congress, which supported an Africans-only resistance as opposed to the African National Congress idea of working with all races; this action circumvented an ANC anti-pass campaign scheduled for a few days later.

in parts like the Transkei[1], a state of emergency is still continuing. Ours is a continent in revolution against oppression. And peace and revolution make uneasy bedfellows. There can be no peace until the forces of oppression are overthrown.

Our continent has been carved up by the great powers; alien governments have been forced upon the African people by military conquest and by economic domination; strivings for nationhood and national dignity have been beaten down by force; traditional economics and ancient customs have been disrupted, and human skills and energy have been harnessed for the advantage of our conquerors. In these times there has been no peace; there could be no brotherhood between men.

But now, the revolutionary stirrings of our continent are setting the past aside. Our people everywhere from north to south of the continent are reclaiming their land, their right to participate in government, their dignity as men, their nationhood. Thus, in the turmoil of revolution, the basis for peace and brotherhood in Africa is being restored by the resurrection of national sovereignty and independence, of equality and the dignity of man.

It should not be difficult for you here in Europe to appreciate this. Your continent passed through a longer series of revolutionary upheavals, in which your age of feudal backwardness gave way to the new age of industrialization, true nationhood, democracy, and rising living standards – the golden age for which men have striven for generations. Your age of revolution, stretching across all the years from the eighteenth century to our own, encompassed some of the bloodiest civil wars in all history. By comparison, the African revolution has swept across three-quarters of the continent in less than a decade; its final completion is within sight of our own generation. Again, by comparison with Europe, our African revolution – to our credit – is proving to be orderly, quick, and comparatively bloodless.

This fact of the relative peacefulness of our African revolution is attested to by other observers of eminence. Professor C. W. de Kiewiet, president of the University of Rochester, U. S. A., in a Hoernlé Memorial Lecture for 1960, has this to say: «There has, it is true, been almost no serious violence in the achievement of political self-rule. In that sense there is no revolution in Africa – only reform...»

Professor D. V. Cowen, then professor of comparative law at the Uni-

1. In East Cape Province of South Africa.

versity of Cape Town, South Africa, in a Hoernlé Memorial Lecture for 1961, throws light on the nature of our struggle in the following words: «They (the Whites in South Africa) are again fortunate in the very high moral caliber of the non-White inhabitants of South Africa, who compare favorably with any on the whole continent.» Let this never be forgotten by those who so eagerly point a finger of scorn at Africa.

Perhaps, by your standards, our surge to revolutionary reforms is late. If it is so–if we are late in joining the modern age of social enlightenment, late in gaining self-rule, independence, and democracy, it is because in the past the pace has not been set by us. Europe set the pattern for the nineteenth- and twentieth-century development of Africa. Only now is our continent coming into its own and recapturing its own fate from foreign rule.

Though I speak of Africa as a single entity, it is divided in many ways– by race, language, history, and custom; by political, economic, and ethnic frontiers. But in truth, despite these multiple divisions, Africa has a single common purpose and a single goal–the achievement of its own indepen- dence. All Africa, both lands which have won their political victories but have still to overcome the legacy of economic backwardness, and lands like my own whose political battles have still to be waged to their conclusion– all Africa has this single aim: our goal is a united Africa in which the standards of life and liberty are constantly expanding; in which the ancient legacy of illiteracy and disease is swept aside; in which the dignity of man is rescued from beneath the heels of colonialism which have trampled it. This goal, pursued by millions of our people with revolutionary zeal, by means of books, representations, demonstrations, and in some places armed force provoked by the adamancy of white rule, carries the only real promise of peace in Africa. Whatever means have been used, the efforts have gone to end alien rule and race oppression.

There is a paradox in the fact that Africa qualifies for such an award in its age of turmoil and revolution. How great is the paradox and how much greater the honor that an award in support of peace and the brother- hood of man should come to one who is a citizen of a country where the brotherhood of man is an illegal doctrine, outlawed, banned, censured, proscribed and prohibited; where to work, talk, or campaign for the realiza- tion in fact and deed of the brotherhood of man is hazardous, punished with banishment, or confinement without trial, or imprisonment; where effective democratic channels to peaceful settlement of the race problem have never existed these 300 years; and where white minority power rests on the most heavily armed and equipped military machine in Africa. This is South Africa.

Even here, where white rule seems determined not to change its mind for the better, the spirit of Africa's militant struggle for liberty, equality, and independence asserts itself. I, together with thousands of my countrymen have in the course of the struggle for these ideals, been harassed and imprisoned, but we are not deterred in our quest for a new age in which we shall live in peace and in brotherhood.

It is not necessary for me to speak at length about South Africa; its social system, its politics, its economics, and its laws have forced themselves on the attention of the world. It is a museum piece in our time, a hangover from the dark past of mankind, a relic of an age which everywhere else is dead or dying. Here the cult of race superiority and of white supremacy is worshiped like a god. Few white people escape corruption, and many of their children learn to believe that white men are unquestionably superior, efficient, clever, industrious, and capable; that black men are, equally unquestionably, inferior, slothful, stupid, evil, and clumsy. On the basis of the mythology that «the lowest amongst them is higher than the highest amongst us», it is claimed that white men build everything that is worthwhile in the country–its cities, its industries, its mines, and its agriculture–and that they alone are thus fitted and entitled as of right to own and control these things, while black men are only temporary sojourners in these cities, fitted only for menial labor, and unfit to share political power. The prime minister of South Africa, Dr.Verwoerd[1], then minister of Bantu Affairs, when explaining his government's policy on African education had this to say: «There is no place for him (the African) in the European community above the level of certain forms of labour.»

There is little new in this mythology. Every part of Africa which has been subject to white conquest has, at one time or another and in one guise or another, suffered from it, even in its virulent form of the slavery that obtained in Africa up to the nineteenth century. The mitigating feature in the gloom of those far-off days was the shaft of light sunk by Christian missions, a shaft of light to which we owe our initial enlightenment. With successive governments of the time doing little or nothing to ameliorate the harrowing suffering of the black man at the hands of slave drivers, men

1. Hendrik Frensch Verwoerd (1901–1966), Nationalist Party leader and prominent advocate of apartheid in the Union of South Africa; native affairs minister (1950–1958); prime minister (1958–1966).

like Dr. David Livingstone[1] and Dr. John Philip[2] and other illustrious men of God stood for social justice in the face of overwhelming odds. It is worth noting that the names I have referred to are still anathema to some South Africans. Hence the ghost of slavery lingers on to this day in the form of forced labor that goes on in what are called farm prisons. But the tradition of Livingstone and Philip lives on, perpetuated by a few of their line. It is fair to say that even in present-day conditions, Christian missions have been in the vanguard of initiating social services provided for us. Our progress in this field has been in spite of, and not mainly because of, the government. In this, the church in South Africa, though belatedly, seems to be awakening to a broader mission of the church in its ministry among us. It is beginning to take seriously the words of its Founder who said: «I came that they might have life and have it more abundantly.»[3] This is a call to the church in South Africa to help in the all-round development of man in the present, and not only in the hereafter. In this regard, the people of South Africa, especially those who claim to be Christians, would be well advised to take heed of the Conference decisions of the World Council of Churches held at Cottesloe, Johannesburg, in 1960, which gave a clear lead on the mission of the church in our day[4]. It left no room for doubt about the relevancy of the Christian message in the present issues that confront mankind. I note with gratitude this broader outlook of the World Council of Churches. It has a great meaning and significance for us in Africa.

There is nothing new in South Africa's apartheid ideas, but South Africa is unique in this: the ideas not only survive in our modern age but are stubbornly defended, extended, and bolstered up by legislation at the time when, in the major part of the world, they are now largely historical and are either being shamefacedly hidden behind concealing formulations or are being steadily scrapped. These ideas survive in South Africa because those who sponsor them profit from them. They provide moral whitewash

1. David Livingstone (1813–1873), Scottish missionary and explorer in Africa.
2. John Philip (1775–1851), British missionary in South Africa; was influential in gaining rights for the natives but had to abandon his plan for independent native states.
3. John 10:10.
4. Meeting from December 8 to 14, 1960, the Council delegates lived and worked together without regard for the color bar and in their final report included criticism of the Union government's racial measures.

for the conditions which exist in the country: for the fact that the country is ruled exclusively by a white government elected by an exclusively white electorate which is a privileged minority; for the fact that eighty-seven percent of the land and all the best agricultural land within reach of town, market, and railways are reserved for white ownership and occupation, and now through the recent Group Areas legislation[1] nonwhites are losing more land to white greed; for the fact that all skilled and highly paid jobs are for whites only; for the fact that all universities of any academic merit are exclusively preserves of whites; for the fact that the education of every white child costs about £64 per year while that of an African child costs about £9 per year and that of an Indian child or colored child costs about £20 per year; for the fact that white education is universal and compulsory up to the age of sixteen, while education for the nonwhite children is scarce and inadequate; and for the fact that almost one million Africans a year are arrested and jailed or fined for breaches of innumerable pass and permit laws, which do not apply to whites.

I could carry on in this strain and talk on every facet of South African life from the cradle to the grave. But these facts today are becoming known to all the world. A fierce spotlight of world attention has been thrown on them. Try as our government and its apologists will, with honeyed words about «separate development» and eventual «independence» in so-called «Bantu homelands»[2], nothing can conceal the reality of South African conditions. I, as a Christian, have always felt that there is one thing above all about «apartheid» or «separate development» that is unforgivable. It seems utterly indifferent to the suffering of individual persons, who lose their land, their homes, their jobs, in the pursuit of what is surely the most terrible dream in the world. This terrible dream is not held on to by a crackpot group on the fringe of society or by Ku Klux Klansmen[3], of whom we have a sprinkling. It is the deliberate policy of a government, supported actively by a large part of the white population and tolerated passively by

1. Legislation permitting the division of residential land in South African cities into sections, each for one racial group.
2. Under the apartheid or «separate development» policy, Bantu «homelands» or Bantustans are areas set aside for Africans only, where, the theory goes, they can preserve their own culture and traditions.
3. Founded in 1915 in Georgia, the «modern» Ku Klux Klan, an anti-Negro, anti-Catholic, anti-Semitic organization, reached its peak of power in the U.S. in the mid-twenties; is now moribund.

an overwhelming white majority, but now fortunately rejected by an encouraging white minority who have thrown their lot with nonwhites, who
are overwhelmingly opposed to so-called separate development.

Thus it is that the golden age of Africa's independence is also the dark
age of South Africa's decline and retrogression, brought about by men who,
when revolutionary changes that entrenched fundamental human rights were
taking place in Europe, were closed in on the tip of South Africa–and so
missed the wind of progressive change.

In the wake of that decline and retrogression, bitterness between men
grows to alarming heights; the economy declines as confidence ebbs away;
unemployment rises; government becomes increasingly dictatorial and intolerant of constitutional and legal procedures, increasingly violent and sup-
pressive; there is a constant drive for more policemen, more soldiers, more
armaments, banishments without trial, and penal whippings. All the trap-
pings of medieval backwardness and cruelty come to the fore. Education is
being reduced to an instrument of subtle indoctrination; slanted and biased
reporting in the organs of public information, a creeping censorship, book-
banning, and blacklisting–all these spread their shadows over the land. This
is South Africa today, in the age of Africa's greatness.

But beneath the surface there is a spirit of defiance. The people of South
Africa have never been a docile lot, least of all the African people. We
have a long tradition of struggle for our national rights, reaching back to
the very beginnings of white settlement and conquest 300 years ago. Our
history is one of opposition to domination, of protest and refusal to submit
to tyranny. Consider some of our great names: the great warrior and nation-
builder Shaka, who welded tribes together into the Zulu nation from which
I spring; Moshoeshoe, the statesman and nation-builder who fathered the
Basuto nation and placed Basutoland beyond the reach of the claws of the
South African whites; Hintsa of the Xosas, who chose death rather than
surrender his territory to white invaders[1]. All these and other royal names,
as well as other great chieftains, resisted manfully white intrusion. Consider
also the sturdiness of the stock that nurtured the foregoing great names. I

1. Shaka [also Chaka] (?-1828), the «Black Napoleon», built the Zulu nation by
conquest between 1816 and 1828, when he was assassinated. Moshoeshoe [also Mos-
hesh] (c.1780-1870) fought off the Zulus and later signed an agreement with the
British, under whose protection and guidance Basutoland has been developing self-
government. Hintsa of the Gcaleka Xosas, a tribal chief, was killed when trying to
«escape» the English in 1835.

refer to our forbears, who, in trekking from the north to the southernmost tip of Africa centuries ago, braved rivers that are perennially swollen; hacked their way through treacherous jungle and forest; survived the plagues of the then untamed lethal diseases of a multifarious nature that abounded in Equatorial Africa; and wrested themselves from the gaping mouths of the beasts of prey. They endured it all. They settled in these parts of Africa to build a future worthwhile for us, their offspring. While the social and political conditions have changed and the problems we face are different, we too, their progeny, find ourselves facing a situation where we have to struggle for our very survival as human beings. Although methods of struggle may differ from time to time, the universal human strivings for liberty remain unchanged. We, in our situation, have chosen the path of nonviolence of our own volition. Along this path we have organized many heroic campaigns. All the strength of progressive leadership in South Africa, all my life and strength, have been given to the pursuance of this method, in an attempt to avert disaster in the interests of South Africa, and [we] have bravely paid the penalties for it.

It may well be that South Africa's social system is a monument to racialism and race oppression, but its people are the living testimony to the unconquerable spirit of mankind. Down the years, against seemingly overwhelming odds, they have sought the goal of fuller life and liberty, striving with incredible determination and fortitude for the right to live as men–free men. In this, our country is not unique. Your recent and inspiring history, when the Axis powers overran most European states, is testimony of this unconquerable spirit of mankind. People of Europe formed resistance movements that finally helped to break the power of the combination of Nazism and Fascism, with their creed of race arrogance and Herrenvolk mentality.

Every people has, at one time or another in its history, been plunged into such struggle. But generally the passing of time has seen the barriers to freedom going down, one by one. Not so South Africa. Here the barriers do not go down. Each step we take forward, every achievement we chalk up, is cancelled out by the raising of new and higher barriers to our advance. The color bars do not get weaker; they get stronger. The bitterness of the struggle mounts as liberty comes step by step closer to the freedom fighter's grasp. All too often the protests and demonstrations of our people have been beaten back by force; but they have never been silenced.

Through all this cruel treatment in the name of law and order, our people, with a few exceptions, have remained nonviolent. If today this peace award is given to South Africa through a black man, it is not because we in South Africa have won our fight for peace and human brotherhood. Far from it. Perhaps we stand farther from victory than any other people in Africa. But nothing which we have suffered at the hands of the government has turned us from our chosen path of disciplined resistance. It is for this, I believe, that this award is given.

How easy it would have been in South Africa for the natural feelings of resentment at white domination to have been turned into feelings of hatred and a desire for revenge against the white community. Here, where every day, in every aspect of life every nonwhite comes up against the ubiquitous sign «Europeans Only» and the equally ubiquitous policeman to enforce it–here it could well be expected that a racialism equal to that of their oppressors would flourish to counter the white arrogance toward blacks. That it has not done so is no accident. It is because, deliberately and advisedly, African leadership for the past fifty years, with the inspiration of the African National Congress, which I had the honor to lead for the last decade or so until it was banned, had set itself steadfastly against racial vaingloriousness. We know that in so doing we passed up opportunities for an easy demagogic appeal to the natural passions of a people denied freedom and liberty; we discarded the chance of an easy and expedient emotional appeal. Our vision has always been that of a nonracial, democratic South Africa which upholds the rights of all who live in our country to remain there as *full* citizens, with equal rights and responsibilities with all others. For the consummation of this ideal we have labored unflinchingly. We shall continue to labor unflinchingly.

It is this vision which prompted the African National Congress to invite members of other racial groups who believe with us in the brotherhood of man and in the freedom of all people to join with us in establishing a nonracial, democratic South Africa. Thus the African National Congress in its day brought about the Congress Alliance and welcomed the emergence of the Liberal Party and the Progressive Party, who to an encouraging measure support these ideals.

The true patriots of South Africa, for whom I speak, will be satisfied with nothing less than the fullest democratic rights. In government we will not be satisfied with anything less than direct, individual adult suffrage and the right to stand for and be elected to all organs of government. In economic matters we will be satisfied with nothing less than equality of opportunity in every sphere, and the enjoyment by all of those heritages which form the resources of the country, which up to now have been appropriated on a racial «whites only» basis. In culture we will be satisfied with nothing less than the opening of all doors of learning in nonsegregated institutions on the sole criterion of ability. In the social sphere we will be satisfied with nothing less than the abolition of all racial bars. We do not demand these things for people of African descent alone. We demand them for all South Africans, white and black. On these principles we are uncompromising. To compromise would be an expediency that is most treacherous to democracy, for in the turn of events, the sweets of economic, political, and social privileges that are a monopoly of only one section of a community turn sour even in the mouths of those who eat them. Thus apartheid in practice is proving to be a monster created by Frankenstein. That is the tragedy of the South African scene.

Many spurious slogans have been invented in our country in an effort to redeem uneasy race relations – «trusteeship», «separate development», «race federation» and elsewhere, «partnership». These are efforts to sidetrack us from the democratic road, mean delaying tactics that fool no one but the unwary. No euphemistic naming will ever hide their hideous nature. We reject these policies because they do not measure up to the best mankind has striven for throughout the ages; they do great offense to man's sublime aspirations that have remained true in a sea of flux and change down the ages, aspirations of which the United Nations Declaration of Human Rights[1] is a culmination. This is what we stand for. This is what we fight for.

In their fight for lasting values, there are many things that have sustained the spirit of the freedom-loving people of South Africa and those in the yet unredeemed parts of Africa where the white man claims resolutely proprietary rights over democracy–a universal heritage. High among them –the things that have sustained us–stand: the magnificent support of the progressive people and governments throughout the world, among whom number the people and government of the country of which I am today guest; our brothers in Africa, especially in the independent African states; organizations who share the outlook we embrace in countries scattered right across the face of the globe; the United Nations Organization jointly and some of its member nations singly. In their defense of peace in the world through actively upholding the quality of man, all these groups have re-

1. Adopted by the General Assembly on December 10, 1948; for details, see presentation speech for Cassin and his Nobel lecture in 1968, pp. 385–407.

inforced our undying faith in the unassailable rightness and justness of our cause. To all of them I say: Alone we would have been weak. Our heartfelt appreciation of your acts of support of us we cannot adequately express, nor can we ever forget, now or in the future when victory is behind us and South Africa's freedom rests in the hands of all her people.

We South Africans, however, equally understand that, much as others might do for us, our freedom cannot come to us as a gift from abroad. Our freedom we must make ourselves. All honest freedom-loving people have dedicated themselves to that task. What we need is the courage that rises with danger.

Whatever may be the future of our freedom efforts, our cause is the cause of the liberation of people who are denied freedom. Only on this basis can the peace of Africa and the world be firmly founded. Our cause is the cause of equality between nations and peoples. Only thus can the brotherhood of man be firmly established. It is encouraging and elating to remind you that, despite her humiliation and torment at the hands of white rule, the spirit of Africa in quest for freedom has been, generally, for peaceful means to the utmost.

If I have dwelt at length on my country's race problem, it is not as though other countries on our continent do not labor under these problems, but because it is here in the Republic of South Africa that the race problem is most acute. Perhaps in no other country on the continent is white supremacy asserted with greater vigor and determination and a sense of righteousness. This places the opponents of apartheid in the front rank of those who fight white domination.

In bringing my address to a close, let me invite Africa to cast her eyes beyond the past and to some extent the present, with their woes and tribulations, trials and failures, and some successes, and see herself an emerging continent, bursting to freedom through the shell of centuries of serfdom. This is Africa's age—the dawn of her fulfillment, yes, the moment when she must grapple with destiny to reach the summits of sublimity, saying: Ours was a fight for noble values and worthy ends, and not for lands and the enslavement of man.

Africa is a vital subject matter in the world of today, a focal point of world interest and concern. Could it not be that history has delayed her rebirth for a purpose? The situation confronts her with inescapable challenges, but more importantly with opportunities for service to herself and mankind. She evades the challenges and neglects the opportunities, to her

shame, if not her doom. How she sees her destiny is a more vital and rewarding quest than bemoaning her past, with its humiliations and sufferings.

The address could do no more than pose some questions and leave it
to the African leaders and peoples to provide satisfying answers and responses
by their concern for higher values and by their noble actions that could
be

> *Footprints on the sands of time.*
> *Footprints, that perhaps another,*
> *Sailing o'er life's solemn main,*
> *A forlorn and shipwrecked brother,*
> *Seeing, shall take heart again.* [1]

Still licking the scars of past wrongs perpetrated on her, could she not be
magnanimous and practice no revenge? Her hand of friendship scornfully
rejected, her pleas for justice and fair play spurned, should she not nonetheless seek to turn enmity into amity? Though robbed of her lands, her
independence, and opportunities–this, oddly enough, often in the name of
civilization and even Christianity–should she not see her destiny as being
that of making a distinctive contribution to human progress and human
relationships with a peculiar new Africa flavor enriched by the diversity
of cultures she enjoys, thus building on the summits of present human
achievement an edifice that would be one of the finest tributes to the genius
of man?

She should see this hour of her fulfillment as a challenge to her to labor
on until she is purged of racial domination, and as an opportunity of re-
assuring the world that her national aspiration lies not in overthrowing white
domination to replace it by a black caste but in building a nonracial democracy that shall be a monumental brotherhood, a «brotherly community» with none discriminated against on grounds of race or color.

What of the many pressing and complex political, economic, and cultural
problems attendant upon the early years of a newly independent state?
These, and others which are the legacy of colonial days, will tax to the
limit the statesmanship, ingenuity, altruism, and steadfastness of African
leadership and its unbending avowal to democratic tenets in statecraft. To
us all, free or not free, the call of the hour is to redeem the name and
honor of Mother Africa.

1. From «A Psalm of Life» by Henry Wadsworth Longfellow (1807–1882), American
poet.

In a strife-torn world, tottering on the brink of complete destruction by man-made nuclear weapons, a free and independent Africa is in the making, in answer to the injunction and challenge of history: «Arise and shine for thy light is come.»[1] Acting in concert with other nations, she is man's last hope for a mediator between the East and West, and is qualified to demand of the great powers to «turn the swords into ploughshares»[2] because two-thirds of mankind is hungry and illiterate; to engage human energy, human skill, and human talent in the service of peace, for the alternative is unthinkable–war, destruction, and desolation; and to build a world community which will stand as a lasting monument to the millions of men and women, to such devoted and distinguished world citizens and fighters for peace as the late Dag Hammarskjöld, who have given their lives that we may live in happiness and peace.

Africa's qualification for this noble task is incontestable, for her own fight has never been and is not now a fight for conquest of land, for accumulation of wealth or domination of peoples, but for the recognition and preservation of the rights of man and the establishment of a truly free world for a free people.

1. Isaiah 60:1.
3. Isaiah 2:4.

Biography

Chief of his tribe and president-general of the African National Congress, Albert John Lutuli (1898?–July 21, 1967) was the leader of ten million black Africans in their nonviolent campaign for civil rights in South Africa. A man of noble bearing, charitable, intolerant of hatred, and adamant in his demands for equality and peace among all men, Lutuli forged a philosophical compatibility between two cultures–the Zulu culture of his native Africa and the Christian-democratic culture of Europe.

Lutuli was heir to a tradition of tribal leadership. His grandfather was chief of his small tribe at Groutville in the Umvoti Mission Reserve near Stanger, Natal, and was succeeded by a son. Lutuli's father was a younger son, John Bunyan Lutuli, who became a Christian missionary and spent most of the last years of his life in the missions among the Matabele of Rhodesia. Lutuli's mother, Mtonya Gumede, spent part of her childhood in the household of King Cetewayo but was raised in Groutville. She joined her husband in Rhodesia where her third son, Albert John, was born in what Lutuli calculates would probably have been 1898. Exactly when her husband died is not known, but by 1906 she and Albert John were back in Groutville.

Supported by a mother who was determined that he get an education, Albert John Lutuli[1] went to the local Congregationalist mission school for his primary work. He then studied at a boarding school called Ohlange Institute for two terms before transferring to a Methodist institution at Edendale, where he completed a teachers' course about 1917. After leaving a job as principal of an intermediate school, which he held for two years– he was also the entire staff, he says in his autobiography[2]–he completed the Higher Teachers' Training Course at Adams College, attending on a

1. Lutuli preferred the spelling of his name used here, although the commonly employed spelling, «Luthuli» appears to be a closer phonetic rendering; he also preferred his Zulu name «Mvumbi» (Continuous Rain) to that of Albert John. See Benson, *Chief Albert Lutuli of South Africa*, p. 3.
2. *Let My People Go*, p. 31.

scholarship. To provide financial support for his mother, he declined a scholarship to University College at Fort Hare and accepted an appointment at Adams, as one of two Africans to join the staff.

A professional educator for the next fifteen years, Lutuli then and afterwards contended that education should be made available to all Africans, that it should be liberal and not narrowly vocational in nature, and that its quality should be equal to that made available to white children. In 1928 he became secretary of the African Teacher's Association and in 1933 its president.

Lutuli was also active in Christian church work, being a lay preacher for many years. As an adviser to the organized church, he became chairman of the South African Board of the Congregationalist Church of America, president of the Natal Mission Conference, and an executive member of the Christian Council of South Africa. He was a delegate to the International Missionary Conference in Madras in 1938 and in 1948 spent nine months on a lecture tour of the United States, sponsored by two missionary organizations.

In 1927 Lutuli married a fellow teacher, Nokukhanya Bhengu. They established their permanent home in Groutville, where in 1929 the first of their seven children was born. In 1933 the tribal elders asked Lutuli to become chief of the tribe. For two years he hesitated, for he was loath to give up his profession and the financial security it afforded. He accepted the call in early 1936 and, until removed from this office by the government in 1952, devoted himself for the next seventeen years to the 5,000 people who made up his tribe. He performed the judicial function of a magistrate, the mediating function of an official acting as representative of his people and at the same time as representative of the central government, the tribal function of a presiding dignitary at traditional festivities, and the executive function of a leader seeking a better life for his people.

As the restrictions imposed by the Union government on nonwhites became increasingly complete, Lutuli's concern for his race transcended the tribal level to encompass the welfare of all black South Africans, and indeed of all South Africans. In 1936 the government disenfranchised the only Africans who had had voting rights–those in Cape Province; in 1948 the Nationalist Party, in control of the government, adopted the policy of «apartheid», or total «apartness»; in the 1950's the laws known as the Pass Laws, circumscribing the freedom of movement of Africans, were tighten ed; and throughout this period laws were added which put limitations on the African in almost every aspect of his life[1].

In 1944 Lutuli joined the African National Congress (ANC), an organization somewhat analogous to the American NAACP[2], whose objective was to secure universal enfranchisement and the legal observance of human rights. In 1945 he was elected to the Committee of the Natal Provincial Division of ANC and in 1951 to the presidency of the Division. The next year he joined with other ANC leaders in organizing nonviolent campaigns to defy discriminatory laws. The government, charging Lutuli with a conflict of interest, demanded that he withdraw his membership in ANC or forfeit his office as tribal chief. Refusing to do either voluntarily, he was dismissed from his chieftainship, for chiefs hold office at the pleasure of the government even though elected by tribal elders.

A month later Lutuli was elected president-general of ANC. Responding immediately, the government sought to minimize his effectiveness as a leader by banning him from the larger South African centers and from all public meetings for two years. Upon the expiration of that ban, he went to Johannesburg to address a meeting but at the airport was served with a second ban confining him to a twenty-mile radius of his home for another two years. When this second ban expired, he attended an ANC conference in 1956, only to be arrested and charged with treason a few months later, along with 155 others. After being held in custody for about a year during the preliminary hearings, he was released in December, 1957, and the charges against him and sixty-four others were dropped.

Lutuli's return to active leadership in 1958 was cut short by the imposition of a third ban, this time a five-year ban prohibiting him from publishing anything and confining him to a fifteen-mile radius of his home. The ban was temporarily lifted while he testified at the continuing treason trials (which ended with a verdict in 1961 absolving ANC of Communist subservience and of plotting the violent overthrow of the government). It was lifted again in March, 1960, to permit his arrest for publicly burning his pass–a gesture of solidarity with those demonstrators against the Pass Laws who had died in the Sharpeville «massacre». The Pan-Africanist Congress, not the African National Congress, had called the demonstration, but in the ensuing state of emergency that was officially declared, Parliament outlawed both

1. For a brief account of Lutuli's struggle against apartheid see Callan, *Albert John Luthuli and the South African Race Conflict*.
2. Noted by C. and M. Legum, *The Bitter Choice*, p. 50.

organizations and apprehended their leaders. Lutuli was found guilty, fined, given a jail sentence that was suspended because of the precarious state of his health, and returned to the isolation of Groutville. One final time the ban was lifted, this time for ten days in early December of 1961 to permit Lutuli and his wife to attend the Nobel Peace Prize ceremonies in Oslo.

A fourth ban to run for five years confining Lutuli to the immediate vicinity of his home was issued in May, 1964, the day before the expiration of the third ban. Still, Lutuli remained undiminished in the public mind. The South African Colored People's Congress nominated him for president, the National Union of South African Students made him its honorary president, the students of Glasgow University voted him their rector, the New York City Protestant Council conferred an award on him. Despite the publication ban, his autobiography circulated in the outside world, and his name appeared on human rights petitions presented to the UN.

For fifteen years or so before his death, Lutuli suffered from high blood pressure and once had a slight stroke. With age, his hearing and eyesight also became impaired—perhaps a factor in his death. For in July, 1967, at the age of sixty-nine, he was fatally injured when he was struck by a freight train as he walked on the trestle bridge over the Umvoti River near his home.

Selected Bibliography

Benson, Mary, *The African Patriots: The Story of the African National Congress in South Africa.* New York, Encyclopaedia Britannica Press, 1964.

Benson, Mary, *Chief Albert Lutuli of South Africa.* London, Oxford University Press, 1963.

Callan, Edward, *Albert John Luthuli and the South African Race Conflict.* Rev. ed. Kalamazoo, Michigan, Institute of International and Area Studies, Western Michigan University, 1965.

Current Biography, 1962.

«Foe of Apartheid», the *New York Times* (October 24, 1961) 22.

Gordimer, Nadine, «Chief Luthuli», *Atlantic Monthly,* 203 (April, 1959) 34–39.

Italiaander, Rolf, *Die Friedensmacher: Drei Neger erhielten den Friedens-Nobelpreis.* Kassel, W.Germany, Oncken, 1965.

Legum, Colin and Margaret, «Albert Lutuli: Zulu Chief, Nobel Peace Prize Winner», in *The Bitter Choice: Eight South Africans' Resistance to Tyranny,* pp.47–72. New York, World, 1968.

Lutuli, Albert John, «Freedom is the Apex.» Cape Town, South African Congress of Democrats, [1960?].

Lutuli, Albert John, *Let My People Go: An Autobiography*. Prepared for publication by Charles and Sheila Hooper. Johannesburg and London, Collins, 1962. Lutuli's life story to 1959; in later printings, sixteen pages, written no earlier than 1964, have been added.

Lutuli, Albert John, «The Road to Freedom Is via the Cross.» Appendix A of *Let My People Go, q.v.* Public statement made after dismissal from his chieftainship by the government in 1952.

Lutuli, Albert John, «What I Would Do If I Were Prime Minister», *Ebony*, 17 (February, 1962) 21–29.

Lutuli, Albert John, and others, *Africa's Freedom*. London, Allen & Unwin, 1964.

Obituary, the *New York Times* (July 22, 1967) 1, 25.

Obituary, the (London) *Times* (July 22, 1967) 12.

Reeves, Ambrose, *Shooting at Sharpeville*, with a Foreword by Chief Luthuli. London, Gollancz, 1960.

Sampson, Anthony, «The Chief», in *The Treason Cage: The Opposition on Trial in South Africa*, pp. 185–197. London, Heinemann, 1958.

Peace 1961

DAG HJALMAR AGNE CARL
HAMMARSKJÖLD

Presentation

by Gunnar Jahn*, Chairman of the Nobel Committee

The Nobel Committee of the Norwegian Parliament has awarded the Peace Prize for 1961 posthumously to Dag Hammarskjöld.

Dag Hammarskjöld was born in 1905, and prior to his appointment as secretary-general to the Secretariat of the United Nations in 1953, he had been associated with the administration of his native Sweden ever since the completion of his education.

He had studied widely, and his knowledge ranged far beyond his chosen field. His special subject, however, was regarded as economics, in which he took his doctor's degree in 1934, with a thesis entitled «Konjunkturspridningen»[1]. He had by then already obtained degrees in philology and in law. In 1936 he entered the Swedish Ministry of Finance, and from 1941 to 1948, he was chairman of the Board of the Swedish Riksbank. In 1945 he became government adviser on trade policy and financial policy and in 1947 joined the Swedish Foreign Office. In 1951 he was appointed a consultative cabinet minister. But as he himself pointed out, he was committed to no particular party, and his cabinet appointment was a professional rather than a political one. In addition to leading various Swedish financial delegations in negotiations with other countries–primarily in connection with trade agreements–he also represented Sweden in UNISCAN[2] negotiations and was for a time vice-chairman of OEEC[3].

* Mr. Jahn delivered this speech on December 10, 1961, in the Auditorium of the University of Oslo, following his presentation of the Peace Prize for 1960 to Mr. Lutuli. At its conclusion he presented the Peace Prize for 1961 to Swedish Ambassador Rolf Edberg as representative of the Hammarskjöld family, five of whose members were present. The English translation of Mr. Jahn's speech is, with certain editorial changes made after collation with the Norwegian text, that published in *Les Prix Nobel en 1961*, which also contains the Norwegian text.

1. Translated in Richard I. Miller, *Dag Hammarskjöld and Crisis Diplomacy* (p. 15), as «Expansion of Market Trends».
2. UNISCAN (United Kingdom-Scandinavia) was a free trade project of the countries concerned, promoted in the early 1950's.
3. OEEC (Organization for European Economic Cooperation), established in 1948,

A brief recapitulation of this kind tells us little about Dag Hammarskjöld the man; nor does his well-merited reputation as a person of outstanding intellectual ability shed much light on his personality. So many men receive this tribute. Those of us who knew him before he became the secretary-general were also impressed by this young man's wide knowledge and indefatigability, as well as by his quiet and unassuming approach to his administrative duties in the service of his country.

In 1953 he assumed his post as secretary-general in the United Nations Secretariat. He had already come into contact with the United Nations as a member and vice-chairman of the Swedish delegation to the General Assembly in 1951 and as chairman of the delegation in 1952. As secretary-general he succeeded Mr. Trygve Lie [1], who had not only built up the United Nations administration and participated in planning its new building, but had also given the post of secretary-general a more important and in-dependent position within the United Nations than had probably been originally envisaged. In other words, he took over an office which had already been given form and an administrative apparatus which had acquired a certain amount of tradition.

There is no doubt that in accepting this high office Dag Hammarskjöld fully realized that the years ahead would not prove easy. He was all too familiar with the difficulties Trygve Lie had encountered to have any il-lusions on that score. Fully aware of the magnitude and complexity of his task, he devoted himself to it completely, exerting all his determination and strength in carrying it out. In a private letter written in 1953 he says: «To know that the goal is so significant that everything else must be set aside gives a great sense of liberation and makes one indifferent to anything that may happen to oneself.»

It has often been said that from the very first he wished to play the role of adviser rather than that of politician, or we might say that he preferred to be the one carrying out what others had decided rather than the one who made the decision.

As far as I can judge, this appraisal is not correct. From the beginning,

helped to coordinate the European Recovery Program and to liberalize trade restric-tions in Western Europe; it was superseded in 1961 by OECD (Organization for Economic Cooperation and Development).
1. Trygve Lie (1896–1968), Norwegian lawyer and statesman; chief representative of the Norwegian delegation at the organizing conference of the UN (1945); chairman of the commission that drafted the Charter; first UN secretary-general (1946–1953).

back in 1953, when he outlined the role and activities of the Secretariat and the secretary-general, he laid down that, while it is clearly the duty of the Secretariat and of the secretary-general to obtain complete and objective information on the aims and problems of the various member nations, the secretary-general must personally form an opinion; he must base it on the rules of the UN Charter and must never for a moment betray those rules, even if this means being at variance with members of the UN.

From the very first he placed great importance on the solution of disputes through the medium of private discussion between representatives of the individual countries, pursuing what has come to be known as «the method of quiet diplomacy». There is, of course, nothing new in this, as informal meetings of this kind have always been and will always be an important part of the work necessary to achieve agreement between conflicting views.

Outwardly it may have looked as if he became more and more active as time went on, but this, I believe, can be ascribed more to the course of events than to any change in his views. In every situation with which he was faced he had one goal in mind: to serve the ideas sponsored by the United Nations. He called himself «an international civil servant», with the emphasis on the word «international»[1]. As such he had only one master, and that was the United Nations.

There can be little doubt that Dag Hammarskjöld achieved a great deal through the informal meetings he took part in, and that in these he demonstrated strong personal initiative; yet his personal contribution was best known to the general public in cases where attempts to reach agreement between members in the United Nations had failed, or where the instructions he had received were not sufficiently clear, and he was compelled personally to point the way, as we shall see. It is impossible to mention in detail the many areas in which he intervened and on which he left his mark during the time he was secretary-general.

The first and most important disputes which fell to his lot to settle arose in the Middle East. The first of these was the conflict between Israel and the Arab States in 1955. As the representative of the UN, he succeeded in easing the tension by negotiating an agreement between each of the parties involved and the UN, setting up demarcation lines and establishing UN observation

1. See, for example, Hammarskjöld's lecture, «The International Civil Servant in Law and in Fact», delivered at Oxford University, May 30, 1961, in Foote, *Servant of Peace*, pp. 329–349.

posts. Personally he did not believe that the relaxation of tension would prove permanent, and he was right in his surmise.

In the following year, in September of 1956, the conflict that arose between Great Britain, France, and Egypt, after Egypt had nationalized the Suez Canal[1], was submitted to the Security Council. In October, 1956, Dag Hammarskjöld tried to find a solution to this dispute through private negotiations conducted by himself, and it looked as if these would lead to a satisfactory result. But at the end of October, 1956, Israel attacked Egypt, and on October 30 the Security Council was called together to deal with the situation that had arisen. This meeting, however, proved abortive when France and Great Britain exercised their veto right to obstruct a resolution calling on Israel to withdraw her troops. On the next day, October 31, France and Great Britain launched their attack on Egypt. At the meeting of the Security Council on October 31, Hammarskjöld was the first person to speak. In a forthright speech he hinted that he would resign unless all member states honored their pledge to abide by all clauses of the Charter.

On October 31 the General Assembly was then convoked, and on November 1 passed a resolution calling on the parties concerned to terminate hostilities immediately and requesting the Secretary-General to keep a close watch on the course of events and to report on the way in which the resolution was being implemented. In reality the Secretary-General was thus vested with far-reaching powers. On November 3 Hammarskjöld was already able to announce that France and Great Britain were willing to suspend hostilities, provided that Israel and Egypt were prepared to accept the establishment of a UN force to ensure and supervise the suspension of hostilities and subsequently to prevent the violation of the Egyptian-Israeli border. The result was that the war was brought to an end, a demarcation line was fixed, and a UN force was established to guard it.

He also made a major contribution to the solution of a crisis between Lebanon, Jordan, and the Arab States in 1958. In this, both the United States and Great Britain were involved.

During these crises, all his qualities were given full scope, particularly his ability to negotiate and to act swiftly and firmly; and to Dag Hammarskjöld must go the principal credit for the fact that all these crises were resolved in the spirit of the United Nations. A state of peace was established in this area.

1. For details of this and other conflicts mentioned, see Miller, *Dag Hammarskjöld and Crisis Diplomacy*.

This was a triumph for the ideal of peace of which the UN is an expression, and in addition undoubtedly greatly strengthened the position of the Secretary-General.

The concept of peace contained in the UN Charter was always to remain Dag Hammarskjöld's guiding principle in tackling such problems as that presented by the liberation of the Congo on June 30, 1960.

There is no time to deal here with all the problems confronting the United Nations in connection with the termination of colonial rule. I must restrict myself to the role which the United Nations was to play in the Congo. When the Congo achieved its independence on June 30, 1960, it was constituted as a unified state. Kasavubu[1] was elected president and Lumumba[2] was made prime minister. Lumumba had always supported the idea of a unified Congo.

The new government was faced with a difficult situation: the administration, which had been in Belgian hands, had broken down; the army had mutinied; a large proportion of the white population had fled; Belgian troops had intervened–in part to protect the white inhabitants; and on July 11 the province of Katanga declared itself an independent state.

All these factors–the collapse of the administration, the mutiny of the armed forces, and finally Katanga's secession from the rest of the Congo– form the background for the request made to the UN by Kasavubu and Lumumba on July 11 for civil assistance and on July 12 for military aid. In a cable dispatched on July 13, Lumumba emphasized that UN military assistance was needed to protect the Congo against an attack by Belgian troops.

Hammarskjöld was in a position to grant the Congo's request for civil aid without referring the case to the Security Council; military aid, however, could be given only by decision of the Security Council, which he summoned on July 13.

This meeting is highly important, for it marks a turning point in the history of the UN. It was the first time that the UN used armed force to intervene actively in the solution of a problem involving the termination of

1. Joseph Kasavubu (1917?–1969), African political leader who favored a Congolese federation rather than a strong central government.
2. Patrice Emergy Lumumba (1925–1961), African political leader who supported strong central government, was out of office two months later and eventually imprisoned in Katanga; killed there in 1961 by parties still unknown, he was considered a martyr by his followers.

colonial rule. In the resolution unanimously adopted by the Security Council, Belgium was ordered to withdraw her troops from Congo territory, and the Secretary-General was authorized in consultation with the Congo government to provide whatever military aid proved necessary until such time as the country's own forces were, in the opinion of the Congo government, in a position to carry out their functions.

The military aid made available to the Congo consisted of contingents from African nations and from neutral Sweden and Ireland. No troops from the Eastern bloc or from the old colonial powers were included. The UN force was to function as a noncombatant peace force; there was to be no intervention in disputes involving matters of internal policy, and arms were to be used only in self-defense.

This form of military aid did not meet the expectations of the Congo government, which had clearly envisaged the expulsion of Belgian troops by UN forces; whereas the UN's action was taken on the assumption that Belgium would comply with the order of the Security Council and withdraw her troops from the Congo.

This Belgium failed to do, despite the fact that a note of July 14 addressed to the Congo government announced that Belgian troops would be withdrawn to two bases in Katanga as soon as UN forces had succeeded in establishing law and order.

Thus, during these first few days, UN intervention had not brought about the result Lumumba had anticipated. The Belgian troops remained in their bases in Katanga, and fresh Belgian troops were dispatched to the Congo.

As a consequence, during the period from July 14 to July 20, 1960, Lumumba made some highly unexpected moves. First of all, as early as July 14 he sent a cable to Khrushchev[1], announcing the possibility of asking for Russian aid if the Western powers continued their aggression against the Congo. On July 15 he had already received an encouraging reply from Khrushchev.

With that, the Congo crisis became a factor in the East-West conflict, rendering the position of Hammarskjöld and the UN in the Congo immensely difficult.

As the days and months went by, their position became no easier. All conceivable obstacles to the success of the UN's Congo venture seemed to pile up: disagreement among the Congolese themselves on the question of

1. Nikita Sergeyevich Khrushchev (1894–1971), Russian premier (1958–1964).

unified state or confederation, the support Katanga received from Belgium, Soviet aid to Lumumba, the dissolution of the central government, the military rule under Mobutu[1], the murder of Lumumba, increasingly violent Russian attacks on Hammarskjöld and UN action. A complete account of all that occurred cannot be given here; but an examination of the available documents covering this period will establish that it was the United Nations alone that worked to realize the establishment of the Republic of the Congo as an independent nation, and that the man who above all others deserves the credit for this is Dag Hammarskjöld. Time and again, in the Security Council and in the meetings of the General Assembly, he fought in defense of his policy and carried the day. He insisted throughout that all aid to the Congo – civil as well as military – must be made available through the medium of the UN. No vested interests representing any of the power blocs must be allowed to exert their influence. Is it then surprising that he was the object of attack, at times from the West but most often and most violently from the Soviet Union, whose charges took the form of an assault on the very idea of the United Nations Organization as a separate power? In the calm and dignified answer which Dag Hammarskjöld made to the Soviet leaders, he said that he would remain at his post as long as this was necessary to defend and strengthen the authority of the United Nations. And he added: It is not Soviet Russia or any of the great powers that need the vigilance and protection of the UN; it is all the others[2].

But he was not destined to live long enough to pursue his policy to its conclusion.

We all know that he perished on his way to a meeting which he hoped would bring an end to the fighting in the Congo between Katanga troops and UN forces, which had just broken out during the attempt to implement the UN resolution of February 21, 1961. This resolution called on UN military forces to take immediate steps to prevent a civil war in the Congo, and to use force only as a last resort. The UN was furthermore enjoined to ensure that all Belgian and other foreign military, political, and other advisers not under UN command should be withdrawn immediately.

1. Joseph Désiré Mobutu (1930–   ), commander of the Congolese army and «front man» of the military regime (September, 1960–February, 1961) set up after the crisis precipitated by Lumumba; became president of the Democratic Republic of the Congo in 1965.
2. See «I Shall Remain in My Post», Statement to the General Assembly, 3 October 1960, in Foote, op.cit., p.319.

Hammarskjöld left for the Congo on September 12, at the invitation of the Congolese government, to discuss the range and details of the UN's program of aid to the Congo. When Dag Hammarskjöld left New York, he knew that the situation in Katanga was difficult, but it was not until he received Dr.Linner's report on September 14 that he learned that Katanga forces and UN troops were fighting one another[1].

Attempts to conclude a truce during the first few days of his visit proved unsuccessful; so Dag Hammarskjöld decided to establish personal contact with the President of Katanga, Tshombe[2]; his purpose, as he explained in a message to Tshombe, was to find the means of settling the immediate conflict in a peaceful manner and thus open the way to a solution of the Katanga problem within the framework of the Congolese state.

The meeting never took place. Dag Hammarskjöld's plane crashed on September 18 on its way to Tshombe. He and all the others aboard perished.

Then–and not till then–criticism of Hammarskjöld and UN policy in the Congo was silenced, but during the period from September 13 to 18, operations in the province of Katanga were severely criticized, this time in Western quarters, with the strongest assault coming from certain English Conservative newspapers.

Dag Hammarskjöld was exposed to criticism and violent, unrestrained attacks, but he never departed from the path he had chosen from the very first: the path that was to result in the UN's developing into an effective and constructive international organization, capable of giving life to the principles and aims expressed in the UN Charter, administered by a strong Secretariat served by men who both felt and acted internationally. The goal he always strove to attain was to make the UN Charter the one by which all countries regulated themselves.

Today this goal may seem remote; as we know, it is remote. Dag Hammarskjöld fully realized this, and in a speech in Chicago in 1960 he said:

1. After landing in Léopoldville and being ceremoniously welcomed by Congolese dignitaries, the laureate went to the home of Sture Linner, head of the UN mission in the Congo, who gave him his first news of the fighting that had begun during his flight to Africa.
2. Moise (Kependa) Tshombe (1919–1969), African political leader whose opposition to strong central government resulted in Katanga's secession from the Democratic Republic of the Congo; signed a cease-fire between Katanga and UN troops a few days after the plane crash, dedicating it to Hammarskjöld. Under UN pressure, Katanga was reintegrated with the Republic in 1963, and Tshombe became premier of the Republic (1964–1965).

«Working at the edge of the development of human society is to work on the brink of the unknown. Much of what is done will one day prove to have been of little avail. That is no excuse for the failure to act in accordance with our best understanding, in recognition of its limits but with faith in the ultimate result of the creative evolution in which it is our privilege to cooperate.»[1]

His driving force was his belief that goodwill among men and nations would one day create conditions in which peace would prevail in the world.

The Nobel Committee of the Norwegian Parliament has today awarded him the Peace Prize for 1961 posthumously in gratitude for all he did, for what he achieved, for what he fought for: to create peace and goodwill among nations and men.

Let us stand in tribute to the memory of Dag Hammarskjöld.

1. These sentences conclude «The Development of a Constitutional Framework for International Cooperation», a speech delivered at the dedication ceremonies of the new buildings of the University of Chicago Law School, May 1, 1960. In Foote, *op. cit.*, pp. 251–260.

Acceptance

by Rolf Edberg*, Swedish Ambassador to Norway

It is with infinite sadness that I have received, at the request of the adminis-
trators of the estate of Dag Hammerskjöld, the prize for the year 1961
awarded posthumously to a friend and fellow countryman.

How thankful I should be if I could present to you what he himself would
have thought and said, were he standing here today.

Surely he would have seen it as symbolic to be called to this stage – where
so much human goodwill has been honored – along with the South African
advocate of nonviolent liberation: two men of different origin and with
different starting points, but both striving toward the same goal.

My compatriot was much concerned with the awakening and fermenting
continent which was to become his destiny. He once said that the next
decade must belong to Africa or to the atom bomb. He firmly believed that
the new countries have an important mission to fulfill in the community of
nations. He therefore invested all his strength of will, and at the end more
than that, to smooth their road toward the future.

Africa was to be the great test for the philosophy he wished to see brought
to life through the United Nations.

Time and again he recurred to the indissoluble connection between peace
and human rights. Tolerance, protection by law, equal political rights, and
equal economic opportunities for all citizens were prerequisites for a harmonious life within a nation. They also became requirements for such a life
among nations.

He would remind us how man once organized himself in families, how
families joined together in tribes and villages, and how tribes and villages
developed into peoples and nations. But the nation could not be the end of

---

* At the award ceremony on December 10, 1961, after Mr.Lutuli had accepted his
Peace Prize, Swedish Ambassador to Norway Rolf Edberg, representing the Ham-
marskjöld family, accepted the Peace Prize for 1961 awarded posthumously to Dag
Hammarskjöld. The English translation of his speech is, with some editorial emenda-
tions, basically that appearing in *Les Prix Nobel en 1961*, which also carries the original
Swedish text.

such development. In the Charter of the United Nations he saw a guide to what he called an organized international community.

With an intensity that grew stronger each year, he stressed in his annual reports to the General Assembly that the United Nations had to be shaped into a dynamic instrument in the service of development. In his last report, in a tone of voice penetrating because of its very restraint, he confronted those member states which were clinging to «the time-honored philosophy of sovereign national states in armed competition, of which the most that may be expected is that they achieve a peaceful coexistence»[1]. This philosophy did not meet the needs of a world of ever increasing interdependence, where nations have at their disposal armaments of hitherto unknown destructive strength. The United Nations must open up ways to more developed forms of international cooperation.

He dated this report August 17 of this year. It now stands as a last testament.

He found the words of the Charter concerning equal rights for all nations, large and small, filled with life and significance. Above all, it was the small nations, and especially the developing countries, which needed the United Nations for their protection and their future. This was why he refused to step down and to throw the organization to the winds when one of the large nations demanded his resignation[2].

It was impossible to witness that scene at the stormy session of last year's General Assembly without recalling some words that he once wrote about his own father. «A man of firm convictions does not ask, and does not receive, understanding from those with whom he comes into conflict»[3], he wrote about Hjalmar Hammarskjöld. «A mature man is his own judge. In the end, his only firm support is being faithful to his own convictions.»[4]

How aptly these words applied to himself when he rose unhesitatingly to defend the idea of a truly international body of civil servants or to uphold the principles of the Charter in the Congo operation!

1. Introduction to the *Annual Report 1960–1961* in Foote, *Servant of Peace*, p.355.
2. The Soviet Union, criticizing Hammarskjöld's actions in the Congo and charging him with bias, suggested in the UN General Assembly on September 23, 1960, that the office of secretary-general be replaced by a committee of three, and on October 3, 1960, repeating the charges, called for Hammarskjöld's resignation. For Hammarskjöld's replies, including his refusal to resign, see Foote, *op.cit.*, pp.314–319.
3. From his inaugural address to the Swedish Academy, December 20, 1954, when he took the seat left vacant by his father's death. Foote, *op.cit.*, p.64.
4. *Ibid.*, p.76.

If he felt any uneasiness, then it was because questions dealing with the peace and welfare of peoples were being treated in an overheated atmosphere. And an eyewitness, looking at him sitting there, deeply serious, with the fingers of his right hand against his cheek, as they always were when he was listening intently, might find himself asking this question: What does he represent, that slender man up there behind the green marble desk? A tradition of polished quiet diplomacy doomed to drown in the rising tide of new clamor? Or is he, with his visions of a world community, a herald of the future?

The latter is what we would like to believe. He himself had no doubt about the convincing force of his ideals. He expressed it thus in the last article that he wrote: «Setbacks in trying to realize the ideal do not prove that the ideal is at fault.»

Such a conviction must be based on a determined philosophy of life. No one who met him could help noticing that he had a room of quiet within himself[1]. Probably no one was ever able really to reach into that room.

But perhaps we can think that he found something that was essential to himself in the last book that he was engaged in translating, the powerful work *Ich und Du* [I and Thou], in which the Jewish philosopher Martin Buber[2] sets forth his belief that all real living is meeting. He himself believed that there were invisible bridges on which people could meet as human beings above the confines of ideologies, races, and nations.

And perhaps we may dare to see something significant in the obscurity and seeming futility of what happened on that African September night. Scattered about in the debris of the airplane were some books. Among them was *Ich und Du*, with some pages just translated into Swedish. Just before the plane took off on its nocturnal flight, he had left behind with a friend Thomas à Kempis' *Imitation of Christ*[3]. Tucked in the pages was the oath of office of the Secretary-General:

1. Probably a reference to the UN Meditation Room (located off the public lobby of the General Assembly Hall), which the laureate designed, and to the inscription on its black marble plaque, which he wrote: This Is A Room Devoted To Peace And Those Who Are Giving Their Lives For Peace. It Is A Room Of Quiet Where Only Thoughts Should Speak. Hammarskjöld also wrote the text of the leaflet given to visitors. Its first sentence reads: «We all have within us a center of stillness surrounded by silence.»
2. Martin Buber (1878–1965), Austrian-born philosopher, writer, and Judaic scholar; after exile from Germany (1938), a professor at Hebrew University in Jerusalem.
3. Thomas à Kempis (c. 1380–1471), German Augustinian canon and writer.

«I, Dag Hammarskjöld, solemnly swear to exercise in all loyalty, discretion and conscience the functions entrusted to me as Secretary-General of the United Nations, to discharge these functions and regulate my conduct with the interest of the United Nations only in view...»

Had he stood here today, he would, I believe, have had something to say about service as a self-evident duty.

My fellow countryman became a citizen of the world. He was regarded as such by the people from whom he came. But on that cool autumn day of falling leaves when he was brought back to the Uppsala of his youth, he was ours again, he was back home. Shyly he had guarded his inner world, but at that moment the distance disappeared and we felt that he came very close to us.

Therefore, I can speak on behalf of an entire people when I submit our respectful thanks for the honor that has been bestowed today upon our fellow citizen, the greatest honor a man can have. The Peace Prize awarded to Dag Hammarskjöld will constitute a fund which will bear his name and which will be used for a purpose that was close to his heart.

Biography

Dag Hjalmar Agne Carl Hammarskjöld (July 29, 1905 – September 18, 1961) was the youngest of four sons of Agnes (Almquist) Hammarskjöld and Hjalmar Hammarskjöld, prime minister of Sweden, member of the Hague Tribunal, governor of Uppland, chairman of the Board of the Nobel Foundation. In a brief piece written for a radio program in 1953, Dag Hammarskjöld spoke of the influence of his parents: «From generations of soldiers and government officials on my father's side I inherited a belief that no life was more satisfactory than one of selfless service to your country–or humanity. This service required a sacrifice of all personal interests, but likewise the courage to stand up unflinchingly for your convictions. From scholars and clergymen on my mother's side I inherited a belief that, in the very radical sense of the Gospels, all men were equals as children of God, and should be met and treated by us as our masters in God. »[1]

Dag Hammarskjöld was, by common consent, the outstanding student of his day at Uppsala University where he took his degree in 1925 in the humanities, with emphasis on linguistics, literature, and history. During these years he laid the basis for his command of English, French, and German and for his stylistic mastery of his native language in which he developed something of the artist's touch. He was capable of understanding the poetry of the German Hermann Hesse and of the American Emily Dickinson; of taking delight in painting, especially in the work of the French Impressionists; of discoursing on music, particularly on the compositions of Beethoven; and in later years, of participating in sophisticated dialogue on Christian theology. In athletics he was a competent performer in gymnastics, a strong skier, a mountaineer who served for some years as the president of the Swedish Alpinist club. In short, Hammarskjöld was a Renaissance man.

His main intellectual and professional interest for some years, however, was political economy. He took a second degree at Uppsala in economics

1. Written for Edward R. Murrow's radio program, «This I Believe», and published in a book of the same name in 1954; reprinted in Foote, *Servant of Peace*, pp. 23–24.

in 1928, a law degree in 1930, and a doctoral degree in economics in 1934.

For one year, 1933, Hammarskjöld taught economics at the University of Stockholm. But both his own desire and his heritage led him to enter public service, to which he devoted thirty-one years–in Swedish financial affairs, Swedish foreign relations, and global international affairs. His success in his first position, that of secretary from 1930 to 1934 to a governmental commission on unemployment, brought him to the attention of the directors of the Bank of Sweden who made him the Bank's secretary in 1935. From 1936 to 1945, he held the post of undersecretary in the Ministry of Finance. From 1941 to 1948, thus overlapping the undersecretaryship by four years, he was placed at the head of the Bank of Sweden, the most influential financial structure in the country.

Hammarskjöld has been credited with having coined the term «planned economy»[1]. Along with his eldest brother, Bo, who was then undersecretary in the Ministry of Social Welfare, he drafted the legislation which opened the way to the creation of the present, so-called «welfare state». In the latter part of this period, he drew attention as an international financial negotiator for his part in the discussions with Great Britain on the postwar economic reconstruction of Europe, in his reshaping of the twelve-year-old United States-Swedish trade agreement, in his participation in the talks which organized the Marshall Plan, and in his leadership on the Executive Committee of the Organization for European Economic Cooperation.

Hammarskjöld's connection with the Swedish Ministry of Foreign Affairs began in 1946 when he became its financial adviser. In 1949 he was named to an official post in the Foreign Ministry and in 1951 became the deputy foreign minister, with cabinet rank, although he continued to remain aloof from membership in any political party. In foreign affairs he continued a policy of international economic cooperation. A diplomatic feat of this period was the avoiding of Swedish commitment to the cooperative military venture of the North Atlantic Treaty Organization while collaborating on the political level in the Council of Europe and on the economic level in the Organization of European Economic Cooperation.

Hammarskjöld represented Sweden as a delegate to the United Nations in 1949 and again from 1951 to 1953. Receiving fifty-seven votes out of sixty, Hammarskjöld was elected secretary-general of the United Nations in 1953 for a five-year term and reelected in 1957. Before turning to the world

1. Van Dusen, *Dag Hammarskjöld*, p. 57.

problems awaiting him, he established a firm base of operations. For his Secretariat of 4,000 people, he drew up a set of regulations defining their responsibilities to the international organization of which they were a part and affirming their independence from narrowly conceived national interests. In the six years after his first major victory of 1954–1955, when he personally negotiated the release of American soldiers captured by the Chinese in the Korean War, he was involved in struggles on three of the world's continents. He approached them through what he liked to call «preventive diplomacy» and while doing so sought to establish more independence and effectiveness in the post of secretary-general itself.

In the Middle East his efforts to ease the situation in Palestine and to resolve its problems continued throughout his stay in office. During the Suez Canal crisis of 1956, he exercised his own personal diplomacy with the nations involved; worked with many others in the UN to get the UN to nullify the use of force by Israel, France, and Great Britain following Nasser's commandeering of the Canal; and under the UN's mandate, commissioned the United Nations Emergency Force (UNEF)–the first ever mobilized by an international organization. In 1958 he suggested to the Assembly a solution to crises in Lebanon and Jordan and subsequently directed the establishment of the UN Observation Group in Lebanon and the UN Office in Jordan, bringing about the withdrawal of the American and British troops which had been sent there. In 1959 he sent a personal representative to Southeast Asia when Cambodia and Thailand broke off diplomatic relations, and another to Laos when problems arose there.

Out of these crises came procedures and tactics new to the UN–the use of the UNEF, employment of a UN «presence» in world trouble spots–and a steadily growing tendency to make the secretary-general the executive for operations for peace.

It was with these precedents established that the United Nations and Hammarskjöld took up the problems stemming from the new independence of various developing countries. The most dangerous of these, that of the newly liberated Congo, arose in July, 1960, when the new government there, faced with mutiny in its army, secession of its province of Katanga, and intervention of Belgian troops, asked the UN for help. The UN responded by sending a peace-keeping force, with Hammarskjöld in charge of operations.

When the situation deteriorated during the year that followed, Hammarskjöld had to deal with almost insuperable difficulties in the Congo and with criticism in the UN[1]. A last crisis for him came in September, 1961, when, arriving in Léopoldville to discuss details of UN aid with the Congolese government, he learned that fighting had erupted between Katanga troops and the noncombatant forces of the UN. A few days later, in an effort to secure a cease-fire, he left by air for a personal conference with President Tshombe of Katanga. Sometime in the night of September 17–18, he and fifteen others aboard perished when their plane crashed near the border between Katanga and North Rhodesia[2].

After his death, the publication in 1963 of his «journal» entitled *Markings* revealed the inner man as few documents ever have. The entries in this manuscript, Hammarskjöld wrote in a covering letter to his literary executor, constitute «a sort of ‹White Book› concerning my negotiations with myself–and with God». There is a delicate irony in this use of the language of the diplomat. The entries themselves are spiritual truths given artistic form. *Markings* contains many references to death, perhaps none more explicit or significant than this portion from the opening entries, written when he was a young man:

> *Tomorrow we shall meet,*
> *Death and I–.*
> *And he shall thrust his sword*
> *Into one who is wide awake.*[3]

Selected Bibliography

Aulén, Gustaf, *Dag Hammarskjöld's White Book: An Analysis of «Markings»*. Philadelphia, Fortress, 1969.

Cordier, Andrew W., and Kenneth L. Maxwell, eds., *Paths to World Order*. New York, Columbia University Press, 1967. Contains, among other Dag Hammarskjöld Memorial Lectures, «Motivations and Methods of Dag Hammarskjöld», by Andrew W. Cordier, pp. 1–21; «Dag Hammarskjöld: The Inner Person», by Henry P. van Dusen, pp. 22–44.

Cordier, Andrew W., and Wilder Foote, eds., *The Quest or Peace: The Dag Hammarskjöld*

1. The story of the UN Congo mission is told in some detail in the presentation speech.
2. Not all of the details of the crash are known; for in-depth discussions see Gavshon, *The Last Days of Dag Hammarskjöld* and Thorpe, *Hammarskjöld: Man of Peace.*
3. Hammarskjöld, *Markings*, p. 31.

Memorial Lectures. New York, Columbia University Press, 1965. Contains «The Dag Hammarskjöld Foundation», by Alva Myrdal, pp. vii–xi and, among other lectures, «Dag Hammarskjöld's Quest for Peace», by Mongi Slim, pp. 1–8; «The United Nations Operation in the Congo», by Ralph J. Bunche, pp. 119–138. This volume is published in shortened form under the title *Quest for Peace*, Racine, Wisc., The Johnson Foundation, 1965.

Current Biography, 1953.

Foote, Wilder, ed., *Servant of Peace: A Selection of the Speeches and Statements of Dag Hammarskjöld, Secretary-General of the United Nations 1953–1961*. New York, Harper & Row, 1962.

Gavshon, Arthur L., *The Last Days of Dag Hammarskjöld*. London, Barrie & Rockliff with Pall Mall Press, 1963.

Hammarskjöld, Dag, *Markings*, translated by Leif Sjöberg and W. H. Auden. London, Faber and Faber, 1964; New York, Knopf, 1964. Originally published in Swedish as *Vägmärken*. Stockholm, Bonniers, 1963.

Kelen, Emery, *Hammarskjöld*. New York, Putnam, 1966.

Kelen, Emery, ed., *Hammarskjöld: The Political Man*. New York, Funk & Wagnalls, 1968.

Lash, Joseph P., *Dag Hammarskjöld: Custodian of the Brushfire Peace*. Garden City, N.Y., Doubleday, 1961.

Miller, Richard I., *Dag Hammarskjöld and Crisis Diplomacy*. New York, Oceana Publications, 1961. Includes bibliographical references at the end of each chapter.

Obituary, the (London) *Times* (September 19, 1961) 13.

Obituary and other articles, the *New York Times* (September 19, 1961) 1, 14.

Paffrath, Leslie, «The Legacy of Dag Hammarskjöld», *Saturday Review* (July 24, 1965) 33, 49.

Settel, T. S., ed., *The Light and the Rock: The Vision of Dag Hammarskjöld*. New York, Dutton, 1966.

Simon, Charlie May, *Dag Hammarskjöld*. New York, Dutton, 1967.

Smith, Bradford, «Dag Hammarskjöld: Peace by Juridical Sanction», in *Men of Peace*, by Bradford Smith, pp. 310–345. Philadelphia, Lippincott, 1964.

Snow, C. P., «Dag Hammarskjöld», in *Variety of Men*, pp. 151–168. London, Macmillan, 1967.

Stolpe, Sven, *Dag Hammarskjöld: A Spiritual Portrait*, English translation by Naomi Walford. New York, Scribner, 1966. Originally published in Swedish as *Dag Hammarskjölds andliga väg*, 1965.

Thorpe, Deryck, *Hammarskjöld: Man of Peace*. Ilfracombe, England, Stockwell, 1969.

Van Dusen, Henry P., *Dag Hammarskjöld: The Statesman and His Faith*. New York, Harper & Row, 1967.

Peace 1962

(Prize awarded in 1963)

LINUS CARL PAULING

Presentation

Gunnar Jahn*, Chairman of the Nobel Committee

Shortly after the atomic bombs were exploded over Hiroshima and Naga-saki[1], Albert Einstein[2] made this statement:

«The time has come now, when man must give up war. It is no longer rational to solve international problems by resorting to war. Now that an atomic bomb, such as the bombs exploded at Hiroshima and Nagasaki, can destroy a city, kill all the people in a city, a small city the size of Minneapolis, say, we can see that we *must* now make use of man's powers of reason, in order to settle disputes between nations.

In accordance with the principles of justice we must develop international law, strengthen the United Nations, and have peace in the world from now on.»

At the time few people heeded these words of Albert Einstein's.

One man, however, never forgot them, the man we welcome among us today, the man whom the Nobel Committee of the Norwegian Parliament has selected for this year's award of the Peace Prize–Linus Carl Pauling, who ever since 1946 has campaigned ceaselessly, not only against nuclear weap-ons tests, not only against the spread of these armaments, not only against their very use, but against all warfare as a means of solving international conflicts.

Linus Pauling is a professor of chemistry; for thirty-nine years he has been on the staff of the California Institute of Technology in Pasadena, where he was made a professor in 1931. In addition to the Nobel Prize in Chemistry, his scientific achievements have won him many distinctions, medals, and

* Mr. Jahn delivered this speech on December 10, 1963, in the Auditorium of the University of Oslo and at its conclusion presented the Peace Prize for 1962 (reserved in that year) to Mr. Pauling. The laureate responded with a brief speech of acceptance. The English translation of Mr. Jahn's speech is, with certain editorial changes made after collation with the Norwegian text, basically that which appears in *Les Prix Nobel en 1963*.
1. Early in August, 1945, in the last days of WWII.
2. Albert Einstein (1879–1955), German-born American theoretical physicist and re-cipient of the Nobel Prize in Physics for 1921.

honors, both in his own country and abroad. His renown as a scientist is beyond dispute.

In 1946, at the request of Albert Einstein, Linus Pauling, together with seven other scientists, formed the Emergency Committee of Atomic Scientists, of which Einstein was chairman[1]. The most important task of this committee was to bring to the notice of people everywhere the tremendous change that had taken place in the world after the splitting of the atom and the production of the atomic bomb had become fact. In the words of the author Robert Jungk, «it was a crusade undertaken by men who were children in political affairs».[2]

The hope cherished by mankind that, once the Second World War was over, an age of peace and disarmament would follow, was not fulfilled. It was not long before differences between East and West emerged in all their stark reality, as the cooperation engendered in time of war crumbled and was replaced by suspicion and mutual fear of aggression.

The result was the armaments race between the two great powers, to see who could produce the most effective nuclear weapons. Gradually the «terror balance» became the tacitly accepted safeguard against war and a guarantee of peace.

It was in August, 1949, that the Soviet Union also succeeded in producing the atom bomb[3].

The armaments race created an atmosphere which not only made it difficult to work for the promotion of disarmament and peace but also threatened to muzzle freedom of speech.

Inevitably, the crusade lost impetus and faded away.

But Linus Pauling marched on; for him, retreat was impossible.

During the first few years, his aim was above all to prevent the hydrogen bomb from becoming a reality. In speeches and lectures he endeavored to open the eyes of his fellowmen to the catastrophe it represented. «This bomb», he declared, «may have a destructive effect, a hundred, a thousand, nay ten thousand times greater than that of the bombs dropped on Hiroshima and Nagasaki. Its effect will depend on how great the bomb is and at

1. The seven other scientists were Hans A. Bethe, Selig Hecht, Thorfin R. Hogness, Philip Morse, Leo Szilard, Harold C. Urey, Victor F. Weisskopf; a few others were added after 1946. The committee ceased activity in 1950.
2. Robert Jungk, *Brighter than a Thousand Suns*, p. 236.
3. In the text this sentence is footnoted as follows: «According to Elis Biörklund's book *Atompolitiken under ett decennium*, 1955, p. 61.»

what height above the earth it is exploded.» This statement was made as early as 1947, and subsequent tests with the hydrogen bomb proved the validity of his predictions.

On February 13, 1950, Pauling spoke to a large audience in Carnegie Hall in New York, this time in protest against the decision to produce the hydrogen bomb. His speech was subsequently published as a brochure entitled *The Ultimate Decision*.

He opened his speech by describing the consequences, should there be a major war involving hydrogen bombs: a thousand million men and women dead, and the earth's atmosphere permeated with toxic radioactive substances, from which no human being, animal, or plant would be safe.

He concludes as follows:

«The solution of the world's problem–the problem of atomic war–is that we must–we *must* bring law and order into the world as a whole...

Our political leaders impelled by the massed feelings of the people of the world must learn that *peace* is the important goal–a peace that reflects the spirit of true humanity, the spirit of the brotherhood of man.

It is not necessary that the social and economic systems in Russia be identical with that in the United States, in order that these two great nations can be at peace with one another. It is only necessary that the people of the United States and the people of Russia have respect for one another, a deep desire to work for progress, a mutual recognition that war has finally ruled itself out as the arbiter of the destiny of humanity. Once the people of the world express these feelings, the East and the West can reach a reasonable and equitable decision about all world affairs and can march together side by side, towards a more and more glorious future.»

This 1950 speech was followed by a series of talks and lectures on the same subject–what would happen if a major nuclear war broke out.

There were many, of course, who recognized the truth of Linus Pauling's warning, but at that time his words aroused no general response from the American public. Outside the ranks of scientists and peace organizations, he was then relatively unknown. And the people themselves? In the United States–as here in Norway at a later period–they found it most convenient to turn a deaf ear to his warnings.

The United States tested its first hydrogen bomb in November, 1952, and the Soviet Union followed suit in August, 1953 [1]. The cold war had now

1. In the text this sentence is footnoted as follows: «According to Elis Biörklund's book *Atompolitiken under ett decennium*, 1955, p.66.»

entered upon a still more uncompromising phase, but the voice of Linus Pauling was not to be silenced. Tireless and undaunted, and supported in his views by numerous scientists, he continued to draw attention to the fearful destruction and mass annihilation of human life that might result if hydrogen bombs were used. «There does not seem», he says, «to be any theoretical limit to the size of these weapons.»

Of the appeals launched at this time bearing Pauling's signature, the Mainau Declaration of July 15, 1955, is the best known. It was signed by fifty-two Nobel prizewinners, most of them scientists. The appeal is such an important document that I should like to quote it.

«We, the undersigned, are scientists of different countries, different creeds, different political persuasions. Outwardly, we are bound together only by the Nobel Prize, which we have been favored to receive. With pleasure we have devoted our lives to the service of science. It is, we believe, a path to a happier life for people. We see with horror that this very science is giving mankind the means to destroy itself. By total military use of weapons feasible today, the earth can be contaminated with radioactivity to such an extent that whole peoples can be annihilated. Neutrals may die thus as well as belligerents.

If war broke out among the great powers, who could guarantee that it would not develop into a deadly conflict? A nation that engages in a total war thus signals its own destruction and imperils the whole world.

We do not deny that perhaps peace is being preserved precisely by the fear of these weapons. Nevertheless, we think it is a delusion if governments believe that they can avoid war for a long time through the fear of these weapons. Fear and tension have often engendered wars. Similarly it seems to us a delusion to believe that small conflicts could in the future always be decided by traditional weapons. In extreme danger no nation will deny itself the use of any weapon that scientific technology can produce.

All nations must come to the decision to renounce force as a final resort of policy. If they are not prepared to do this, they will cease to exist.»

In the harsh political atmosphere then prevailing, it was not surprising that Linus Pauling gradually became isolated and ostracized, primarily on suspicion of being a Communist.

On several occasions during the 1950's, the authorities withheld his passport, even when he wished to travel abroad to attend conferences of a purely scientific nature, as for example in 1952. It is only fair to record that, upon making his application direct to Washington, he was granted his passport.

In 1955 Dr. Pauling appeared before a committee of the United States Senate that was investigating the work of the Passport Office. He was then questioned on his alleged associations with Communists or Communist sympathizers, a term which at that time was applied to many people. When asked whether he himself was a Communist, Linus Pauling repeated what he had so often declared under oath: that he was not a Communist, that he had not been a Communist, that he was not a crypto-Communist nor a theoretical Marxist, that he had never wittingly helped the Communist Party or followed the party line. The senator conducting the investigation remarked that it was his own impression that «it was the Communists who had followed Pauling's line». This was as far as the committee could get, and for a few years Pauling was left in peace.

Anyone familiar with Linus Pauling and his views, anyone who has heard him speak or has read his works, should know that he is by no means a Communist.

Meanwhile, as the United States, Great Britain, and the Soviet Union stepped up their nuclear tests, radioactive fallout in the earth's atmosphere increased.

Soon more and more scientists, alive to the dangerous effects of radioactive fallout on human health and hereditary factors, were protesting against these tests.

Linus Pauling was one of the first to perceive the danger, and from the middle of the 1950's he devoted the better part of his time and energy to his campaign against test explosions. He constantly maintained that these tests must be terminated by an agreement signed by the countries possessing the atomic bomb and the hydrogen bomb, and that the agreement must be enforced by means of effective international supervision.

It was during his struggle to end tests of nuclear weapons that Linus Pauling's name became well known all over the world – and also controversial.

In order to assess in terms of figures the effect radioactive fallout would have on future generations, Linus Pauling carried out his own investigations and calculations, calculations which he always submits with reservation, because of the many unknown factors involved.

Time and again he states: «Maybe my figures are many times too high, maybe they are many times too low.» But his calculations were supported by many others. I need only remind you of Albert Schweitzer's message[1] broadcast by the Oslo radio station on April 23, 1957.

The opposition Pauling encountered came first of all from two scientists, E. Teller[2] and W. F. Libby[3], of the U. S. Atomic Energy Commission.

They seem to differ not so much on the resultant calculations themselves as on the conclusion to be drawn from these calculations.

Teller and Libby readily admit that radioactive fallout is harmful, but they consider this fact relative, weighing it against the risk taken by being unable to secure ever more effective defensive armaments through nuclear tests.

Pauling's views on test explosions, on the other hand, are not dependent on whether there are few or many people who would suffer from radioactive fallout.

On May 15, 1957, in a speech to students at Washington University in St. Louis, he dealt with what was known about the effect of radioactivity on human hereditary factors. Among other things, he said: «I believe that no human being should be sacrificed to a project; and in particular I believe that no human being should be sacrificed to the project of perfecting nuclear weapons that could kill hundreds of millions of human beings, could devastate this beautiful world in which we live.»

It was after this speech that he drew up the appeal which, more than anything else, attracted the attention of the public. This appeal was signed by more than 2,000 American scientists and was later circulated and signed by over 8,000 foreign scientists, from forty-nine different countries.

In his book No More War!, published in 1958, Linus Pauling has described how he collected these signatures.

The petition was the result of the efforts of individual scientists. No organization was responsible for circulating the petition or gathering signatures. The whole job was done by a mere handful of people.

In January, 1958, Linus Pauling and his wife, Ava Helen Pauling, sub-

1. Albert Schweitzer (1875–1965), recipient of the Nobel Peace Prize for 1952, issued his «Declaration of Conscience», appealing for an end to testing of nuclear weapons, under the auspices of the Nobel Committee. See Pauling, No More War!, pp. 225–237.
2. Edward Teller (1908–   ), Hungarian-born American physicist who helped to develop both the A-bomb and the H-bomb; for his views on nuclear testing, see his book Our Nuclear Future: Facts, Dangers, and Opportunities, written in collaboration with Albert L. Latter, 1958.
3. Willard Frank Libby (1908–   ), American chemist and recipient of the Nobel Prize in Chemistry for 1960.

mitted the appeal, with its 11,021 signatures, to the secretary-general of the United Nations Organization, Dag Hammarskjöld. The Pauling Appeal reads as follows:

«We, the scientists whose names are signed below, urge that an international agreement to stop the testing of nuclear bombs be made now.

Each nuclear bomb test spreads an added burden of radioactive elements over every part of the world. Each added amount of radiation causes damage to the health of human beings all over the world and causes damage to the pool of human germ plasm such as to lead to an increase in the number of seriously defective children that will be born in future generations.

So long as these weapons are in the hands of only three powers, an agreement for their control is feasible. If testing continues, and the possession of these weapons spreads to additional governments, the danger of outbreak of a cataclysmic nuclear war through the reckless action of some irresponsible national leader will be greatly increased.

An international agreement to stop the testing of nuclear bombs now could serve as a first step toward a more general disarmament and the ultimate effective abolition of nuclear weapons, averting the possibility of a nuclear war that would be a catastrophe to all humanity.

We have in common with our fellowmen a deep concern for the welfare of all human beings. As scientists we have knowledge of the dangers involved and therefore a special responsibility to make those dangers known. We deem it imperative that immediate action be taken to effect an international agreement to stop the testing of all nuclear weapons.»

And then, in 1958, without entering into any prior agreement, the Soviet Union, followed by the United States and Great Britain, discontinued nuclear tests.

Just what effect the warnings of scientists–foremost among them Linus Pauling and Albert Schweitzer–may have had in this connection, would be difficult to say with any certainty. But there is no doubt that both of them, together with other scientists, have contributed to familiarizing people with the dangers nuclear tests involve; and every government is bound to take into consideration public opinion, whether openly expressed or not.

Pauling's campaign had aroused a tremendous amount of attention both at home and abroad.

Once again the Internal Security Subcommittee of the United States

Senate summoned him for interrogation. The first interview took place on June 21, 1960, and the second on October 11 of the same year.

At Pauling's request, the hearings were held in public, and the proceedings published for everyone to read.

The primary purpose of the subcommittee was to discover how the 11,000 signatures had been obtained. There were many who believed that the appeal was Communist inspired, and once again Linus Pauling found himself facing the old charge of communism.

Pauling answered every question frankly and clearly. Questioned on his own attitude to communism he said: «At a meeting in Pasadena, I testified under oath that a statement that I had prepared to the effect that I was not a Communist, never had been a Communist, and never had been associated with the Communist Party, was true.»

Later on in the course of the proceedings, he stated: «I would like to know more about Marxism than I know. I believe that we never can know too much about anything... I do not understand dialectical materialism, either. But I do not believe in censorship. I believe in freedom of publication.»

He gave the subcommittee all the facts on how the appeal signed by the 11,021 scientists came about.

But when the subcommittee asked to be supplied with a list of names of those who had assisted him in collecting signatures, he replied: «I think that my reputation and example may well have led many young people to work for peace in this way. My conscience does not allow me to protect myself by sacrificing these idealistic and hopeful people. And I am not going to do it... For (he continued later) anyone called before this committee is rendered vulnerable. He may lose his job.»

It was a serious matter for Linus Pauling to refuse to answer questions put to him by the subcommittee, and he realized that he risked a prison sentence for contempt of Congress.

Pauling endeavored to secure a court ruling that the subcommittee's demand that he submit the names of those who had helped him to collect signatures violated the constitutional right of every citizen to appeal to the authorities. Pauling failed to secure a favorable verdict in two instances. His appeal to the Supreme Court did not materialize, for the Senate subcommittee dropped the matter. It merely published its findings in a report which, incidentally, was strongly criticized in some of the major American newspapers as being too one-sided and not particularly fair to Pauling.

Although encountering opposition in various quarters, Pauling's name and his views became even better known, and the manner in which his hearings had been conducted gained him added support, as is so often the case when a good cause is attacked.

Undaunted, Linus Pauling and his wife, Ava Helen Pauling, continued their campaign, delivering as many as a hundred speeches and lectures a year. His wife has been a great source of inspiration for Pauling, and the assistance she renders him is invaluable. Her own peace lectures, with their special appeal to women, have been influential.

It is impossible in a short address to touch upon all the speeches Linus Pauling has made and all the conferences in which he has participated. I must confine myself to a few of the international disarmament and peace conferences, such as the Conference against Atomic and Hydrogen Bombs held in Hiroshima in 1959, where he personally wrote the resolution which was issued after the meeting.

This states that an international agreement must be reached in which the nations pledge themselves to terminate all tests with nuclear weapons and not to produce new ones. Nor should these weapons be distributed to other nations. A neutral zone should be established between East and West. Among the countries to remain neutral, mention is made of East and West Germany, with adjoining countries, and Japan, but naturally not China.

In May, 1961, Linus Pauling and his wife convened in Oslo an international Conference against the Spread of Nuclear Weapons. Scientists from fifteen countries attended, and the main point in the resolution adopted was that nuclear weapons must not be allowed to spread to other countries, since such a spread would inevitably increase the danger of some power's willfully unleashing nuclear warfare. Furthermore, the spread of these weapons would also reduce the chance of a disarmament agreement.

On September 1, 1961, the Soviet Union resumed nuclear testing in the atmosphere and announced plans for detonating a fifty-megaton nuclear bomb. On October 18, Pauling sent a telegram to Premier Khrushchev[1], earnestly entreating him not to carry out this plan. At the same time he sent a telegram to President Kennedy[2], requesting that the United States government declare that no test explosions would be undertaken in the atmosphere

1. Nikita Sergeyevich Khrushchev (1894–1971), premier of the U.S.S.R. (1958–1964).
2. John Fitzgerald Kennedy (1917–1963), U.S. president (1961–1963).

provided the Soviet Union revoked its plan to detonate the fifty-megaton bomb.

He received a long letter from Khrushchev, dated October 26, 1961, the gist of which was that the Soviet Union considered itself regrettably forced to carry out new tests with nuclear weapons, and he was therefore sorry that he was unable to reverse the decision already made. The reasons given were that the Western powers were arming, and that the Soviet Union considered its security threatened.

And so, despite his efforts, Linus Pauling did not succeed.

At this time he was also deeply involved in the problem of shelters in the event of nuclear attack. He maintained that shelters would not be able to reduce the number of dead and wounded in a nuclear war because their construction might give people the false impression that nuclear warfare was not, after all, so dangerous. He strove in articles and speeches to enlighten the general public on this point.

In November, 1961, Pauling and his wife were invited by the Academy of Science in Moscow to attend its second centenary celebration. While they were there, they were both asked to lecture on disarmament and peace. Pauling's lecture was based on the same arguments he had used in the United States, but he emphasized the danger of the new nuclear tests in the Soviet Union. He was confronted with the argument that the Soviet Union was compelled to continue its tests in order to be in a position to obtain weapons capable of preventing the outbreak of a nuclear war. Pauling pointed out that this was the very argument used by those in the United States who insisted on continuing nuclear tests.

During this visit in Moscow, Pauling applied for a personal interview with Premier Khrushchev. When this was refused, he sent the Russian leader two letters and a draft of an agreement for a ban on nuclear tests. In the main, his proposal tallies with the test ban agreement of July 25, 1963.

On March 1, 1962, the United States resumed nuclear tests in the atmosphere.

In October, 1962, Pauling was in a position to state that the tests undertaken in the Soviet Union and in the United States during the course of the previous year or so had released twice as much radioactive fallout as all the tests undertaken during the sixteen preceding years.

In 1963, however, after what had long appeared a state of permanent deadlock, discussions on a nuclear test ban finally made some headway when the United States, the Soviet Union, and Great Britain entered into an agreement. This was signed in Moscow on July 25, 1963, and went into effect on October 10 of this year. Most countries have now signed, the most important exceptions being France and China. The agreement covers all tests of nuclear weapons except those carried out underground.

In his magnificent speech to the American people on July 26 of this year[1], the late President John F. Kennedy stated: «Even then, the number of children and grandchildren with cancer in their bones, with leukemia in their blood, or with poison in their lungs might seem statistically small to some, in comparison with natural health hazards. But this is not a natural health hazard, and it is not a statistical issue. The loss of even one human life, or the malformation of even one baby – who may be born long after we are gone – should be of concern to us all.»

In his speech President Kennedy revealed that his views on nuclear tests were based on the same moral attitude that Linus Pauling has consistently maintained.

No one would suggest that Linus Pauling is actually responsible for the nuclear test ban itself or for the efforts of the great powers to arrive at an agreement acceptable to all parties.

But does anyone believe that this treaty would have been concluded now if there had been no responsible scientist who, tirelessly, unflinchingly, year in year out, had impressed on the authorities and on the general public the real menace of nuclear tests?

In his speech President Kennedy likewise stressed the great danger of spreading nuclear weapons to more and more countries. These were his words: «I ask you to stop and think for a moment what it would mean to have nuclear weapons in so many hands, in the hands of countries, large and small, stable and unstable, responsible and irresponsible, scattered throughout the world. There would be no rest for anyone then, no stability, no real security, and no chance of effective disarmament.»[2]

Even though the Test Ban Treaty has been effected, this is only the first small step toward an agreement on complete disarmament and peace.

Though the road may be long and difficult, Linus Pauling has an un-shakable belief that one day mankind will succeed in banning war: «I

1. This telecast speech was published in *The Department of State Bulletin*, Vol. 49, No. 1259 (August 12, 1963) 234–239, under the title «The Nuclear Test Ban Treaty: A Step toward Peace». (Washington, D.C.: Supt. of Documents, U.S. Government Printing Office, 1963.) The quotation is on p. 236.
2. *Ibid.*, p. 237.

believe that there is a greater power in the world than the evil power of military force, of nuclear bombs – there is the power of *good*, of *morality*, of *humanitarianism*.»[1]

In his opinion, it will be possible by enlisting these forces to build a world community in which the actions of all nations will be subject to just supervision and control, through the medium of international law and justice.

As far as I know, Linus Pauling has not drawn up any concrete plan for the future. But one thing is certain: he has great faith in the role of science, as he shows in his suggestion for establishing a World Peace Research Organization which would be affiliated with the United Nations, and which would represent every branch of science, including the natural sciences and the humanities[2].

An organization of this kind must be based on knowledge and wisdom. It is for this reason that Pauling has now left his position at the California Institute of Technology in Pasadena and joined the Center for the Study of Democratic Institutions at Santa Barbara. He has taken this step, he tells us, because this institution allows him greater freedom to continue his work for peace.

He wants to use this opportunity for research in drawing up concrete plans for the future.

It is Linus Pauling's highly ethical attitude toward life – the deepest driving force within him – that drew him into the fight against nuclear weapons.

Through his campaign, Linus Pauling has manifested the ethical responsibility which he believes science should bear for the fate of mankind, today and in the future.

The scientist's urge to wrest Nature's secrets from her, is one Linus Pauling can never satisfy. As long as the world exists, there will always be bold, adventurous minds and new campaigns to be carried on for new goals.

Should Linus Pauling, through his tireless efforts, have contributed – if only a little – to restoring to science its ideals, then his campaign will in itself have been of such value that we living today can scarcely appreciate the full extent of the debt we owe him.

1. Pauling, *No More War!*, p.193.
2. *Ibid.*, pp.201–208.

LINUS PAULING

Science and Peace

Nobel Lecture*, *December 11, 1963*

I believe that there will never again be a great world war–a war in which the terrible weapons involving nuclear fission and nuclear fusion would be used. And I believe that it is the discoveries of scientists upon which the development of these terrible weapons was based that is now forcing us to move into a new period in the history of the world, a period of peace and reason, when world problems are not solved by war or by force, but are solved in accordance with world law, in a way that does justice to all nations and that benefits all people.

Let me again remind you, as I did yesterday in my address of acceptance of the Nobel Peace Prize for 1962, that Alfred Nobel wanted to invent «a substance or a machine with such terrible power of mass destruction that war would thereby be made impossible forever»[1]. Two thirds of a century later scientists discovered the explosive substances that Nobel wanted to invent– the fissionable substances uranium and plutonium, with explosive energy ten million times that of Nobel's favorite explosive, nitroglycerine, and the fusionable substance lithium deuteride, with explosive energy fifty million times that of nitroglycerine. The first of the terrible machines incorporating these substances, the uranium-235 and plutonium-239 fission bombs, were exploded in 1945, at Alamogordo, Hiroshima, and Nagasaki[2]. Then in 1954, nine years later, the first of the fission-fusion-fission superbombs was exploded, the 20-megaton Bikini bomb, with energy of explosion one thousand times greater than that of a 1945 fission bomb.

This one bomb, the 1954 superbomb, contained less than one ton of nuclear explosive. The energy released in the explosion of this bomb was

---

* The laureate delivered this lecture in the Auditorium of the University of Oslo. The text is taken from *Les Prix Nobel en 1963*.

1. From a conversation in 1876 with Bertha von Suttner (recipient of the Nobel Peace Prize for 1905), who recorded it in her journal.

2. The desert near Alamogordo, New Mexico, was the site of the first test of the atomic bomb in July, 1945. The cities of Hiroshima and Nagasaki in Japan were the victims of such bombs in August, 1945, in the last days of WWII.

greater than that of all of the explosives used in all of the wars that have taken place during the entire history of the world, including the First World War and the Second World War.

Thousands of these superbombs have now been fabricated; and today, eighteen years after the construction of the first atomic bomb, the nuclear powers have stockpiles of these weapons so great that if they were to be used in a war hundreds of millions of people would be killed, and our civilization itself might not survive the catastrophe.

Thus the machines envisaged by Nobel have come into existence, and war has been made impossible forever.

The world has now begun its metamorphosis from its primitive period of history, when disputes between nations were settled by war, to its period of maturity, in which war will be abolished and world law will take its place. The first great stage of this metamorphosis took place only a few months ago–the formulation by the governments of the United States, Great Britain, and the Soviet Union, after years of discussion and negotiation, of a treaty[1] banning the testing of nuclear weapons on the surface of the earth, in the oceans, and in space, and the ratification and signing of this treaty by nearly all of the nations in the world.

I believe that the historians of the future may well describe the making of this treaty as the most important action ever taken by the governments of nations, in that it is the first of a series of treaties that will lead to the new world from which war has been abolished forever.

We see that science and peace are related. The world has been greatly changed, especially during the last century, by the discoveries of scientists. Our increased knowledge now provides the possibility of eliminating poverty and starvation, of decreasing significantly the suffering caused by disease, of using the resources of the world effectively for the benefit of humanity. But the greatest of all the changes has been in the nature of war– the several millionfold increase in the power of explosives and corresponding changes in methods of delivery of bombs.

These changes have resulted from the discoveries of scientists, and during the last two decades scientists have taken a leading part in bringing them to the attention of their fellow human beings and in urging that vigorous action be taken to prevent the use of the new weapons and to abolish war from the world.

1. In Moscow in July, 1963.

The first scientists to take actions of this sort were those involved in the development of the atomic bomb. In March, 1945, before the first nuclear explosion had been carried out, Leo Szilard prepared a memorandum[1] to President Franklin Delano Roosevelt[2] in which he pointed out that a system of international control of nuclear weapons might give civilization a chance to survive. A committee of atomic scientists, with James Franck[3] as chairman, on June 11, 1945, transmitted to the U.S. Secretary of War a report urging that nuclear bombs not be used in an unannounced attack against Japan, as this action would prejudice the possibility of reaching an international agreement on control of these weapons[4].

In 1946 Albert Einstein, Harold Urey, and seven other scientists[5] formed an organization to educate the American people about the nature of nuclear weapons and nuclear war. This organization, the Emergency Committee of Atomic Scientists (usually called the Einstein Committee), carried out an effective educational campaign over a five-year period. The nature of the campaign is indicated by the following sentences from the 1946 statement by Einstein:

«Today the atomic bomb has altered profoundly the nature of the world as we know it, and the human race consequently finds itself in a new habitat to which it must adapt its thinking... Never before was it possible for one nation to make war on another without sending armies across borders. Now with rockets and atomic bombs no center of population on the earth's surface is secure from surprise destruction in a single attack... Few men have ever seen the bomb. But all men if told a few facts can understand that this bomb and the danger of war is a very real thing, and not something far away. It directly concerns every person in the civilized world. We cannot leave it to generals, senators, and diplomats to work out a solution over a

1. Leo Szilard (1898–1964), Hungarian-born physicist, after 1943 an American citizen; with Metallurgical Laboratory, University of Chicago (1942–1946), and then professor at the university. The text of his memorandum is published in *The Atomic Age* (see selected bibliography), pp. 13–18.
2. Franklin Delano Roosevelt (1882–1945), U.S. president (1933–1945).
3. James Franck (1882–1964), German-born American physicist; co-recipient of the Nobel Prize in Physics for 1925; professor at the University of Chicago (1938–1947).
4. Published in *The Atomic Age*, pp. 19–27.
5. Harold Clayton Urey (1893–   ), American chemist and recipient of the Nobel Prize in Chemistry for 1934; director of the Manhattan Bomb Project (1940–1945); professor at the University of Chicago (1945–1958). For Einstein and the other committee members, see p. 259, fn. 2, and p. 260, fn. 1.

period of generations... There is no defense in science against the weapon which can destroy civilization. Our defense is not in armaments, nor in science, nor in going underground. Our defense is in law and order... Future thinking *must* prevent wars.» [1]

During the same period and later years, many other organizations of scientists were active in the work of educating people about nuclear weapons and nuclear war; among them I may mention especially the Federation of American Scientists (in the United States) [2], the Atomic Scientists' Association (Great Britain), and the World Federation of Scientific Workers (with membership covering many countries).

On July 15, 1955, a powerful statement, called the Mainau Declaration, was issued by fifty-two Nobel laureates [3]. This statement warned that a great war in the nuclear age would imperil the whole world, and ended with the sentences: «All nations must come to the decision to renounce force as a final resort of policy. If they are not prepared to do this, they will cease to exist.»

A document of great consequence, the Russell-Einstein Appeal, was made public by Bertrand Russell [4] on July 9, 1955. Russell, who for years remained one of the world's most active and effective workers for peace, had drafted this document some months earlier, and it had been signed by Einstein two days before his death, and also by nine other scientists. The Appeal began with the sentence: «In the tragic situation which confronts humanity, we feel that scientists should assemble in conference to appraise the perils that have arisen as a result of the development of weapons of mass destruction...» And it ended with the exhortation: «There lies before us, if we choose, continual progress in happiness, knowledge, and wisdom. Shall we, instead, choose death, because we cannot forget our quarrels? We appeal, as human beings, to human beings: Remember your humanity, and forget the rest. If you can do so, the way lies open to a new Paradise; if you cannot, there lies before you the risk of universal death.» [5]

This Appeal led to the formation of the Pugwash Continuing Committee,

1. From «Only Then Shall We Find Courage» (in an interview with Michael Amrine), published in the *New York Times Magazine*, June 23, 1946, and later in pamphlet form by the Emergency Committee of Atomic Scientists.
2. Of which the laureate was one of the leaders.
3. For complete text, see presentation speech, p.262. For the 52 laureates (all scientists), see Pauling, *No More War!*, pp.223–224.
4. Bertrand Arthur William Russell, third Earl Russell (1872–1970), English philosopher and mathematician, and recipient of the Nobel Prize in Literature for 1950.
5. The complete text can be found in *The Atomic Age*, pp.539–541.

with Bertrand Russell as chairman, and to the holding of a series of Pugwash Conferences (eleven during the years 1957 to 1963). Financial support for the first few conferences was provided by Mr. Cyrus Eaton[1], and the first conference was held in his birthplace, the village of Pugwash, Nova Scotia.

Among the participants in some of the Pugwash Conferences have been scientists with a close connection with the governments of their countries, as well as scientists without government connection. The Conferences have permitted the scientific and practical aspects of disarmament to be discussed informally in a thorough, penetrating, and productive way and have led to some valuable proposals. It is my opinion that the Pugwash Conferences were significantly helpful in the formulation and ratification of the 1963 Bomb Test Ban Treaty.

Concern about the damage done to human beings and the human race by the radioactive substances produced in nuclear weapons tests was expressed with increasing vigor in the period following the first fission-fusion-fission bomb test at Bikini on March 1, 1954. Mention was made of radioactive fallout in the Russell-Einstein Appeal and also in the statement of the First Pugwash Conference. In his Declaration of Conscience issued in Oslo on April 24, 1957, Dr. Albert Schweitzer described the damage done by fallout and asked that the great nations cease their tests of nuclear weapons[2]. Then on May 15, 1957, with the help of some of the scientists in Washington University, St. Louis, I wrote the Scientists' Bomb Test Appeal, which within two weeks was signed by over two thousand American scientists and within a few months by 11,021 scientists, of forty-nine countries. On January 15, 1958, as I presented the Appeal to Dag Hammarskjöld[3] as a petition to the United Nations, I said to him that in my opinion it represented the feelings of the great majority of the scientists of the world.

The Bomb Test Appeal consists of five paragraphs. The first two are the following:

« We, the scientists whose names are signed below, urge that an international agreement to stop the testing of nuclear bombs be made now.

Each nuclear bomb test spreads an added burden of radioactive elements over every part of the world. Each added amount of radiation causes damage to the health of human beings all over the world and causes damage to the

1. Cyrus Stephen Eaton (1883–   ), Canadian-born Cleveland industrialist.
2. See presentation speech, p. 264.
3. Dag Hammarskjöld (1905–1961), Swedish secretary-general of the UN (1953– 1961); posthumously awarded the Nobel Peace Prize for 1961.

pool of human germ plasm such as to lead to an increase in the number of seriously defective children that will be born in future generations.»[1]

Let me now say a few words to amplify the last statement, about which there has been controversy. Each year, of the nearly 100 million children born in the world, about 4,000,000 have gross physical or mental defects, such as to cause great suffering to themselves and their parents and to constitute a major burden on society. Geneticists estimate that about five percent, 200,000 per year, of these children are grossly defective because of gene mutations caused by natural high-energy radiation–cosmic rays and natural radio-activity, from which our reproductive organs cannot be protected. This numerical estimate is rather uncertain, but geneticists agree that it is of the right order of magnitude.

Moreover, geneticists agree that any additional exposure of the human reproductive cells to high-energy radiation produces an increase in the number of mutations and an increase in the number of defective children born in future years, and that this increase is approximately proportional to the amount of the exposure.

The explosion of nuclear weapons in the atmosphere liberates radioactive fission products–cesium 137, strontium 90, iodine 131, and many others. In addition, the neutrons that result from the explosion combine with nitrogen nuclei in the atmosphere to form large amounts of a radioactive isotope of carbon, carbon 14, which then is incorporated into the organic molecules of every human being. These radioactive fission products are now damaging the pool of human germ plasma and increasing the number of defective children born.

Carbon 14 deserves our special concern. It was pointed out by the Soviet scientist O.I.Leipunsky in 1957 that this radioactive product of nuclear tests would cause more genetic damage to the human race than the radioactive fallout (cesium 137 and other fission products), if the human race survives over the 8,000-year mean life of carbon 14. Closely agreeing numerical estimates of the genetic effects of bomb-test carbon 14 were then made independently by me and by Drs.Totter, Zelle, and Hollister of the United States Atomic Energy Commission[2]. Especially pertinent is the fact that the so-called «clean» bombs, involving mainly nuclear fusion, produce when they are tested more carbon 14 per megaton than the ordinary fission bombs or fission-fusion-fission bombs.

1. The remaining three paragraphs are given later in the lecture, p.279.
2. Established in 1946 to direct the use of atomic energy to peaceful ends.

A recent study by Reidar Nydal, of the Norwegian Institute of Technology in Trondheim, shows the extent to which the earth is being changed by the tests of nuclear weapons. Carbon 14 produced by cosmic rays is normally present in the atmosphere, oceans, and biosphere, in amount as to be responsible for between one and two percent of the genetic damage caused by natural high-energy radiation. Nydal has reported that the amount of carbon 14 in the atmosphere has been more than doubled because of the nuclear weapons tests of the last ten years, and that in a few years the carbon-14 content of human beings will be two or three times the normal value, with a consequent increase in the gene mutation rate and the number of defective children born.

Some people have pointed out that the number of grossly defective children born as a result of the bomb tests is small compared with the total number of defective children and have suggested that the genetic damage done by the bomb tests should be ignored. I, however, have contended, as have Dr. Schweitzer and many others, that every single human being is important and that we should be concerned about every additional child that is caused by our actions to be born to live a life of suffering and misery. President Kennedy in his broadcast[1] to the American people on July 26, 1963, said: «The loss of even one human life, or the malformation of even one baby–who may be born long after we are gone–should be of concern to us all. Our children and grandchildren are not merely statistics towards which we can be indifferent.»

We should know how many defective children are being born because of the bomb tests. During the last six years I have made several attempts to estimate the numbers. My estimates have changed somewhat from year to year, as new information became available and as continued bomb testing increased the amount of radioactive pollution of the earth, but no radical revision of the estimates has been found necessary.

It is my estimate that about 100,000 viable children will be born with gross physical or mental defects caused by the cesium 137 and other fission products from the bomb tests carried out from 1952 to 1963, and 1,500,000 more, if the human race survives, with gross defects caused by the carbon 14 from these bomb tests. In addition, about ten times as many embryonic, neonatal, and childhood deaths are expected–about 1,000,000 caused by the fission products and 15,000,000 by carbon 14. An even larger number of children

1. See p. 269, fn. 1.

may have minor defects caused by the bomb tests; these minor defects, which are passed on from generation to generation rather than being rapidly weeded out by genetic death, may be responsible for more suffering in the aggregate than the major defects.

About five percent of the fission-product effect and 0.3 percent of the carbon-14 effect may appear in the first generation; that is, about 10,000 viable children with gross physical or mental defects, and 100,000 embryonic, neonatal, and childhood deaths.

These estimates are in general agreement with those made by other scientists and by national and international committees. The estimates are all very uncertain because of the deficiencies in our knowledge. The uncertainty is usually expressed by saying that the actual numbers may be only one-fifth as great or may be five times as great as the estimates, but the errors may be even larger than this.

Moreover, it is known that high-energy radiation can cause leukemia, bone cancer, and some other diseases. Scientists differ in their opinion about the carcinogenic activity of small doses of radiation, such as produced by fallout and carbon 14. It is my opinion that bomb-test strontium 90 can cause leukemia and bone cancer, iodine 131 can cause cancer of the thyroid, and cesium 137 and carbon 14 can cause these and other diseases. I make the rough estimate that, because of this somatic effect of these radioactive substances that now pollute the earth, about 2,000,000 human beings now living will die five or ten or fifteen years earlier than if the nuclear tests had not been made. The 1962 estimate of the United States Federal Radiation Council was 0 to 100,000 deaths from leukemia and bone cancer in the U.S. alone, caused by the nuclear tests to the end of 1961.

The foregoing estimates are for 600 megatons of bombs. We may now ask: At what sacrifice is the atmospheric test of a single standard 20-megaton bomb carried out? Our answer, none the less horrifying because uncertain, is: with the sacrifice, if the human race survives, of about 500,000 children, of whom about 50,000 are viable but have gross physical or mental defects; and perhaps also of about 70,000 people now living who may die prematurely of leukemia or some other disease caused by the test.

We may be thankful that most of the nations of the world have, by subscribing to the 1963 treaty, agreed not to engage in nuclear testing in the atmosphere. But what a tragedy it is that this treaty was not made two years earlier! Of the total of 600 megatons of tests so far, three-quarters of the testing, 450 megatons, was done in 1961 and 1962. The failure to formulate a treaty in 1959 or 1960 or 1961 was attributed by the governments of the United States, Great Britain, and the Soviet Union to the existing differences of opinion about methods of inspection of underground tests. These differences were not resolved in 1963; but the treaty stopping atmospheric tests was made. What a tragedy for humanity that the governments did not accept this solution before taking the terrible step of resuming the nuclear tests in 1961!

I shall now quote and discuss the rest of the nuclear test ban petition of six years ago.

«So long as these weapons are in the hands of only three powers, an agreement for their control is feasible. If testing continues, and the possession of these weapons spreads to additional governments, the danger of outbreak of a cataclysmic nuclear war through the reckless action of some irresponsible national leader will be greatly increased.

An international agreement to stop the testing of nuclear bombs now could serve as a first step toward a more general disarmament and the ultimate effective abolition of nuclear weapons, averting the possibility of a nuclear war that would be a catastrophe to all humanity.

We have in common with our fellowmen a deep concern for the welfare of all human beings. As scientists we have knowledge of the dangers involved and therefore a special responsibility to make those dangers known. We deem it imperative that immediate action be taken to effect an international agreement to stop the testing of all nuclear weapons.»

How cogent is this argument? Would a great war, fought with use of the nuclear weapons that now exist, be a catastrophe to all humanity?

Consideration of the nature of nuclear weapons and the magnitude of the nuclear stockpiles gives us the answer: it is Yes.

A single 25-megaton bomb could largely destroy any city on earth and kill most of its inhabitants. Thousands of these great bombs have been fabricated, together with the vehicles to deliver them.

Precise information about the existing stockpiles of nuclear weapons has not been released. The participants in the Sixth Pugwash Conference, in 1960, made use of the estimate 60,000 megatons. This is 10,000 times the amount of explosive used in the whole of the Second World War. It indicates that the world's stockpile of military explosives has on the average doubled every year since 1945. My estimate for 1963, which reflects the continued manufacture of nuclear weapons during the past three years, is 320,000 megatons.

This estimate is made credible by the following facts. On November 12, 1961, the U.S. Secretary of Defense[1] stated that the U.S. Strategic Air Command then included 630 B-52's, 55 B-58's, and 1,000 B-47's, a total of 1,685 great bombers. These bombers carry about 50 megatons of bombs apiece–two 25-megaton bombs on each bomber. Accordingly, these 1,685 intercontinental bombers carry a load totalling 84,000 megatons. I do not believe that it can be contended that the bombs for these bombers do not exist. The Secretary of Defense also stated that the United States has over 10,000 other planes and rockets capable of carrying nuclear bombs in the megaton range. The total megatonnage of nuclear bombs tested by the Soviet Union is twice that of those tested by the United States and Great Britain, and it is not unlikely that the Soviet stockpile is also a tremendous one, perhaps one-third or one-half as large as the U.S. stockpile.

The significance of the estimated total of 320,000 megatons of nuclear bombs may be brought out by the following statement: if there were to take place tomorrow a 6-megaton war, equivalent to the Second World War in the power of the explosives used, and another such war the following day, and so on, day after day, for 146 years, the present stockpile would then be exhausted–but, in fact, this stockpile might be used in a single day, the day of the Third World War.

Many estimates have been made by scientists of the probable effects of hypothetical nuclear attacks. One estimate, reported in the 1957 Hearings before the Special Subcommittee on Radiation of the Joint Committee on Atomic Energy of the Congress of the United States, was for an attack on population and industrial centers and military installations in the United States with 250 bombs totalling 2,500 megatons. The estimate of casualties presented in the testimony, corrected for the increase in population since 1957, is that sixty days after the day on which the attack took place ninety-eight million of the 190 million American people would be dead, and twenty-eight million would be seriously injured but still alive; many of the remaining seventy million survivors would be suffering from minor injuries and radiation effects.

This is a small nuclear attack made with use of about one percent of the existing weapons. A major nuclear war might well see a total of 30,000

1. Robert Strange McNamara (1916–   ), U.S. secretary of defense (1961–1968).

megatons, one-tenth of the estimated stockpiles, delivered and exploded over the populated regions of the United States, the Soviet Union, and the other major European countries. The studies of Hugh Everett and George E. Pugh[1], of the Weapons Systems Evaluation Division, Institute of Defense Analysis, Washington, D.C., reported in the 1959 Hearings before the Special Subcommittee on Radiation, permit us to make an estimate of the casualties of such a war. This estimate is that sixty days after the day on which the war was waged, 720 million of the 800 million people in these countries would be dead, sixty million would be alive but severely injured, and there would be twenty million other survivors. The fate of the living is suggested by the following statement by Everett and Pugh: «Finally, it must be pointed out that the total casualties at sixty days may not be indicative of the ultimate casualties. Such delayed effects as the disorganization of society, disruption of communications, extinction of livestock, genetic damage, and the slow development of radiation poisoning from the ingestion of radioactive materials may significantly increase the ultimate toll.»

No dispute between nations can justify nuclear war. There is no defense against nuclear weapons that could not be overcome by increasing the scale of the attack. It would be contrary to the nature of war for nations to adhere to agreements to fight «limited» wars, using only «small» nuclear weapons—even little wars today are perilous, because of the likelihood that a little war would grow into a world catastrophe.

The only sane policy for the world is that of abolishing war.

This is now the proclaimed goal of the nuclear powers and of all other nations.

We are all indebted to the governments of the United States, the Soviet Union, and Great Britain for their action of formulating a test ban agreement that has been accepted by most of the nations of the world. As an American, I feel especially thankful to our great President, John F. Kennedy, whose tragic death occurred only nineteen days ago. It is my opinion that this great international agreement could not have been formulated and ratified except for the conviction, determination, and political skill of President Kennedy.

The great importance of the 1963 Test Ban Treaty lies in its significance as

1. Hugh Everett III and George E. Pugh, «The Distribution and Effects of Fallout in Large Nuclear-Weapon Campaigns», in *Biological and Environment Effects of Nuclear War* (see selected bibliography).

the first step toward disarmament. To indicate what other steps need to be taken, I shall now quote some of the statements made by President Kennedy in his address to the United Nations General Assembly on the 26th of September, 1961.

«The goal (of disarmament) is no longer a dream. It is a practical matter of life or death. The risks inherent in disarmament pale in comparison to the risks inherent in an unlimited arms race...

Our new disarmament program includes:...

First, signing the test-ban treaty by all nations...

Second, stopping production of fissionable materials and preventing their transfer to (other) nations;...

Third, prohibiting the transfer of control over nuclear weapons to other nations;

Fourth, keeping nuclear weapons from outer space;

Fifth, gradually destroying existing nuclear weapons;

And Sixth, halting... the production of strategic nuclear delivery vehicles, and gradually destroying them.»

The first of these goals has been approached, through the 1963 treaty, but not yet reached. Six weeks ago, by the vote ninety-seven to one, the Political Committee of the United Nations General Assembly approved a resolution asking that the eighteen-nation Disarmament Committee take supplementary action to achieve the discontinuance of all test explosions of nuclear weapons for all time. We must strive to achieve this goal.

The fourth action proposed by President Kennedy, that of keeping nuclear weapons from outer space, was taken two months ago, in the United Nations, through a pledge of abstention subscribed to by many nations.

Action on the third point, the prevention of the spread of nuclear weapons, could lead to a significant diminution in international tensions and in the chance of outbreak of a world war. The 1960 treaty making Antarctica a nuclear-free zone provides a precedent. Ten Latin American nations have proposed that the whole of Latin America be made into a second zone free of nuclear weapons; and a similar proposal has been made for Africa. Approval of these proposals would be an important step toward permanent peace.

Even more important would be the extension of the principle of demilitarization to Central Europe, as proposed by Rapacki, Kennan[1], and others several years ago. Under this proposal the whole of Germany, Poland, and Czechoslovakia, and perhaps some other countries would be largely demilitarized, and their boundaries and national integrity would be permanently assured by the United Nations. I am not able at the present time to discuss in a thorough way the complex problem of Berlin and Germany; but I am sure that if a solution other than nuclear destruction is ever achieved, it will be through demilitarization, not remilitarization.

President Kennedy, President Johnson, Chairman Khrushchev, Prime Minister Macmillan[2], and other national leaders have proclaimed that, to prevent the cataclysm, we must move toward the goal of general and complete disarmament, we must begin to destroy the terrible nuclear weapons that now exist, and the vehicles for delivering them. But instead of destroying the weapons and the delivery vehicles, the great nations continue to manufacture more and more of them, and the world remains in peril.

Why is no progress being made toward disarmament? I think that part of the answer is that there are still many people, some of them powerful people, who have not yet accepted the thesis that the time has now come to abolish war. And another part of the answer is that there exists a great nation that has not been accepted into the world community of nations–the Chinese People's Republic, the most populous nation in the world. I do not believe that the United States and the Soviet Union will carry out any major stage of the process of disarmament unless that potentially great nuclear power, the Chinese People's Republic, is a signatory to the disarmament agreement; and the Chinese People's Republic will not be a signatory to such a treaty until she is accepted into the community of nations under conditions worthy of her stature[3]. To work for the recognition of China is to work for world peace.

We cannot expect the now existing nuclear weapons to be destroyed for several years, perhaps for decades. Moreover, there is the possibility,

1. Adam Rapacki (1909–   ), who, as Polish foreign minister, presented a plan for Central European denuclearization to the UN General Assembly in October, 1957. George Frost Kennan (1904–   ), American diplomat, expert in Russian relations with the West.
2. Lyndon Baines Johnson (1908–   ), U.S. president (1963–1969). Nikita Sergeyevich Khrushchev (1894–1971), Russian premier (1958–1964). (Maurice) Harold Macmillan (1894–   ), British prime minister (1957–1963).
3. The People's Republic of China was admitted to the UN in 1971.

mentioned by Philip Noel-Baker in his Nobel lecture in 1959, that some nuclear weapons might be concealed or surreptitiously fabricated, and then used to terrorize and dominate the disarmed world[1]; this possibility might slow down the program of destroying the stockpiles.

Is there no action that we can take immediately to decrease the present great danger of outbreak of nuclear war, through some technological or psychological accident or as the result of a series of events such that even the wisest national leaders could not avert the catastrophe?

I believe that there is such an action, and I hope that it will be given consideration by the national governments. My proposal is that there be instituted, with the maximum expedition compatible with caution, a system of joint national-international control of the stockpiles of nuclear weapons, such that use could be made of the American nuclear armaments only with the approval both of the American government and of the United Nations, and that use could be made of the Soviet nuclear armament only with the approval both of the Soviet government and of the United Nations. A similar system of dual control would of course be instituted for the smaller nuclear powers if they did not destroy their weapons.

Even a small step in the direction of this proposal, such as the acceptance of United Nations observers in the control stations of the nuclear powers, might decrease significantly the probability of nuclear war.

There is another action that could be taken immediately to decrease the present great hazard to civilization. This action would be to stop, through a firm treaty incorporating a reliable system of inspection, the present great programs of development of biological and chemical methods of waging war.

Four years ago the scientists participating in the Fifth Pugwash Conference concluded that at that time the destructive power of nuclear weapons was far larger than that of biological and chemical weapons, but that biological and chemical weapons have enormous lethal and incapacitating effects against man and could also effect tremendous harm by the destruction of plants and animals. Moreover, there is a vigorous effort being made to develop these weapons to the point where they would become a threat to the human race equal to or greater than that of nuclear weapons. The money expended for research and development of biological and chemical warfare by the United States alone has now reached 100 million dollars per year, an increase of sixteenfold in a decade, and similar efforts are probably being exerted in the Soviet Union and other countries.

1. See p. 200.

To illustrate the threat, I may mention the plans to use nerve gases that, when they do not kill, produce temporary or permanent insanity, and the plans to use toxins such as the botulism toxin, viruses such as the virus of yellow fever, or bacterial spores such as of anthrax, to kill tens or hundreds of millions of people.

The hazard is especially great in that, once the knowledge is obtained through a large-scale development program such as is now being carried out, it might well spread over the world and might permit some small group of evil men, perhaps in one of the smaller countries, to launch a devastating attack.

This terrible prospect could be eliminated now by a general agreement to stop research and development of these weapons, to prohibit their use, and renounce all official secrecy and security controls over microbiological, toxicological, pharmacological, and chemical-biological research. Hundreds of millions of dollars per year are now being spent in the effort to make these malignant cells of knowledge. Now is the time to stop. When once the cancer has developed and its metastases have spread over the world, it will be too late.

The replacement of war by law must include not only great wars but also small ones. The abolition of insurrectionary and guerrilla warfare, which often is characterized by extreme savagery and a great amount of human suffering, would be a boon to humanity.

There are, however, countries in which the people are subjected to continuing economic exploitation and to oppression by a dictatorial government, which retains its power through force of arms. The only hope for many of these people has been that of revolution, of overthrowing the dictatorial government and replacing it with a reform government, a democratic government that would work for the welfare of the people.

I believe that the time has come for the world as a whole to abolish this evil, through the formulation and acceptance of some appropriate articles of world law. With only limited knowledge of law, I shall not attempt to formulate a proposal that would achieve this end without permitting the possibility of the domination of the small nations by the large nations. I suggest, however, that the end might be achieved by world legislation under which there would be, perhaps once a decade, a referendum, supervised by the United Nations, on the will of the people with respect to their national government, held, separately from the national elections, in every country in the world.

It may take many years to achieve such an addition to the body of world law. In the meantime, much could be done through a change in the policies of the great nations. During recent years insurrections and civil wars in small countries have been instigated and aggravated by the great powers, which have moreover provided weapons and military advisers, increasing the savagery of the wars and the suffering of the people. In four countries during 1963 and several others during preceding years, democratically elected governments, with policies in the direction of social and economic reform, have been overthrown and replaced by military dictatorship, with the approval, if not at the instigation, of one or more of the great powers. These actions of the great powers are associated with policies of militarism and national economic interest that are now antiquated. I hope that the pressure of world opinion will soon cause them to be abandoned and to be replaced by policies that are compatible with the principles of morality, justice, and world brotherhood.

In working to abolish war, we are working also for human freedom, for the rights of individual human beings. War and nationalism, together with economic exploitation, have been the great enemies of the individual human being. I believe that, with war abolished from the world, there will be improvement in the social, political, and economic systems in all nations, to the benefit of the whole of humanity.

I am glad to take this opportunity to express my gratitude to the Norwegian Storting [Parliament] for its outstanding work for international arbitration and peace during the last seventy-five years. In this activity the Storting has been the leader among the parliaments of nations. I remember the action of the Storting in 1890 of urging that permanent treaties for arbitration of disputes between nations be made, and the statement that «the Storting is convinced that this idea has the support of an overwhelming proportion of our people. Just as law and justice have long ago replaced the rule of the fist in disputes between man and man, so the idea of settling disputes among peoples and nations is making its way with irresistible strength. More and more, war appears to the general consciousness as a vestige of prehistoric barbarism and a curse to the human race.»

Now we are forced to eliminate from the world forever this vestige of prehistoric barbarism, this curse to the human race. We, you and I, are privileged to be alive during this extraordinary age, this unique epoch in the history of the world, the epoch of demarcation between the past millennia of war and suffering, and the future, the great future of peace, justice,

morality, and human well-being. We are privileged to have the opportunity of contributing to the achievement of the goal of the abolition of war
and its replacement by world law. I am confident that we shall succeed in
this great task; that the world community will thereby be freed not only
from the suffering caused by war but also, through the better use of the
earth's resources, of the discoveries of scientists, and of the efforts of mankind, from hunger, disease, illiteracy, and fear; and that we shall in the
course of time be enabled to build a world characterized by economic,
political, and social justice for all human beings and a culture worthy of
man's intelligence.

Biography

Linus Pauling (February 28, 1901–), the only person who has won two undivided Nobel Prizes[1], was born in Portland, Oregon, the son of a pharmacist, Henry H. W. Pauling, and Lucy (Darling) Pauling. He attended Washington High School in Portland but because of a technicality did not receive his diploma until 1962, long after he had received his bachelor's degree from Oregon State College in 1922, his doctorate from the California Institute of Technology in 1925, and honorary degrees from universities in seven countries.

With the help of a National Research Council fellowship in 1925–1926 and a Guggenheim Foundation fellowship in 1926–1927, he studied with three physicists: Arnold Sommerfeld in Munich, Erwin Schrödinger in Zurich, and Niels Bohr in Copenhagen. From 1927 until 1964, he was a member of the professorial staff of California Institute of Technology, earning a reputation as a gifted teacher – articulate, enthusiastic, with a talent for simplification and a willingness to engage in controversy. For twenty-two of those thirty-seven years, he was chairman of the Division of Chemistry and Chemical Engineering, as well as director of the Gates and Crellin Laboratories of Chemistry.

From 1963 to 1967, Pauling was attached to the Center for the Study of Democratic Institutions at Santa Barbara, California, as a research professor; from 1967 to 1969, he was a professor of chemistry at the University of California at San Diego; since 1969 he has been on the professorial staff of Stanford University.

From his graduate days until the mid-thirties, Pauling was interested primarily in physical chemistry, especially in molecular spatial configurations and their relevance to molecular behavior. In 1939 he published the results of over ten years of research in *The Nature of the Chemical Bond and the Structure of Molecules and Crystals*. When he won the Nobel Prize in Chemistry for 1954, he was cited «for his research into the nature of the chemical

1. The Nobel Prize in Chemistry for 1954 and the Peace Prize for 1962. Marie S. Curie won the Prize in Chemistry for 1911 and shared the Prize in Physics for 1903.

bond and its application to the elucidation of the structure of complex substances».

Pauling's interest in the «behavior» of molecules led him from physical chemistry to biological chemistry, from an absorption in the architecture of molecules to their functioning, especially in the human body. He began with proteins and their main constituents, the amino acids, which are called «the building blocks of life». He studied the abnormal in structure as well as the normal, even creating abnormalities in order to observe effects. From his creation of synthetic antibodies formed by altering molecules of globulin in the blood, came the development of a substitute for blood plasma. In 1950 he constructed the first satisfactory model of a protein molecule, a discovery which has implications for the understanding of the living cell. He has studied and published papers on the effects of certain blood cell abnormalities, the relationship between molecular abnormality and heredity, the possible chemical basis of mental retardation, the functioning of anesthetics. Looking to the future, he said in the last edition of *The Nature of the Chemical Bond*, «We may ask what the next step in the search for an understanding of the nature of life will be. I think that it will be the elucidation of the nature of the electromagnetic phenomena involved in mental activity in relation to the molecular structure of brain tissue. I believe that thinking, both conscious and unconscious, and short-term memory involve electromagnetic phenomena in the brain, interacting with the molecular (material) patterns of long-term memory, obtained from inheritance or experience.»[1]

Pauling's latest chemical-medical-nutritional study has been published in a 1970 book entitled *Vitamin C and the Common Cold*, in which he maintains that the common cold can be «controlled almost entirely in the United States and some other countries within a few years, through improvement of the nutrition of the people by an adequate intake of ascorbic acid [vitamin C]»[2].

During World War II, Pauling participated in scientific enterprises deemed vital to the protection of the country. Early in the war he was a consultant to the explosives division of the National Defense Research Commission and from 1945 to 1946 a member of the Research Board for National Security. For his contributions, which included work on rocket propellants, on an oxygen deficiency indicator for pressurized space, such as that in submarines

1. Third edition, 1960, p. 570.
2. P. 6. The book won the 1971 ΦBK Book Award in Literature of Science.

and aircraft, and on a substitute for human serum in medical treatment, he was awarded the Presidential Medal of Merit in 1948.

The use of the atomic bomb near the end of the war turned Pauling in a new direction. As one who had long worked on the structure of molecules, both normal and abnormal, on their behavior in the human body, and on their transmission through heredity, he took an immediate and intense interest in the potentially malignant effects of nuclear fallout on human molecular structures, as well as in the forces of blast and fire released by an exploding bomb. From the late forties on, Pauling, as a member of Einstein's Emergency Committee of Atomic Scientists, which was active from 1946 to 1950, as a supporter of many peace organizations, and as an individual, has waged a constant campaign against war and its now nuclear nature. He calculated estimates on the probable frequency of congenital deformity in future generations resulting from carbon 14 and radioactive fission products released by nuclear testing, and publicized them; protested the production of the hydrogen bomb; advocated the prevention of the spread of nuclear weapons; promoted the banning of tests of nuclear weapons as a first step toward multilateral disarmament[1].

In the early fifties and again in the early sixties, he encountered accusations of being pro-Soviet or Communist, allegations which he categorically denied. For a few years prior to 1954, he had restrictions placed by the Department of State on his eligibility to obtain a passport.

In 1958, on January 15, he presented to the UN the celebrated petition signed by 9,235 scientists from many countries in the world protesting further nuclear testing[2]. In that same year he published No More War!, a book which presents the rationale for abandoning not only further use and testing of nuclear weapons but also war itself, and which proposes the establishment of a World Peace Research Organization within the structure of the UN to «attack the problem of preserving the peace»[3].

When the Soviet Union announced a resumption of nuclear testing in August, 1961, after the nuclear powers had voluntarily withheld testing for three years, Pauling redoubled his efforts to convince the Russian, American, and British leaders of the necessity of a test ban treaty. He spoke as a man of

1. Detailed accounts of Pauling's activities in connection with the effort to secure an international agreement to ban nuclear testing are given in the presentation speech and in the Nobel lecture.
2. Pauling, No More War!, p. 160. The petition eventually carried 11,021 signatures.
3. Ibid., p. 201.

science. His intellectual position is summarized in a communication published in *Harper's Magazine* in 1963 [1]: «I have said that my ethical principles have caused me to reach the conclusion that the evil of war *should* be abolished; but my conclusion that war *must* be abolished if the human race is to survive is based not on ethical principles but on my thorough and careful analysis, in relation to international affairs, of the facts about the changes that have taken place in the world during recent years, especially with respect to the nature of war.»

The Nuclear Test Ban Treaty, outlawing all but underground nuclear testing, was signed in July, 1963, and went into effect on October 10, 1963, the same day on which the Norwegian Nobel Committee announced that the Peace Prize reserved in the year 1962 was to be awarded to Linus Pauling.

Selected Bibliography

The Atomic Age: Scientists in National and World Affairs, edited and with Introductions by Morton Grodzins and Eugene Rabinowitch. New York, Basic Books, 1963. This collection of articles from the *Bulletin of the Atomic Scientists*, 1945–1962, includes two by Harry Kalven, Jr., on Pauling's Congressional hearings (pp. 466–493), as well as some articles by various scientists referred to in the presentation and lecture.

Biological and Environment Effects of Nuclear War. Hearings before the Special Subcommittee on Radiation of the Joint Congressional Committee on Atomic Energy, June 22–26, 1959. Washington, D.C., U.S. Government Printing Office, 1959.

Current Biography Yearbook. New York, H.W. Wilson, 1964.

Gilpin, Robert, *American Scientists and Nuclear Weapons Policy.* Princeton, N.J., Princeton University Press, 1962.

Jacobson, Harold Karan, and Eric Stein, *Diplomats, Scientists, and Politicians: The United States and the Nuclear Test Ban Negotiations.* Ann Arbor, University of Michigan Press, 1966.

Jungk, Robert, *Brighter than a Thousand Suns: A Personal History of the Atomic Scientists* [*Heller als tausend Sonnen*], translated by James Cleugh. New York, Harcourt, Brace & World, 1958.

The Nature of Radioactive Fallout and Its Effects on Man. 2 vols. Hearings before the Special Subcommittee on Radiation of the Joint Congressional Committee on Atomic Energy, May 27–June 7, 1957. Washington, D.C., U.S. Government Printing Office, 1957.

Pauling, Linus, *The Architecture of Molecules.* With Roger Hayward. San Francisco, Freeman, 1964.

1. *Harper's Magazine*, 226 (May, 1963) 6.

Pauling, Linus, *The Nature of the Chemical Bond and the Structure of Molecules and Crystals: An Introduction to Modern Structural Chemistry*. Ithaca, N.Y., Cornell University Press, 1939. Third ed., 1960. A shortened version appeared in 1967: *The Chemical Bond: A Brief Introduction to Modern Structural Chemistry*.

Pauling, Linus, *No More War!* New York, Dodd, Mead, 1958. Second ed. in 1962.

Pauling, Linus, *Our Choice: Atomic Death or World Law*. A lecture delivered during the Fifth World Conference against A-and H-Bombs in Hiroshima, August, 1959. Toronto, Canadian Peace Congress, 1959.

Pauling, Linus, *Science and World Peace*. Azad Memorial Lectures for 1967. New Delhi, Indian Council for Cultural Relations, 1967.

Pauling, Linus, *Vitamin C and the Common Cold*. San Francisco, Freeman, 1970.

Pauling, Linus, and E. Bright Wilson, Jr., *Introduction to Quantum Mechanics: With Applications to Chemistry*. New York, McGraw-Hill, 1935.

Pauling, Linus, and Harvey A. Itano, eds., *Molecular Structure and Biological Specificity*. A symposium sponsored by the Office of Naval Research and arranged by the American Institute of Biological Sciences, held in Washington, D.C., October 28–29, 1955. Washington, D.C., American Institute of Biological Sciences, 1957.

Peace 1963

THE INTERNATIONAL COMMITTEE
OF THE RED CROSS

THE LEAGUE OF RED CROSS
SOCIETIES

Presentation

by Carl Joachim Hambro*, Member of the Nobel Committee

The Nobel Committee of the Norwegian Storting [Parliament] has decided to divide the Peace Prize for 1963 between the two sister organizations of the Red Cross: the International Red Cross Committee and the League of Red Cross Societies.

It is most appropriate that such a decision should be taken this year, for it marks the centennial of the Red Cross. That it should have been possible to constitute the Red Cross and start its work in 1863 is one of the great miracles in human history.

It was after the French-Sardinian-Austrian war and on the background of the terrible massacres on the battlefields of northern Italy that the Red Cross came into existence. On June 24, 1859, 300,000 French, Sardinian, and Austrian soldiers fought, at Solferino in northern Italy, the most merciless battle of the war; and more than 40,000 dying, dead, and wounded were herded into the little village of Castiglione. There was no organized medical aid and no medical supplies, and there was no water. The heat was suffocating; and in this hell on earth an idealistic and pious young Swiss businessman from Geneva, Henri Dunant[1] (he was later called by Dickens «the man in white»), worked day and night among the dead and the dying and pressed into his service every man and woman of the neighborhood. The Italian peasant women came to his aid and helped even the enemies,

---

* Mr. Hambro delivered this speech on December 10, 1963, in the Auditorium of the University of Oslo, following Mr. Jahn's presentation of the prize for 1962 to Linus Pauling. At the conclusion of Mr. Hambro's remarks, Mr. Jahn, chairman of the Committee, presented the Nobel diplomas and medals to Léopold Boissier as representative of the International Committee of the Red Cross and to John A. MacAulay as representative of the League of Red Cross Societies. Both men responded with brief speeches of acceptance, which included tributes to some earlier prizewinners and to the Norwegian Red Cross. The English text of Mr. Hambro's speech, with some minor emendations, is that appearing in *Les Prix Nobel en 1963*.
1. Jean Henri Dunant (1828–1910), co-recipient of the Nobel Peace Prize for 1901. See biography, Vol. 1, p. 5.

and repeated the words which Dunant adopted: «Tutti fratelli». We are all brothers.

Dunant had come to Italy for a conference with Napoleon III[1], but followed the call of his heart and conscience.

The earlier decades of the nineteenth century had seen wars in every country of Europe, and from the days of the disasters of the great French armies, the minds of statesmen and soldiers were busy with the idea of how to prevent wars and how to fight the disorder and disorganization which followed in the wake of war.

Fifty years before Solferino, General Döbeln, the great hero of the Swedish war in Finland[2], wrote in his diary: «Happy the country where nothing is regarded as little things, neither in peace nor in war.»

Dunant saw in Castiglione the indescribable suffering that came as a result of the lack of preparation and the neglect of what had been regarded as little things; and when later the idea of the Red Cross was accepted with open hearts in England, it was because the importance of «the little things» had been understood as a result of Florence Nightingale's work[3], and there were public meetings very much like those that were later arranged for the Red Cross. For such a meeting in 1845 a young English authoress, Miss Craigie, presented a poem called «Little Things»[4], which became very popular and was recited in the schools of England and America and accepted as an introduction to work for the Red Cross.

> *Little drops of water,*
> *Little grains of sand,*
> *Make the mighty ocean*
> *And the pleasant land.*
>
> *Thus the little minutes,*
> *Humble though they be,*
> *Make the mighty ages*
> *Of eternity.*

1. Louis Napoleon Bonaparte (1808–1873), emperor of the French (1852–1870).
2. War between Sweden and Russia (1808–1809) through which Russia acquired Finland from Sweden.
3. Florence Nightingale (1820–1910), English nurse and hospital reformer who organized hospital units during the Crimean War (1853–1856).
4. By Julia A. Fletcher Carney (1823–1908), American verse writer.

Thus our little errors
Make a mighty sin;
Drop by drop the evil
Floods the heart within.

Little deeds of kindness,
Little words of love,
Make our earth an Eden,
Like the heaven above.

Never have little things given greater results. Last summer there were Red Cross societies in eighty-eight countries, with a membership of nearly 170 millions.

Henri Dunant had learnt to see the importance of little things, and when in 1862 he published his book, *Un Souvenir de Solférino*[1], which was a tremendous shock to public opinion in Europe, he launched the idea to start, before any war broke out, organizations of peaceful, idealistic women and men to work for help to the wounded in war, friends and enemies alike. And should it not be possible to bring about an international convention to declare that wounded and medical personnel should be regarded as neutral and under protection of the governments at war? His book made an impression like that of *Uncle Tom's Cabin* by Harriet Beecher Stowe[2], and stirred the conscience of responsible people all over Europe.

In his native city of Geneva, La Société genevoise d'utilité publique [the Geneva Public Welfare Society] appointed a committee of five–among whom was Dunant–to make his idea a reality. And these five private individuals, without any official status, really succeeded in arranging a conference at Geneva in October, 1863, in which sixteen countries participated– among them Norway and Sweden. Here the Red Cross was organized, and in honor of Dunant it adopted as its international emblem the inverted Swiss flag–the red cross on white.

Until then every country–if it had any organized military medical service at all–had had its own flag and symbols, and there was general confusion behind the battlefields.

1. See Dunant's biography, Vol. 1, p.6.
2. Harriet Beecher Stowe (1811–1896), American author whose novel *Uncle Tom's Cabin* (serial form, 1851; book form, 1852) did much to solidify public opinion in the North against slavery.

In 1864, the year after, delegates of twelve states, invited by the Swiss government on the initiative of the Committee of Five, met at Geneva and adopted the first Geneva Convention for protection of sick and wounded in land warfare.

Gradually–and in the early years slowly – the Red Cross became the mighty institution which it is today.

It is wholly independent of any government and completely neutral. Its highest authority is the Red Cross Conference which usually meets every four years and consists of delegates from the National Red Cross Societies, the International Red Cross Committee, the League of Red Cross Societies and representatives of the governments which have signed the Geneva Convention. The delegation of each national Red Cross has only one vote. The decisions of the Conference bind the National Red Cross Societies morally, but the Conference can only give advice and express wishes.

The first International Red Cross Conference was in Paris in 1867, and the most recent one was in New Delhi in 1957 on the invitation of the Indian Red Cross.

A permanent International Red Cross Commission of nine members has been established to discuss every problem which arises between the conferences and to decide when and where the next conference shall meet. Five of the nine are elected by the Conference from the national Red Cross organizations, two are appointed by the Committee and two by the League.

The work of the International Committee has two branches, the General Affairs Division and the Executive Division. The General Affairs Division has worked to spread knowledge of the Geneva Conventions and the principles of the Red Cross, a work which has been of particular importance in all the new states; at the same time the Committee has tried to make governments improve and extend the Geneva Convention, which did not correspond to the modern form of war, and four new conventions were adopted at a conference in 1949, for the protection of the victims of sea warfare, for the shipwrecked, for prisoners of war, and for the protection of nonmilitary persons in time of war. But governments proved most reluctant to accept any conventions that would forbid atomic warfare and use of weapons whose destruction cannot be controlled by those who make use of them.

The Red Cross Conference at New Delhi again adopted such resolutions, and they were sent to the governments of all countries, with the remarks of the International Committee. Most governments have given no answer, and Mr. Boissier has commented that it is not difficult to understand this silence. «It will be necessary to fight fear and hatred.» And in this work is the future of the Red Cross.

In many quarters there has been an idea that the Committee as a Swiss body is more completely neutral and impartial than the League. It was the Committee that was asked to take care of all transportation and distribution of aid in Hungary after the uprising of the people[1], but it was the League that took care of the refugees, at a cost of more than 100 million Swiss francs; and corresponding large sums of money were given to the Algerian refugees[2] and to the Congo[3]–and it was a delegate of the Committee who was killed at Katanga.

It was the Committee that was permitted by the government of Nepal to give aid to the refugees from Tibet[4]–for Switzerland, not being a member of the United Nations, had taken no part in any decision against Communist China.

In the same way it was on the invitation of the Japanese Red Cross, that the Committee repatriated North Korean prisoners of war in Japan. Up to 1962 some 75,000 had been brought back to their home country, and in Europe the Committee has been active in repatriating refugees in even greater numbers and bringing together families that had been dispersed. And the Committee under the peace treaty with Japan has distributed the compensation given to those who had been prisoners of war in Japan, and in Europe to the victims of medical experiments in Germany.

The work of the Committee is so closely coordinated with that of the League that to all practical purposes they form a unity, and in many fields they work hand in hand with the United Nations.

The great worldwide humanitarian work of the League falls outside the sphere of the Peace Prize, but the cooperation between the Red Cross So-

1. The Hungarian uprising of October, 1956, against Soviet domination was put down by Russian troops early in November.
2. The Algerian refugee problem arose as a result of Algerian revolt against France, the ensuing war between France and Algeria, and finally of civil strife, once independence had been agreed upon in the early 1960's.
3. The new independent Republic of the Congo, created in 1960, was immediately torn by regional and tribal rivalries, with the province of Katanga seceding but eventually being subdued by UN troops and reintegrated with the Republic.
4. Many Tibetans became refugees as a result of unrest after the Chinese Communists assumed dominance over Tibet in the early 1950's and of the failure of a full-scale Tibetan revolt in 1959.

cieties of ninety different countries of different races, creeds, and color is of very real importance for international understanding and peace.

In Mohammedan countries the Red Cross became the Red Half-Moon on white, in Iran the Red Lion and Sun. But they all work loyally together, and the successful efforts of the Red Cross Societies in China and Japan which led to the repatriation of 30,000 Japanese prisoners in China in 1952 promoted peace in the Far East, and corresponding efforts which led to an exchange of prisoners between Poland and West Germany in 1955 had real importance. Particular stress has been laid on the work of the Junior Red Cross Societies. The Red Cross youth movement started in the U.S. in 1923 and has been in constant evolution. Today there are some sixty-two million members, and it cannot be doubted that if millions of young women and men are taught in the schools that we are all brothers–«Tutti fratelli»– and that little deeds of friendship and little words of love should bind the world together, the ideas of Nobel will triumph.

LÉOPOLD BOISSIER

Some Aspects of the Mission of the International Committee of the Red Cross

Nobel Lecture*, December 11, 1963

The International Committee of the Red Cross, being an institution unique of its kind, I feel I should say a few words about what it is and what its activities are. It is a private, independent body, composed only of Swiss citizens.

At the present time there are eighteen members who were recruited by co-optation, that is to say invited by the Committee itself, to become members. The International Committee is, therefore, completely national by composition, but international in its mission.

This is not a contradiction.

The International Committee is admitted on the territory of belligerents for the sole reason that its members are citizens of a small country, with no political ambitions but with a tradition of complete neutrality. Governments can, therefore, have full confidence in its impartiality.

The International Committee has no material power. It has no arms and would not even know how to resort to diplomatic maneuver. But its apparent weakness is offset by its moral authority. For just one hundred years now, governments have considered the existence of the International Committee useful.

They expect it to carry out tasks which cannot be accomplished by anyone else.

They know that, in a world where selfish or ideological interests are in conflict, one institution alone stands apart from struggles of this nature, even in the climax of war, and that it will always act, without any thought of self-interest, in complete independence and in obedience to its belief that

* Mr. Boissier (1893–1968), Swiss jurist, professor, and diplomat, a former secretary-general of the Interparliamentary Union, a member of the International Committee of the Red Cross since 1946 and its president 1955–1964, delivered this Nobel lecture in the name of the International Committee on December 11, 1963, in the Auditorium of the University of Oslo. The text is taken from *Les Prix Nobel en 1963*.

suffering, being a cruel reality, must be alleviated without prejudice of any kind.

The practical activities of the International Committee are threefold: protection of war victims, information on missing persons, relief in countries afflicted by war.

To discharge its first function of giving protection, the International Committee sends out delegates, who are all Swiss also, to the countries at war, particularly in order to visit prisoner-of-war camps and ensure humane treatment to those who are held captive. These delegates watch over the situation in the detention quarters, diet, medical care, working and living conditions.

They interview prisoners without witness. Detailed reports are then sent to the detaining power and to the government of the prisoner's country of origin. The delegates submit on the spot requests for any necessary improvements. If need be, the International Committee itself takes the matter up with the higher authorities, using the principle of reciprocity as a lever to achieve its aim.

During the Second World War the International Committee's delegates carried out some eleven thousand camp visits.

The Geneva Conventions of 1949 added strength to the International Committee in its role as the protector of prisoners of war.

These Conventions [1] extended its field of activity to all civilians who might be interned, in time of war, for any reason whatsoever, and the camps –I mean the concentration camps–where they are interned are now also open to inspection.

To carry out its second function of supplying information on missing persons, the International Committee has been entrusted with setting up and running the Central Tracing Agency for prisoners of war and civilians.

This Agency communicates to anxious families news of their kin, held captive or who are missing. During the last World War, the Agency assembled some forty million information cards.

It brought news to as many as six thousand families a day.

The Agency is now a permanent establishment.

1. The Geneva Conventions of August 12, 1949, covered the following: (1) The Amelioration of the Condition of the Wounded and Sick in Armed Forces in the Field; (2) The Amelioration of the Condition of Wounded, Sick, and Shipwrecked Members of the Armed Forces at Sea; (3) The Treatment of Prisoners of War; (4) The Protection of Civilian Persons in Time of War.

Furthermore, the Committee manages the International Tracing Service at Arolsen, in the Federal Republic of Germany, whose duty it is to supply information on persons missing from concentration camps and, also, to issue certificates of incarceration to those who survived. A staff of over two hundred and fifty persons is necessary for this colossal task.

The third aspect of the Committee's work is to supply material relief.

During the Second World War it distributed, to the camps in which Allied soldiers were detained in Germany, for instance, relief in the form of food, clothing, medical supplies, and books, to a value of some three and a half billion Swiss francs. In order to transport this material through the blockade, the International Committee had to organize a fleet of fourteen ships which sailed the seas under the Red Cross flag.

Since the war this activity has continued. Two examples are the supplies to Hungary, at the time of the 1956 uprising[1], and, at the present time, the setting up, in the heart of the Arabian desert, of a field hospital, in order to bring relief to the victims of the cruel war of which the Yemen is the theatre[2].

But there are also tasks of a more general order which the International Committee has to perform.

It is the recognized guardian of the Red Cross ideal. It must, therefore, exercise vigilance to ensure respect for humanitarian principles: non discrimination, independence, and neutrality, which are the common heritage of our universal movement.

Yet a further, primary duty is to work for the development of international humanitarian law which protects the human person in the time of war. As early as 1864, the International Committee persuaded governments to conclude the first Geneva Convention[3] for—as its title indicates—the Amelioration of the Condition of the Sick and Wounded in the Field.

This treaty was strengthened in 1929 by a second Convention, relative to the Treatment of Prisoners of War. This Convention affected the lives of millions of captives during the Second World War. In order to demonstrate its usefulness, let me say that wherever it was applied the mortality rate did not exceed ten percent!

1. Against Soviet domination.
2. Between the forces of the Imam in Yemen and an army group which seized power in 1962, proclaiming Yemen a republic.
3. See history of the Red Cross, Vol. 1, p. 284; see also selected bibliography, Vol. 1, p. 286.

In the concentration camps for civil prisoners–where the Committee's delegates never penetrated, despite repeated appeals to Hitler himself–the mortality rate was as high as ninety percent!

That is why it was absolutely necessary to revise and extend these Conventions. This was done in 1949 when two new Conventions were also drawn up.

The first of these brought humanitarian protection to the victims of war at sea, whilst the second–of capital importance–extended it to civilians. In fact, despite all the efforts of the International Committee, no complete, up-to-date Convention to protect civilians was in force when the Second World War broke out. Civilians were, therefore, in some countries, subject to deportation and even to extermination!

This tragic gap has now been bridged. Civilians have been given the status and the guarantees which were previously so cruelly lacking. They are now entitled to treatment of at least the same standard as that which is given to prisoners of war.

What is even more important is that this fourth Convention, as well as the three others, contains a common article, which is revolutionary in international law.

This is Article Three.

It gives certain guarantees to combatants in civil wars. It prohibits the taking of hostages and summary executions without fair trial. It lays down humane conditions of internment and the right to protection by the International Committee.

Article Three has enabled the International Committee to intervene in the civil wars which have ravaged various countries during the past fifteen years. I am thinking, more particularly, of the subcontinent of India at the time of its division into two great countries: India and Pakistan. Also in Latin America, Algeria, Vietnam, Laos, and recently again, in the Congo.

The new Geneva Conventions were soon signed and ratified by nearly every country in the world. Ninety-eight governments have ratified so far. The International Committee has drawn up detailed commentaries of these Conventions.

It has also undertaken to ensure their diffusion, for they must be known to all those who will be called upon to apply them.

Here in Oslo, two years ago, I explained how the International Committee's mission has developed in civil wars. I shall, therefore, not dwell on this point. I would, however, like to add a further example to those I have just mentioned.

It is a venture, the scene of which is set in the burning sands of Arabia and the Yemen, where civil war is raging.

These are the only regions in the world where the Red Cross and the Geneva Convention have not yet penetrated. But they are doing so now, little by little.

This exploration in unknown territory, I assure you, is most exalting. Indeed, the heads of the two opposing forces have decided to give up their traditional practice of slaughtering the vanquished.

And now, for my example. A sheikh in the desert found himself suddenly face to face with an enemy officer. In the course of the fight both were wounded, but the sheikh, who was less seriously hurt, was able to bandage the wounds of his opponent. He leant over the man who a moment before had sought to kill him and took care of him. Then he brought him as his prisoner to his own tribe. But there, all his family and warrior friends insulted him, urging him to put the enemy to death. «If you are a man, prove it!» shouted his mother. But the sheikh was steadfast and delivered his prisoner to his king. Thus a life–and several hundred others–was saved, and the flag of the Red Cross flies over the mysterious landscapes of Arabia.

There is a point I would like to make here in connection with the intervention of the United Nations in civil wars, not only in the Yemen, but also, for instance, at the frontiers of Israel and in the Congo.

It may be presumed that they will be called upon, more and more frequently, to maintain or to reestablish peace and that the troops they send for that purpose may sometimes be in action in the trouble spots of the world.

The United Nations Organization, as such, is not, however, a party to the Geneva Conventions.

Already, in 1956 immediately after the Suez crisis[1], the International Committee made known to the late–and regretted–Mr. Hammarskjöld[2], its concern with this question. It repeated this in 1960, when the United Nations acted in the Congo. Each time the Committee received the assurance that the United Nations intended to observe the broad principles–that was the

1. Precipitated by Gamal Abdel Nasser (1918–1970), president of Egypt (1956–1970), in July, 1956, when he announced the nationalization of the Suez Canal.
2. Dag Hammarskjöld (1905–1961), recipient, posthumously, of the Nobel Peace Prize for 1961; secretary-general of the UN (1953–1961).

word used–of the Geneva Conventions. But incidents which resulted in the tragic death of three Red Cross workers, including an International Committee delegate, proves that the problem is far from being solved.

It was again raised at the Centenary Congress of the International Red Cross which was held this summer in Geneva. The Congress passed a unanimous resolution. I give you the essential passages:

(a) «The Council of Delegates–of the International Red Cross–recommends: that the United Nations be invited to adopt a solemn declaration, accepting that the Geneva Conventions equally apply to their Emergency Forces, as they apply to the forces of States parties to the said Conventions;

(b) That the Governments of countries providing contingents to the United Nations should, as a matter of prime importance, give them before departure from their country of origin, adequate instruction on the Geneva Conventions, as well as orders to comply with them...»

In this way, the International Committee hopes that this important question will be brought to a satisfactory conclusion, thanks to the goodwill of all concerned.

Despite the great extension of the Geneva Conventions they still do not cover the whole field of human suffering. We have just seen that, since 1949, there exists an Article Three, common to all four Geneva Conventions, for the protection of the victims of civil wars. This article, however, is only applicable in the event of armed conflicts, but governments often deny the existence of such conflicts on their territory.

The International Committee is, therefore, trying to extend the scope of humanitarian law further still. The first objective is to bring assistance to persons interned in their own countries as a result of internal tensions.

Here the International Committee is on difficult ground.

Indeed, this raises the problem of intervention in matters affecting national sovereignty or the superior interests of the state.

Today, individuals are often treated in their own countries less favorably than enemy soldiers captured with weapons in their hands. Paradoxically, therefore, it seems that humanitarian law might, sometimes, be applied to the domestic affairs of states.

Experts of international renown, consulted by the Committee, have recognized the legitimacy of the intervention of the Red Cross in this particular field. They laid down a definition of humane treatment which should be applied to detainees in such cases. On the basis of this, the Committee has been able to act, in the course of disturbances or troubles, in several countries on the American, African, and Asian continents. Thus law and fact, theory and practice, give support the one to the other and to the work of the Red Cross.

But there is a greater problem still: the evolution of war towards an ever increasingly «total» form. It approaches this climax through the development of aviation and explosives, via systematic bombing, V-two, and napalm to the hydrogen bomb, which threatens to destroy all humanity and civilization.

The rules of air warfare, drawn up in 1907 and laid down in the Hague Conventions[1], were already, at the time of the first air raid in 1911, outmoded and buried beneath the ruins of the towns laid waste.

But governments, in the face of the menacing progress of nuclear physics, are doing nothing to revise and restore these regulations.

The International Committee had, therefore, the duty to do something. It proceeded from the fact that the wholesale bombing of towns during the Second World War did not «pay» from a purely military point of view. Indeed, in the bombed industrial regions, factories never ceased work and even increased production. If governments, therefore, do not admit that total, indiscriminate war is criminal, they will, perhaps, heed the argument that it is not good tactics.

The International Committee has had an idea which may perhaps provide the key to the problem: It should not concentrate its effort against any particular weapon, such as the atom bomb, as this would go unheeded by governments and would, in any case, be insufficient. What must be done is to oppose a particular form of war.

In fact, the bombing of Hamburg resulted in as many victims as the bombing of Hiroshima.

Once a weapon is prohibited, an even more frightful one will be invented to take its place. In the French village of Oradour, where the entire population was burnt alive in the church, the weapon was a mere box of matches!

The principle to be established is, therefore, that whatever weapons are employed, the civilian population must not be harmed or at least not exposed to risks out of all proportion to the military objectives.

With the assistance of experts, the International Committee drew up draft regulations which were approved, in principle, by the last International Red Cross Conference in 1957.

1. At the Hague Peace Conference of 1907.

This draft was then communicated to governments.

But alas, the answer was silence! The time was, perhaps, not ripe. The Red Cross, however, never lets itself be discouraged. When one door is closed, it seeks to open others.

We shall not abandon our intention of protecting the civilian population.

In autumn, 1962, the International Committee was asked to act and to step beyond the limits of its traditional mission. This was during the Cuban crisis[1]. You will recall that the world was then on the brink of disaster.

War was liable to break out from one minute to the next–a «press button» war, involving extermination on a massive scale, by remote-controlled thermonuclear rockets.

Faced by this ghastly prospect, the United Nations turned to the International Committee as the only organization still, perhaps, able to maintain peace.

It was asked to set up a system to control the ships bound for Cuba, to ensure, through a force of some thirty inspectors, that no long-range atomic weapons were being delivered to Cuba.

The International Committee did not see how it could refuse to undertake this task.

Indeed, when the Red Cross movement codified the «Red Cross principles» in 1961, defining its fundamental doctrine, an additional duty was embodied, that is, to promote mutual understanding, friendship, cooperation and a lasting peace amongst all peoples.

No one intended this principle to remain a dead letter.

So it came about that, in the grave tensions of the Cuban crisis, the International Committee was called upon to perform a task which it alone perhaps could undertake: to maintain peace in the world.

For at least two days there was every reason to fear the worst, that a conflict breaking out under these conditions would soon become an atomic war which would inevitably have caused the loss of millions of human lives, inflicted untold suffering and terrible destruction.

At the same time, the Red Cross itself was likely to see its work reduced to nought or rendered impossible.

The International Committee mustered all the conditions which its ex-

1. The crisis, involving the U.S. and the USSR, arose over the building of Russian missile sites in Cuba in 1962; it ended when the USSR agreed to withdraw offensive weapons threatening U.S. security.

perience and the principle of neutrality demanded. The first step was to obtain the consent of the three parties concerned–the United States, the Soviet Union, and Cuba–which was given.

The International Committee, thereupon, delegated one of its members to the United Nations. There he examined, with the Secretary-General, the further conditions for possible action by the Committee: among others that there be a real threat of atomic war and that the International Committee be in a position to give its assistance, in an effective manner, within the framework of the Red Cross principles.

These principles are consistent with those of international public law. One of the most important of the latter principles is the freedom of the high seas. That is why the International Committee also laid down the prior condition that the control which it was called upon to carry out be accepted by all maritime powers whose ships call at Cuba.

Had this last condition been better known by the public at large, the opposition to the International Committee's intervention, which was raised in several countries having large merchant fleets, would certainly have been withdrawn.

Tension over Cuba subsided without the International Committee's having to intervene in fact. But the Committee's cooperative attitude facilitated the easing of tension.

By contributing to the maintenance of peace, it remained faithful to its mission.

Every institution, like every individual, should contribute to the crusade for peace, with the means at its disposal, The Red Cross, for its part, struggles against war by making it less inhuman; does it not rescue war victims, even on the battlefield? But, given the present state of the world, it cannot pretend to be able to eliminate the scourge of war; it therefore tries to alleviate its evils.

By promoting the first Geneva Convention, the Red Cross dealt war one of the first and most serious blows it has ever received. In August, 1864, states sacrificed a fraction of their sovereignty for the benefit of human needs. This was the price paid in order to force a breach in the ancestral hatred of man for man. War gave ground to law.

The first Geneva Convention, which was revolutionary at the time, is the basis of all humanitarian law which aims at protecting the victims of hostilities. Within a century, the mortality rate of wounded on the battlefield fell from sixty percent to two percent. These figures speak louder than words.

The impetus created by this Convention resulted in the conclusion of the Hague Conventions which govern the conduct of hostilities and restrict the use of certain weapons[1].

On the moral plane also, the Red Cross promotes understanding amongst peoples by developing an active sense of brotherhood and by promoting a feeling of mutual responsibility for the good of mankind. The Red Cross knows better than anyone the wounds caused by war, for it is the Red Cross which heals those wounds; it reveals to men the hideous aspect of war and turns them from it.

The achievements of the Red Cross have a symbolic value and stand out as an example. Its accomplishments at the height of battle are acts of peace.

When war creates its tragic gap between nations, the Red Cross remains the last link. Its struggle against suffering is a vivid reproach to those who inflict it. It intervenes in the midst of violence but does not have recourse thereto. The Red Cross, therefore, makes a powerful appeal to all men in favor of peace.

1. See Renault's Nobel lecture, Vol. 1, pp. 150–155.

JOHN A. MACAULAY

The Red Cross in a Changing World

Nobel Lecture*, December 11, 1963

To this hall tonight have been invited men and women representative of the four corners of our world. Each person present has rendered some service to the cause of peace. Such an undertaking imposes humility and suggests that we speak simply to this world forum about the common purpose that concerns us all.

Goodwill is often inarticulate. Fortunately, we are blessed with individuals and organizations to express the longings of little peoples in all lands. The gift of great and continuing institutions is a splendid gift. We are «inheritors of a tradition», and in our hands is responsibility that the lustre does not dim, nor the shadow shrink.

Before making any reference to the League of Red Cross Societies, I would like to speak in the highest terms of the work which has been done for the past one hundred years by the International Committee of the Red Cross and for the work it continues to carry on ever with increased fervor. The International Committee is that great body of Swiss citizens which acts as intermediary between belligerents in the time of war, and as arbitrators of disputes in time of peace. To quote Mr. Boissier, president of the International Committee, at the inauguration ceremony [1] of the Centenary of the Red Cross, «The International Committee will endeavor, with untiring perseverance, to obtain universal acceptance and application of the Geneva Conventions. These conventions, instruments fashioned and perfected by experience, were forged to protect and save innocent victims of

* This Nobel lecture was delivered in the Auditorium of the University of Oslo by John Alexander MacAulay (1895–   ), who spoke on behalf of the League of Red Cross Societies. Mr. MacAulay, a Canadian jurist, businessman, and for many years an active volunteer worker in the Canadian Red Cross Society and a member of its Central Council (president, 1950–1951), was at this time chairman of the Board of Governors of the League of Red Cross Societies in Geneva, a post he held 1959–1965. The text is that in *Les Prix Nobel en 1963*, with some statistical corrections and stylistic changes made after collation with the Red Cross Centenary text.
1. In Geneva on September 1, 1963.

war. Each victim is considered as a separate entity and assisted in his individual suffering, from which it is necessary to save him by stretching out a helping hand. In this fashion, the text of the Convention is transformed into a veritable causeway along which representatives from Geneva travel to bring comfort and perhaps salvation to the wounded or imprisoned.»

The League of Red Cross Societies was founded on May 5, 1919. The League is described in its constitution as the International Federation of National Red Cross Societies, an association of unlimited duration having the legal status of a corporate body. In referring to National Red Cross Societies, the constitution also and equally refers to the corresponding National Societies of the countries using in the place of the Red Cross the other emblems recognized by the Geneva Conventions, namely the Red Crescent, and the Red Lion and Sun[1].

National Societies emerged and developed as a direct consequence of the attitude and philosophy of Henri Dunant. The first National Society was founded in 1863. For the realization of his dreams, he proposed the formation of relief societies which would always be available for the performance of an ever increasing number of tasks. His ideas respecting the function of relief committees were conveyed in his own words as follows:

«To render great services by their permanent existence during periods of epidemics, floods, great fires, and other unforeseen disasters; the philanthropic spirit which brought them into being would prompt them to action in all circumstances where they could be of service.»[2]

This year, Red Cross celebrated its centenary. The Red Cross begins its second century with 102 active National Red Cross Societies, comprising approximately 170,000,000 individual members of local societies. Fourteen of these National Societies became members of the League of Red Cross Societies during the last meeting of the Board of Governors held in Geneva in August, 1963. The formation throughout the world of new National Societies gives increased vitality, a deeper and more realistic meaning to the Red Cross principles of universality, humanity, and impartiality. These National Societies are all working according to principles laid down in Geneva one hundred years ago by the founding fathers of Red Cross. Thus

1. See history of the Red Cross, Vol. 1, p. 285.
2. Jean Henri Dunant (1828–1910), co-recipient of the Nobel Peace Prize for 1901. The quotation is a translation of fn. 1, p. 152, of the third edition of Dunant's *Un Souvenir de Solférino* (Genève, 1863).

have the humanitarian ideas of one man, Henri Dunant, taken root and flourished.

Red Cross members, unified in their own National Societies and federated in the League, belong to something more significant than a series of benevolent societies. These individuals are guided by international agreements and basic humanitarian principles which give their work a special significance. The League represents millions of voluntary workers, to whom the movement owes an extreme debt of gratitude. The officers of the League have the honor of representing these volunteer members on this very important occasion.

The League of Red Cross Societies, the National Societies of Red Cross, and the members of all National Societies regard with pride the history of the Red Cross, and anticipate with confidence and humility the great new tasks which are ahead. They remember with thankful respect the founding fathers of the International Red Cross.

What does the future hold for the Red Cross? Whatever the developments may be in the world in the coming decades, there will be a tremendous opportunity for this humanitarian organization. Without changing its principles, it must adapt itself to a changing world. There will be a great responsibility for the League and for the National Societies.

«We are a civilization which knows how to make War, but no longer knows how to make Peace», the Italian Guglielmo Ferrero wrote in his book, *The Problem of Peace*. During the past ten years this provocative declaration has been tested by partial and localized conflicts in many parts of the world. There is a condition of continuous tension arising from the antagonism of ideologies and the fear of a world war. And yet, there is not a person in the world who does not yearn for peace. What then, in the twentieth century, in this world which is a prey to the most violent convulsions and to the most unexpected upheavals, are the ways to create a climate of understanding and fraternity between men? How do we learn to make peace?

As the seventeenth International Conference of the Red Cross affirmed in Stockholm in 1948, «The history of mankind shows that the campaign against the terrible scourge of war cannot achieve success if it is limited to the political sphere.» The Red Cross, to which quite special appeals have been made in these last ten years, has demonstrated that it is one of the rare institutions capable of marshaling great numbers of men and women, and the necessary material resources, to action for peaceful purposes. It has made a contribution to development of a climate of agreement over and above all ideological, racial, and religious considerations. The Red Cross has always devoted itself to ignoring the antagonisms, whatever they may be, in order to unite all men in one and the same movement of solidarity.

Since its founding in 1919, the League has sent out 168 appeals for international help. The response has not been only from a few prosperous societies. Every society, large or small, young or old, rich or poor, responds to the call for help with eagerness and generosity. After the recent Agadir disaster[1], where 17,000 people were killed and 1,700 injured, sixty-one Red Cross Societies participated in relief work. From all corners of the globe teams of surgeons, doctors, and nurses made every effort to bring relief to the victims. Foodstuffs and medicaments were provided to a total value of millions of Swiss francs. Following the disaster emergency, the reconstruction of a hospital complex in Agadir remains as a memorial of Red Cross cooperation.

The list of disasters in the last ten years is impressive. It illustrates the distress of populations who require continuous relief in many instances for several months. To a greater extent than any other body, the League has been called upon to devote its attention to the fate of needy populations and to draw up long-term programs, often at the request of UN specialized agencies, and even governments. Within the broad plan «each victim is considered as a separate entity and assisted in his individual suffering, from which it is necessary to save him by stretching out a helping hand».

The paralysis epidemic in Morocco in 1959 presented the League with the opportunity of bringing relief to a population and demonstrating the solidarity of this world movement. Everyone recalls the innocent consumption of adulterated cooking oil by a section of the Moroccan population[2]. There were 10,466 paralysis victims, but after training centers were set up, manned by expert personnel for a period of eighteen months, all but 120 were rehabilitated and orthopedic surgery was arranged for these. In the midst of the disturbances, doctors from Federal and Democratic Germany worked in the same operating theatres; Polish, Canadian, and Czechoslovakian nurses bandaged and treated the same patients, without discrimination.

Among distressed populations, there is a category of people who are most destitute among the destitute, namely the refugees. Often obliged to flee

1. The severe earthquake of 1960.
2. Moroccan merchants bought surplus mineral oil used for rinsing engines, mixed it with cooking oil, and sold it as table oil.

from their own countries, with no official status and with pride hurt, the refugees are left to their own devices. At this time when some countries are persecuting these human beings, and other countries ignoring them, the League, in pursuance of its principles of humanity and impartiality, rushes to their support. In 1956–1957, 180,000 Hungarians fled from their country. For eleven months the League, with the help of the Austrian and Yugoslav governments and the Office of the United Nations High Commissioner for Refugees, devoted itself to coordinating relief and administering temporary camps. Millions of dollars were put to use in this vast operation, in which fifty-two National Societies participated, and for which the League received the Nansen medal.

The largest relief operation ever undertaken by the League remains without doubt the one from which 285,000 Algerian refugees benefitted. These refugees, installed in Tunisia and Morocco from 1958 to 1962, received regular care from medical teams and were provided with foodstuffs and clothing. Fifty-seven National Societies made gifts during these four years to the total amount of 90,000,000 Swiss francs. This massive assistance was given until the repatriation of the refugees which was effected in 1962 under the auspices of the Office of the United Nations High Commissioner for Refugees. And later, for some months, the League was engaged in a large-scale program of assistance to two million needy Algerians.

The mission of the League is to bring relief on all fronts. One has only to recall the appeal of the League in 1960 to provide medical teams for the civilian hospitals of the Congo, the relief given to the Angolan refugees, and the medical care and foodstuffs provided for the Watusi tribes from Ruanda-Urundi, who were not only given assistance in the form of medical care and foodstuffs, but were also resettled and equipped.

These are only a few of the actions undertaken by the League during recent years. Others are too numerous to mention except by names–floods in Italy, The Netherlands, England, Belgium, and other countries; hurricanes in Thailand, Madagascar, the Caribbean; earthquakes in Japan, Iran, Turkey, and more recently, in Yugoslavia, where the city of Skoplje was destroyed in July, 1963. The League undertook to assist the Yugoslav Red Cross by providing 27,000 children and 3,000 mothers with food and clothing while their homes were being rebuilt.

These examples illustrate this vast movement of solidarity, which the League always tries to promote and develop between nations. The generosity of National Societies, which between 1950 and 1960 contributed to eighty-

eight relief actions to the extent of some sixty million dollars, is certainly
not a negligible factor in the search for peace. In Austria, Chile, the Congo,
and Viet Nam, men of all races and different ideologies have united their
efforts, here to build a dispensary, there to set up a milk station, and everywhere to alleviate suffering. A great philosopher has said: «Force them to
build a tower together and you will change them into brothers.» This is
the most important aspect. Specialists from all corners of the globe have
studied together a rare illness. They have taken the measure of human suffering to find a remedy.

Even more than the thousands of cases of clothing and foodstuffs, with
labels from many nations, which lie together in the holds of ships, these
human contacts which the League does not cease to encourage are those
that best contribute to the justification of its motto: «Per humanitatem ad
pacem». Such is the great, the noble task which the League never ceases
to pursue.

International mutual aid is not limited to the field of relief but includes
also the development of other sister Societies. The League needs constantly
to extend its network of humanitarian actions, and many new countries
have recently gained their independence. The Red Cross Development
Program is to promote by material and financial aid the organization and
development of the different services to sister Societies in need of help. This
program, dynamic and flexible enough to be adapted to local conditions,
also aims at developing international understanding between sister Societies,
between the old and the new. Study seminars and the loan of technical
experts help to train the leaders of future Societies, or Societies recently
founded.

The Junior Red Cross enables children, ignoring the quarrels of adults,
to smile at each other across national borders. A symbol of this broad approach to international service and understanding is the «Henri Dunant
House» in Woudschoten, near Zeist, in The Netherlands. Founded by teams
of young people on the occasions of the disasters[1] which struck Holland
in 1953, it has become a house of solidarity–welcoming groups of handicapped adolescents.

It should not be forgotten that the meetings of the League bring peoples
together and create better understanding. To these meetings all the National Societies send their representatives, and this serves not only to strength-

1. The floods of 1953.

en the links between members of the Red Cross but also to provide fruitful contact with statesmen who belong to the Red Cross and whose influence may be considerable. Thousands of families, the members of which were dispersed throughout the world as a result of the last war, have been reunited through contact with the National Societies.

On many occasions resolutions relevant to peace have been adopted by various Red Cross Conferences. In addition, the League has intervened directly to remedy to the extent possible the consequences of a conflict. Thus, in 1952 the League took the initiative in arranging semiofficial discussions between the Red Cross Societies of Japan and the People's Republic of China. In a few months, 30,000 Japanese detained in China were able to return to their country, thanks to the goodwill and understanding of these two societies. In December, 1952, following suspension of the armistice negotiations in Korea, the League appealed to the belligerents to take immediate steps, under the Geneva Conventions, to ensure repatriation of prisoners. The difficulties were immense, but the League's appeal prepared the way for a solution which, if it had been delayed for long, would have caused new and pointless suffering.

In 1955 the German Red Cross of the Federal Republic of Germany negotiated the repatriation of 11,000 Germans detained in Poland.

The League of Red Cross Societies launches through its activities a daily challenge to misery and despair. It succeeds when it establishes a field of understanding, where men of goodwill speak together in the spirit of human heart.

No finer homage has ever been paid to the League than by the late Mr. Dag Hammarskjöld[1], secretary-general of the United Nations, when he declared: «The Red Cross, with its affiliated Red Crescent and Red Lion and Sun Societies, has become the symbol of complete impartiality in rendering help wherever help is needed. The technical achievements of the League have been outstanding, but even greater has been its work in strengthening the ideal of the human race as one family by translating into practical terms the humanitarian concern for the welfare of our fellow men.»

Since the birth of the League, it has seen wars and major human catastrophes. The blind forces of nature have on many occasions overwhelmed the puny breastworks of man. In each and every instance, from every corner of the globe, the response came flooding in to meet the challenge.

1. Dag Hammarskjöld (1905–1961), recipient, posthumously, of the Nobel Peace Prize for 1961.

It would be an impervious being who would not note that this outpouring of the spirit of helpfulness is not present in all the dealings between the scattered members of our human family. Many have been the attempts to scale the heights, or pierce the thick darkness, where Peace resides. History, civilized and primitive, is stained with the blood of those who had the determination to attain peace, or impose it upon their adversaries. Too often, idealism has found itself steeped in cruelty and twisted in hate. The path to Peace is deep in dead. The entrails of youth are strewn on our battlefields. What matters it to Death and Despair that our protestations are pure, and our declared motives blameless.

In such a world it is to be wondered that the Red Cross has survived. Is it merely that a referee is needed who will serve as liaison and be impartial? Is there place for a doctor who will stanch the bleeding of those who may still be saved? Is it merely as a convenience of the combatants that Red Cross is able to penetrate the exclusions of nationalism to keep alive the fact of mercy? Is Red Cross in wartime a flickering flame to remind us of our continuing brotherhood? Is it a gesture to declare, despite appearances, that we are derived from the Godhead; that we may lay waste our bodies but cannot cast aside, entirely, our souls?

It is this contrast between the work of the Red Cross in peace and in war that provides an endless fascination. In peace, it is the strong support of beneficent service, and in emergencies a wave and pillar of succor for the distressed. In war, it is a liaison, a medium of practical help to the wounded and the prisoner, a symbol that beyond the knives and guns, the larks and the angels are watching.

Why is it that the Red Cross must work in two such disparate worlds? How is it that the same people who rush to the relief of the stranger in a peacetime emergency will grant merely treaty rights in time of war? These rights have been hard won and have yielded important returns in the relief of suffering. But it is the contrast in moods that is impressive.

The Red Cross, acting on behalf of mercy, touches a vibrant chord of outwelling sympathy that stretches from land to land, from black to white, red to yellow, from creed to creed, from heart to heart. There is no delay, no finely weighed counting up of plus and minus, no calculation of the terms of trade, or estimate of what we get for what we give. It is like the mechanism of the human body responding to an infection; like a human family pooling its resources for the member who has met catastrophe.

Perhaps we do not live in two worlds. Rather we live in a divided world where we alarm our neighbors with terrible threats, and evoke the horrors of retaliation. That very same world and those very same people are ready to rush to the aid of those very same neighbors when nature lets loose her terrors. Great wells and springs of sympathy and understanding exist. They are tapped and made into reservoirs in times of need.

Happily, there is some evidence that the closing years of the twentieth century may see great progress made towards the goal of human brotherhood and away from the practices of hate and deception. You may be tolerant if we place before you certain of the reasons of our convictions, and even hopes:

(1) The expansion of knowledge about the world, the universe, and man himself has shown how fascinating can be the discovery and enjoyment of this vast workshop and playroom. War and destruction are idiotic in circumstances where the potential is boundless for the sharing of achievement. Why quarrel over pebbles when we can share diamonds; why create destruction when we could be partners in abundance?

(2) The great religions of the world are indicating a realization that they are the keepers of a viewpoint about man and his meaning. Archaic arrogance and conflicting finalities are yielding to a nicer grasp of what matters and should be enshrined. The past is not being forsaken, it is being winnowed; the truth is not being abandoned, it is being rediscovered in modern terms; differences are not being disregarded, they are being reconciled. From this alchemy may come diminution of the estrangement of reason from belief, and the alienation of good men over suppositional certainties.

(3) The habit of cooperation is growing among the nations. The United Nations is a fact and a symbol for man's determination to talk and act together. Projects like the International Geophysical Year[1] draw men from everywhere, together in furtherance of a common interest. The Thinkers Conference[2], at Pugwash, Canada, could be proliferated in topics and place

1. The IGY (July, 1957, through December, 1958) was a period of cooperative study of earth and its cosmic environment by scientists throughout the world.
2. Cyrus S. Eaton, a Cleveland industrialist, convened or sponsored at his estate at Pugwash, Nova Scotia, various conferences of intellectuals for the exchange of ideas on contemporary life and issues. The independently organized Pugwash Conference on Science and World Affairs held its first meeting (1957) at Pugwash at Mr. Eaton's invitation.

to great advantage. The Peace Corps[1] and the Peace Institute[2] have seeds of promise. Common interest is a common denominator and is the solution of many problems. Happily, there is more coming and going, and more understanding should be a consequence.

(4) The improvement in the means of communications and the increase in the resources for wealth creation have multiplied the capacity to help the less fortunate. Much has been said recently about the shortcomings of the colonial powers in the nineteenth century. It is clear that it is possible today to do more for backward peoples than in the days of sailing ships, and supply more than bare subsistence for the masses in the countries of Europe. Factories are springing up in Africa. Exchange students are numerous on university campuses, and these students will return to enrich their respective homelands.

(5) We are moving into a climate of world opinion where idealism is becoming practical politics, an acknowledged fact of life. It is no longer a subject to be discussed in hushed voice and undertaken, by a strange and select coterie, under penalty of ridicule. Young people who follow idealistic courses are no longer regarded as eccentric by their contemporaries. Idealism is no longer «far out»; it is approaching a norm. In this significant change many organizations and many individuals, moving in the slow step of time, have brought to bear their influence. The far corners of the earth are responding to the breath and the touch of brotherhood.

Here tonight, we can make entries in the ledger of hopeful trends. We will include our own auditor's notes of caution about the terrifying consequences of false or slanted propaganda; of how the ghosts of history can rise to haunt us; and that insane desires or even misunderstandings can loose the horrors of unlimited calamity.

We can take solace and courage from awareness that the good of all men is within our reach. Many forces are in motion. Is there any further way we can tip the balance in the tug between a Paradise Lost and a Paradise Gained?

1. The U.S. Peace Corps, an organization of trained men and women sent to assist foreign countries in meeting skilled manpower needs, was established by President J.F. Kennedy in 1961.
2. The International Institute for Peace was founded in 1957 in Vienna to promote peace through publications, through serving those working for peace, through establishing contact with religious, political, and cultural groups with like aims, as well as with the UN and other international organizations.

It would seem that a practical gain might be achieved if we could set up an agreed international relationship between the resources we direct to the means of destruction, and those we direct to the relief of distress, the increase in well-being of the less fortunate, and the continued unveiling of nature. A friendly competition in getting a higher percent of our national resources used for human betterment might be an approach to a lower percent being used for destruction. Most human beings would rather relieve distress than create it.

A famous poet once inquired: «Where are the snows of yesteryear?»[1] Perhaps we shall live to the day when men will ask: «Where are the hates of yesteryear?» For, in the long run, the power of kindness can redeem beyond the power of force to destroy. There is a vast reservoir of kindness that we can no longer afford to disregard.

The curtain is lifting. We can have Triumph or Tragedy – for we are the playwrights, the actors, and the audience. Let us book our seats for Triumph – the world is sickened of Tragedy.

1. François Villon (1431–c. 1463), French poet, in «Ballade des dames du temps jadis» in his *Grand Testament*.

Peace 1964

MARTIN LUTHER KING, JR.

Presentation

by Gunnar Jahn*, Chairman of the Nobel Committee

Not many years have passed since the name Martin Luther King became known all over the world. Nine years ago, as leader of the Negro people in Montgomery in the state of Alabama, he launched a campaign to secure for Negroes the right to use public transport on an equal footing with whites.

But it was not because he led a racial minority in their struggle for equality that Martin Luther King achieved fame. Many others have done the same, and their names have been forgotten.

Luther King's name will endure for the way in which he has waged his struggle, personifying in his conduct the words[1] that were spoken to mankind:

> *Whosoever shall smite thee on thy right cheek,*
> *turn to him the other also!*

Fifty thousand Negroes obeyed this commandment in December, 1955, and won a victory. This was the beginning. At that time Martin Luther King was only twenty-six years old; he was a young man, but nevertheless a mature one.

His father is a clergyman, who made his way in life unaided and provided his children with a good home where he tried to shield them from the humiliations of racial discrimination. Both as a member of the National Association for the Advancement of Colored People and as a private citizen, he has been active in the struggle for civil rights, and his children have followed in his footsteps. As a boy Martin Luther King soon learned the

---

* Mr. Jahn delivered this speech on December 10, 1964, in the Auditorium of the University of Oslo. This text in English translation, with some minor emendations, is taken from *Les Prix Nobel en 1964*. Dr. King, who was present, received his award from Mr. Jahn, accepting in the name of a civil rights movement determined to establish «a reign of freedom and a rule of justice» and terming the award a recognition of nonviolence as the «answer to the crucial political and moral question of our time – the need for man to overcome oppression and violence without resorting to violence and oppression».

1. Matthew 5:39.

role played by economic inequality in the life of the individual and of the community.

From his childhood years this left its indelible mark on him, but there is no evidence to suggest that as a boy he had yet made up his mind to devote his life to the struggle for Negro rights.

He spent his student years in the northern states, where the laws provided no sanction for the discrimination he had encountered in the South, but where, nevertheless, black and white did not mix in their daily lives. Yet living in the northern states – especially in a university milieu – was like a breath of fresh air. At Boston University, where he took a doctor's degree in philosophy, he met Coretta Scott, who was studying singing. She was a Negress from his own state of Alabama, a member of the black middle class which also exists in the South.

The young couple, after being married, were faced with a choice: should they remain in the North where life offered greater security and better conditions, or return to the South? They elected to go back to the South where Martin Luther King was installed as minister of a Baptist congregation in Montgomery.

Here he lived in a society where a sharp barrier existed between Negroes and whites. Worse still, the black community in Montgomery was itself divided, its leaders at loggerheads and the rank and file paralyzed by the passivity of its educated members. As a result of their apathy, few of them were engaged in the work of improving the status of the Negro. The great majority were indifferent; those who had something to lose were afraid of forfeiting the little they had achieved.

Nor, as Martin Luther King discovered, did all the Negro clergy care about the social problems of their community; many of them were of the opinion that ministers of religion had no business getting involved in secular movements aimed at improving people's social and economic conditions. Their task was «to preach the Gospel and keep men's minds centered on the heavenly!»

Early in 1955 an attempt was made to unite the various groups of blacks. The attempt failed. Martin Luther King said that «the tragic division in the Negro community could be cured only by some divine miracle!»

The picture he gives us of conditions in Montgomery is not an inspiring one; even as late as 1954 the Negroes accepted the existing status as a fact, and hardly anyone opposed the system actively. Montgomery was a peaceful town.

But beneath the surface discontent smoldered. Some of the black clergy, in their sermons as well as in their personal attitude, championed the cause of Negro equality, and this had given many fresh confidence and courage.

Then came the bus boycott of December 5, 1955.

It looks almost as if the boycott was the result of a mere coincidence. The immediate cause was the arrest of Mrs. Rosa Parks for refusing to give up her seat on a bus to a white man. She was in the section reserved for Negroes and was occupying one of the seats just behind the section set aside for whites, which was filled.

The arrest of Mrs. Parks not only aroused great resentment, but provoked direct action, and it was because of this that Martin Luther King was to become the central personality in the Negro's struggle for human rights.

In his book *Stride toward Freedom* he has described not only the actual bus conflict, but also how, on December 5 after the boycott had been started, he was elected chairman of the organization formed to conduct the struggle[1].

He tells us that the election came as a surprise to him; had he been given time to think things over he would probably have said no. He had supported the boycott when asked to do so on December 4, but he was beginning to doubt whether it was morally right, according to Christian teaching, to start a boycott. Then he remembered David Thoreau's essay on «Civil Disobedience», which he had read in his earlier years and which had made a profound impression on him. A sentence by Thoreau[2] came back to him: «We can no longer lend our cooperation to an evil system.»

But he was not convinced that the boycott would be carried out. As late as the evening of Sunday, December 4, he believed that if sixty percent of the Negroes cooperated, it would prove reasonably successful.

During the morning of December 5, as bus after bus without a single Negro passenger passed his window, he realized that the boycott had proved a hundred percent effective.

But final victory had not yet been won, and as yet no one had announced that the campaign was to be conducted in accordance with the slogan: «Thou shalt not requite violence with violence.» This message was given to his people by Martin Luther King in the speech he made to thousands

1. Martin Luther King, Jr., *Stride toward Freedom*, chap. 4 and *passim*.
2. See *The Works of Thoreau*, ed. by H.S. Canby (Boston: Houghton Mifflin, 1946). King's sentence is a paraphrase of Thoreau's main point in the essay «Civil Disobedience».

of them on the evening of December 5, 1955. He calls this speech[1] the most decisive he ever made. Here are his own words:

«We have sometimes given our white brothers the feeling that we liked the way we were being treated. But we come here tonight to be saved from that patience that makes us patient with anything less than freedom and justice.

But [he continues] our method will be that of persuasion not coercion. We will only say to the people, ‹Let your conscience be your guide.› Our actions must be guided by the deepest principles of our Christian faith... Once again we must hear the words of Jesus[2] echoing across the centuries: ‹Love your enemies, bless them that curse you, and pray for them that despitefully use you.› »

He concludes as follows:

«If you will protest courageously and yet with dignity and Christian love, when the history books are written [in future generations], the historians will [have to pause and] say: ‹There lived a great people–a black people–who injected new meaning and dignity into the veins of civilization.› This is our challenge and our overwhelming responsibility.»

This battle cry–for such it was–was enthusiastically received by the audience. This was «Montgomery's moment in history», as Martin Luther King calls it[3].

His words rallied the majority of Negroes during their active struggle for human rights. All around the South, inspired by this slogan, they declared war on the discrimination between black and white in eating places, shops, schools, public parks, and playgrounds.

How was it possible to obtain such strong support?

To answer this question we must recall the strong position enjoyed by the clergy among the Negroes. The church is their only sanctuary in their leisure hours; here they can rise above the troubles and cares of everyday life. Nor would the appeal that they go into battle unarmed have been followed, had not the blacks themselves been so profoundly religious.

Despite laws passed by Congress and judgments given by the American Supreme Court, this struggle has not proved successful everywhere, since

1. This speech, delivered at the Holt Street Baptist Church in Montgomery, Alabama, is described and excerpted by King in *Stride toward Freedom*, pp. 61–64.
2. Matthew 5:44. «Love your enemies, bless them that curse you, do good to them that hate you, and pray for them which despitefully use you, and persecute you.»
3. *Stride toward Freedom*, p. 70.

these laws and judgments have been sabotaged, as anyone who has followed the course of events subsequent to 1955 knows.

Despite sabotage and imprisonment, the Negroes have continued their unarmed struggle. Only rarely have they acted against the principle given to them by requiting violence with violence, even though for many of us this would have been the immediate reaction. What can we say of the young students who sat down in an eating place reserved for whites? They were not served, but they remained seated. White teenagers mocked and insulted them and stubbed their lighted cigarettes out on their necks. The black students sat unmoving. They possessed the strength that only belief can give, the belief that they fight in a just cause and that their struggle will lead to victory precisely because they wage it with peaceful means.

Martin Luther King's belief is rooted first and foremost in the teaching of Christ, but no one can really understand him unless aware that he has been influenced also by the great thinkers of the past and the present. He has been inspired above all by Mahatma Gandhi[1], whose example convinced him that it is possible to achieve victory in an unarmed struggle. Before he had read about Gandhi, he had almost concluded that the teaching of Jesus could only be put into practice as between individuals; but after making a study of Gandhi he realized that he had been mistaken.

«Gandhi», he says, «was probably the first person in history to lift the love ethic of Jesus above mere interaction between individuals to a powerful and effective social force...»[2]

In Gandhi's teaching he found the answer to a question that had long troubled him: How does one set about carrying out a social reform?

«... I found», he tells us, «in the nonviolent resistance philosophy of Gandhi... the only morally and practically sound method open to oppressed people in their struggle for freedom.»[3]

Martin Luther King has been attacked from many quarters. Greatest was the resistance he encountered from white fanatics. Moderate whites and even the more prosperous members of his own race consider he is proceeding too fast, that he should wait and let time work for him to weaken the opposition.

1. Mohandas Karamchand Gandhi (1869–1948), Hindu religious leader and Indian nationalist who advocated home rule for India and practiced nonviolent resistance against the British government.
2. *Stride toward Freedom*, p.97.
3. *Ibid.*

In an open letter in the press eight clergymen reproached him for this and other aspects of his campaign. Martin Luther King answered these charges in a letter written in Birmingham Jail in the spring of 1963. I should like to quote a few lines:

«Actually time itself is neutral... Human progress never rolls in on wheels of inevitability. It comes through the tireless efforts of men, willing to be co-workers with God, and without this hard work time itself becomes an ally of the forces of social stagnation.»[1]

In answer to the charge that he has failed to negotiate, he replies:

«You are quite right in calling for negotiation. Indeed, this is the very purpose of direct action. Nonviolent direct action seeks to... foster such a tension that a community which has constantly refused to negotiate is forced to confront the issue.»[2]

He reminds them that the Negroes have not won a single victory for civil rights without struggling persistently to achieve it in a lawful way without recourse to violence. When reproached for breaking the laws in the course of his struggle, he replies as follows:

«There are two types of laws: just and unjust... An unjust law is a code that is out of harmony with the moral law...

An unjust law is a code that a numerical or power majority group compels a minority group to obey but does not make binding on itself...

One who breaks an unjust law must do so openly, lovingly, and with a willingness to accept the penalty.»[3]

Martin Luther King also takes the church to task. Even during the bus conflict in Montgomery he had expected that white clergy and rabbis would prove the Negroes' staunchest allies. But he was bitterly disappointed. «All too many others», he recalls, «have been more cautious than courageous and have remained silent behind the anesthetizing security of stained-glass windows.»[4]

It is not difficult to understand Martin Luther King's disappointment with the white church, for what is the first commandment of Christian teaching if not «Thou shalt love thy neighbor»?

Yet even if victory is won in the fight against segregation, discrimination will still persist in the economic field and in social intercourse. Realistic

1. Martin Luther King, Jr., *Why We Can't Wait*, p. 89.
2. *Ibid.*, p. 81.
3. *Ibid.*, pp. 84–86, *passim*.
4. *Ibid.*, p. 94.

as he is, Martin Luther King knows this. In his book *Strength to Love* he writes[1]:

«Court orders and federal enforcement agencies are of inestimable value in achieving desegregation, but desegregation is only a partial, though necessary, step towards the final goal which we seek to realize, genuine intergroup and interpersonal living...

But something must touch the hearts and souls of men so that they will come together spiritually because it is natural and right...

True integration will be achieved by true neighbors who are willingly obedient to unenforceable obligations.»

Martin Luther King's unarmed struggle has been waged in his own country; its result has been that an obdurate, centuries-old, and traditional conflict is now nearing its solution.

Is it possible that the road he and his people have charted may bring a ray of hope to other parts of the world, a hope that conflicts between races, nations, and political systems can be solved, not by fire and sword, but in a spirit of true brotherly love?

Can the words of our poet Arnulf Överland[2] come true?

> *The unarmed only*
> *can draw on sources eternal.*
> *The spirit alone gives victory.*

It sounds like a dream of a remote and unknown future; but life is not worth living without a dream and without working to make the dream reality.

Today, now that mankind is in possession of the atom bomb, the time has come to lay our weapons and armaments aside and listen to the message Martin Luther King has given us through the unarmed struggle he has waged on behalf of his race. Luther King looks *also* beyond the frontiers of his own country. He says:

«More than ever before, my friends, men of all races and nations are today challenged to be neighborly... No longer can we afford the luxury of passing by on the other side. Such folly was once called moral failure; today it will lead to universal suicide...

If we assume that mankind has a right to survive, then we must find an alternative to war and destruction. In our days of space vehicles and

1. Martin Luther King, Jr., *Strength to Love*, p. 23.
2. Arnulf Överland (1889–1968).

guided ballistic missiles, the choice is either nonviolence or nonexistence.»

Though Martin Luther King has not personally committed himself to the international conflict, his own struggle is a clarion call to all who work for peace.

He is the first person in the Western world to have shown us that a struggle can be waged without violence. He is the first to make the message of brotherly love a reality in the course of his struggle, and he has brought this message to all men, to all nations and races.

Today we pay tribute to Martin Luther King, the man who has never abandoned his faith in the unarmed struggle he is waging, who has suffered for his faith, who has been imprisoned on many occasions, whose home has been subject to bomb attacks, whose life and the lives of his family have been threatened, and who nevertheless has never faltered.

To this undaunted champion of peace the Nobel Committee of the Norwegian Parliament has awarded the Peace Prize for the year 1964.

MARTIN LUTHER KING, JR.

The Quest for Peace and Justice

Nobel Lecture*, December 11, 1964

It is impossible to begin this lecture without again expressing my deep appreciation to the Nobel Committee of the Norwegian Parliament for bestowing upon me and the civil rights movement in the United States such a great honor. Occasionally in life there are those moments of unutterable fulfillment which cannot be completely explained by those symbols called words. Their meaning can only be articulated by the inaudible language of the heart. Such is the moment I am presently experiencing. I experience this high and joyous moment not for myself alone but for those devotees of nonviolence who have moved so courageously against the ramparts of racial injustice and who in the process have acquired a new estimate of their own human worth. Many of them are young and cultured. Others are middle aged and middle class. The majority are poor and untutored. But they are all united in the quiet conviction that it is better to suffer in dignity than to accept segregation in humiliation. These are the real heroes of the freedom struggle: they are the noble people for whom I accept the Nobel Peace Prize.

This evening I would like to use this lofty and historic platform to discuss what appears to me to be the most pressing problem confronting mankind today. Modern man has brought this whole world to an awe-inspiring threshold of the future. He has reached new and astonishing peaks of scientific success. He has produced machines that think and instruments that peer into the unfathomable ranges of interstellar space. He has built gigantic bridges to span the seas and gargantuan buildings to kiss the skies. His airplanes and spaceships have dwarfed distance, placed time in chains, and carved highways through the stratosphere. This is a dazzling picture of modern man's scientific and technological progress.

Yet, in spite of these spectacular strides in science and technology, and

* Dr. King delivered this lecture in the Auditorium of the University of Oslo. This text is taken from *Les Prix Nobel en 1964*. The text in the *New York Times* is excerpted. His speech of acceptance delivered the day before in the same place is reported fully both in *Les Prix Nobel en 1964* and the *New York Times*.

still unlimited ones to come, something basic is missing. There is a sort of poverty of the spirit which stands in glaring contrast to our scientific and technological abundance. The richer we have become materially, the poorer we have become morally and spiritually. We have learned to fly the air like birds and swim the sea like fish, but we have not learned the simple art of living together as brothers.

Every man lives in two realms, the internal and the external. The internal is that realm of spiritual ends expressed in art, literature, morals, and religion. The external is that complex of devices, techniques, mechanisms, and instrumentalities by means of which we live. Our problem today is that we have allowed the internal to become lost in the external. We have allowed the means by which we live to outdistance the ends for which we live. So much of modern life can be summarized in that arresting dictum of the poet Thoreau[1]: «Improved means to an unimproved end». This is the serious predicament, the deep and haunting problem confronting modern man. If we are to survive today, our moral and spiritual «lag» must be eliminated. Enlarged material powers spell enlarged peril if there is not proportionate growth of the soul. When the «without» of man's nature subjugates the «within», dark storm clouds begin to form in the world.

This problem of spiritual and moral lag, which constitutes modern man's chief dilemma, expresses itself in three larger problems which grow out of man's ethical infantilism. Each of these problems, while appearing to be separate and isolated, is inextricably bound to the other. I refer to racial injustice, poverty, and war.

The first problem that I would like to mention is racial injustice. The struggle to eliminate the evil of racial injustice constitutes one of the major struggles of our time. The present upsurge of the Negro people of the United States grows out of a deep and passionate determination to make freedom and equality a reality «here» and «now». In one sense the civil rights movement in the United States is a special American phenomenon which must be understood in the light of American history and dealt with in terms of the American situation. But on another and more important level, what is happening in the United States today is a relatively small part of a world development.

We live in a day, says the philosopher Alfred North Whitehead[2], «when

1. Henry David Thoreau (1817–1862), American poet and essayist.
2. Alfred North Whitehead (1861–1947), British philosopher and mathematician, professor at the University of London and Harvard University.

civilization is shifting its basic outlook: a major turning point in history where the presuppositions on which society is structured are being analyzed, sharply challenged, and profoundly changed.» What we are seeing now is a freedom explosion, the realization of «an idea whose time has come», to use Victor Hugo's phrase[1]. The deep rumbling of discontent that we hear today is the thunder of disinherited masses, rising from dungeons of oppression to the bright hills of freedom, in one majestic chorus the rising masses singing, in the words of our freedom song, «Ain't gonna let nobody turn us around.»[2] All over the world, like a fever, the freedom movement is spreading in the widest liberation in history. The great masses of people are determined to end the exploitation of their races and land. They are awake and moving toward their goal like a tidal wave. You can hear them rumbling in every village street, on the docks, in the houses, among the students, in the churches, and at political meetings. Historic movement was for several centuries that of the nations and societies of Western Europe out into the rest of the world in «conquest» of various sorts. That period, the era of colonialism, is at an end. East is meeting West. The earth is being redistributed. Yes, we are «shifting our basic outlooks».

These developments should not surprise any student of history. Oppressed people cannot remain oppressed forever. The yearning for freedom eventually manifests itself. The Bible tells the thrilling story of how Moses stood in Pharaoh's court centuries ago and cried, «Let my people go.»[3] This is a kind of opening chapter in a continuing story. The present struggle in the United States is a later chapter in the same unfolding story. Something within has reminded the Negro of his birthright of freedom, and something without has reminded him that it can be gained. Consciously or unconsciously, he has been caught up by the *Zeitgeist*, and with his black brothers of Africa and his brown and yellow brothers in Asia, South America, and the Caribbean, the United States Negro is moving with a sense of great urgency toward the promised land of racial justice.

Fortunately, some significant strides have been made in the struggle to end the long night of racial injustice. We have seen the magnificent drama of independence unfold in Asia and Africa. Just thirty years ago there were

1. «There is one thing stronger than all the armies in the world and that is an idea whose time has come.» Translations differ; probable origin is Victor Hugo, *Histoire d'un crime*, «Conclusion–La Chute», chap. 10.
2. «Ain't Gonna Let Nobody Turn Me Around» is the title of an old Baptist spiritual.
3. Exodus 5:1; 8:1; 9:1; 10:3.

only three independent nations in the whole of Africa. But today thirty-five African nations have risen from colonial bondage. In the United States we have witnessed the gradual demise of the system of racial segregation. The Supreme Court's decision of 1954 outlawing segregation in the public schools gave a legal and constitutional deathblow to the whole doctrine of separate but equal[1]. The Court decreed that separate facilities are inherently unequal and that to segregate a child on the basis of race is to deny that child equal protection of the law. This decision came as a beacon light of hope to millions of disinherited people. Then came that glowing day a few months ago when a strong Civil Rights Bill became the law of our land[2]. This bill, which was first recommended and promoted by President Kennedy, was passed because of the overwhelming support and perseverance of millions of Americans, Negro and white. It came as a bright interlude in the long and sometimes turbulent struggle for civil rights: the beginning of a second emancipation proclamation providing a comprehensive legal basis for equality of opportunity. Since the passage of this bill we have seen some encouraging and surprising signs of compliance. I am happy to report that, by and large, communities all over the southern part of the United States are obeying the Civil Rights Law and showing remarkable good sense in the process.

Another indication that progress is being made was found in the recent presidential election in the United States. The American people revealed great maturity by overwhelmingly rejecting a presidential candidate who had become identified with extremism, racism, and retrogression[3]. The voters of our nation rendered a telling blow to the radical right[4]. They defeated those elements in our society which seek to pit white against Negro and lead the nation down a dangerous Fascist path.

Let me not leave you with a false impression. The problem is far from

1. «Brown *vs.* Board of Education of Topeka», 347 U.S. 483, contains the decision of May 17, 1954, requiring desegregation of the public schools by the states. «Bolling *vs.* Sharpe», 347 U.S. 497, contains the decision of same date requiring desegregation of public schools by the federal government; *i.e.* in Washington, D.C. «Brown *vs.* Board of Education of Topeka», Nos. 1-5. 349 U.S. 249, contains the opinion of May 31, 1955, on appeals from the decisions in the two cases cited above, ordering admission to «public schools on a racially nondiscriminatory basis with all deliberate speed».
2. Public Law 88-352, signed by President Johnson on July 2, 1964.
3. Both *Les Prix Nobel* and the *New York Times* read «retrogress».
4. Lyndon B. Johnson defeated Barry Goldwater by a popular vote of 43,128,956 to 27,177,873.

solved. We still have a long, long way to go before the dream of freedom is a reality for the Negro in the United States. To put it figuratively in biblical language, we have left the dusty soils of Egypt and crossed a Red Sea whose waters had for years been hardened by a long and piercing winter of massive resistance. But before we reach the majestic shores of the Promised Land, there is a frustrating and bewildering wilderness ahead. We must still face prodigious hilltops of opposition and gigantic mountains of resistance. But with patient and firm determination we will press on until every valley of despair is exalted to new peaks of hope, until every mountain of pride and irrationality is made low by the leveling process of humility and compassion; until the rough places of injustice are transformed into a smooth plane of equality of opportunity; and until the crooked places of prejudice are transformed by the straightening process of bright-eyed wisdom.

What the main sections of the civil rights movement in the United States are saying is that the demand for dignity, equality, jobs, and citizenship will not be abandoned or diluted or postponed. If that means resistance and conflict we shall not flinch. We shall not be cowed. We are no longer afraid.

The word that symbolizes the spirit and the outward form of our encounter is *nonviolence*, and it is doubtless that factor which made it seem appropriate to award a peace prize to one identified with struggle. Broadly speaking, nonviolence in the civil rights struggle has meant not relying on arms and weapons of struggle. It has meant noncooperation with customs and laws which are institutional aspects of a regime of discrimination and enslavement. It has meant direct participation of masses in protest, rather than reliance on indirect methods which frequently do not involve masses in action at all.

Nonviolence has also meant that my people in the agonizing struggles of recent years have taken suffering upon themselves instead of inflicting it on others. It has meant, as I said, that we are no longer afraid and cowed. But in some substantial degree it has meant that we do not want to instill fear in others or into the society of which we are a part. The movement does not seek to liberate Negroes at the expense of the humiliation and enslavement of whites. It seeks no victory over anyone. It seeks to liberate American society and to share in the self-liberation of all the people.

Violence as a way of achieving racial justice is both impractical and immoral. I am not unmindful of the fact that violence often brings about momentary results. Nations have frequently won their independence in battle. But in spite of temporary victories, violence never brings permanent peace. It solves no social problem: it merely creates new and more complicated ones. Violence is impractical because it is a descending spiral ending in destruction for all. It is immoral because it seeks to humiliate the opponent rather than win his understanding: it seeks to annihilate rather than convert. Violence is immoral because it thrives on hatred rather than love. It destroys community and makes brotherhood impossible. It leaves society in monologue rather than dialogue. Violence ends up defeating itself. It creates bitterness in the survivors and brutality in the destroyers.

In a real sense nonviolence seeks to redeem the spiritual and moral lag that I spoke of earlier as the chief dilemma of modern man. It seeks to secure moral ends through moral means. Nonviolence is a powerful and just weapon. Indeed, it is a weapon unique in history, which cuts without wounding and ennobles the man who wields it.

I believe in this method because I think it is the only way to reestablish a broken community. It is the method which seeks to implement the just law by appealing to the conscience of the great decent majority who through blindness, fear, pride, and irrationality have allowed their consciences to sleep.

The nonviolent resisters can summarize their message in the following simple terms: we will take direct action against injustice despite the failure of governmental and other official agencies to act first. We will not obey unjust laws or submit to unjust practices. We will do this peacefully, openly, cheerfully because our aim is to persuade. We adopt the means of nonviolence because our end is a community at peace with itself. We will try to persuade with our words, but if our words fail, we will try to persuade with our acts. We will always be willing to talk and seek fair compromise, but we are ready to suffer when necessary and even risk our lives to become witnesses to truth as we see it.

This approach to the problem of racial injustice is not at all without successful precedent. It was used in a magnificent way by Mohandas K. Gandhi to challenge the might of the British Empire and free his people from the political domination and economic exploitation inflicted upon them for centuries. He struggled only with the weapons of truth, soul force, non-injury, and courage[1].

In the past ten years unarmed gallant men and women of the United

1. For a note on Gandhi, see p. 329, fn. 1.

States have given living testimony to the moral power and efficacy of non-violence. By the thousands, faceless, anonymous, relentless young people, black and white, have temporarily left the ivory towers of learning for the barricades of bias. Their courageous and disciplined activities have come as a refreshing oasis in a desert sweltering with the heat of injustice. They have taken our whole nation back to those great wells of democracy which were dug deep by the founding fathers in the formulation of the Constitution and the Declaration of Independence. One day all of America will be proud of their achievements[1].

I am only too well aware of the human weaknesses and failures which exist, the doubts about the efficacy of nonviolence, and the open advocacy of violence by some. But I am still convinced that nonviolence is both the most practically sound and morally excellent way to grapple with the age-old problem of racial injustice.

A second evil which plagues the modern world is that of poverty. Like a monstrous octopus, it projects its nagging, prehensile tentacles in lands and villages all over the world. Almost two-thirds of the peoples of the world go to bed hungry at night. They are undernourished, ill-housed, and shabbily clad. Many of them have no houses or beds to sleep in. Their only beds are the sidewalks of the cities and the dusty roads of the villages. Most of these poverty-stricken children of God have never seen a physician or a dentist. This problem of poverty is not only seen in the class division between the highly developed industrial nations and the so-called under-developed nations; it is seen in the great economic gaps within the rich nations themselves. Take my own country for example. We have developed the greatest system of production that history has ever known. We have become the richest nation in the world. Our national gross product this year will reach the astounding figure of almost 650 billion dollars. Yet, at least one-fifth of our fellow citizens – some ten million families, comprising about forty million individuals – are bound to a miserable culture of poverty. In a sense the poverty of the poor in America is more frustrating

1. For accounts of the civil rights activities by both whites and blacks in the decade from 1954 to 1964, see Alan F. Westin, *Freedom Now: The Civil Rights Struggle in America* (New York: Basic Books, 1964), especially Part IV, «The Techniques of the Civil Rights Struggle»; Howard Zinn, *SNCC: The New Abolitionists* (Boston: Beacon Press, 1964); Eugene V. Rostow, «The Freedom Riders and the Future», *The Reporter* (June 22, 1961); James Peck, *Cracking the Color Line: Nonviolent Direct Action Methods of Eliminating Racial Discrimination* (New York: CORE, 1960).

than the poverty of Africa and Asia. The misery of the poor in Africa and Asia is shared misery, a fact of life for the vast majority; they are all poor together as a result of years of exploitation and underdevelopment. In sad contrast, the poor in America know that they live in the richest nation in the world, and that even though they are perishing on a lonely island of poverty they are surrounded by a vast ocean of material prosperity. Glistening towers of glass and steel easily seen from their slum dwellings spring up almost overnight. Jet liners speed over their ghettoes at 600 miles an hour; satellites streak through outer space and reveal details of the moon. President Johnson, in his State of the Union Message[1], emphasized this contradiction when he heralded the United States' «highest standard of living in the world», and deplored that it was accompanied by «dislocation, loss of jobs, and the specter of poverty in the midst of plenty».

So it is obvious that if man is to redeem his spiritual and moral «lag», he must go all out to bridge the social and economic gulf between the «haves» and the «have nots» of the world. Poverty is one of the most urgent items on the agenda of modern life.

There is nothing new about poverty. What is new, however, is that we have the resources to get rid of it. More than a century and a half ago people began to be disturbed about the twin problems of population and production. A thoughtful Englishman named Malthus wrote a book[2] that set forth some rather frightening conclusions. He predicted that the human family was gradually moving toward global starvation because the world was producing people faster than it was producing food and material to support them. Later scientists, however, disproved the conclusion of Malthus, and revealed that he had vastly underestimated the resources of the world and the resourcefulness of man.

Not too many years ago, Dr. Kirtley Mather, a Harvard geologist, wrote a book entitled *Enough and to Spare*[3]. He set forth the basic theme that famine is wholly unnecessary in the modern world. Today, therefore, the question on the agenda must read: Why should there be hunger and privation in any land, in any city, at any table when man has the resources and the scientific know-how to provide all mankind with the basic necessities

1. January 8, 1964.
2. Thomas Robert Malthus (1766–1834), *An Essay on the Principle of Population* (1798).
3. Kirtley F. Mather, *Enough and to Spare: Mother Earth Can Nourish Every Man in Freedom* (New York: Harper, 1944).

of life? Even deserts can be irrigated and top soil can be replaced. We cannot complain of a lack of land, for there are twenty-five million square miles of tillable land, of which we are using less than seven million. We have amazing knowledge of vitamins, nutrition, the chemistry of food, and the versatility of atoms. There is no deficit in human resources; the deficit is in human will. The well-off and the secure have too often become indifferent and oblivious to the poverty and deprivation in their midst. The poor in our countries have been shut out of our minds, and driven from the mainstream of our societies, because we have allowed them to become invisible. Just as nonviolence exposed the ugliness of racial injustice, so must the infection and sickness of poverty be exposed and healed–not only its symptoms but its basic causes. This, too, will be a fierce struggle, but we must not be afraid to pursue the remedy no matter how formidable the task.

The time has come for an all-out world war against poverty. The rich nations must use their vast resources of wealth to develop the underdeveloped, school the unschooled, and feed the unfed. Ultimately a great nation is a compassionate nation. No individual or nation can be great if it does not have a concern for «the least of these». Deeply etched in the fiber of our religious tradition is the conviction that men are made in the image of God and that they are souls of infinite metaphysical value, the heirs of a legacy of dignity and worth. If we feel this as a profound moral fact, we cannot be content to see men hungry, to see men victimized with starvation and ill health when we have the means to help them. The wealthy nations must go all out to bridge the gulf between the rich minority and the poor majority.

In the final analysis, the rich must not ignore the poor because both rich and poor are tied in a single garment of destiny. All life is interrelated, and all men are interdependent. The agony of the poor diminishes the rich, and the salvation of the poor enlarges the rich. We are inevitably our brothers' keeper because of the interrelated structure of reality. John Donne interpreted this truth in graphic terms when he affirmed[1]:

> No man is an Iland, intire of its selfe: every
> man is a peece of the Continent, a part of the
> maine: if a Clod bee washed away by the Sea,

1. John Donne (1572?–1631), English poet, in the final lines of «Devotions» (1624).

Europe is the lesse, as well as if a Promontorie
were, as well as if a Mannor of thy friends
or of thine owne were: any mans death
diminishes me, because I am involved in
Mankinde: and therefore never send to know
for whom the bell tolls: it tolls for thee.

A third great evil confronting our world is that of war. Recent events have vividly reminded us that nations are not reducing but rather increasing their arsenals of weapons of mass destruction. The best brains in the highly developed nations of the world are devoted to military technology. The proliferation of nuclear weapons has not been halted, in spite of the Limited Test Ban Treaty[1]. On the contrary, the detonation of an atomic device by the first nonwhite, non-Western, and so-called underdeveloped power, namely the Chinese People's Republic[2], opens new vistas of exposure of vast multitudes, the whole of humanity, to insidious terrorization by the ever-present threat of annihilation. The fact that most of the time human beings put the truth about the nature and risks of the nuclear war out of their minds because it is too painful and therefore not «acceptable», does not alter the nature and risks of such war. The device of «rejection» may temporarily cover up anxiety, but it does not bestow peace of mind and emotional security.

So man's proneness to engage in war is still a fact. But wisdom born of experience should tell us that war is obsolete. There may have been a time when war served as a negative good by preventing the spread and growth of an evil force, but the destructive power of modern weapons eliminated even the possibility that war may serve as a negative good. If we assume that life is worth living and that man has a right to survive, then we must find an alternative to war. In a day when vehicles hurtle through outer space and guided ballistic missiles carve highways of death through the stratosphere, no nation can claim victory in war. A so-called limited war will leave little more than a calamitous legacy of human suffering, political turmoil, and spiritual disillusionment. A world war–God forbid!–will leave only smoldering ashes as a mute testimony of a human race whose folly

1. Officially called «Treaty Banning Nuclear Weapons Tests in Atmosphere, in Outer Space, and Underwater», and signed by Russia, England, and United States on July 25, 1963.
2. On October 16, 1964.

led inexorably to ultimate death. So if modern man continues to flirt un-hesitatingly with war, he will transform his earthly habitat into an inferno such as even the mind of Dante could not imagine.

Therefore, I venture to suggest to all of you and all who hear and may eventually read these words, that the philosophy and strategy of nonviolence become immediately a subject for study and for serious experimentation in every field of human conflict, by no means excluding the relations be-tween nations. It is, after all, nation-states which make war, which have produced the weapons which threaten the survival of mankind, and which are both genocidal and suicidal in character.

Here also we have ancient habits to deal with, vast structures of power, indescribably complicated problems to solve. But unless we abdicate our humanity altogether and succumb to fear and impotence in the presence of the weapons we have ourselves created, it is as imperative and urgent to put an end to war and violence between nations as it is to put an end to racial injustice. Equality with whites will hardly solve the problems of either whites or Negroes if it means equality in a society under the spell of terror and a world doomed to extinction.

I do not wish to minimize the complexity of the problems that need to be faced in achieving disarmament and peace. But I think it is a fact that we shall not have the will, the courage, and the insight to deal with such matters unless in this field we are prepared to undergo a mental and spiritual reevaluation – a change of focus which will enable us to see that the things which seem most real and powerful are indeed now unreal and have come under the sentence of death. We need to make a supreme effort to generate the readiness, indeed the eagerness, to enter into the new world which is now possible, «the city which hath foundations, whose builder and maker is God»[1].

We will not build a peaceful world by following a negative path. It is not enough to say «We must not wage war.» It is necessary to love peace and sacrifice for it. We must concentrate not merely on the negative ex-pulsion of war, but on the positive affirmation of peace. There is a fascinating little story that is preserved for us in Greek literature about Ulysses and the Sirens. The Sirens had the ability to sing so sweetly that sailors could not resist steering toward their island. Many ships were lured upon the rocks, and men forgot home, duty, and honor as they flung themselves

1. Hebrews 11:10.

into the sea to be embraced by arms that drew them down to death. Ulysses, determined not to be lured by the Sirens, first decided to tie himself tightly to the mast of his boat, and his crew stuffed their ears with wax. But finally he and his crew learned a better way to save themselves: they took on board the beautiful singer Orpheus whose melodies were sweeter than the music of the Sirens. When Orpheus sang, who bothered to listen to the Sirens?

So we must fix our vision not merely on the negative expulsion of war, but upon the positive affirmation of peace. We must see that peace represents a sweeter music, a cosmic melody that is far superior to the discords of war. Somehow we must transform the dynamics of the world power struggle from the negative nuclear arms race which no one can win to a positive contest to harness man's creative genius for the purpose of making peace and prosperity a reality for all of the nations of the world. In short, we must shift the arms race into a «peace race». If we have the will and determination to mount such a peace offensive, we will unlock hitherto tightly sealed doors of hope and transform our imminent cosmic elegy into a psalm of creative fulfillment.

All that I have said boils down to the point of affirming that mankind's survival is dependent upon man's ability to solve the problems of racial injustice, poverty, and war; the solution of these problems is in turn dependent upon man squaring his moral progress with his scientific progress, and learning the practical art of living in harmony. Some years ago a famous novelist died. Among his papers was found a list of suggested story plots for future stories, the most prominently underscored being this one: «A widely separated family inherits a house in which they have to live together.» This is the great new problem of mankind. We have inherited a big house, a great «world house» in which we have to live together—black and white, Easterners and Westerners, Gentiles and Jews, Catholics and Protestants, Moslem and Hindu, a family unduly separated in ideas, culture, and interests who, because we can never again live without each other, must learn, somehow, in this one big world, to live with each other.

This means that more and more our loyalties must become ecumenical rather than sectional. We must now give an overriding loyalty to mankind as a whole in order to preserve the best in our individual societies.

This call for a worldwide fellowship that lifts neighborly concern beyond one's tribe, race, class, and nation is in reality a call for an all-embracing and unconditional love for all men. This oft misunderstood and misinterpreted concept so readily dismissed by the Nietzsches of the world as a weak and cowardly force, has now become an absolute necessity for the survival of man. When I speak of love I am not speaking of some sentimental and weak response which is little more than emotional bosh. I am speaking of that force which all of the great religions have seen as the supreme unifying principle of life. Love is somehow the key that unlocks the door which leads to ultimate reality. This Hindu-Moslem-Christian-Jewish-Buddhist belief about ultimate reality is beautifully summed up in the First Epistle of Saint John[1]:

> *Let us love one another: for love is of God; and everyone*
> *that loveth is born of God, and knoweth God.*
> *He that loveth not knoweth not God; for God is love.*
> *If we love one another, God dwelleth in us, and His*
> *love is perfected in us.*

Let us hope that this spirit will become the order of the day. As Arnold Toynbee[2] says: «Love is the ultimate force that makes for the saving choice of life and good against the damning choice of death and evil. Therefore the first hope in our inventory must be the hope that love is going to have the last word.» We can no longer afford to worship the God of hate or bow before the altar of retaliation. The oceans of history are made turbulent by the ever-rising tides of hate. History is cluttered with the wreckage of nations and individuals that pursued this self-defeating path of hate. Love is the key to the solution of the problems of the world.

Let me close by saying that I have the personal faith that mankind will somehow rise up to the occasion and give new directions to an age drifting rapidly to its doom. In spite of the tensions and uncertainties of this period something profoundly meaningful is taking place. Old systems of exploitation and oppression are passing away, and out of the womb of a frail world new systems of justice and equality are being born. Doors of opportunity are gradually being opened to those at the bottom of society. The shirtless and barefoot people of the land are developing a new sense of «somebodiness» and carving a tunnel of hope through the dark mountain of despair. «The people who sat in darkness have seen a great light.»[3] Here and

1. I John 4:7-8, 12.
2. Arnold Joseph Toynbee (1889–   ), British historian whose monumental work is the 10-volume *A Study of History* (1934–1954).
3. This quotation may be based on a phrase from Luke 1:79, «To give light to them

there an individual or group dares to love, and rises to the majestic heights of moral maturity. So in a real sense this is a great time to be alive. Therefore, I am not yet discouraged about the future. Granted that the easygoing optimism of yesterday is impossible. Granted that those who pioneer in the struggle for peace and freedom will still face uncomfortable jail terms, painful threats of death; they will still be battered by the storms of persecution, leading them to the nagging feeling that they can no longer bear such a heavy burden, and the temptation of wanting to retreat to a more quiet and serene life. Granted that we face a world crisis which leaves us standing so often amid the surging murmur of life's restless sea. But every crisis has both its dangers and its opportunities. It can spell either salvation or doom. In a dark confused world the kingdom of God may yet reign in the hearts of men.

that sit in darkness and in the shadow of death»; or one from Psalms 107:10, «Such as sit in darkness and in the shadow of death»; or one from Mark Twain's *To the Person Sitting in Darkness* (1901), «The people who sit in darkness have noticed it... ».

Biography

Martin Luther King, Jr., (January 15, 1929–April 4, 1968) was born Michael Luther King, Jr., but later had his name changed to Martin. His grandfather began the family's long tenure as pastors of the Ebenezer Baptist Church in Atlanta, serving from 1914 to 1931; his father has served from then until the present, and from 1960 until his death Martin Luther acted as co-pastor. Martin Luther attended segregated public schools in Georgia, graduating from high school at the age of fifteen; he received the B.A. degree in 1948 from Morehouse College, a distinguished Negro institution of Atlanta from which both his father and grandfather had been graduated. After three years of theological study at Crozer Theological Seminary in Pennsylvania where he was elected president of a predominantly white senior class, he was awarded the B.D. in 1951. With a fellowship won at Crozer, he enrolled in graduate studies at Boston University, completing his residence for the doctorate in 1953 and receiving the degree in 1955. In Boston he met and married Coretta Scott, a young woman of uncommon intellectual and artistic attainments. Two sons and two daughters were born into the family.

In 1954, Martin Luther King accepted the pastorate of the Dexter Avenue Baptist Church in Montgomery, Alabama. Always a strong worker for civil rights for members of his race, King was, by this time, a member of the executive committee of the National Association for the Advancement of Colored People, the leading organization of its kind in the nation. He was ready, then, early in December, 1955, to accept the leadership of the first great Negro nonviolent demonstration of contemporary times in the United States, the bus boycott described by Gunnar Jahn in his presentation speech in honor of the laureate. The boycott lasted 382 days. On December 21, 1956, after the Supreme Court of the United States had declared unconstitutional the laws requiring segregation on buses, Negroes and whites rode the buses as equals. During these days of boycott, King was arrested, his home was bombed, he was subjected to personal abuse, but at the same time he emerged as a Negro leader of the first rank. In 1957 he was elected president of the Southern Christian Leadership Conference, an organization formed to provide new leadership for the now burgeoning civil rights movement. The ideals for this organization he took from Christianity; its operational techniques from Gandhi. In the eleven-year period between 1957 and 1968, King traveled over six million miles and spoke over twenty-five hundred times, appearing wherever there was injustice, protest, and action; and meanwhile he wrote five books as well as numerous articles. In these years, he led a massive protest in Birmingham, Alabama, that caught the attention of the entire world, providing what he called a «coalition of conscience» and inspiring his «Letter from a Birmingham Jail», a manifesto of the Negro revolution; he planned the drives in Alabama for the registration of Negroes as voters; he directed the peaceful march on Washington, D.C., of 250,000 people to whom he delivered his address, «I Have a Dream»; he conferred with President John F. Kennedy and campaigned for President Lyndon B. Johnson; he was arrested upwards of twenty times and assaulted at least four times; he was awarded five honorary degrees, was named Man of the Year by *Time* magazine in 1963, and became not only the symbolic leader of American blacks but also a world figure.

At the age of thirty-five, Martin Luther King, Jr., was the youngest man to have received the Nobel Peace Prize. When notified of his selection, he announced that he would turn over the prize money of $ 54,123 to the furtherance of the civil rights movement.

On the evening of April 4, 1968, while standing on the balcony of his motel room in Memphis, Tennessee, where he was to lead a protest march in sympathy with striking garbage workers of that city, he was assassinated.

Selected Bibliography

Adams, Russell, *Great Negroes Past and Present*, pp. 106–107. Chicago, Afro-Am Publishing Co., 1963.

Bennett, Lerone, Jr., *What Manner of Man: A Biography of Martin Luther King, Jr.* Chicago, Johnson, 1964.

I Have a Dream: The Story of Martin Luther King in Text and Pictures. New York, Time-Life Books, 1968.

King, Martin Luther, Jr., *The Measure of a Man*. Philadelphia, The Christian Education Press, 1959. Two devotional addresses.

King, Martin Luther, Jr., *Strength to Love*. New York, Harper & Row, 1963. Sixteen sermons and one essay entitled «Pilgrimage to Nonviolence».

King, Martin Luther, Jr., *Stride toward Freedom: The Montgomery Story*, New York, Harper, 1958.

King, Martin Luther, Jr., *The Trumpet of Conscience*. New York, Harper & Row, 1968.

King, Martin Luther, Jr., *Where Do We Go from Here: Chaos or Community?* New York, Harper & Row, 1967.

King, Martin Luther, Jr., *Why We Can't Wait*. New York, Harper & Row, 1963.

«Man of the Year», *Time*, 83 (January 3, 1964) 13–16; 25–27.

«Martin Luther King, Jr.», in *Current Biography Yearbook 1965*, ed. by Charles Moritz, pp. 220–223. New York, H. W. Wilson.

Reddick, Lawrence D., *Crusader without Violence: A Biography of Martin Luther King, Jr.* New York, Harper, 1959.

Peace 1965

THE
UNITED NATIONS CHILDREN'S FUND
(UNICEF)

Presentation

by Aase Lionaes*, Member of the Nobel Committee

The death of Alfred Nobel at San Remo on December 10, 1896, robbed the world of a highly talented person. At the same time the world was enriched by a document, a testament, which has provided growth and stimulus to the ideals and the compelling desire for research that provided the guiding star in Alfred Nobel's rich but lonely life.

In his will Nobel directed that the interest on his fortune should be divided among those persons who have rendered the greatest services to mankind. On the subject of the Peace Prize he categorically states that it is to be awarded to the person who has done most to promote brotherhood among the nations.

Alfred Nobel, particularly in the later years of his life, was much preoccupied with the problem of peace. This emerges *inter alia* from his correspondence with Bertha von Suttner[1], the author of the pacifist novel *Lay Down Your Arms*. Many people imbued with constructive ideas have, like Nobel, both before and after his time, devoted their attention to this apparently simple but as yet unsolved problem, that of promoting brotherhood among men and building a world free from war. During the course of time many profound theories have been developed to show how international relations should be organized in order to ensure the attainment of peace.

Personally, I have found no answer either in the works of the philosophers or in those of the legal experts. Maybe, after all, the only valid solution

* Aase Lionaes, at this time president of the Lagting (a section of the Norwegian Parliament), delivered this speech on December 10, 1965, in the Auditorium of the University of Oslo. Mr. Gunnar Jahn, chairman of the Committee, presented the Nobel medal and diploma to Mr. Henry R. Labouisse, the executive director of UNICEF, who responded in behalf of the organization with a short speech of acceptance. The English translation of Mrs. Lionaes' speech used here is basically that appearing in *Les Prix Nobel en 1965*, with certain editorial changes, as well as some emendations made after collation with the Norwegian text in *Les Prix Nobel*.
1. Bertha von Suttner (1843–1914), recipient of the Nobel Peace Prize for 1905.

is to be found in the simple words our own poet Bjørnstjerne Bjørnson[1] wrote as he lay on his deathbed in Paris in 1910. These words formed the first line of a poem which was never completed but which begins as follows: «Good deeds save the world.»

We have come together here today to pay tribute, by the award of the Nobel Peace Prize, to an organization – UNICEF – because in giving life to Bjørnstjerne Bjørnson's words, it has fulfilled the condition of Nobel's will, the promotion of brotherhood among the nations.

UNICEF was set up by a United Nations resolution on December 11, 1946. The resolution was unanimous, but I well remember[2] that in United Nations circles in New York that autumn we had a great many discussions with various politicians as to whether the UN really ought to organize a children's fund. The United Nations, many maintained, was a political forum which was not justified in dealing with such «minor» peripheral problems as aid to children. During the war the organization UNRRA had carried out large-scale humanitarian work for children, prisoners, and refugees in Europe and in China; for various reasons it was now being liquidated[3]. A number of people expressed the opinion that, now that peace was a fact, national children's organizations should take over the work of caring for the children of each country.

Today there is no disagreement on justifying UNICEF as part of the United Nations.

As you know, it is not always easy to achieve unanimity in the United Nations. This is understandable when one considers that we are dealing here with 118 member states representing every race, nation, political ideology, and religious creed. But everyone has understood the language of UNICEF, and even the most reluctant person is bound to admit that in action UNICEF has proved that compassion knows no national boundaries. As soon as all the resolutions relative to the form of organization, mandate, and financing of UNICEF were clarified, the organization set to work.

It was a blessing for UNICEF and the millions of children it took to

1. Bjørnstjerne Bjørnson (1832–1910), Norwegian poet, dramatist, and novelist; recipient of the Nobel Prize in Literature for 1903.
2. Mrs. Lionaes was a Norwegian delegate to the UN 1946–1965.
3. The UN Relief and Rehabilitation Administration, established in 1943, was discontinued in Europe in 1947 and in China in 1949, its work being taken over by the UN Food and Agriculture Organization (FAO) and the International Refugee Organization (IRO).

its heart that from the very first day of its existence it had a leader like Mr. Maurice Pate[1]. He was UNICEF's never slumbering conscience. He never allowed formalities to impede him in his work; in his opinion the essential object was that good deeds should be carried out as swiftly and as effectively as possible. He recruited his fellow-workers from among those who were prepared uncompromisingly, to quote Bjørnson, to pursue «the policy of compassion». Maurice Pate was the head of UNICEF for eighteen years, up to his death this year. He was an unassuming person, but on the road that leads to peace, where politicians are still groping their way in the dark, Maurice Pate has lit many a candle.

He has been succeeded by Henry Labouisse[2], a man eminently qualified by experience for this task, who was chosen by Maurice Pate, nominated by the Secretary-General, and unanimously approved by the Executive Board[3].

UNICEF's first field of operations was in Europe.

What did Europe look like in 1946? And how were Europe's children living at the conclusion of the World War? The Swedish poet Hjalmar Gullberg provides us with an unforgettable picture in his poem «Europe's Children»:

> *That we had fixed the padlock on our gate,*
> *That hardly mattered;*
> *Though finespun dreams had lulled the very soul,*
> *Our peace of mind was shattered:*
> *Beyond the palings Europe's children hold aloft*
> *Their begging-bowl.*

These were the children UNICEF came to help in Europe during that fearful, bitter winter of 1947–undernourished, ill, clad in rags, homeless, and starved after five years of war and occupation. We came across them everywhere–in the ruins of cities, in refugee camps, in bombed villages in

1. Maurice Pate (1894–1965), executive director of UNICEF from its founding in 1946 until his death a few months before he was to retire.
2. Henry R. Labouisse (1904–   ), American attorney and diplomat.
3. This paragraph in the Norwegian text reads as follows: «Maurice Pate himself chose the man to succeed him as the leader of the organization–Henry Labouisse. Director Labouisse's superb qualifications and his devotion to UNICEF's aims made it natural for UN Secretary-General U Thant to nominate him as Maurice Pate's successor. We have the honor and pleasure of having Director Labouisse with us here today to receive the Nobel Peace Prize on behalf of UNICEF.»

Hungary, Yugoslavia, Albania, Poland, Italy, Greece, Rumania, and Austria.

UNICEF itself calculated that in Europe in 1947 the number of needy children amounted to twenty million. It was for these children in fourteen different countries that UNICEF provided a lifeline–a stream of food, medicine, clothes, and footwear. Never before had we witnessed an international relief campaign for children on such a scale. During the winter of 1947–1948 UNICEF was able to report that it gave six million children and mothers one meal every day.

Fortunately the economic reconstruction of Europe after the war proceeded relatively quickly. After four or five years our countries were able to look after their children themselves.

But no sooner did the European aid program approach a point of solution than the outlines of another menacing specter appeared, the inconceivable social misery of the developing countries.

As each of these countries solved its problem of national independence, the plight of their child population came more sharply into focus. Suddenly in one single year, 1960, we find seventeen new states inscribed on the map of Africa. In a matter of a few years the membership of the United Nations rose from fifty-one states to 118. The majority of these new states are what *we* call developing countries.

Various factors, among them, the modern mass media of communication –TV and broadcasting–with their dissemination of factual information on the social misery endured in these countries, made it a moral imperative for the wealthy nations of the West to come to the assistance of these countries.

The United Nations Economic and Social Council soon realized the scope of this task, and the efforts of its many specialist organizations, such as the World Health Organization, FAO, and UNICEF, were directed to this work.

In 1946 UNICEF had been organized as a provisional emergency organization. In 1953 the United Nations General Assembly decided to make UNICEF its permanent child-aid organization, with the emphasis on work in the developing countries.

UNICEF now took up the second great task in its history, that of improving the indescribably miserable conditions in which hundreds of millions of children lived in the developing countries.

UNICEF cannot do this work on its own. It can work only in countries whose governments solicit its aid, and the countries receiving this aid must contribute at least as much as UNICEF itself in carrying out aid programs. While the aid given by UNICEF generally consists of technical assistance, and of commodities and equipment which must be purchased with foreign currency, the recipient country makes its contribution in the form of its own products, local personnel, transport services, and so on. The interest in UNICEF's aid programs for children has been so great that the contribution of governments now comprises two and a half dollars for every UNICEF dollar that is given. In fact, the aim of UNICEF's work is precisely to provide a spur to self-help.

The aid given must cover all children in an area, regardless of race, creed, nationality, or political conviction.

At the head of UNICEF today there is a board consisting of representatives from thirty member countries; it is this board that lays down the broad outlines of the work to be carried out, evaluates requests for help, and decides the extent of such help. Today UNICEF's Secretariat consists of some 600 persons, some of them working at the headquarters in New York, and some at the thirty regional offices in Europe, America, Asia, and Africa.

UNICEF is financed by gifts from governments, private individuals, and organizations. In 1964, 118 countries contributed a total of thirty-three million dollars.

What does UNICEF accomplish with this money?

First of all, it must be borne in mind that the field of work to be covered is enormous, embracing over 115 developing countries, with a total population of 750 million children, whose needs for better food, better health, and better teaching are far, far greater than the modest 200 million kroner now at the disposal of UNICEF. This sum corresponds approximately to the amount which is spent in the world today every two hours for armaments.

However, let us not be dismayed at the thought of the still inadequate amounts of money available. What is most important is that for the first time in history we possess an international device capable of tackling the giant task of liberating the children of the developing countries–who are, all of them, our joint responsibility–from ignorance, disease, malnutrition, and starvation. The most important thing is not the precise amount in terms of hard cash; what is far more important is the breakthrough of the idea of international cooperation that UNICEF represents.

The English historian Arnold Toynbee says that our century will probably be remembered, not for its two world wars, but as the period in history when, for the first time, the idea of mutual help between people, aimed at raising the standard of living everywhere, was accepted.

Today, through its work, UNICEF is helping to confirm this conception of the twentieth century.

When UNICEF started operations in the developing countries, the task appeared so overwhelming that it was difficult to know where to begin. To people aware of the tremendous advances made by medical science in the countries of the West and the comprehensive health services enjoyed by the inhabitants of these countries, it seemed outrageous that hundreds of millions of children should be suffering from diseases which we today have means of combating. This group wanted to give first priority to the campaign against such national scourges as malaria, trachoma, tuberculosis, and yaws.

Others pointed to the limitless extent of undernourishment and malnutrition on the one hand, and the tremendous surplus stores of grain and meat in Western countries on the other hand. They would have preferred to concentrate on the campaign to raise the standard of nutrition.

A third group pointed to the necessity of overcoming illiteracy, since an ignorant population could not possibly achieve the economic growth that was needed.

Which of these courses did UNICEF choose?

It can be said that all three problems were approached simultaneously, for it was realized that these evils–disease, starvation, and ignorance–form arcs of the same vicious circle.

When we consider the results that UNICEF has achieved today, we must keep in mind that they have been achieved in fruitful cooperation with the World Health Organization, with FAO, UNESCO, and the various technical aid organizations within the United Nations.

Cooperating with the World Health Organization, UNICEF has made a sizeable contribution in the fight against malaria, a disease which by 1955 attacked an estimated 200 million victims annually, of whom two million died. When one hears these staggering figures, he asks himself: Is there any use at all in taking up the fight?

One of the best examples of the progress that has been achieved comes to us from Mexico, where UNICEF, together with other UN organs, was able to call on the services of 2,800 men who, on foot, on horseback, and in motorboats, traversed the length and breadth of the country, disinfecting three million houses with DDT in the course of 1960 alone. Not a single death due to malaria was reported in 1960. Agricultural production, too, went up; and the government is now planning to move several million people from the central, overpopulated highland areas down to the areas along the coast which are now free from malaria.

In combating the painful and sinister disease of yaws, UNICEF has made a major contribution. In 1946 this scourge afflicted a total of fifty million victims; while the disease is not fatal, it results in the stunting and disfigurement of the human body. And yet this sickness, which brings so much misery to the individual, can be completely cured by a single shot of penicillin at a cost of five kroner.

When Indonesia became independent in 1949, its government asked UNICEF to assist in the fight against yaws. It was calculated in 1950 that ten million people in Indonesia suffered from this ailment. With the World Health Organization, UNICEF has succeeded in liberating whole villages from this disease; and in a few years' time yaws will be completely eradicated in Indonesia.

We could also mention the ten million children who were treated for the tremendously infectious eye malady known as trachoma, or the treatment given to millions of lepers in as many as thirty-five countries. Mass examinations of the population and anti-TB vaccinations have also been carried out on a massive scale.

In the prosperous parts of the world we are concerned with our diet problem. Many people are concerned because they eat too much, and they worry about the ill effects. In the developing countries, unfortunately, the problem is the very opposite. Experts calculate that in these countries half the population are undernourished or suffer from malnutrition. One of the results is an infant mortality rate of up to four hundred per thousand. In Norway it is seventeen per thousand.

UNICEF has launched a number of projects in an endeavor to improve the nutrition of mothers and children. This work is carried on through information work in the nearly 20,000 health centers for mothers and children that UNICEF has organized. It is also done by granting financial aid for the building of dairies, of factories for the production of dried milk and for the conservation of milk, or – as in Chile – for building a factory for the production of large quantities of fishmeal. The aim is primarily to encourage the production of foodstuffs rich in protein, such as fish, which can be bred on a large scale in fish farms or in paddy fields under water.

UNICEF's initiative in these areas is important because it represents the first systematic attempt ever made to coordinate scientific endeavors all over the world to produce food rich in protein for children in the developing countries.

I have mentioned a third area: the struggle against illiteracy, to which UNICEF, in collaboration with UNESCO, has made a notable contribution.

If we review UNICEF's activities, we shall find that during these years it has carried out hundreds of aid programs in developing countries in the health-nutrition-and-education field.

Today UNICEF is about to embark on a third stage in its development.

At the moment there is a tremendous interest in most developing countries in working out nationwide schemes of economic planning. In the discussion revolving around these development plans, the primary matter of interest is how large investments can be made in industry, agriculture, and communications. And yet, maybe these words of Nehru[1] contain a dangerous truth: «In one way or another in all our thinking on development plans for factory plants and machinery, we lose sight of the fact that, in the last analysis, development depends on the human factor.»

It is this fundamental viewpoint that prompts UNICEF's efforts at the present time to ensure that the interests of the children are safeguarded in the development plans now being drawn up. UNICEF is here building on the principle of the child's right to social security and education and of other rights adopted by the United Nations in 1959 in the Declaration of the Rights of the Child[2]. And in the same way as we have seen the fundamental principles of the Declaration of Human Rights[3] incorporated in the constitutions of many of the new countries, it is hoped that it will be possible to incorporate the rights of the child in the economic and social structure of these new states.

It is this hope that inspired the invitation that was sent out to attend the

1. Jawaharlal Nehru (1889–1964), Indian statesman; prime minister of India (1947–1964).
2. A declaration setting forth the world's obligations to its children, including those of giving children affection and security and of bringing them up «in a spirit of understanding, tolerance, friendship among peoples, peace, and universal brotherhood» (Principle 10).
3. For the Universal Declaration of Human Rights, adopted by the UN in 1948, see Cassin's Nobel lecture, pp.394–407.

round table conference in Italy, initiated by UNICEF in 1964. Those who took part in this conference were ministers, economists, and child-welfare experts. The conclusion arrived at was that, in the long run, no economic development is possible unless the growth of a healthy and enlightened generation of children is given priority in the plans for development.

Maximum aid must be given by the prosperous countries if this gigantic task is to be accomplished; and we possess the material and technical potential for giving this aid. The miracles of technology seem to be limitless; we have within our grasp the possibility of satisfying practically every material need on earth. In fact, in our ambition we move beyond the confines of this world, literally stretching our arms toward the moon. On the other hand, there are millions of people who do not possess a spade for digging their meager soil.

Today the people of the developing countries are fully alive to their own misery; and they are determined to leave it behind. They contemplate the riches of the West—our surplus food, our fantastic technology, the health and good things that we enjoy in life, all our material well-being—and they compare them with the misery of their own children.

This contrast creates a dangerous tension factor which threatens the peace of the world.

The aim of UNICEF is to spread a table, decked with all the good things that nature provides, for all the children of the world. For this reason the organization is a peace factor of great importance. UNICEF has realized that children provide the key to the future; the children of today make the history of the future. UNICEF is now forging a link of solidarity between the rich and the poor countries. In an age when so many people are terrified of the destructive effects of the forces that science has placed in our hands, UNICEF offers young people in all countries an alternative worth living and working for—a world with:

Freedom for all people,
Equality between all races,
Brotherhood among all men.

Acceptance

by Henry R.Labouisse, Executive Director of UNICEF

After receiving the prize from Mr.Jahn, Henry Richardson Labouisse (1904–
   ), American attorney and diplomat and former U.S.ambassador to
Greece, who, before becoming executive director of UNICEF in 1965,
had held several United Nations posts, including that of director of the UN
Relief and Works Agency for Palestine Refugees, responded in behalf of
UNICEF with the following speech of acceptance[1].

It is a great privilege to represent here today the United Nations Children's
Fund and, on its behalf, to receive the Nobel Peace Prize for 1965. I speak
for the entire staff of UNICEF and for our Executive Board in expressing
our profound gratitude to the Nobel Committee of the Norwegian Storting.

   May I also say how very much we wish that my predecessor, Maurice
Pate[2], could be here with us. This great practical idealist was UNICEF's
architect and builder. To the work for children, Maurice Pate devoted much
of his life and at that work he died last January, a few months before his
scheduled retirement. We miss him poignantly in Oslo today.

   Created in 1946 to provide urgent relief for the children of war-ravaged
Europe, UNICEF was soon given the task of assisting the children of the
developing countries who live in the shadow of disease, hunger, ignorance,
and poverty.

   We know from Alfred Nobel's own childhood what care and tireless
effort can mean in enabling a fragile, sickly boy to attain great heights in
later life. Nobel's parents succeeded in overcoming the ill fortune which
beset their son; everything that could be done for him was done. He lived,
and his name today is associated with mankind's highest achievements.

   Had Alfred Nobel been born not in 1833 but even in 1965, in a steamy,
isolated village of Asia, Africa, Latin America, what would be his chances
of survival and of success?

   The hard reality is that, in more than one hundred developing countries

1. The text is taken from *Les Prix Nobel en 1965*.
2. Maurice Pate (1894–1965), the first executive director of UNICEF.

of the world, the odds that confront the *average* child today–not to say a sickly one–are still overwhelming. They are four to one against his receiving any medical attention, at birth or afterwards. Even if he survives until school age, the chances are two to one that he will get no education at all; if he does get into school, the chances are about four to one that he will not complete the elementary grades. Almost certainly he will have to work for a living by the time he is twelve. He will work to eat–to eat badly and not enough. And his life will, on the average, end in about forty years.

Such statistics make us face the staggering waste of human energy and talent which drains, year in, year out, the very nations which need them the most. The developing countries are making a courageous effort to catch up with the industrial ones. To them, to us, the word «development» is a symbol of hope: it brings to mind new roads, power plants, and steel mills, stepped up production in farming and industry. But development means, above all, *people*–not numbers of people but quality of people. One of the crucial factors in the progress of a country is the development of the child, the adult of tomorrow–tomorrow's engineers, doctors, progressive farmers, teachers, scientists, social leaders. That is the great task in which UNICEF is taking a share.

Now, an underprivileged child may benefit from many different things: from a mass vaccination campaign, from improved nutrition, from a new well in his village providing clean water to drink, from a book, from a good teacher in a modernized school, from a small clinic serving his neighborhood. In its efforts to help meet these needs, UNICEF concentrates on helping governments establish or expand *their own* services for children. Assisted governments contribute, on the average, more than two and a half times as much as does UNICEF to each given project. Our agency's contribution consists of such things as medicines and medical equipment, jeeps and bicycles for public health and community development workers, science kits, and other equipment for pilot schools, tools for vocational training, pipes and pumps for village sanitation, the stipends to pay for the training of teachers–or of teacher's teachers.

UNICEF aid comes marvelously alive in the field when you see, for instance, a whole pilot region raising its standards simultaneously in education, nutrition, sanitation, and health, with everyone lending a hand, from the local teachers and doctors to the poorest families of the jungle villages– all this with the help of our supplies and of advice from United Nations experts. The «fraternity of nations» that Alfred Nobel, in his will, dreamt to see promoted is truly there in action. On our UNICEF staff we have men and women of seventy-one different nationalities and on our Board, thirty nations; 121 governments contribute on a purely voluntary basis to our budget, and 118 countries receive our assistance while, in turn, doing their share of the financing and of the work. Such worldwide cooperation contributes, in itself, to a better understanding within the family of Man.

But to me, the great, the most important meaning of this Nobel award is the solemn recognition that the welfare of today's children is inseparably linked with the peace of tomorrow's world. The sufferings and privations to which I have referred do not ennoble; they frustrate and embitter. The longer the world tolerates the slow war of attrition which poverty and ignorance now wage against 800 million children in the developing countries, the more likely it becomes that our hope for lasting peace will be the ultimate casualty.

It is not just in those countries, of course, but in all countries, rich and poor alike, that we adults should constantly ask ourselves: is our society doing, or failing to do, all that is possible to equip our children with the weapons for peace? When our children grow up, will they have trained and informed minds, liberated from the old prejudices and hatreds? Will they trust their own civilization? Will they be prepared to trust and understand others? This is an area way beyond the mandate of our agency—but not beyond the probing of our own conscience, as individuals.

We of UNICEF accept the Nobel Prize for Peace with humility, knowing how little we are able to do and how immense are the needs. We accept it with gratitude toward the governments who are the fountainheads of our financing, toward the Specialized Agencies of the United Nations that provide us with their advice, toward the national committees, nongovernmental organizations, and the very many individuals who give us invaluable support. The people and the government of Norway deserve our special thanks—for Norway, in 1964, gave us the highest contribution per capita of population of all our contributing governments. We are proud of your interest and your trust.

To all of us in UNICEF the prize will be a wonderful incentive to greater efforts in the name of peace. You have given us new strength. You have reinforced our profound belief that each time UNICEF contributes, however modestly, to giving today's children a chance to grow into useful and happier citizens, it contributes to removing some of the seeds of world tension and future conflicts.

Zena Harman

UNICEF: Achievement and Challenge

Nobel Lecture*, December 11, 1965

If Alfred Nobel had been alive today, I venture to believe that he would have welcomed the award of his Peace Prize to the United Nations Children's Fund. He would have commended its purpose, its effectiveness, and achievement. He would have understood the infusion of new hope which this recognition will bring to millions of deprived and tragic children. His own childhood was, as he put it, «every day a renewed fight for survival». But he did not suffer the pangs of hunger, nor did he know the cruel vicissitudes of grim poverty. He experienced the warm love of a devoted mother, the comforts of a good home. Andriette Nobel, tender and calm, brave and intelligent, sustained him throughout his life. The symbol of UNICEF, a mother clasping her child, exulting in the healthy baby held high in her arms, would have touched him significantly.

The love that infuses the mother–child relationship is the most positive expression of human hope; it is the wellspring of human life. Baroness Bertha von Suttner[1], the great woman who influenced Nobel's thinking, said, «An abundance of maternal love is wanted to shield and guide the whole of humanity.» There is no dearth of maternal love, no lack of tenderness for the young, only a great yearning for a better future. Would that there were in equal measure food and clothing, shelter, medicines and doctors, schools and teachers.

The UNICEF Executive Board at a special meeting convened in the United Nations on November 19, 1965, expressed its deep appreciation of

---

* This lecture was delivered in the auditorium of the Nobel Institute by Zena Harman (Mrs. Abraham Harman), speaking for UNICEF in her capacity as chairman of its Executive Board. At one time assistant director of the Technical Assistance Department of the Prime Minister's Office in Israel and later director of the Division for International Organizations in Israel's Ministry for Foreign Affairs, Mrs. Harman had served on the UNICEF Executive Board as Israel's representative from 1952 to 1959 and again from 1962, chairing the Program Committee several times during these years before becoming chairman of the Executive Board in 1964. The text of Mrs. Harman's lecture is taken from *Les Prix Nobel en 1965*.

1. Bertha von Suttner (1843–1914), recipient of the Nobel Peace Prize for 1905.

the Nobel Peace Prize award in a resolution. It considered the award a recognition of the importance of the welfare and rearing of children in a spirit of friendship among nations for peace in the world, and a tribute to cooperation on behalf of children among governments, United Nations agencies, and other international organizations; an acknowledgment of the efforts of millions of volunteers, both as individuals and as members of nongovernmental organizations, and of the devotion and competence of the UNICEF staff; and expressed the hope that this award will encourage all countries to increase their cooperative efforts to improve the condition of children in their own countries and throughout the world.

Alfred Nobel once said, «If you could only understand that we can help a human being without any ulterior motive.» It is precisely this spirit that has animated UNICEF's work and made possible a record of unique cooperation. Differences of view have been welded, almost always, into an accepted concensus in the search for agreement on the best methods of providing assistance to alleviate the agony of children who are victims of cruel circumstance. The nations of the world agreed, when they approved unanimously the Declaration of the Rights of the Child, that «mankind owes the child the best it has to give.» It is UNICEF's responsibility to help them make that best a worthy and effective contribution to ensure healthy growth and development, to translate an acknowledged duty into programs of practical action.

A man of science, Nobel understood the potential of technical progress and scientific discovery. He knew that they could be applied to dispel ignorance, fight disease, and eliminate hunger. He realized the implications of scientific understanding for the welfare of mankind and the ability of men of science to influence, even determine, human destiny. At a recent meeting of scientists with politicians and policy makers, convened to explore ways of accelerating progress through the application of science to everyday needs, a Christian minister from an African country brought the great men back to a tragic and stark reality. «I come from a country», he said, «in which, while it is of great interest and importance to talk about nuclear fission, solar energy, and all of these things, it is of even greater interest to know how to save our babies... We cannot believe that nature, God, call it what you like, loves children of other countries more than African children. Is typhoid caused by drinking dirty water or by someone who has bewitched you? Are babies dying because they are not fed properly or because your enemy put sickness into them? Men of science, men of

goodwill,» he implored, «help the African people to develop and understand.» This simple, moving appeal is some indication of the immense chasm
that must be traversed before the gap of centuries, in terms of civilization,
can be successfully navigated. UNICEF is immensely challenged.

UNICEF was born of the tragedy of war to become a major implement
of peace. It was brought into existence on December 11, 1946, by a resolution of the General Assembly, as the International Children's Emergency
Fund, charged with responsibility to prevent epidemics and stave off the
worst consequences of malnutrition among millions of children who had
been exposed to the ravages of war. It brought supplies of food, clothing,
and drugs to these young victims of man-made upheaval and conflagration,
which tore at the roots of European civilization.

It was soon acknowledged, however, that many more children were victims of a hostile environment, of poverty, inertia and neglect. Children in
Asia, the Middle East, Africa, and Latin America died in their millions of
sickness and starvation, abandoned in the backwash of history, left behind
in the surge of time. Child suffering could not be distinguished by virtue
of its cause or origin. Children in desperate need anywhere and everywhere
required help and attention. In December, 1950, the General Assembly directed UNICEF to use its resources for «the purpose of meeting, through
the provision of supplies, training and advice, the emergency and long-
range needs of children and their continuing needs, particularly in underdeveloped countries, with a view to strengthening, wherever this may be
appropriate, the permanent child-health and child-welfare programs of the
countries receiving assistance». In yet another resolution, passed unanimously in December, 1953, the Assembly decided to continue the work
of the Fund indefinitely, to drop the word Emergency in its name, and
to all intents and purposes, treat it as a permanent organ of the United
Nations, charged with responsibility for the child, recognizing that there
would undoubtedly be continuing, unmet needs for many decades.

An Executive Board of twenty-five members, subsequently increased in
1957 to thirty, elected by the Economic and Social Council for three-year
terms, representative of all regions of the world, establishes policy and sets
the criteria for the deployment of funds. A program committee of sixteen
and an administrative budget committee of ten, elected from the Board's
membership, accelerate its work. In its deliberations, the Board has invari-
ably viewed its task as an historic opportunity to influence, in some measure, the nature and character of tomorrow's citizens. The child of today

is the farmer, the teacher, the politician, and the worker of tomorrow. The child, indeed, is the father of the man, or, as is said in Proverbs 22:6, «Train up a child in the way he should go and when he is old, he will not depart from it.»

It was understood from the outset that whilst UNICEF could stimulate and encourage action, the vital decisions would need to be taken by governments themselves, committed to ensuring the welfare of their peoples. UNICEF cannot provide ready-made motivation nor ensure that the people themselves are inspired to make a supreme effort in their own behalf. Improving conditions for the child involves a ceaseless, long-term effort. Neither the capacity nor the will to succeed can be supplied from without. There is no substitute for an indigenous leadership which understands that real wealth is found in the happiness and security of individual human beings.

The UNICEF Secretariat, with headquarters at the United Nations in New York, became the nerve center of a network of offices established in the different regions of the world. Maurice Pate, the first executive director, who died early this year, provided incomparable leadership. A man of compassion, he was imbued with a love of people; he had infinite faith in them and saw good in everyone. With wisdom, dignity, and tact, he inspired universal respect and invoked confidence. He not only selected his staff on the basis of professional qualification, but sought in each of them special qualities of heart, a willingness to subordinate self to a labor of love, in which hours and physical frailty did not figure. A dedicated team was assembled, inspired always by the selflessness of Mr. Pate himself and his certain conviction that he and his colleagues had been entrusted with a task of sacred dimension. It is appropriate that the Executive Board should have decided to link his name to the Nobel Peace Prize, which will constitute the nucleus of a Maurice Pate Scholarship Fund. His successor, Mr. Labouisse, was selected in the knowledge that he possessed the same qualities of mind and heart, reinforced by important experience, to ensure that the work continue with the same sense of commitment and complete objectivity.

The tasks have always seemed vast and limitless, the resources infinitesimal in relation to the need. The establishment of priorities has represented a continuous challenge, although from the outset the primacy of government responsibility was acknowledged. Whilst it has been necessary to concentrate on basic, fundamental needs, the evolution of UNICEF's work has been marked by a flexibility of approach, which has taken account of diversity and local realities. It has been generally recognized that real progress must be expressed in the character and idiom of each nation's personality and aspiration. In order to ensure the government's interest and involvement, as well as to increase the resources available, the matching rule was adopted. Thus, every dollar invested by UNICEF must be matched by at least one dollar or its equivalent. In practice, over the years, the government investment has exceeded, by far, UNICEF's contribution.

A close relationship was established with the Specialized Agencies from the beginning, in the first period specifically with WHO and the FAO[1]. There are joint policy committees with these two agencies, comprising five representatives of each body, which meet annually to determine mutually acceptable lines of approach. All UNICEF projects require the technical approval of the relevant agency, which also recruits the professional personnel for the different projects when outside expert advice is called for. As policy has developed in response to need, suitable arrangements have also been made with UNESCO and ILO[2]. This inter-agency collaboration, as well as the cooperation that has always existed with the United Nations Department of Economic and Social Affairs, has provided an excellent example of teamwork, which has proved mutually beneficial, as each agency seeks to achieve its own goals. Within the United Nations family UNICEF alone has sole responsibility for focusing attention on the child as a complete human being.

The provision of badly needed supplies, which must be imported, is at the center of UNICEF's operation. A large packing, assembly, and distribution center in Copenhagen is today the headquarters of a dramatic supply undertaking, which keeps ships constantly sailing the high seas carrying vital cargoes destined for some 118 countries which receive UNICEF aid. The goods are purchased in different parts of the world as a result of bids and tenders, which seek only to ensure the best quality and the lowest prices. UNICEF ships hundreds of items, including midwifery and tool kits, jeeps and mobile X-ray units, bicycles, drugs and DDT, teaching aids and sew-

1. The World Health Organization (WHO) was initiated in 1946 and affiliated with the UN in 1948. The Food and Agriculture Organization (FAO) was initiated in 1945 and affiliated with the UN in 1946.
2. The United Nations Educational, Scientific, and Cultural Organization (UNESCO) was initiated in 1945 and formally established in 1946. The International Labor Organization (ILO) was created in 1919 by the Versailles Peace Treaty, was affiliated with the League of Nations, and finally made a specialized agency of the UN in 1946; it received the Nobel Peace Prize for 1969.

ing machines, sheets, milk powder and soap. In many countries, UNICEF's readiness to supply previously unavailable items of essential equipment has sparked the construction of schools, clinics, and community centers and has facilitated the development of vital services for children.

UNICEF's original mandate stressed the importance of child health generally. The basic needs of the child are, indeed, protection against disease, adequate food, clean water, shelter and clothing, and an environment conducive to healthy emotional and social development. The first need, however, is to ensure the survival of the infant and its mother. Over 30,000 health centers, providing maternal and child health services, have been set up and equipped with UNICEF assistance in different developing areas of the world, representing a UNICEF investment of over seventy million dollars over the years. They are becoming increasingly part of a centrally directed and financed public health service. Yet it is doubtful whether more than five to ten percent of the mothers and children actually come under their direct care. The impact on the community of these programs has frequently resulted in a chain reaction of developing services; but whilst millions of mothers and infants have received attention and instruction, the coverage is small in relation to the appalling need.

In approving certain projects for assistance, the Board was concerned that the requesting government regard them as having a relatively high priority in the scale of need. It wanted assurance that heavy loss of children's lives or the serious impairment of health would be checked. It preferred projects of long-term value in preference to those of short-term relief and it was pleased if other countries were able to benefit too. The attraction of the mass campaigns against infectious communicable diseases, which not only account for millions of child deaths but lead to permanent physical defect and weakness, was obvious. They had the additional advantage of having a low per capita cost–one cent could buy enough BCG vaccine to protect a child against tuberculosis, ten cents enough penicillin to cure four children of yaws, twenty-five cents enough antibiotics to cure two children of trachoma, fifty cents enough DDT to protect seven children from malaria for a year, and seventy-five cents enough sulfone tablets to treat a leprosy case for three years. UNICEF has, over the years, expended about one-third of its total aid on disease control programs. It has, in close cooperation with the World Health Organization and, in the early days, with the Danish and Swedish Red Cross and the Norwegian Relief for Europe, assisted campaigns to combat tuberculosis (200 million BCG vaccinations alone have been given). It has helped campaigns to eradicate malaria; it has been instrumental in curing millions of cases of yaws; it has provided drugs for leprosy and trachoma. Certain endemic diseases which have been almost entirely eliminated in the industrialized world are responsible for rampant child sickness and still take a shocking toll of child life. Progress will be slow and halting as long as clean, piped water is unavailable and the rules of elementary hygiene are unknown, as long as environmental sanitation remains a blueprint for the future.

Of the 600 million children today believed to be living at, or below, the minimum subsistence level, some sixteen and a half million still die before they attain their first birthdays. Despite the progress of the last decade, mortality rates among infants in the less developed regions are still as much as five times higher than in the developed areas; they are up to forty times higher for children in the one to five age group.

It is estimated that some 500 million children have actually experienced hunger or suffer from varying degrees of starvation or malnutrition. The grim picture of the emaciated child, misshapen, with its swollen belly and tragic questioning eyes, has left an indelible mark on those sensitive to harrowing misery. UNICEF in its early years supported many feeding programs. In fact, the glass of milk became a symbol of its activities to many. Large quantities of milk powder, supplemented by vitamins A and D, did much to modify the gnawing pains of hunger and the effects of malnutrition. At the same time, milk conservation projects were assisted to ensure the availability of permanent supplies of clean and safe low-cost milk. A food and agricultural policy was urged that would make provision for growing protective foods, so important for the diet of the child and his family, giving them a suitable priority vis-à-vis cash crops. Attention was also drawn to the high incidence of protein malnutrition in early childhood leading, inevitably, to stunted growth and physical disability.

In the course of the years, UNICEF's assistance was made available to encourage priority for comprehensive nutrition programs. Together with FAO and WHO, it supported surveys to ascertain food habits and estimate need, on the basis of what was feasible, against a background of local tradition and custom. It helped applied nutrition programs, community projects, including horticulture, the raising of small animals and poultry, fisheries, home economics, and food preservation. It was intent on ensuring that the child was fed properly because the mother had acquired a new understanding of its nutritional needs, and that the government was committed to an agricultural policy that would make available the foods necessary to healthy survival. A further development is in the direction of processing cheap protein concentrates from fish and readily available crops, such as soybean, peanuts, sesame and cotton seed. Such concentrates are being used to fortify low-cost weaning food mixtures.

The plight of the child continued to cause anxiety. The conscience of the world was shaken by the knowledge of the excruciating suffering of its most vulnerable citizens. In 1959, the General Assembly again underlined its deep concern in the Declaration of the Rights of the Child, which stressed the child's right to maternal protection, health, adequate food, shelter, and education. Members of UNICEF's Executive Board and Secretariat were convinced, on the basis of accumulated experience, that little real progress would result from an *ad hoc* approach to meeting pressing, immediate need. Systematic analysis, appraisal, evaluation, and research were required if the overall needs of the child were to be fully understood and progress made. It became clear that the child had to be prepared for life in all its manifestations as well as protected against its hazards.

A study prepared by the Secretary-General in connection with the United Nations Decade of Development[1] has defined development as «growth plus change». Children and young people are the primary agents of change. Indeed, much of the change that takes place in their lifetime will be influenced by the sum total of their efforts and actions.

Children and young people are growing up today in a period of rapid, revolutionary transition, shattering century-old norms and patterns of life. New political realities, new freedom, the responsibilities implicit in newly acquired independence find apathy, fatalism, and indifference to be major stumbling blocks. Modern development envisages growth in every sphere, political, economic, social, cultural, and educational. UNICEF became increasingly aware of the importance of preparing the child for the exigencies of life from its earliest childhood. It began to examine its role in the light of the crucial need to invest in human resources, to develop the abilities inherent in people, to increase their capacity to produce and fend for themselves.

In 1961 an important shift occurred in UNICEF's policy. It had become abundantly clear that, despite all the assistance rendered, the statistics of need had not diminished. On the contrary, millions more children were in need of help due, in part, to the rapid increase in population, which offset much

1. The decade of the 1960's.

of the real achievement in terms of relief that could be brought to the individual child. Barely half of the child population, aged five to fourteen, attended school, and many of these were unable to complete the full primary cycle. Teacher training and the provision of minimal school equipment, textbooks, visual aids, paper, and pencils were often beyond the strained budget of the country struggling to contend with a growing number of competing needs. The health of children and young people could not be viewed as a separate field of work, nor could their nutrition requirements, their education, or their emotional development. Children could not be regarded as a separate entity, but rather as an integral part of the population, the family, and the community, requiring certain priority consideration in national, economic, and social development planning. Services for the child should be taken for granted as a vitally important aspect of government responsibility to ensure economic viability, progress, and stability.

The condition of the child would certainly be influenced in direct proportion to the progress made in the general economy as prosperity increased. UNICEF was fully aware of its own inability to do little more than inject some help judiciously at the right time. Its budget of less than thirty-five million dollars had brought remarkable dividends and been put to maximum use, but the limitations were obvious. No occasion was allowed to pass without emphasizing the importance of encouraging every effort to raise standards of living and improve prospects. UNICEF appealed to all agencies within the family of nations, to bilateral assistance, and the army of volunteers engaged in pioneering efforts in nongovernmental organizations to concern themselves with those aspects of development in their undertakings which could also have relevance for the child. In general, it might be said that the guiding principle in investing UNICEF's resources was to ensure that they related to the key problems of children, concentrated on basic needs, and integrated with larger economic and social development plans.

In the earlier days, most of the work undertaken was in rural areas. The growth of towns and the new industrialization had led to the appearance of brutal slums, exposing children to deprivation and dangers often more terrible in their consequences than the stagnation and dejection of the primitive village. UNICEF was unable to ignore the special needs of the new city urchins. In this context, consideration had to be given to social welfare activities, day-care centers, community and neighborhood centers, and mothers' clubs.

I have already referred to grim figures of child mortality among the one to five age group. The stark fact of ignorance and neglect, and its consequences for the helpless toddler, brought yet another problem to UNICEF for urgent attention. The plight of these young children, roaming the dirt-infested alleyways of both towns and villages, highlighted once again the shocking dilemma of the mother, ignorant of elementary health, nutrition, and hygiene needs, harassed by her many offspring and endlessly nursing a new infant, confounded and perplexed by the new demands made upon her as the security of her old world cracked and crumbled. Habit and superstition die hard, and a deep fear of change brings obstinate resistance to it. It was clear that considerably more would have to be done to help the neglected young child and that national policies for children would have to take special account of the critical needs of early childhood.

Maternal and child health centers, hospitals and health services, schools, day-care centers, and community undertakings require, above all, competent, trained staffs. Equipment and supplies can be made available with relative speed. It may take years to prepare professional personnel for its role, which goes beyond the acquisition of expertise. Warm human sympathy, endless patience and understanding, and a deep, abiding faith that a better day is possible–all of these are necessary in order to make the new knowledge meaningful to the resistant and the confused.

At first the UNICEF Board was unwilling to spend its meager resources on local training costs, which it felt should be the obligation of the local government. When progress lagged for lack of trained midwives, nurses, auxiliary workers, nutritionists, teachers, doctors, pediatricians, social workers, club and community workers, it could no longer avoid the realization that no form of investment was likely to be more productive. It began to expend more of its funds on training in the form of stipends for personnel at all levels, including the trainers and the supervisors. Some scholarships were given for advanced study abroad, but emphasis was placed on people preparing to serve their own communities in the idiom of their own traditions and patterns of life. Numerous courses were designed to meet the needs of each local situation. In extending its assistance to the field of education, stress was laid on training for teachers and on those subjects that would have a direct bearing on preparing the child for the contingencies of life. Help provided for certain vocational and prevocational programs also included an important element of training. The availability of efficient, trained personnel will continue to be the touchstone of UNICEF's ability to make a fundamental contribution to improving the lot of the child. UNICEF's field staffs and the experts of the different agencies working with them (project personnel) have had to translate their own experience and attitudes into local concepts. They have often shown extraordinary sensitivity and wisdom, but they cannot substitute for the local people themselves, as they acquire a new competence and understanding.

It is among the ironies of fate that where need is greatest, there is the least possibility of absorbing assistance. Outside help cannot be really effectively utilized unless minimal services and a minimum budget are available. The Board decided recently to enable certain countries in the early stages of their development, particularly in Africa, to prepare projects for assistance which envisaged dispensing with the usual requirement of matching funds, to be provided subsequently on a sliding scale. It was disappointing and frustrating to learn that even this concession did not go far enough. Much will still have to be done to strengthen administrative structures and train personnel before help can be made effective.

One hundred twenty-one governments now contribute regularly to UNICEF's budget, and volunteer groups and private individuals raised as much as six million dollars in 1964. Yet there is little hope at the present rate of contributions for an annual budget from all sources exceeding a total of thirty-five million dollars. This amount can be reinforced not only by government matching but by the positive nature of governmental policy and the extent of its commitment to development programs that give cognizance to the crucial importance of providing for the child in planning for the future. At its June, 1965, meeting, the Executive Board was able to allocate only ten percent of its program funds for new programs. Ninety percent was required for continuing ongoing projects, sixty-three percent of which continue to be in the field of maternal and child health and disease control. Possibilities for viable projects far exceed UNICEF's financial capabilities, and it has been necessary to impose a ceiling on allocations. It is an agonizing predicament to know that millions of children will die each year, who might have lived were it not for lack of funds.

We live in a world dedicated to progress and capable of incredible achievement. Universal declarations, giving lip service to the dignity of man and human justice, have never been more numerous and more loudly proclaimed. In a world of unbelievable affluence, millions flounder and struggle for survival, as they suffer indescribable need. The child, the most vulnerable of human beings and the least able to fend for itself, surely agitates the conscience of a world that acknowledges the right of every human being to equal consideration and prospects. To quote again from the Declaration of the Rights of the Child, «He shall be brought up in a spirit of understanding, tolerance, friendship among peoples and universal brotherhood, and in the full consciousness that his energy and talents should be devoted to the service of his fellow men.» Would that he be given the chance!

The International Conference on the Economic Aspects of Disarmament, meeting in Oslo[1], heard from a survey prepared for it that 180 billion dollars are being spent annually on arms. Each atomic submarine costs approximately 160 million dollars and the latest supersonic fighter planes are priced at several millions of dollars. A Polaris nuclear-powered submarine costs 200 million dollars.

UNICEF, together with all those engaged in the struggle for social betterment and the raising of standards of living, the governments, the organizations, and individuals who have understood its purposes and provided moral and material support, has the formula to put life and substance into the words of the Declaration. If only the nations of the world could together agree to spend a fraction of their outlay on building «deterrent strengths» to develop the capacity of the young generation to adjust in health and happiness to the needs of a dynamic society! Perhaps each abortive disarmament conference would set itself a penalty–a contribution to UNICEF, the equivalent cost of one submarine or a dozen fighter planes. Today's children are surely the central factor in the strategy for peace and survival. This is what Alfred Nobel in his greatness and his vision would have understood.

1. Sponsored by the Peace Research Institute of Oslo.

Historical Note[*]

Established by the United Nations General Assembly on December 11, 1946, and originally known as the United Nations International Children's Emergency Fund (UNICEF), the UN Children's Fund has employed three approaches in discharging its mandate.

For the postwar period 1946 to 1950, the «emergency needs approach» meant swift action to meet the food, clothing, and health needs of children, particularly in Europe. At an expenditure of $ 112,000,000, UNICEF distributed various articles of clothing to five million children in twelve countries, vaccinated eight million against tuberculosis, rebuilt milk processing and distribution facilities, and, at the climax of its effort in Europe, provided a daily supplementary meal to millions of children.

During the period 1951–1960, UNICEF continued to meet emergency needs, but at the same time moved into the «long-range benefit approach». To protect the health of children, UNICEF conducted campaigns against tuberculosis, yaws, leprosy, and malaria; made provisions for environmental sanitation; encouraged maternal and child health care education. To raise nutritional standards for children, UNICEF helped countries produce and distribute low-cost, high-protein foods and fostered programs to educate people in their use. To provide for the social welfare of children, UNICEF instituted informal training of mothers in child rearing and home improvement, aided services for children through day-care and neighborhood centers, family counseling, and youth clubs. The expenditures during this period totaled $ 150,000,000.

UNICEF broadened its policy during the 1961–1970 period by adopting a concept of allying aid for children to the development of the nation. In

---

[*] Since the presentation speech, the acceptance speech, and the lecture provide historical information on UNICEF, this note is designed only to outline the main periods of UNICEF's history, to update it to 1971, and, by using representative statistics, to summarize its contributions. The editor gratefully acknowledges the kindness of UNICEF in providing for his information a soon-to-be-issued history, but he is, of course, solely responsible for this note.

recognition of the interconnection between aspects of national policy and programs of aid to children, this approach, called the «country approach», permitted UNICEF to implement in appropriate ways the priorities established by each nation in meeting the needs of its children. Consequently, becoming concerned with the intellectual, psychological, and vocational needs of children as well as with their physical needs, UNICEF provided assistance for teacher education and curriculum reform, allocated funds for prevocational training in usable skills, promoted information on the uses of technology. UNICEF projects, in short, reflected «a comprehensive view of the child», seeing him as «a future agent for economic and social change»[1]. In this decade UNICEF's total expenditures were in excess of $ 300,000,000.

In the decade of the seventies, UNICEF will attempt to elevate the quality of life of children in the developing nations, coordinating its efforts with those of the governments concerned. UNICEF hopes to increase its assistance during the decade, aiming at an annual level of $ 100,000,000 by 1975, and to enlist complementary support from international, multinational, and nongovernmental agencies.

Stark statistics for UNICEF's twenty-five-year history reveal only a facet of the constructive work accomplished, but they provide some indication of its scope: 71,000,000 children examined for trachoma and 43,000,000 treated; 425,000,000 examined for yaws and 23,000,000 treated; 400,000,000 vaccinated against tuberculosis, many millions protected from malaria, and 415,000 discharged as cured of leprosy; 12,000 rural health centers and several thousand maternity wards established in eighty-five countries; help given to provide equipment for 2,500 teacher training schools, 56,000 primary and secondary schools, 965 prevocational training schools, 31 schools for training prevocational instructors, 600 for training dietary personnel; equipment supplied for 4,000 nutrition centers and community gardens, and for 9,000 school gardens and canteens; equipment given to 2,500 day-care centers, 3,000 women's clubs, and 3,500 community centers; supplementary meals dispensed in the billions and articles of clothing in the high millions; emergency aid furnished to hundreds of thousands victimized by floods, earthquakes, and other natural disasters.

1. *General Progress Report of the Executive Director*, 1971, p.6.

Selected Bibliography

Films. UNICEF releases films for group showings. These films include four in English: *Nomad Boy* (Somalia), *Beneath the Dreams* (Hong Kong), *Meet Tasani* (Thailand), *Starting from Scratch* (United Republic of Tanzania); a number of Spanish versions of UNICEF films on Latin American countries; films produced by the European office—among them, two fifteen-minute documentaries, *L'Eau sauvage* (Ceylon) and *Le Chemin de la paix* (Nigeria) and four shorts on child life. Films scheduled for release in 1971 include a documentary on UNICEF, a documentary on problems of urbanization as it affects children, and one on the story of a UNICEF greeting card from design to sale.

General Progress Report of the Executive Director. New York, United Nations (E/ICEF/ 608), 1971.

Heilbroner, Robert L., *Mankind's Children: The Story of UNICEF.* New York, Public Affairs Committee, 1959.

Keeny, Spurgeon M., *Half the World's Children: A Diary of UNICEF at Work in Asia.* New York, Association Press, 1957.

Progress Begins with the Child: Statement by the Executive Director to the Third Committee of the General Assembly, December, 1968. New York, United Nations (printed leaflet), 1969.

A Short Guide to UNICEF. New York, United Nations (UNICEF/Misc. 131), 1967.

Strategy for Children: A Study of UNICEF Assistance Policies. New York, United Nations (E/ICEF/559/Rev. 1), 1967.

Yates, Elizabeth, *Rainbow round the World: A Story of UNICEF.* Indianapolis, Bobbs-Merrill, 1954.

Peace 1966 - 1967

Prizes not awarded

Peace 1968

RENÉ-SAMUEL CASSIN

Presentation

by Aase Lionaes*, Chairman of the Nobel Committee

The last time the Nobel Peace Prize was awarded to an individual was in 1964. The prize for that year was given to Martin Luther King. Today he is no longer alive. On April 4 of this year, so bitter a year for human rights, he fell at his post as leader of the Negroes' nonviolent struggle for their rights. His death was one of the most grievous losses ever suffered by the world's champions of peace and goodwill.

The Nobel Committee of the Norwegian Parliament gratefully remembers Martin Luther King and invokes peace for his memory.

On November 27, 1895, in the Swedish Club of Paris Alfred Nobel signed his testament which later became so famous. This was almost exactly one year before his death on December 10, 1896, at San Remo in Italy.

As is well known, Nobel decided that the income from his fortune should be divided into five equal parts and given as prizes to those who had made the greatest contributions to mankind. There is one sentence in this very short testament of his which makes us think of this year's Peace Prize laureate, Professor René Cassin. That sentence is: «It is my express wish that in awarding the prizes no consideration whatever shall be given to the nationality of the candidates, so that the most worthy shall receive the prize, whether he be a Scandinavian or not.»

It is this respect for human worth, irrespective of nationality, race, religion, sex, or social position, which animates Professor Cassin's life and work. And it is primarily for his contribution to the protection of human worth and the rights of man, as set forth in the Universal Declaration of Human Rights, that the Nobel Committee of the Norwegian Parliament today awards the Nobel Peace Prize to René Cassin.

* Mrs. Lionaes, Lagtingspresident (the Lagting being a section of the Norwegian Parliament), delivered this speech on December 10, 1968, in the Auditorium of the University of Oslo. At its conclusion she presented the prize to the laureate who responded with a brief speech of acceptance. The translation of Mrs. Lionaes' speech is based on the Norwegian text in *Les Prix Nobel en 1968*, which also carries a French translation.

René Cassin was born in 1887 in Bayonne in southern France. He drafted the United Nations' Declaration of Human Rights which was adopted on December 10, 1948, exactly twenty years ago today. At that time Cassin was about sixty years old. But although it was only then that his name became internationally known, he already had a long and rich life of service to mankind behind him.

Shortly after Cassin had completed his legal education, he was mobilized in the First World War. In 1916 a German bullet made him a war invalid and from then on he was mobilized in the demanding struggle for peace.

Let me mention the great efforts he made during the aftermath of the war in behalf of the disabled soldiers, the war widows, and the 800,000 orphaned French children. The organization which he formed and directed for their benefit had nearly one million members[1]. And it was Cassin who was the driving force behind the social legislation which assured these war victims the social and economic protection they had a right to.

His work for those affected by the war was not limited to France. In 1921 and the years following he arranged several conferences of war veterans from Italy, Poland, Germany, Czechoslovakia, and Austria. As late as 1932 and 1933 large demonstrations were organized in support of the Disarmament Conference[2]. Because of the disastrous political developments during the 1930's in Europe – the growing fascism and nazism – these attempts to establish a climate of peace and understanding among the war veterans from all countries came to an end.

From 1924 until 1938 Cassin worked within the League of Nations for disarmament.

When the war in France in 1940 led to an armistice after a few months, René Cassin was the first civilian to leave Bordeaux in response to General de Gaulle's appeal. On June 20 he reached London, where he became de Gaulle's minister of justice in exile. Here he prepared, among other things, the agreement between Winston Churchill and de Gaulle which was to

1. The laureate was a founder or member of several veterans organizations, probably the one referred to here being the Union fédérale des associations des mutilés et d'anciens combattants; he was also vice-chairman of the Conseil supérieur des pupilles de la nation.
2. The conference was held under the auspices of the League of Nations, beginning in February, 1932, and continuing for the next several years, although Germany's withdrawal from the League in 1933 in effect destroyed its efforts.

become the charter of the Free French forces[1]. The Vichy government[2] then deprived him of his French citizenship and sentenced him to death in absentia.

The end of the Second World War was the beginning of perhaps the most important stage in René Cassin's life. It was at this time that the people of all countries first came to understand clearly what the dimensions and what the nature of Hitler's war had been. It had not been merely a total war for a political objective. It had been an annihilation of ethnic groups, a genocide which the world had never before experienced.

Public opinion was stunned by the reports of the atrocities in the concentration camps and of the extermination of those of Jewish origin. The general horror found expression in demands made on the governments of all nations to prevent a repetition of this assault on the value of human beings by adopting an international Bill of Rights.

This idea was realized in 1945 when the United Nations included the establishment of a Commission on Human Rights in its Charter. The Commission's task was to compose a Universal Declaration of Human Rights and an international convention which would bind the states to make these rights a reality.

Through one of history's whims it was a representative of France, René Cassin, and a representative of the United States, Eleanor Roosevelt[3], who became the architects of the Declaration of Human Rights. Over a hundred years before, both of these nations had adopted declarations guaranteeing the basic rights of man. I am referring to the American Declaration of Independence in 1776 and the French Declaration of the Rights of Man in 1789.

But the Declaration of Human Rights, which Eleanor Roosevelt and René Cassin were to leave their marks upon so firmly, moved the stakes

1. Charles de Gaulle (1890–1970), French general and statesman, who, opposing the 1940 armistice, fled to England where Winston Churchill (1874–1965), then prime minister, agreed to support him and the Free French movement he instigated; he was later president of France (1945–1946; 1958–1969).
2. The French government set up in 1940 at Vichy, headed by Marshal Pétain and subservient to the Germans, administered that part of France not occupied by Germany; after 1942 when Hitler occupied all of France, Pierre Laval, who had become virtual dictator of France a few months earlier, was a puppet ruler for the Germans.
3. (Anna) Eleanor Roosevelt (1884–1962), wife of U.S. President F.D.Roosevelt; U.S. delegate to the UN (1945–1952) and chairman of the UN Commission on Human Rights.

farther ahead than had either the American Declaration of Independence
in 1776 or the French Declaration of the Rights of Man in 1789 – that is,
it was also in the articles which dealt with economic and social rights, being
influenced by the Russian Declaration of Rights of 1918 [1].

Eleanor Roosevelt was the chairman of the Commission on Human
Rights, and René Cassin its vice-chairman. But it was Cassin who drew
up the Declaration.

Perhaps some will say that the work for the rights of man, the struggle
against discrimination toward the colored races, toward minorities, religious
groups, and women – that all of this is noble, but does it have anything to
do with peace?

No one has given a better, more truthful answer than Nordahl Grieg [2]
has given in these words in his poem «To Youth»:

> *Here is your protection against violence,*
> *Here is your sword,*
> *The belief in our life,*
> *The worth of mankind.*

The fifty nations which adopted the United Nations' Charter in San Francisco in April, 1945, were also fully cognizant of the fact that lasting peace
had to be built upon respect for the rights and worth of the individual
human being. For what kind of peace can there be in a country where the
people are not free – where they cannot express their thoughts or print their
words, where they are not equal before the law, where they are subject to
torture and degrading treatment?

In the Preamble of the Charter it is established that the objectives are
peace and security. In the next section the member countries confirm their
belief in the fundamental rights of man and the worth of the individual.
It was this firm belief in the relation between respect for the rights of man
and preservation of peace which lay behind the United Nations' decision
to work out this first universal declaration of human rights.

The Commission on Human Rights was confronted by a very difficult
task.

To be sure, the United Nations Charter does mention several times that

1. Contained in the first Soviet Constitution of July 10, 1918, and in the Constitution
of May 11, 1925. See Aulard and Mirkine-Guetzevitch, *Les Déclarations des droits de
l'homme*, p. 172 (Paris, 1929).
2. Nordahl Grieg (1902–1943), Norwegian poet.

it will promote human rights. But we do not find these rights defined any-where in the Charter. So the question was: what did *human rights* mean to the people from these fifty or sixty nations, coming as they did from all parts of the world and from different levels of cultural development, with diverse traditions, religions, and ideologies. The West European peoples have a somewhat similar understanding of this concept. But what do the Chinese, the Indonesians, and the people on Haiti see in the words *freedom, equality,* and *cultural and economic rights*? Were there in general any points of contact between the welfare states' conception of these terms and that of the developing countries? For example, in the European countries, we can agree rather readily on what we mean by «the woman's legal position in society». But how is it interpreted by the people in those parts of the world where a woman's value is equated with that of four camels?

In view of all these difficulties, it is not surprising that it took the Com-mission two years to work out formulations which everyone could accept at the United Nations' General Assembly at Paris in 1948. But even there, where a completely prepared draft was presented to us[1], we spent two months in ninety-seven meetings discussing the Declaration. And a total of 1,200 ballots was taken on proposed amendments before the Declaration, with its thirty articles, was finally adopted.

But we had thus brought into existence a Declaration which stands as a standard for the common values of man, wherever he may live in the world, whatever the social system he may live under. The countries which voted for the Declaration did not commit themselves, but declared them-selves in agreement that all people should have the right to life, liberty, and security of person; that all are equal before the law; that everyone is entitled to freedom of conscience, of religion, of expression, and of as-sembly; that everyone is entitled to the right to work, to equal compensa-tion for equal work, to reasonable working hours, and to free education. Finally, the last article, Article 30, states: «Nothing in this Declaration may be interpreted as implying for any State, group or person any right to en-gage in any activity or to perform any act aimed at the destruction of any of the rights and freedoms set forth herein.»

To us who sit here, these rights sound like self-evident truths. A glance at conditions in the world around us will convince us, however, that in

1. Mrs. Lionaes was a Norwegian delegate to the UN (1946–1965) and therefore participated in the discussions.

many states, yes, in most states, the promises of this simple Declaration are written in sand.

In the area of international law, however, the Declaration was a product of new thought. Whereas earlier treaties had regulated the relationships between nations and governments, this new Declaration made the individual himself the focus.

Man should be guaranteed these rights in whatever system of social organization he may live. Therefore, we can say that the Declaration of Human Rights is the constitution of a world society. It expresses our common ideals, and it embodies a goal which everyone can strive to attain. It is a standard by which we can measure the quality of the political system of any country.

The Declaration puts, therefore, a dividing line in history. It breaks away from the old, set doctrines of international law; yes, it allows us to look out over the boundaries of the old sovereign states toward a world society.

I know that the skeptics and pessimists will be quick to say that this lies a long way off. And I know they are right. But let us look for some bright spots. For they are there. We can see how the principles in the Declaration of Human Rights have already taken root in men's minds. Many of the seventy or eighty new sovereign states established since the war have incorporated parts of or even the entire Declaration in their constitutions.

From a historical point of view I still believe that it is correct to say that the adoption of the Declaration of Human Rights on December 10, 1948, marked the beginning of a new era. It might very well be the beginning of a revolutionizing evolution which will realize President Roosevelt's dream–a world with freedom from fear and freedom from want[1].

The Commission on Human Rights spent two years on the rough draft of the Declaration. In its extremely laborious work, in which each and every concept and the validity of each and every word were thoroughly aired in all languages, Professor Cassin held a key position. He formulated, defined, and clarified. He was crystal clear in his formulations and steadfast in his goal, but always cooperative and tolerant of the opinions of others. He upheld his ideas vigorously, but whenever he realized they had no immediate chance of being accepted, he was wise enough not to force the

1. Franklin Delano Roosevelt (1882–1945), U.S. president (1933–1945), whose annual message to Congress of January 6, 1941, contained the often quoted passage on looking forward «to a world based on four essential freedoms... freedom of speech and expression... freedom of every person to worship God in his own way... freedom from want... freedom from fear... ».

issue but to bide his time. The years that followed, which saw many new nations and new needs arise, proved to be ready for several of the proposals initially rejected in 1948 but now integrated in the text of the Convention.

Cassin also played a positive role as a mediator between the Western European way of thought, which emphasized civil and political rights, and the Eastern European viewpoint, which laid more weight on economic, social, and cultural rights.

And so when the Declaration of Human Rights–that bridge between many minds, many religions, many ideologies, and many hearts–was finally constructed, it was primarily the engineering feat of René Cassin. Then, how satisfied is Professor Cassin today with his work? In an article in the *Jerusalem Post* several weeks ago he says:

«The Declaration holds up an ideal for us, and it draws the guide lines for our actions.

But a glance at reality today is enough to show us that we are far from the ideal. No country, not even the most advanced, can pride itself on fulfilling all the articles of the Declaration. Once the war and the ideals for which we fought have faded in the distance and new states have gained their independence, they are inclined to conduct their domestic affairs as they wish without regard to human rights.

We are witnessing the violation of the right to live. Murders and massacres are perpetrated with impunity. The exploitation of women, mass hunger, disregard for freedom of conscience and for freedom of speech, widespread racial discrimination–all these evils are far too prevalent to be overlooked.»[1]

But Professor Cassin does not despair over these shortcomings. He points to the significance of educational work, not only among children, but also among adults, in producing fertile soil for the growth of the Declaration's ideas. And it was no coincidence that Cassin also became one of the authors of the UNESCO[2] Charter.

1. Also see Cassin, «How the Charter on Human Rights Was Born», *UNESCO Courier*, 21 (January, 1968) 6, col. 2.
2. United Nations Educational, Scientific, and Cultural Organization, constituted in 1945 and formally established as a specialized agency of the UN in 1946; the laureate was a founder-delegate at its initial conferences and a delegate to several of its later ones.

In the work of making the Declaration of Human Rights legally binding on the states, René Cassin has actively participated in the preparation of the two Covenants, which, eighteen years after the Declaration, were u-nanimously adopted by the United Nations' General Assembly on December 16, 1966.

During the eighteen years separating acceptance of the Declaration in 1948 and realization of the Convention in 1966, an important political development has taken place in individual countries and in the world as a whole.

As an indication of this development, one can cite the fact that approximately sixty new countries became members of the United Nations between 1948 and 1966.

These new states had some interests entirely different from those of the older states in the United Nations. For them it was not a question of the Old World's classical political rights but of the principles concerning the right of self-determination for their countries and of control over their economic development. Consequently, one can say perhaps that these emerging nations stood at the beginning of a development which the industrialized countries had long since completed.

This strong new element in the United Nations also left its imprint on the texts of the two Covenants, giving them a wider scope than the Declaration had originally aimed at. Nevertheless, for the first time in history, two international conventions intended to give man certain fundamental rights were unanimously adopted.

No country has yet ratified these two Covenants, one on civil and political rights and one on economic, social, and cultural rights. Thirty-five states must ratify them before they are valid. It should be mentioned as a hopeful sign that the Norwegian government has declared itself willing to submit to the Parliament a proposal for the ratification of the Convention as soon as it is technically possible. It is reasonable to expect that the other Scandinavian countries will do the same.

It was on just such a cold December day as this, exactly twenty years ago, that, a little before midnight in the Palais de Chaillot, this historic declaration on human worth and human rights was adopted by the General Assembly of the United Nations.

To the millions of people who live today in the darkness of oppression, this document was unknown. But a small light was lit, and the moral commandments contained in the Declaration, like those written on the tablets of Moses, will in the years to come play a forceful role in reforming the conscience of man and his understanding of what is right and wrong.

Today, where there is no respect for human rights and freedom, there is no peace either. Every day youth falls on the battlefield. Every day prisoners are led to prisons and torture chambers. They fight and they suffer for the ideals which the Declaration of Human Rights proclaims.

But the demand is made not only of them. It is made also of each and every one of us who live in such secure conviction that we have received these rights as inalienably our own. It is this very year of 1968 – precisely the Year of Human Rights [1] – that has given us the tragic proof of the old truth: Peace, like freedom, is indivisible; it must be captured anew by everyone every single day.

1. To mark the twentieth anniversary of the adoption of the Universal Declaration of Human Rights, the UN designated 1968 as International Human Rights Year.

RENÉ CASSIN

The Charter of Human Rights

Nobel Lecture*, December 11, 1968

In the course of the December tenth session, I had the privilege of paying tribute to the Norwegian nation in the person of its King, to Alfred Nobel, founder of the Peace Prize, who died on December 10, 1896, and to all the laureates honored since 1901 for their services to humanity. But I am aware of not having properly expressed my gratitude to the members of the Nobel Peace Prize Committee and in particular to its chairman, Mrs. Aase Lionaes, who represented Norway in 1948 at the General Assembly of the United Nations whose [Third] Committee deliberated on the Universal Declaration of Human Rights.

So before I begin, I should like to make amends for what must seem an unwarrantable omission. The independence and the rigorous impartiality which the Committee has consistently shown have steadily increased the worldwide prestige of the Nobel Peace Prize, and increased also for its recipient–institution or individual–the distinction of being selected. Furthermore, when public opinion and men representing the highest moral values concur in the Nobel Committee's choice, the goal sought by the founder of the prize is more closely approached.

If it is the responsibility of the Nobel Committee to weigh carefully and to communicate to the public the reasons for its choice, the laureate has the obligation on his own part to set forth publicly the motives which have inspired his work for peace in general or on behalf of one or the other of its elements. It is only after having discharged that obligation of conscience that he has the right to cast a backward glance at the progress made to date, in the hope of convincing his listeners–and all others–of the necessity, as well as the possibility, of advancing toward the creation of a more humane world.

I shall confess at the outset that it was only shortly after the beginning of this century that I entered active life–with a somewhat precocious capacity

* The laureate delivered this lecture in the auditorium of the Nobel Institute. The translation is based on the French text in *Les Prix Nobel en 1968*.

for involvement. To be sure, I was at an early age engrossed in education, interested in international affairs and in reading about social issues. And as a child I was filled with passionate admiration for acts of civic courage I had seen performed by an elderly military doctor, who was a friend of my family. I was likewise deeply moved a little later by the injurious injustice done not only to Captain Dreyfus[1] but also to persons less in the public eye. Nevertheless during the whole period of my preparation for a professorship through advanced studies in law and letters, because of a sort of reticence or even distrust of my impulses, I avoided dealing with subjects of an avowedly political nature, even though the technical law of contracts and obligations is of course dominated by moral principles, notably that of good faith. Similarly, the problem of the rights of the state in the disposition of inheritances left by individuals presents social aspects of the first importance.

It was really the War of 1914–1918 which upset my temporarily comfortable moral equilibrium, or–to be less severe on myself–my carefully disciplined self-limitation. *That war put its indelible and unmistakable stamp on me, as it did on many of my contemporaries.* But it wasn't so much the spectacular horror of the battlefields or the suffering in the hospitals that marked us, as it was the agonized perception of the lasting and wasteful consequences of the war: the disabled soldiers, the families deprived of their last supporting member–dead for the welfare of all. I was not able to accept the idea that national solidarity with those victims should limit itself to a kind of charitable alms. That is why I soon joined those who fought–and victoriously–for recognition of the right to compensation for personal damages incurred in the service of the national community. Human dignity and the general welfare of our country, then depleted in manpower, demanded that, in addition to being given the traditional pensions, our numerous disabled veterans be reintegrated into society by such measures as artificial limb banks, professional retraining programs, and loans for establishing small businesses, and that our 800,000 orphaned minors be brought up and educated under the special protection of the nation.

It was as a result of that first undertaking that my most eminent colleagues and I *decided it was essential to go back to first principles and to foster*

1. The conviction and imprisonment of Captain Alfred Dreyfus (1859–1935) for treason in 1894 and the ensuing debate on his innocence or guilt eventually constituted a political issue in the years that followed, dividing all France; after a pardon in 1899, Dreyfus won complete legal clearance in 1906.

respect for the supreme commitment of those who had sacrificed themselves that this war might be «the last». As soon as the compensatory legislation was assured passage, we began to lay the groundwork for the future.

Our first gesture was to support the creation of the International Labor Organization[1] by bringing together, as early as 1921, representatives of the disabled veterans organizations from the two sides so recently enemies. Under the auspices of Albert Thomas[2] we began to coordinate our social legislation, both that already in effect and that in the planning stage, and also to coordinate our needs for and our aspirations toward peace.

We were thus led to organize ourselves, as men who had fought the war together, in order to support those statesmen who had truly understood the lessons of that World War, thus attempting to prevent its recurrence. The extent of our effort was vividly indicated by the massive enrollment of our French veterans groups into the French Association for the League of Nations in 1922 and by the founding during 1925–1926 of a Conférence internationale des associations des mutilés et d'anciens combattants (CIA-MAC) [International Confederation of Disabled Veterans], whose deeply sincere leaders risked their influence, their freedom, and often their lives when the hatemongers and the champions of violence raised their heads once again and seized power in Germany and elsewhere. Personally, I have never forgotten the speech made at Munich in that black year of 1934 – on July 6, 1934, to be exact – by Rudolph Hess[3], the friend of Hitler, in which he announced that the Nazi regime, already the abettor of widely publicized assassinations, was preparing to break down the morale of veterans in free countries; he was only too correct, alas! It was in vain that some of us attempted to ward off this preparatory maneuver toward future wars of aggression.

The peacemaking efforts of the CIAMAC at that time were brought to the attention of the Nobel Peace Prize Committee. But the invasion of Poland had already begun to set Europe aflame. As a privileged survivor of the First World War, I hope I may be allowed to interject here a deeply felt tribute to those who were not fortunate enough to succeed, but who shared the signal honor of trying to the last to salvage peace.

1. Recipient of the Nobel Peace Prize for 1969.
2. Albert Thomas (1878–1932), prominent French Socialist; in French cabinet during WWI; first director-general of the International Labor Office (1919–1932).
3. (Walter Richard) Rudolf Hess (1894–   ), German Nazi leader; made deputy Führer in 1933.

Meanwhile, crucial problems began to assail the League of Nations itself. It had finally become necessary to exclude Japan. But Hitler's Germany was quite a different matter. Concerned over a complaint about violations of agreements on minorities, the Geneva Assembly of 1933 settled on a very moderate text which invited all states, «whether or not they were bound by special covenants», to respect the fundamental rights of all those over whom they had jurisdiction. Hitler was unable to tolerate such an affirmation. He made it an excuse for a clamorous break with the League of Nations and thus escaped any check on his then clandestine armament program, which he was subsequently to develop on a massive scale.

I bring this event up not because it was the sole cause of the Second World War but because it illuminated from that moment on the true nature of all the heinous acts which precipitated a catastrophe in which seventy-two million people perished. For those peoples forced to fight in order to halt that immense machine geared for the destruction of human liberty and dignity, the Second World War constituted a genuine «crusade for human rights». I also mention it, alas, because today, barely a quarter of a century after that victorious crusade, we still hear too many national leaders expressing themselves on the subject of the absolute and exclusive sovereignty of the state over the human beings under its jurisdiction, enunciating principles which threaten again to lead the world into a state of anarchy and to plunge it into wars, supposedly local and limited in scope, but in reality damaging to all of humanity.

When France resolved, along with England, to lend assistance in the legitimate defense of Poland, the realization burst on us that a conflict of awesome proportions was inevitable. As early as the winter of 1940, but simply as a professor, I denounced «the Leviathan State against man and the human community»[1], and I ranked respect for human rights as one of the essential goals of the sacrifices to which we were all committed. The following year, in September of 1941, having become, after the temporary disaster in my country, the representative of Fighting France at the Allied Conference in London, I swelled the voices of the occupied countries as we joined those of Churchill and Roosevelt in proclaiming the need to establish all future peace on a basis of human rights[2]. How is it that, once victory took form

1. The title of an article by the laureate in *Nouveaux Cahiers* (avril, 1940).
2. The Allied Conference endorsed the Atlantic Charter of peace aims issued in August by British Prime Minister Winston Churchill (1874–1965) and U.S. President Franklin D. Roosevelt (1882–1945).

and the horrible spectacle of the extermination camps was revealed, we could have shamelessly broken the promises given to the peoples in those years of ordeal?

I have felt the need to describe–perhaps too lengthily–the stages through which my first international activities passed, between 1920 and the beginning of the Second World War, before going on to consider the importance for international peace of respecting the rights of all men, and before devoting myself more completely to this vast problem during the rest of my remarks. Since the Nobel Committee, through its chairman's speech, has fully reviewed the efforts I have been able to make in this domain during the last twenty-five years, I shall try to avoid chronicling them again.

On the other hand, and principally because I consider myself doubly privileged, not only to work in the area of human rights, but also to work within it on three separate planes–national, international, and regional–I would like to draw some conclusions and lessons from the experience I have acquired.

Until 1940, the collective effort of the community of man in behalf of human rights had been devoted to the struggle against the scourge of slavery and slave-trading, with pacts of an humanitarian order ranging from the 1864 Charter of the International Red Cross[1] to the Hague Conventions on the laws of war[2]. To this nucleus might be added certain covenants concerning contagious diseases or those intended to curb counterfeiting, the traffic in arms, white slavery, and, later, terrorism. Besides these matters, interventions «on behalf of humanity» were brought into play occasionally, but they either seemed to come too late–the Armenian massacres[3]–or else they turned into colonialist exploitations.

The Covenant of the League of Nations had envisaged sponsoring only the protection of certain categories of men: national minorities and populations of territories controlled by other countries. The International Labor

1. The first Geneva Convention (1864) concerned treatment of wounded and sick military personnel during war, guaranteed neutrality for medical personnel, and provided for the official adoption of the emblem of the Red Cross.
2. Adopted by the first (1899) and second (1907) Hague Peace Conferences.
3. The sporadic massacres of the Armenians by the Turks from 1894 to 1915 were often the result of Armenian revolt precipitated by unfulfilled promises of reform; although the European powers intervened, they failed to agree on action for securing the reforms.

Organization was the only agency with a broad mandate, limited moreover to the protection of the rights of workers as such.

Abruptly, a world which had witnessed the serious, systematic, and innumerable violations that could be committed at the orders of a veritable gang found itself facing a problem of unsuspected amplitude: *to protect the whole man and to protect the rights of all men*. In this light we must not be surprised at the hesitation felt by the representatives of all nations convened at San Francisco in 1945 to adopt the Charter of the United Nations. To be sure, they included, as promised, the respect for and the promotion of human rights among the essential ends of the new organization, along with international peace. They conferred prerogatives in this domain on certain principal organs. But they were extremely cautious, if not timid. They did not dare to enact precise statements of purpose like those stipulated in the Statute of the International Labor Organization. They adopted phraseology that was rather weak or even equivocal–«to encourage human rights», for example. Article 2:7, on matters dealing essentially with the jurisdiction of the states, is in contradiction to Articles 13, 65, 56, and 62 of the Charter. Finally, they did indeed create under Article 68 a special body to assure the progress of human rights, namely, the Commission on Human Rights; but they failed to define its powers, with the result that from 1946 on, the Economic and Social Council of the United Nations accorded it a status identical to that of all the other commissions that are auxiliary organs of the United Nations.

As a consequence of these hesitations and of the vague character of such innovations, the Commission on Human Rights itself had doubts from the beginning about its role and its functions in general. The single outstanding exception was the broad yet precise mandate communicated by the General Assembly in 1946 to prepare as soon as possible the Charter of Human Rights which the San Francisco Conference had not had the time or the courage to draw up.

The Commission, originally composed of eighteen members of different nationalities and diverse occupations, was guided by an accurate instinct in its decision to work out before anything else an international Declaration having the character of a manifesto of organized mankind. In less than eighteen months, it prepared a first draft which it submitted to the General Assembly and which, at the end of one hundred sessions of elevated, often impassioned discussion, was adopted in the form of thirty articles on December 10, 1948.

By its very existence this Declaration, which was thereafter called «Universal» and which does not have a juridically obligatory character, constituted a historical event of the first magnitude. It is the first document of an ethical sort that organized humanity has ever adopted, and precisely at a time when man's power over nature became vastly increased because of scientific discoveries and when it was essential to decide to what constructive ends these powers should be put. Its moral and political repercussions have been considerable. Of the eight states[1] abstaining, as against forty-eight voting, at the time of the ballot, six invoke the Declaration as if they had voted. All the states subsequently admitted to the United Nations have actively supported it, if not inserted parts of it in their constitutions.

The Declaration loses none of its authority under close analysis. *It proclaims as principles the whole body of rights and options without whose exercise man cannot fully realize his physical, moral, and intellectual individuality.* After sometimes heated debates in the Commission, over which Mrs. Eleanor Roosevelt presided from beginning to end, the Universal Declaration went even beyond the scope of the classic national declarations of England, North America, and France concerning corporal, judicial, religious, and political liberties. As corollaries to the right of every individual to life and to full participation in society, the Declaration incorporated in the list of human rights the right to work and a certain number of economic, social, and cultural rights. In short, thanks to formulas like that of Article 22 covering the body of these latter rights, it established a careful balance between them and the old liberties, a balance difficult to establish and to maintain in practice when dependent on individual regimes, but a balance of principles set up as an ideal for all countries.

The other salient characteristic of the Declaration is its *universality: it applies to all human beings without any discrimination whatever; it also applies to all territories*, whatever their economic or political regime. It expatiates on the position of the individual in the various social groups of which he is a part, especially on his duties to the community and the other members of society, but in terms postulating a democratic society and excluding the omnipotence of a totalitarian state.

Although the composition and adoption of the Declaration were relatively easy and happily successful, it is common knowledge that the other two leaves of the triptych making up the Charter of Human Rights were

1. The Soviet bloc, Saudi Arabia, and the Union of South Africa.

much more difficult and time-consuming to work out. It was six years before the Commission on Human Rights could submit to the Assembly the drafts of the twin Covenants it had prepared: one concerning civil and political rights; the other concerning economic, social, and cultural rights. There were, as a matter of fact, two difficulties to surmount.

The first to be favorably dealt with was the problem of deciding whether the right of peoples to self-determination, which had previously been considered a principle of a political and essentially collective nature, should be inserted in the Covenants intended to implement the rights proclaimed in the Universal Declaration, which was concerned only with the rights exercised, separately or communally, by the individual. The solution arrived at can be explained historically by the movement toward decolonization and, more exactly, toward the political emancipation of territorial entities, which was a logical outcome of the victorious libertarian principles fostered in the course of the Second World War.

Although seemingly of a simple methodological character, the second difficulty was resolved only after long deliberations at the end of which the General Assembly of the United Nations, after having gone on record in 1950 as favoring the drafting of a single Covenant embodying all the rights proclaimed by the Declaration, changed its mind in 1951 and thereafter directed the Commission to prepare two separate Covenants, each to include substantive provisions on the obligations of the state and the respective measures of application. In the course of time it has been confirmed that this system best fits the peculiarities of each of the two categories of rights.

The debates before the General Assembly of the United Nations went on for eighteen years[1]. Their slowness can be explained in part by the fact that each year the newly independent nations which entered the Third Committee of the General Assembly[2] needed to form an opinion of the usefulness of the Covenants in general and of the eventual effect of these Covenants on their own institutions. But that explanation is only partially valid. The most powerful cause of this delay was the desire of certain powers to put off as long as possible discussion of the–paradoxically quite modest–en-

1. That is, during the 6 years of drafting the Covenants and the almost 13 years of considering them.
2. One of the main UN committees, it deals with social, humanitarian, and cultural affairs, being primarily concerned with the activity of the Economic and Social Council, under which the Commission on Human Rights was established.

forcement measures voted by the Commission on Human Rights, which were considered encroachments on the sovereignty of the states. The final vote attained unanimity in 1966 only because it became inconceivable on the very eve of the International Human Rights Year to prolong the filibuster any further. Moreover, a heavy price has been paid. The implementation measures of both Covenants, but especially those of the Covenant concerning civil and political rights, were considerably weakened to the point where they assumed an optional character. The only compensation, gained through the influence of nongovernmental organizations, consisted in slightly broadening for private individuals the possibility of access and appeal to the agencies enforcing the Covenant concerned with civil and political rights.

Thus, since the unanimous vote of the General Assembly, the Charter of Human Rights has become a unified whole. As Secretary-General U Thant stated, «It is completed.»

Are we justified today, twenty years after the Universal Declaration, in declaring ourselves satisfied?

When one considers the confusion, not to say anarchy, from which the nations of the world have just emerged, as well as the difficulties that have had to be surmounted one after the other, the adoption, however belated, of the Charter of Human Rights is a happy event which prepares the way for a veritable juridical revolution. Henceforth, there should be no doubt about the fundamental question, that of knowing whether the various sovereign states have retained or lost their traditionally exclusive sphere of authority over the manner of dealing with those under their jurisdiction. That jurisdiction of the states will always be a fundamental principle. It will remain basic. But it will no longer be exclusive. It will in some situations, as in the case of a complaint formulated under certain conditions and presented before certain international agencies, be possible to transfer it to these agencies, that is to say to the whole of juridically organized mankind. This will mean two things: first, the permanent accession of every human being to the rank of member of human society – in legal parlance one would say to the rank of subject of international law; second, it will mean that the states consent to exercise their sovereignty under the authority of international law, as Pope John XXIII[1] pointed out in the Encyclical *Pacem in terris*, which is his testament.

1. John XXIII (1881–1963), pope (1958–1963).

But is this result within reach? Here we must appeal to the sense of responsibility of leaders of peoples and at the same time to the aspirations of the common man who helps to shape public opinion.

The delays which hampered the adoption of the draft Covenants and the completion of the Charter of Human Rights were on the whole very prejudicial to the progress of human rights guarantees. They allowed the administrations of all countries to revert to old ways of thinking—without formulating them in a necessarily threatening manner—very like the ones Hitler had expressed at Geneva in 1933 through Goebbels[1].

As a matter of fact, these delays have not been fatal for humanity, and their inauspicious effects have been mitigated to a certain extent. For one thing, when urgent questions were brought up and taken to heart by energetic groups, conventions of universal scope on limited areas of concern were speedily proposed or even ratified, and are now in force or soon will be. I cite as an example slavery, against which a convention was adopted in 1956 complementing the agreement of 1926. I might also mention several covenants aimed at improving the condition of women (with respect to nationality, political rights, freedom of consent to marriage, wages, etc.) and the struggle against discrimination in employment and job categories (ILO, 1958), and in education (UNESCO, 1960 and 1962), and, more recently, against racial discrimination, voted on in December, 1965, at the UN, and now about to become operative.

As a valuable compensatory advantage of the delays, I call attention to the opportunity thus given to states recently come to or returned to independence, to discuss these Covenants and to make their contribution to them. No one can forget the very active initiative taken by certain delegates of these young nations in smoothing out difficulties and carrying the final vote.

The third fact which I feel I should emphasize is that on November 4, 1950, the member states of the Council of Europe[2] adopted a so-called safeguard of human rights. This European Convention for the Protection of Human Rights and Fundamental Freedoms, which, along with its Ad-

1. Joseph Paul Goebbels (1897–1945), German Nazi propaganda minister (1933–1945).
2. The Council of Europe was created in 1949 to obtain European unity in protecting and realizing principles common to its members and to facilitate economic and social progress. It has been considered a possible first step toward a United States of Europe.

ditional Protocol[1] and the European Social Charter[2], aims at the effective application of the *Universal Declaration*, has been in force since 1953. It works. It has already had a twofold effect. On the one hand, its provisions have been made binding within the member nations, thus influencing their national law. On the other hand, its execution is under the supervision of European institutions created for that purpose: the European Commission of Human Rights, the Committee of Ministers, and the European Court of Human Rights. These agencies all function smoothly with regard to states and individuals. The number of cases submitted to them is already considerable. For the first time, one is confronted with the orders of a Court—few as they may be—which have conclusive authority and which the nations who are parties to the Convention find it important to observe punctually. Despite what confirmed pessimists say about the matter, there is at least one continent where an impressive array of states has committed itself to heeding the lessons of the Second World War. Unfortunately it must be conceded that part of Europe remains outside the zone of influence of the Convention. Even among the members of the Council there is a disparity in the strength of their compliance. Eleven states have accepted the possibility of complaints being directed against them by individuals or by groups. But some have accepted the Convention only insofar as it binds them with respect to other states. Two others, including my own country, have not yet ratified. And finally, one member state is at the present moment the subject of petitions from other member states for not respecting the Convention.

At the point now reached, strengthened by the experience acquired through continued analysis of the situation on three planes—national, international, and regional—we are in a position to draw some conclusions.

First of all, it is essential that a system of guarantees, and especially of due process before independent judiciaries, be organized within each state for the benefit of all individuals, without discrimination. The surest means by which *a state may avoid outside intervention is to recognize and itself insure respect for fundamental rights and liberties in the territories under its jurisdiction*.

Second, there must be no question of permitting any diminution of the universality of the *Declaration*. There are fundamental liberties and rights common to all human beings, without possible discrimination. It is the most

1. Of 1952.
2. Of 1961.

oppressed, the weakest of these individuals who would be threatened by any attempts to fragmentize the effective scope of the Declaration.

Third, the universality of the Declaration's principles creates no reasonable obstacles to the establishment of regional systems for applying those principles. Europe has really offered a good example after the turning point of 1948, and I, a determined universalist, was able to conclude that certain means of implementation are more readily accepted if they are organized among neighboring nations of similar culture. Communities of law and customs are not invented arbitrarily. It is to be hoped that the New World will also form regional associations. In Asia, Africa, and the socialist world these concepts are being discussed. But there are as yet no results.

In the fourth place, it is extremely desirable that the Charter of Human Rights go into effect as soon as possible. To accomplish that, the ratification of thirty-five states of the world is necessary for each Covenant. At the present time, to my knowledge, not a single government has ratified, even with reservations. So let us not allow it to be said that the United Nations Organization is at fault and does nothing; the jurists have, for the moment, done their part. It is up to public opinion everywhere to persuade the various governments to do theirs.

At this point I should like to address a special appeal to the European peoples. Despite the benefits received from most of the guarantees of the regional 1950 Convention, the differences which separate this text from that of the Universal Covenant on civil and political rights are not, in the considered judgment of European governmental experts, so significant that they present serious obstacles to a ratification of this Covenant by the European states.

It would be a magnificent example to give to all peoples if they acted in concert for such a ratification. It seems to me that they would insure a sorely needed future for human rights on the other continents. This Covenant's becoming operative constitutes, in my opinion, the most important advance for which we can hope in the immediate future.

I have until now confined my conclusions to matters concerning the Universal Declaration and the Covenants in general, or to limited consequential objectives.

Nongovernmental civic organizations should not cease studying projects for broader juridical reform–such as the creation of a High Commissioner of Human Rights, a freer access for individuals to the channels of international recourse, the establishment of an International Court of Criminal

Law, and others–but I think it is essential that they concentrate their main
effort for as long a time as necessary to bring about tangible results from
this work already done by the United Nations. Then, when the mechanisms
provided by the Covenants have been tested in practice, it will be time
to coordinate and reinforce them. Not to implement the measures already
worked out, even if they are insufficient, would be playing into the hands
of those who wish to block any progress. I do not believe there will be
any «nights of August fourth» in this tense and bitter world of uneasy
transition. We must seize every opportunity to strengthen its unity.

Meanwhile, in addition to this crucial problem of the implementation
of the agreements, several others should be faced without delay.

One of them is restating the role and the methods of the Commission
on Human Rights. After the accomplishment of its mandate to draft the
Declaration and the Covenants, this agency has very properly continued
to work on the preparation of a whole series of conventions against discrimination of various kinds. But for the last two years it has been groping its
way and has been tending to become an agency for providing information
or advice on specific cases, a function which is not outside its theoretical
role but which it is not equipped to handle efficiently. It is necessary, too,
that the Commission stress its essentially significant role of examiner of the
periodic reports which the states must file on the manner in which they
respect human rights. It is the responsibility of the chairman of the Commission to see that their obligations are met.

Other even more urgent measures must, it seems to me, be taken to
protect the agents and the activities of the International Red Cross. Since
the Geneva Conventions of 1949, the role of the Red Cross has been expanded to include all cases of armed conflict, even those not designated as
foreign wars. Now several times in the last few years and most recently
in Biafra, it has been authenticated that agents of the Red Cross sent
on humanitarian missions were molested, threatened, or even killed, and
that it has sometimes been necessary to withdraw them to insure their
safety.

I have not been able to read or to hear such accounts without shame.
In my opinion there is no task of safeguarding human rights more urgent
than that of foreseeing such outrages and preventing them. Humanity owes
it to itself to watch over, guard, and protect those who represent it and
who devote their lives to beneficent activities.

I have been able today to approach only a single, if vast, aspect of the conditions of international peace. It would be shortsighted of anyone to forget the others, such as education, disarmament, technical and financial cooperation.

Ultimately, of course, the organizing of peace must be based on considerations of reason and concern. It presupposes tremendous efforts to modify through education some longstanding mental attitudes–to work toward limitation of armaments, to manifest solidarity with the hungry, to cooperate in the strengthening of family or societal units. But reason alone is not enough. Emotional factors and especially the sense of justice must not be left to those who pervert them to the service of hate and destruction.

It is with great feeling that I take my leave of this country where peace and law are so highly esteemed. So perhaps you will permit a French citizen committed to the service of peace and law to recall, as indicative of faith in mankind, these two lines from a French poet who received one of the first prizes, the Nobel Prize in Literature[1]:

> *My country imbues me with a love that overflows its borders,*
> *And the more French I am, the more I feel a part of mankind[2].*

During the years of anguish when the freedom of whole peoples was in jeopardy, they were asked to persevere to the last. The time has come to proclaim that, for the establishment of peace and human dignity, each of us must work and fight to the last.

1. Sully Prudhomme (1839–1907), recipient of the first Nobel Prize in Literature (1901).
2. From Sonnet IX in *La France: Sonnets*, p. 160 of *Poésies de Sully Prudhomme: 1872–1878*, Vol. 3 of the *Oeuvres* (Paris: Lemerre, 1883–1904). The lines read:
«*Je tiens de ma patrie un coeur qui la déborde,*
   Et plus je suis français, plus je me sens humain.»

Biography

A jurist, humanitarian, and internationalist, René-Samuel Cassin (October 5, 1887–   ) is one of the world's foremost proponents of the legal as well as the moral recognition of the rights of man. Neither a pessimist nor an optimist, the peace laureate, eighty-one years old when awarded the prize in 1968, confessed that «men are not always good»[1], but he has based much of his life's work on the premise that human responses can be constructive if states will transform the conditions that breed ill will into those that recognize the dignity of man.

Cassin was born in Bayonne (Basses-Pyrénées), the son of Gabrielle (Dreyfus) Cassin and Henri Cassin, a merchant. Having established a record of intellectual brilliance at the Lycée of Nice, he added to it in his advanced studies at the University of Aix-en-Provence where, in 1908, he received a degree in the humanities, along with one in law. He took first place in the competitive examination given by the Law Faculty and in 1914 received the doctorate in juridical, economic, and political sciences.

Cassin has made his career in law as practitioner, professor, scholar, administrator, and promoter. The legal career which he began in 1909 in Paris, where he was a counsel at the Court of Paris, was brought to an end when he was inducted into the infantry in 1914. Severely wounded in 1916 by German shrapnel, he survived, but only because his mother, serving as a nurse in the field hospital to which he had been carried, persuaded the doctors to perform surgery. Although the injury he sustained was to give him acute discomfort throughout his life, he recovered, married Simone Yzombard of Marseilles, and entered upon his career as a professor of law at Aix late in 1916.

He moved to a professorship in law at Lille in 1920 and in 1929 to the chair of fiscal and civil law at the University of Paris, where he remained until his retirement from formal teaching in 1960. His teaching career included various scholarly assignments that took him to other countries. He

1. The *New York Times* (October 10, 1968), p.14.

lectured at the National School of Overseas Territories; undertook academic missions in Europe, French Africa, the Middle East, and the Far East; lectured at the Academy of International Law at The Hague, and at the University Institute of Advanced International Studies in Geneva.

Meanwhile, he made extensive contributions to legal scholarship, writing technical treatises on contracts, inheritance, the conception of domicile, and the inequality between men and women in civil legislation; he also published dozens of articles, many of topical concern, such as those dealing with aspects of human rights.

Cassin has been an administrator of academic affairs as well. For the embryonic French government-in-exile during World War II, he was the commissioner of public instruction. With the liberation of France in 1945, he became president of the Council of the National School of Administration [Conseil de l'école nationale d'administration] and in 1960 president of the French National Overseas Center of Advanced Studies [Centre national des hautes-études de la France d'outre-mer].

As a member of the Permanent Conference of Allied Ministers of Education (1942–1945), he encouraged the retention of instruction in the French language and the dissemination of French culture throughout the world In the next two decades or so, he promoted education and law by serving as the president of several organizations–among them, the French branch of the World Federation of Democratic Jurists (1949), the Society of Comparative Legislation (1952–1956), the International Institute of Administrative Sciences (1953–1956), the International Institute of Diplomatic Studies and Research (1956), and the French Association for the Development of International Law (1962–1967).

Cassin has occupied high posts in the judiciaries of France and Europe. From 1944 to 1960, he was vice-president of the Council of State, a body which exercises ultimate jurisdiction in cases involving administrative personnel and administrative law. For the next ten years he was on the Constitutional Council, a court which, akin to the American Supreme Court, rules on questions of the constitutionality of laws passed by the legislature. He was president of the Court of Arbitration at The Hague from 1950 to 1960 and a member (1959–1965) and president (1965–1968) of the European Court of Human Rights at Strasbourg.

After World War I, Cassin devised practical outlets for his humanitarian instincts. In 1918 he founded the French Federation of Disabled War Veterans [l'Union fédérale des associations des mutilés et d'anciens combattants] and until 1940 served it in the capacity of president or of honorary president. To benefit children orphaned by the war, he accepted the office of vice-president of the High Council for Wards of the Nation [Conseil supérieur des pupilles de la nation]. In 1926 he founded and until the outbreak of World War II was the permanent reporter for the International Conference of Associations of Disabled War Veterans [Conférence internationale des associations de mutilés et d'anciens combattants].

Cassin has participated in the political life of his country in various ways, but not in the usual one of seeking elective office or of acting as the leader or representative of a political party. He is a patriot and an internationalist at the same time. From 1924 to 1938, he was a French delegate to the League of Nations, serving at the Disarmament Conference and supporting various moves in the Assembly to advance the formulation and application of international procedures for reasonable accommodation of problems arising out of clashing national interests.

Cassin is said to have been the first civilian to leave Bordeaux to join General de Gaulle in response to his appeal from London after the armistice of June, 1940, between Germany and the capitulating French government. A mainstay for de Gaulle, he drafted all of the legal texts of his incipient government and conducted delicate negotiations with Great Britain, including the Churchill-de Gaulle accord which became the «Charter» of the Free French forces. He held important positions–among them, permanent secretary of the Council of Defense of the Empire (1940–1941), National Commissioner of Justice and Public Instruction (1941–1943), president of the Juridical Committee of the Provisional Government (1943–1945) and vice-president of the Upper House [Haute Assemblée]; he was a delegate to the United Nations Commission on Inquiry into War Crimes (1943–1945) and chairman (1944) of the legislative committee for the Consultative Assembly set up as part of the government-in-exile in Algiers in 1943.

In the period following World War II, Cassin not only occupied the judicial posts already mentioned, but also continued the international work he had begun in the League of Nations. On five occasions–1946, 1948, 1950, 1951, 1968–he was a French delegate to the Assembly of the United Nations, and for many years between 1945 and 1960 a delegate to the UNESCO conferences.

In his work on human rights, Cassin fused his legal knowledge, his humanitarian instinct, and his belief in internationalism. He was a member

of the United Nations Commission on Human Rights from its creation in
1946: vice-chairman from 1946 to 1955, a period which included Eleanor
Roosevelt's chairmanship (1946–1953), chairman from 1955 to 1957, and
again vice-chairman in 1959. The workhorse of the Commission, he was
the one most responsible for the draft of the Declaration of Human Rights
approved by the General Assembly on December 10, 1948[1]. In a series of
lectures delivered in 1951 at The Hague Academy of International Law[2],
Cassin provides a thorough discussion of the Declaration and of the early
problems of drafting the Covenants: he analyzes the pertinent clauses in the
Charter of the UN, the mandate of the Commission, the preparation and
acceptance of the Declaration; he then provides a lawyer's insight into definition of the rights, the limitations imposed, the problems of enforcing
the proposed Covenants, measures needed for the examination of possible
complaints, and procedures required for international surveillance and constructive control. In an article written to mark the International Human
Rights Year of 1968, Cassin concludes with a simple admonition: «Now
that we possess an instrument capable of lifting or easing the burden of
oppression and injustice in the world, we must learn to use it.»[3]

Selected Bibliography

Cassin, René, *La Conception des droits de l'état dans les successions d'après le code civil suisse.*
    Paris, Sirey, 1914.
Cassin, René, «Le Contentieux des victimes de la guerre: Étude de la jurisprudence
    concernant les pensions de guerre et l'adoption des pupilles (1924–1925).» Paris,
    n.d.
Cassin, René, «La Declaration universelle et la mise en oeuvre des droits de l'homme»,
    in Académie de droit international de La Haye: *Recueil des cours.* Tome 2 en 1951,
    pp.239–367. Tome 79 de la Collection. Paris, Sirey, 1952. Contains a brief bio-
    graphical notice and a bibliography.
Cassin, René, *Pour la défense de la paix.* Paris, 1936.
Cassin, René, «18 [*i.e.*Dix-huit] mois de France libre.» Conférence prononcée le 14
    janvier 1942 à Beyrouth au cercle de l'Union française. 1942. In Harvard University
    Library.

1. Both the Nobel lecture and the presentation speech contain details of the drafting
and adoption of the Declaration.
2. Cassin, «La Déclaration universelle et la mise en oeuvre des droits de l'homme.»
3. Cassin, «How the Charter on Human Rights Was Born», p.6.

Cassin, René, «L'État Léviathan contre l'homme et la communauté humaine», *Nouveaux Cahiers* (avril, 1940).

Cassin, René, «How the Charter on Human Rights Was Born», *UNESCO Courier*, 21 (January, 1968) 4–6.

Cassin, René, *L'Inégalité entre l'homme et la femme dans la législation civile*. Marseille, Barlatier, 1919.

Cassin, René, «La Nouvelle Conception du domicile dans le règlement des conflicts de lois», in Académie de droit international de La Haye: *Recueil des cours*. Tome 4 en 1930, pp. 657–809. Tome 34 de la Collection. Paris, Sirey, 1931.

Cassin, René, «Le Réveil de l'empire français.» Conférence faite à l'Institut français du Royaume-Uni à Londres, le 15 janvier 1941. [London?, 1941?]

de Gaulle, Charles, *The Complete War Memoirs of Charles de Gaulle*, translated from the French by Jonathan Griffin. New York, Simon & Schuster, 1964.

Dictionnaire biographique français contemporain, 1950.

The *New York Times* (October 10, 1968) 1, 14.

Nouveau dictionnaire national des contemporains. Troisième édition, 1964.

The (London) *Times* (October 10, 1968) 8.

Peace 1969

THE INTERNATIONAL LABOR ORGANIZATION

Presentation

by Aase Lionaes*, Chairman of the Nobel Committee

When Alfred Nobel died on December 10, 1896, his will and testament revealed that he had instituted five Nobel prizes: one for physics, one for chemistry, one for literature, one for medicine, and a peace prize.

While Swedish institutions were entrusted with the task of awarding the first four prizes, Nobel decided, for reasons not exactly known, that a committee of five members, appointed by the Norwegian Parliament, should be entrusted with the great honor and responsibility of awarding the Peace Prize.

Alfred Nobel not only specified *who* was to award the Peace Prize, but he also laid down the rules to be followed by the committee in choosing a candidate for the prize. He states in his will that the Peace Prize is to be awarded to the person who has done most to promote fraternity among the nations.

With this consideration in mind, the Nobel Committee of the Norwegian Parliament has awarded the Peace Prize for 1969 to the International Labor Organization.

Beneath the foundation stone of the ILO's main office in Geneva lies a document on which is written: «*Si vis pacem, cole justitiam.*» If you desire peace, cultivate justice.

There are few organizations that have succeeded to the extent that the ILO has, in translating into action the fundamental moral idea on which it is based.

Why, we may ask, did the demand for social justice receive such a tremendous impetus when the ILO was founded fifty years ago?

* Mrs. Lionaes, president of the Norwegian Lagting, delivered this speech on December 10, 1969, in the Auditorium of the University of Oslo. She then presented the Nobel medal and diploma to Mr. David A. Morse who, as director-general of the ILO, made a brief speech of acceptance on behalf of the ILO. The English translation of Mrs. Lionaes' speech is essentially that appearing in *Les Prix Nobel en 1969*, with certain editorial changes, as well as some minor emendations made after collation with the original Norwegian text which also appears in *Les Prix Nobel en 1969*.

I think the answer is to be found in the fact that at the conclusion of
the First World War in 1918, the underprivileged members of the community were in the historical position of being able not only to obtain the
ear of Europe's leading politicians for social justice, but also of being strong
enough, should the need arise, to back their demands with force.

During the war, the working class had loyally set aside their own claims
in order to serve their national cause, and they had in full measure borne
the sufferings and privations of war.

But at trade union congresses held in 1916, 1917, and 1918, the demand
was made that the trade union movement should participate in discussing
the future peace treaty. It was emphasized that workers should be guaranteed
a minimum standard of working conditions after the war and that a permanent body to ensure the carrying out of international legislation in this
respect should be established.

In the wake of hostilities came a spate of violent social and political upheavals. It is sufficient to remind you of the Russian Revolution of 1917
and the German Revolution of 1918.

With such a background, it was something of a political imperative, when
the peace treaties in Versailles in 1919 were to be drafted, to include clauses
which aimed to secure peace not only among nations but also among classes
in the various countries.

At its very outset the Peace Conference took the unprecedented step of
setting up an international committee for labor legislation. The committee
consisted not only of government delegates but also of employers and employees, including Samuel Gompers[1], the U.S.A. trade union leader, and
France's Léon Jouhaux[2]. Politicians were represented by Harold Butler[3] of
the United Kingdom and Eduard Beneš[4] of Czechoslovakia.

In this way the ILO, along with the League of Nations, became part
of the Versailles treaties, in which guidelines for international socio-political
cooperation were laid down[5].

1. Samuel Gompers (1850–1924), president of American Federation of Labor (1886–
1895; 1896–1924).
2. Léon Jouhaux (1879–1954), recipient of the Nobel Peace Prize for 1951.
3. Harold Beresford Butler (1883–1951), secretary to British Ministry of Labor (1917),
deputy director (1920–1932) and director of International Labor Office (1932–1938);
British minister to U.S.A. (1942–1946).
4. Eduard Beneš (1884–1948), Czech foreign minister (1918–1935); president (1935–
1938; 1945–1948).
5. This paragraph is not included in the Norwegian text.

Reading this special section of the Versailles Treaty and bearing in mind that it was written in 1919, one is compelled to agree with Paal Berg[1] when he declares that this was one of the most remarkable diplomatic documents ever seen. In the Treaty, for instance, is the following:

... the League of Nations has for its object the establishment of universal peace, and such a peace can be established only if it is based upon social justice;

And whereas conditions of labor exist involving such injustice, hardship, and privation to large numbers of people as to produce unrest so great that the peace and harmony of the world are imperiled; and an improvement of those conditions is urgently required: as, for example, by the regulation of the hours of work, including the establishment of a maximum working day and week, the regulation of the labor supply, the prevention of un-employment, the provision of an adequate living wage, the protection of the worker against sickness, disease and injury arising out of his employment, the protection of children, young persons and women, provision for old age and injury, protection of the interests of workers when employed in countries other than their own, recognition of the principle of freedom of association, the organization of vocational and technical education and other measures; the failure of any nation to adopt humane conditions of labor is an obstacle in the way of other nations which desire to improve the con-ditions in their own countries.[2]

This statement is followed by the guidelines for the ILO and the principal tasks this organization should aim to accomplish. These are summed up in nine points, which have often been called the «Magna Charta» of the working class. Among other things these include: the principle that labor is not a piece of merchandise; the right of employees, as well as of employers, to organize themselves; the right of workers to receive a reasonable wage; the eight-hour day or the forty-eight-hour week; a ban on child labor; equal pay for men and women for the same work; and every country is furthermore to organize a system of labor inspection in which women, too, are to play their part in ensuring that labor legislation is adhered to.

The ILO was organized as a specialized organization, under the League of Nations, to carry out this program.

1. Paal Olav Berg (1873–1968), Norwegian jurist and politician; cabinet minister and head of the Ministry of Social Affairs (1919).
2. From the Preamble of Part XIII of the Versailles Treaty.

And what has been the result? Have the fine words in a solemn document come true, or were they merely writing in the sand, a remote vision glimpsed by impractical dreamers?

As we look at the world around us today, we must admit that many of the aims that the ILO set itself have been achieved in many parts of the industrialized world.

Working earnestly and untiringly, the ILO has succeeded in introducing reforms that have removed the most flagrant injustices in a great many countries, particularly in Europe. By means of a leveling of income and a progressive policy of social welfare, the ILO has played its part in these countries in bridging the gap between rich and poor.

How has the ILO succeeded in carrying out such significant parts of its program?

I believe that part of the answer is to be found in the special form of organization peculiar to the ILO.

The ILO's resolutions, passed at the annual Labor Conferences, are backed by discussions and negotiations in which not only government delegates participate, but also independent representatives of leading employers' and employees' organizations in every single country.

Joint discussions of problems between these three independent interest groups create a possibility of arriving at realistic solutions of important social problems, as well as of deciding how these measures are to be carried out in practice in the various countries.

This is the structure of the organization. But its decisive feature, what makes the mechanism work, is naturally the people themselves, farseeing men of goodwill, inspired with a belief in the possibility of building a peaceful world based on social justice.

What means are at the disposal of the ILO in order to implement its program?

In the first place, the ILO aims to create international legislation ensuring certain norms for working conditions in every country.

In the course of its fifty years of existence the ILO has adopted a total of 128 conventions and 132 recommendations. These cover a wide range, from working hours to equal pay for equal work, from health insurance to the abolition of forced labor, from social security for foreign workers to the task of securing the rights of trade unions.

But are these measures respected in the various countries, are they incorporated as part and parcel of the national laws? Or do delegates in

Geneva vote for the most sweeping resolutions, which are then consigned to the bottom drawer in some government department after the delegates go home?

It is precisely in this area that the ILO, one of the first international organizations in the world to do so, has pioneered in the international sphere, by creating organs which carry out the work of supervising the implementation of the conventions adopted by member states and their embodiment in national law and practice.

Time does not permit me to illustrate this important point in detail. Let me merely mention that the ILO's constitution obliges member states to draw up annual reports, stating what measures have been taken to observe the provisions contained in the ratified conventions.

Another important point is that the ILO constitution gives the organizations in a country the right to lodge a complaint if a government fails to carry out the conventions which the authorities of that country have ratified. The right to lodge a complaint also includes the right of a state to prosecute a member state for violating provisions in conventions that both states have ratified.

During these fifty years the ILO has adopted over 250 conventions and recommendations. And even though not all its 121 member countries have come anywhere close to ratifying all the conventions, I believe we are justified in saying that the ILO has permanently influenced the social welfare legislation of every single country.

Norway has not ratified all the conventions as yet, but I am glad to be able to state that Norway occupies seventh place among all member countries of the ILO with regard to the number of ratifications, having ratified a total of sixty-three out of 128 conventions.

The Norwegian minister of social welfare, Mr. Aarvik, declared at this year's Labor Conference in Geneva that, «out of sixty-three agreements that our country has ratified, not less than forty-three have had an important influence on the development of working conditions and social welfare in Norway.»

When war broke out in 1939, the ILO was naturally faced with great difficulties. The organization moved to Montreal in Canada, where it continued its work for freedom and democracy against Nazism and dictatorship.

One of the most important events in the activities of the ILO during the war was the Labor Conference held in Philadelphia in 1944 on the occasion of the twenty-fifth jubilee of the organization.

Forty-one states, among them Norway, were represented at this conference. The Philadelphia Conference constitutes an historic milestone in the development of the ILO, because, apart from confirming the principles of the organization as adopted in 1919, it also drafted a declaration expressing a new and more dynamic conception of the ILO's aims and responsibilities with regard to combating insecurity and poverty.

At the invitation of President Roosevelt the conference was concluded with a meeting in the White House in Washington. In a speech to the conference, Roosevelt stated that the Philadelphia Declaration was an historic document on a level with the United States' own Declaration of Independence in 1776.

When the war was over and the United Nations Organization was established in 1945, the ILO was linked to UNO as an independent specialized organization.

The ILO now had a far wider field of action than it had enjoyed during its first twenty-five years.

Just as it may be said that one of the motivating forces for the foundation and constitution of the ILO in 1919 was the social and political upheaval that followed in the wake of the First World War, so we can say that shifts in the international political balance of power after the Second World War proved deciding factors in expanding the aims of the ILO from 1945 on.

The old European colonial powers disintegrated, and over sixty new states were given independent status on the map of the world and in time, too, in the ILO. The ILO was no longer an essentially European organization dominated by the special conditions in industrialized Europe. The ILO had become primarily a global organization, whose membership represented practically all races and religions in the world, whose traditions, culture, and history, economic and social problems were entirely different from those with which the ILO had had to deal before the war.

After the First World War the main task of the ILO was to build a bridge between the poor and the rich within individual countries. After the Second World War its task was a far more formidable one, that of building a bridge between the poor and the rich nations.

Today it can be said that the dominant feature in the work of the ILO during the last twenty years has been technical aid programs in the developing countries. Working in close cooperation with UNO and its many specialized organizations – such as FAO, UNESCO, the World Health Organization, the International Atomic Energy Commission, and others–

and with financial support from UNO, the ILO has succeeded in carrying out research projects and making basic investments in developing countries, with a view to developing their agriculture, industry, and other sides of their economic life.

The birth of new states in Africa and Asia has not only enlarged the ILO's scope of activity; it has also created a certain internal political tension in the Organization, which we sincerely hope can be overcome.

The basic reason for this tension is that the ILO's special form of organization, with independent representatives for governments, for free trade union organizations, and for employers' associations, has created problems with regard to the membership of new countries because many of them have not as yet developed free labor organizations. In these new countries, governments nominate both workers' and employers' representatives. This is in complete violation of one of the fundamental principles on which the whole organizational structure of ILO is based. As yet we do not know how this conflict will develop, but it is vital to the whole future of the ILO that it should be solved in such a way that the independent and political neutrality of the ILO can be preserved.

It is primarily the economic and social problems in the developing countries that have confronted the ILO with the tremendous task which it has undertaken to accomplish during the next ten years and which has been called the «World Employment Program».

In the rich industrialized countries we consider an ample supply of labor a sign of wealth. Since the war we have also gradually learned the technique of controlling the economic climate in such a way that we have avoided the unemployment with which, as a mass phenomenon, we were familiar before the war.

In the developing countries, on the other hand, unemployment and under-employment are today social evils which hold millions of people in the grip of hopeless poverty.

A certain growth can be noted in the economic life of these countries, but on the other hand a population explosion is taking place which prevents this growth from promoting a rise in the standard of living of the whole nation.

Millions of people consequently live on the borderline of the physical subsistence level without any hope of enjoying their share in a progressive development.

The ILO calculates that by 1970 the population of the world will have reached a figure of 3,600,000,000 people. Of these, 1,510,000,000 will comprise able-bodied men and women. But in the course of the decade commencing in 1970, the able-bodied population of the world will increase by 280,000,000 people. It is disturbing to contemplate that the bulk of this growth, namely, 226,000,000 people, will take place in countries with the least possibility for finding them employment; whereas the industrialized countries, in which today there is frequently a pressing need to increase the labor force, will show an increase of only 56,000,000 people.

How then will the ILO tackle this gigantic task of finding work for the whole population of the world? And what possibilities has the ILO of solving the problem which has loomed largest during our century, that of reducing, nay, removing, the gap between the rich and the poor nations of the world, and of adjusting the population explosion to a harmonious, economic, and social evolution?

At the ILO's Fiftieth-Jubilee Conference in Geneva this summer the director-general of the ILO, Mr. David A. Morse, expressed the hope he entertains for carrying out this plan in these words:

«Let us make it possible for future generations to look back on this fifty years' jubilee conference as the prelude to an epoch, an epoch where the instinctive solidarity between the people of the world is mobilized in a joint worldwide attack on poverty.»

This massed campaign against poverty will not only be organized by the ILO–it will be supported by all the UNO special organizations, as part of UNO's Second Development Decade.

The first task of the ILO will be to send experts to those parts of the world covered by the project–Latin America, Asia, and Africa–to work with national authorities in drawing up a long-term plan formulating objectives for vocational training and employment of the population.

The other task will be to participate in a program of action which will give effect to the plans that have been drawn up.

The ILO cannot, of course, on its own create new jobs; but it can give advice and help to countries desirous of putting their populations to work.

The ILO can assist in such areas as the implementation of agrarian reforms, agricultural projects, industrialization, public works, the development of training and vocational guidance programs, choice of investment possibilities, development of trade, and so on.

For this reason the ILO's plan does not consist merely of collecting statistical data on the population aspects of the problems involved. It will also have a direct bearing on the entire economic and social development in these areas.

Through this work the ILO is endeavoring to promote the capacity of developing countries to help themselves. No help from outside, however well-intentioned and selfless it may be, can take the place of the developing countries' own will to help themselves.

For this reason, carrying through the World Employment Program will prove a challenge both to the developing countries and to the industrialized countries; if they can work realistically together, they will also achieve their ideal aim, a world living in peaceful coexistence.

The ILO's main task will be to ensure that this new world is based on social justice; in other words, to fulfil the command that is inscribed on the document in Geneva: «*Si vis pacem, cole justitiam.*» If you desire peace, cultivate justice.

And let us add, as a summing up of our experience during these fifty eventful years and as a guideline for the future: «Just as peace is indivisible, so also is justice.»

D A V I D   A . M O R S E

ILO
and the Social Infrastructure of Peace

Nobel Lecture*, December 11, 1969

«Universal and lasting peace can be established only if it is based upon social justice.» This statement, which opens the preamble to the ILO's constitution, clearly and unmistakably places on the ILO a major role in the maintenance of peace. It shows that the founders of our organization in 1919 were convinced that there was an essential link between social justice within countries and international peace, and that this link was so strong and significant as to make it indispensable that an organization to deal with labor matters should be set up as an integral part of the new institutional framework for the promotion and protection of world peace after the First World War.

The founders of the ILO had good reason indeed to hold this belief. For the century which preceded the establishment of the ILO had been one of profound economic and social change in Europe which had played a large part in bringing about the war that Europe had just passed through. Industrialization had in particular led to an unprecedented growth of the economic power of European nations and to increasingly fierce competition between them, a competition which soon had an impact on the political plane and, ultimately, contributed to the outbreak of war. It had also led to serious social tensions within nations. By the end of this century a large industrial working class had become an organized, vociferous, and in many cases revolutionary force in society, often in open conflict with the established order.

Throughout the nineteenth century, however, and in the early years of the twentieth century, some farsighted men had raised their voices in an

---

* This Nobel lecture was delivered in the auditorium of the Nobel Institute by David A. Morse, who spoke in behalf of the International Labor Organization. Mr. Morse (1907–   ), American lawyer and former assistant secretary, undersecretary, and acting secretary of labor (successively in the period 1945–1948), had been the director-general of ILO since August 24, 1948, an office which he held until 1970. The text of his lecture is taken from *Les Prix Nobel en 1969*.

attempt to avoid the social and political catastrophe towards which Europe appeared to be heading. As early as the 1830's and the 1840's, such humanitarian industrialists as Charles Hindley[1] in England and Daniel Le Grand[2] in France had proposed that coordinated action should be taken at an international level to regulate conditions of labor in order to ensure that no country which provided its workers with improved conditions would be at a competitive disadvantage in the international market.

These men were ahead of their times. But as trade unions emerged as an organized political and social force in Europe's industrialized states, they were able not only to make some notable social gains for their members at home, but also to begin forging links of international solidarity among workers in different countries. The first International Working Men's Association had been formed in 1864, and although this and similar subsequent attempts to achieve true and lasting unity among the working classes of Europe were to fail, the workers nevertheless rapidly became a force to be reckoned with, internationally as well as nationally. Their attempts to prevent the outbreak of war between their countries were recognized by the Nobel Committee of the Norwegian Parliament itself when it awarded the Nobel Peace Prize in 1903 to the British trade unionist and pacifist, Sir William Randal Cremer, and much later, in 1951, to the great French trade unionist, my good friend the late Léon Jouhaux. The revulsion against war and the aspirations for peace on the part of workers were clearly and forcefully expressed by Jouhaux when he was here eighteen years ago to receive the Nobel Peace Prize. «War», he said, «not only kills workers by thousands and millions, and destroys their homes... but also, by increasing men's feelings of impotence before the forces of violence, it holds up considerably the progress of humanity toward the age of justice, welfare, and peace.»[3]

But the workers' movement had from the beginning been divided, as it still is today, between those who preached revolution and those who thought that greater social justice could and should be brought about by practical political and social reforms within the existing framework of society. And there were many men who at the end of the last century and the beginning

1. Charles Hindley (1800–1857), cotton spinner, founder of Aston and Dukinfield Mechanics Institute; member of Parliament (1835–1857).
2. Daniel Le Grand (1783–1859), French industrialist, philanthropist, and writer; early advocate of better labor conditions.
3. See p. 14.

of this were deeply alarmed at the prospects of revolutionary upheavals in society and the threat that this might present to the peace of the world. Alfred Nobel himself, in one of his most famous phrases, warned in 1892 of the dangers of an impending social revolution, of a «new tyranny... lurking in the shadows», and of its threat to world peace; and Frédéric Passy, the founder of the Ligue internationale de la paix, who was awarded the first Nobel Peace Prize in 1901, stressed the need for governments to ensure internal stability through social reforms if international peace was to be preserved. Thus, even before the First World War very different trends in thought and action among very different classes of the population had led the peace movement to become inextricably linked with a movement for international action to promote improved conditions of labor.

When the First World War came to an end in 1918, many of the industrialized countries were passing through a critical period of social tension and unrest. The old regime in Russia had been overthrown, and revolution seemed on the point of engulfing much of Europe. The demands from the workers that the peace settlement should include measures to promote international labor legislation and trade union rights were so insistent that delegations to the Peace Conference included leading trade unionists such as Samuel Gompers [1] from the United States and Léon Jouhaux from France. In these conditions it was hardly surprising that one of the main concerns of the Peace Conference should have been with «unrest so great that the peace and harmony of the world are imperiled»; or that one of its concrete – and, as it turned out, most lasting – achievements was the establishment of a permanent international organization to promote improved conditions of labor.

Thus was the ILO born fifty years ago – a product of several different currents in nineteenth-century and early twentieth-century humanitarian, reformist and socialist thought and action in Europe. Its structure and its action since its inception have reflected these different – and in many ways conflicting – currents. The workers' demands for effective international action have often been in contrast with the views of governments which have seen in the ILO an instrument for strengthening the stability of the sovereign nation state. And while the ILO has of course lived and operated

1. Samuel Gompers (1850–1924), president of American Federation of Labor (1886–1895; 1896–1924).

in a world of sovereign states, it has nevertheless gradually extended the scope and possibilities of transnational action. In this way, and in spite of the political calamities, failures, and disappointments of the past half-century, it has patiently, undramatically, but not unsuccessfully, worked to build an *infrastructure of peace*.

The ILO has provided the nations of the world with a meeting ground, an instrument for cooperation and for dialogue among very different interests, at times when men were more disposed to settle their differences by force than by talk. Let us consider in this connection two essential features of the ILO's structure: tripartism and universality.

Tripartism was both the most daring and the most valuable innovation of the Peace Conference when it set up the ILO. The ILO's constitution provides that each member state shall send to the International Labor Conference a delegation consisting of two government delegates and two delegates representing respectively the employers and workers, each of whom is entitled to vote individually and independently of each other. It further provides that the Governing Body, which has the responsibility of planning, reviewing, and coordinating the activities of the Organization, shall have this same tripartite composition, its members being elected independently by the three groups at the Conference. This composition is reflected here by the presence of the officers of the Governing Body who have accompanied me to Oslo for the Nobel Peace Prize ceremony, H.E.Mr.Gros Espiell[1], chairman of the Governing Body, and Mr.Gullmar Bergenström[2] and Mr.Jean Möri[3], respectively the leaders of the Employers' and Workers' groups of the Governing Body.

If the ILO had done nothing more than offer the world a forum for tripartite discussion, it would already have rendered a great service to the cause of peace. In 1919 the concept of tripartism was hardly known, even at the national level. By insisting on tripartite delegations to its Conferences and meetings, the ILO made it essential for governments and employers to accept trade unions as equals and as valid bargaining partners, at least

1. Héctor Gros Espiell, Uruguayan professor and diplomat; chairman of the ILO Governing Body.
2. Stig Gullmar Bergenström (1909–   ), Swedish administrator; president of the Executive Committee of the International Organization of Employers (1963–   ); employers' vice-chairman of the ILO Governing Body.
3. Jean Möri (1902–   ), Swiss trade union official; secretary of Swiss Federation of Trade Unions (1946–   ); workers' vice-chairman of the ILO Governing Body.

for the purposes of representation at the ILO. And if the concept could be accepted and applied in Geneva, why not at home?

The implications of this were far-reaching. It resulted in trade unions and organizations of employers acquiring a position at home which they would not otherwise have had, and encouraged the growth of independent interest groups where they might otherwise never have developed. It also gave the world a new approach to the resolution of social conflict, an approach based on dialogue between the two sides of industry, and between them and the state. The ILO in short offered the world an alternative to social strife; it provided it with the procedures and techniques of bargaining and negotiation to replace violent conflict as a means of securing more human and dignified conditions of work.

If the ILO has in this way helped to create the conditions for labor peace within countries, its tripartite structure has also enabled it to broaden the scope of cooperation between countries. The ILO is still the only world-wide organization where international cooperation is the business not only of diplomats and government representatives, but also of the representatives of employers and workers. It thus provides opportunities for contacts and for greater understanding within as well as among the three groups. It is only in the ILO that the different trends in the international trade union movement, which is today as divided as it was a hundred years ago, can come together to seek common solutions to common problems. And it is only in the ILO that free enterprise employers meet regularly with managers of state enterprises in socialist countries.

This brings me to the second aspect of the ILO's structure which has enabled it to make an important contribution to peace—its universality. The members and leaders of the ILO have constantly striven to make it a world-wide organization—universal in composition, in spirit, and in influence. They have done so because, as the preamble to the constitution states: «the failure of any nation to adopt humane conditions of labor is an obstacle in the way of other nations which desire to improve conditions in their own countries»; or, in the succinct words of the Declaration of Philadelphia, adopted in 1944: «poverty anywhere constitutes a danger to prosperity everywhere». Today, with 121 member states, we are far along towards the goal of universal membership.

A question which has often been raised in this connection is whether the ILO can properly aspire to universality. The very concept of tripartism, it is argued, presupposes an organization of society which is peculiar to

countries which have so-called «market economies». Is the system in socialist countries not incompatible with membership in the ILO? And in
the developing countries, which now form the majority of the ILO's membership, are not trade unions often too weak or too severely controlled by
governments, to play an active, independent role in the ILO? In other
words, can the ILO be both tripartite and universal?

Experience during the past few years has shown that it can; not only
that it can, but also that it *must* if it is to make a major contribution to
peaceful cooperation and mutual understanding among all the nations of
the world. The fact of the matter is that while tripartism may not have
the same meaning or take the same form in all countries of the world, and
while governments, employers, and trade unions may perform different
functions in society in different countries, they nevertheless face a number
of similar problems. Today, despite the very great differences among the
ILO's member states, governments, workers, and employers have at least
learned to live together in the ILO, and, after years of mutual suspicion,
are beginning to find a larger measure of common ground.

Thus, the ILO has not only served as a meeting ground for the nations
of the world, as a «market place» for ideas and ideologies, and as an instrument for adjusting conflicting interests. It has also put forward a set
of goals, and programs for attaining these goals, with which the entire ILO
membership can be identified. It has constantly sought to widen the areas
of «common ground» in order to focus the attention of the nations of the
world on those problems in which they have common interests and concerns, and to unite them in a major international effort to eliminate poverty
and injustice wherever they exist.

There are two elements in the ILO's program of activities to which I
would draw particular attention in this respect–its international labor standards and its technical cooperation activities.

The setting of international labor standards–that is, internationally recognized principles and objectives of social policy–is the traditional function that the ILO was originally set up to carry out. These standards which
are adopted by the International Labor Conference–that is, by the entire
membership of the ILO–take the form of Conventions (which are open
to ratification by governments) and Recommendations (which create no
formal obligation for governments, but which are intended to guide their
social policies).

The original aim of this international legislative function was to *protect* the worker against exploitation and against excessively hard and unjust working conditions (for example, his hours of work, his protection against industrial accidents, the elimination of child labor). As a result of progress in the elimination of such unjust and inhuman practices, increasing emphasis has been placed, particularly since 1945, on the *promotion* of effective measures guaranteeing him such basic human rights as freedom of association, freedom from forced labor, freedom from discrimination, and on the *promotion* of policies for social advancement which contribute to the achievement of economic development–relating, for example, to employment policy, minimum standards of social security, and labor–management relations in the enterprise.

The ILO has not been content simply to set these standards; it has also sought to supervise their effective application in member states, by pioneering a unique system of enforcement machinery. Thus, governments are obliged to report annually on the effect given to ratified Conventions; and their reports are analyzed by an independent Committee of Experts whose conclusions are submitted to a special Committee of the Conference. In addition, special machinery and procedures have been set up to ensure respect for the ILO's standards and principles on freedom of association, which are essential to the functioning of the ILO's tripartite machinery.

While it is impossible to measure in *precise* terms the impact which these standards have had on national legislation and practice, there can be few countries, if any, whose social legislation and whose practices in the formulation and implementation of social policy do not bear the imprint of at least some of the ILO's standards.

In this way the ILO has made a major contribution to international law, in broadening its scope to cover almost every conceivable area of social and labor policy and in seeking to ensure its wide and effective application. The ILO has thus proved that, despite the continuing primacy of the sovereign state, moral persuasion and moral pressure can be highly effective instruments to secure the observance of the rule of law at the international level, at least in the fields of social policy in which the ILO is competent.

While standard–setting remains an important function of the ILO today, it has been supplemented by another form of action, namely the provision of direct technical assistance to the developing countries. For, as more and more of these countries became independent and joined the ILO as full members, it became clear that the problems they faced in giving effect to the ILO's principles and standards were often due not to perverse and reactionary policies on their part but rather to the degree of backwardness and stagnation of their economies.

The idea of giving direct assistance to member countries was not new to the ILO. During the prewar years, and even during the Second World War, the ILO was occasionally called upon by its member countries to give advice and assistance, particularly in the field of social security. It was not, however, until the 1950's, with the launching of the United Nations Expanded Program of Technical Assistance, and subsequently the Special Fund (which are now merged in the United Nations Development Program) that sufficient funds became available to the ILO for it to take a major role in the massive attack on poverty in the developing countries. This has made it possible for the ILO to contribute actively and on a relatively large scale to what the Administrator of the United Nations Development Program has called the «peace-building» activities of the whole United Nations family of organizations.

In what way does assistance to the developing countries constitute an effort of «peace-building»? It could be argued, and with some justification, that economic development results in social changes and social tensions in a developing nation that can, and often do, have very serious consequences for both internal stability and international peace. But this should not, I suggest, be taken as an argument against assistance for development. After all, what is the alternative? Many developing countries are so weak, politically and economically, and so lacking in social cohesion and stability, that they could offer little resistance to subversion or aggression by an ambitious outside power. To provide these countries with the resources, the technical and managerial know-how, and the institutional and administrative framework which are essential for viable nationhood in the modern world, while at the same time providing their populations with the benefits of some social progress during the difficult transitional period of modernization–this, it seems to me, is an essential aspect of the problem of peace-building in the modern world. And it is for this reason that the ILO gives top priority in its work today to the strengthening of developing nations.

It may even seem paradoxical that the ILO, which has devoted so much effort to enlarging the scope and effectiveness of *international* action, should at the same time be giving priority to strengthening the *nation state* in the developing world. But the paradox is more apparent than real. We are strengthening the nation state because it is still the only viable framework within which economic and social progress can take place. And it is only if each developing nation can become independent in fact as well as in law that each can play its full part in the institutions of the wider international community.

Where do we stand today in our efforts to build a more peaceful world? The day which Alfred Nobel predicted seventy-seven years ago «when two army corps can annihilate one another in one second» has long since come. It is now almost possible for whole nations to be annihilated in one second. But this has not, as the inventor of dynamite optimistically predicted it would, led all nations to «recoil from war and discharge their troops». Quite the contrary. The major powers continue to build up their stockpiles of weapons of mass destruction, while even many small countries are investing heavily in the production and acquisition of weapons and the strengthening of their armed forces. The peace of today's world rests on a «balance of terror» which is based on the assumption that the destructive capability of modern weapons is such that no country will dare to be the first to use them. But this balance is now widely recognized as a precarious one.

Some small progress towards disarmament and towards limiting the spread of nuclear weapons has been and is being made. This is certainly of great importance. But full and effective disarmament cannot take place until we have eliminated the need for armaments, until we have laid the *infrastructure of peace* and thus established a climate of confidence in relations between nations and among men. For the tragedy of the modern world is that the immense progress that has been achieved in various branches of science and technology, and which is rightly recognized by the award of other prizes from Alfred Nobel's bequest, has not been paralleled by similar progress in social, human, and international relations.

As I have already stressed, very considerable efforts have been deployed to assist in the development and modernization of the developing countries. This has been a vast and unprecedented effort of international solidarity to which the ILO has been proud to contribute. What has been the result of this effort? Significant economic progress has clearly been made. Many developing countries achieved quite respectable rates of economic growth during the past decade–the first United Nations Development Decade–and creditable progress was made in building up the administrative and institutional framework necessary for development and modernization. But the balance sheet has a negative side which provides us with some somber warnings for the future.

What concerns the ILO in particular is the fact that the economic progress which has been achieved has benefited only a small sector of the population. To some extent, the ILO itself may have contributed to this situation. By assisting in the development of institutions similar to those existing in the industrialized societies of Europe and North America–such as social security systems, trade unions, and collective bargaining–it may have helped to strengthen the position of the privileged sectors of society–the civil servants, the managers, and the skilled workers. I am not suggesting that the ILO should now abandon its fundamental principles; but I am suggesting that it should make every effort to redress the alarming imbalances that have arisen in the societies of developing countries.

Rural areas have been left to stagnate, while dynamic modern industries have provided jobs for only a small proportion of the urban population. Large numbers of rural dwellers have abandoned the land in the hope of finding jobs and higher standards of living in the cities–a hope which all too often turns out to be vain, with the result that they swell the ranks of the unemployed and live in conditions of appalling squalor in vast slum areas. The slums, and the countryside in some areas, have become a breeding ground for seething violence, frustration, and discontent. Revolutionary movements are developing, particularly among younger people. And the problem is compounded by the explosive growth of the population in these countries, which is adding a new element of discontent to a turbulent social situation.

There is no need for me to stress to an audience such as this the dangers of this situation for the stability and prosperity of developing countries and hence for world peace. In my view, it is of the utmost urgency that a way be found of making economic development a meaningful term for the dispossessed masses before it is too late. That is why the ILO has decided to make the creation of higher levels of employment and employment opportunity the cornerstone of its action in the next decade–through a World Employment Program. For employment is a prime source of income, and a family's very existence will depend on whether or not the breadwinner is able to earn a decent livelihood from work. Today some 300 million workers are deprived of this opportunity in the developing countries. During the next decade we estimate that an additional 226 million men and women will be added to the ranks of job-seekers. That is the magnitude of the challenge before us.

The ILO will be tackling the problem on several different fronts at once. We shall try to contribute to the reduction or halting of the drift of the population to the cities by making rural areas more attractive for the peasant, the agricultural laborer, and the artisan, through enabling them to earn a better living off the land, and encouraging the growth of industries in the countryside. We shall encourage the use of labor-intensive techniques of agricultural and industrial production wherever it is economically feasible to do so. We shall attempt to mobilize the energies and enthusiasm of young people by giving them a role to play and a livelihood to earn in their country's development.

When I say «we», I refer, of course, not only to the ILO, since we cannot do this job by ourselves. I refer particularly to the governments of the ILO's member states, who have unanimously committed themselves to the objectives of the World Employment Program, and who will now, with the stimulus and support of the ILO, be called upon to fulfil that commitment by making policies for employment a central feature of their development policies. I refer also to the whole United Nations family of organizations and the regional organizations who have agreed to assist the ILO in the task of implementing the World Employment Program, and whose collaboration, within the framework of the Second Development Decade which is expected to begin in 1970, will be an essential ingredient in the success of the program. We will also look to workers' and employers' organizations for active support and for the kind of innovative thinking that the World Employment Program will require.

While the creation of productive and remunerative employment will be the ILO's principal concern in the developing countries during the next decade, we shall also be concerned with the adoption of other measures which will raise the living standards of the very poor—for example, the extension of social security schemes to new categories of workers, the provision of housing, and improved living and working conditions. And we shall continue to encourage the establishment and improvement of such vital institutions as trade unions and cooperatives and other rural organizations which will facilitate the participation of all sectors of society—rather than just a privileged few—in the economic and social life of their countries. In all these ways we hope to make our contribution to improving the social climate and defusing the potentially explosive situation in the developing world today.

While the developing countries have claimed, and will rightly continue for a long time to claim, the priority attention of the international community, it would be erroneous to assume that all is well in the so-called advanced nations. The ILO must continue to be concerned with the problems here as well. In fact, the way in which the issues with which we are concerned in the developed countries are resolved will to a large extent determine the future balance of relationships with the developing countries and directly affect man's efforts to build a peaceful world.

I would like to elaborate on this point for a moment. For the majority of the population in Europe and North America, the past half-century has brought impressive improvements in standards of living, in economic security, and in material comforts. Unemployment is no longer regarded as an unavoidable evil; on the contrary, full employment has now been embraced as a central goal of economic policy-making in most of these countries, and unemployment has in most cases been reduced to very small proportions, thanks very largely to the development of active labor market policies in which Scandinavian countries have played a pioneering role. Social security and welfare programs, in which the Scandinavian countries have again given the world a lead, have been adopted to cover virtually the entire population; and numerous indices–such as the growing numbers of private cars, and the purchases of consumer goods such as television sets and washing machines–point to high incomes from work among large sectors of the population.

These are extremely encouraging developments. And yet there are two broad groups of problems which give cause for alarm in our industrialized societies. There is first of all the plight of those who live, often in misery, on the fringe of affluence–the lowest paid workers; the racial or religious minorities; the migrant workers and their families from the countries of southern Europe or from other continents; the unemployed in the so-called «backward regions» and in the slum areas of some of our large cities; the elderly people, many of whom end their lives with pitifully small pensions, unprotected against rising prices and forgotten by a society to whose affluence today they contributed yesterday. Some of these–the elderly, for example–may not present a serious danger to social peace and stability. That may be why they are sometimes overlooked by society, although it is certainly no reason why they should be. For one test of the success of any political or economic system must surely be the extent to which the weakest and most defenseless elements in society are cared for and are made to feel deeply involved in the aspirations of that society. But others among the disinherited do present such a danger. In recent years and months we have been forcibly reminded that certain categories of the population are not sharing in the benefits of our technological societies; to enable them to do so is a challenge of some magnitude for many industrialized states. And the ILO must consider one of its most important tasks in the coming years to be the promotion of policies to eliminate discrimination in all its forms, and to ensure a decent standard of living for *all* the inhabitants of the developed nations. For, unlike the developing countries, they have at present adequate resources to banish poverty among their citizens for good if there is a political will to do so. By so doing, they will at the same time lay the groundwork for a deeper sense of international solidarity; for only when the poor and the weak are properly cared for in their own countries can the need for helping the poor and the weak in the world as a whole be given the full attention it requires.

There is a second problem area in the developed countries which is particularly difficult to solve, in part because it has not yet been successfully defined. I refer to the growing social unrest among young people, many of whom can scarcely be considered underprivileged in any material sense. Universities and youth organizations have, of course, long been an arena where the most vocal forms of discontent with existing systems of authority have developed. But what is new in the present situation is that unrest among the young has found an echo among other sections of the population—especially among workers.

This is a novel situation, because the men and women involved are not revolting because they are the victims of poverty, injustice, or oppression. While it has not yet been possible to define precisely the cause of the present malaise in industrial societies, many eminent social scientists have attempted to do so. I venture to suggest that it may be a sign of widespread boredom and frustration at the colorless technological civilization in which we live and in which we are prepared to make too many sacrifices to material progress; that it may be a reaction against the horrifying human, material, and moral waste of war; that it may be frustration over the seeming inability of the existing institutions of industrial societies to seize the almost unlimited opportunities offered by today's technology, opportunities for greater freedom and for all people to lead fuller and richer lives in a spiritual as well as a material sense. Whatever the reasons, it is clear that the creation of all the comforts and the security, of all the social and medical services of the modern welfare state, important as they are, is not enough to satisfy the deepest-felt needs of the population. The challenge before us now is to make industrialized societies more human, to make man the master rather than the slave of modern technology, to offer more possibilities for the constructive use of leisure, for greater freedom, for greater participation, for more effective dialogue. For there is a serious danger that the fabric of these societies will be torn asunder by the complete disruption of the economic, social, and political life of the nation, unless ways can be found of developing new institutions, new forms of authority, even new social values, which are acceptable to the population as a whole.

This raises far-reaching questions concerning the organization and structure of society, many of which are far beyond the ILO's competence, though none are beyond our concern. But there is one important aspect of this vast problem that does directly involve the ILO—the organization of life and work in industry and in particular the relationships between employers and workers and between workers and trade unions. The days of the autocratic and paternalistic employer are long since past; the employer can no longer claim to be, and is no longer accepted as, the sole source of authority in the enterprise. The workers and their organizations demand to share in the authority as well as the responsibilities of management. But at the same time, new problems of communications have arisen between workers on the shop floor and the leaders of the organizations representing their interests; workers sometimes even appear to see their own trade unions as part of the «establishment» against which they are in revolt. The resulting situation, at least in certain countries, is alarming: greater absenteeism, more and more wildcat strikes, in short an erosion of industrial discipline which is the basis on which rests the progress and prosperity of society and, ultimately, of the workers themselves.

This, I suggest, is a major problem for consideration by the ILO and its membership in many industrialized states. And it can only be resolved if there is far more informed and meaningful dialogue: more dialogue between employers and workers, on a far wider range of questions concerning the undertaking as a whole, than is yet the case; more dialogue between the trade unions and their members, so that the eventual terms of a plant-level or nationwide settlement concluded by the leadership are broadly acceptable to the members. Such dialogue has unfortunately all too frequently been lacking; but it is the only means by which the workers' grievances and frustrations—whether or not they are substantial—can be known and understood. It is the only means by which the industrial enterprise can be humanized and the element of drudgery in work can be reduced.

But we also need more dialogue with and between those not represented in the giant organizations of modern society; and this may entail a thorough-going revision of the structures and decision-making processes of society. For these are the only means that I can see by which the growing frustrations and discontent can be prevented from becoming a truly explosive–or at least seriously erosive–force in society.

The ILO has given the world the concept of the industrial dialogue; in the years to come it must seek to broaden the scope, and increase the substance, of that dialogue. And it will be for other organizations–national and international–to transpose both the concept and the substance to all aspects of national life–to the schools and universities, to the churches, to the political parties and central and local government, to the youth clubs and welfare services–if society as a whole is to attain the cohesion and the sense of collective responsibility which are so essential to its survival.

Much has been achieved over the past half-century. There has been a growing awareness and acceptance of man's economic, social, political, and civil rights; a far greater effort than ever before has been made to give each man a decent standard of living and a dignified place in society; men have become far readier to accept and live with people of different races, interests, and ideologies; and there has been growing recognition of the need for a truly worldwide solidarity in the fight against poverty and injustice, with the aim of building a more peaceful world.

The ILO is proud to have played its part in these achievements. But as we know and as you see from the horizon that I have sketched, the task is still far from finished. The goal of «social justice» which the ILO's founding fathers wrote into the Treaty of Versailles has proved to be a dynamic concept. As soon as one problem has been successfully tackled, new and unforeseen problems arise which present a major challenge to the social conscience of mankind. Thus, the ILO has never seen, and will never see, its role as that of a defender of the status quo; it will continue to seek to promote social evolution by peaceful means, to identify emerging social needs and problems and threats to social peace, and to stimulate action to deal with such problems. For there are still, to paraphrase the words of Frédéric Passy, dangerous explosives in the hidden depths of the community–the national community and the world community. To the defusing of these explosives, to the building of a truly peaceful world order based on social justice, the ILO, with the immense encouragement it derives from the unique distinction of the Nobel Peace Prize, solemnly dedicates its second half-century of existence.

History*

The International Labor Organization was created in 1919 by Part XIII of the Versailles Peace Treaty ending World War I. It grew out of nineteenth-century labor and social movements which culminated in widespread demands for social justice and higher living standards for the world's working people. In 1946, after the demise of the League of Nations, the ILO became the first specialized agency associated with the United Nations. The original membership of forty-five countries in 1919 has grown to 121 in 1971.

In structure, the ILO is unique among world organizations in that the representatives of the workers and of the employers have an equal voice with those of governments in formulating its policies. The annual International Labor Conference, the ILO's supreme deliberative body, is composed of four representatives from each member country: two government delegates, one worker and one employer delegate, each of whom may speak and vote independently. Between conferences, the work of the ILO is guided by the Governing Body, comprising twenty-four government, twelve worker and twelve employer members, plus twelve deputy members from each of these three groups. The International Labor Office in Geneva, Switzerland, is the Organization's secretariat, operational headquarters, research center, and publishing house. Its operations are staffed at headquarters and around the world by more than 3,000 people of some 100 nationalities. Activities are decentralized to regional, area, and branch offices in over forty countries.

The ILO has three major tasks, the first of which is the adoption of international labor standards, called Conventions and Recommendations, for implementation by member states. The Conventions and Recommendations contain guidelines on child labor, protection of women workers, hours of work, rest and holidays with pay, labor inspection, vocational guidance and training, social security protection, workers' housing, occupational health

---

* This history is adapted from one kindly supplied by the ILO.

and safety, conditions of work at sea, and protection of migrant workers. They also cover questions of basic human rights, among them, freedom of association, collective bargaining, the abolition of forced labor, the elimination of discrimination in employment, and the promotion of full employment. By 1970, 134 Conventions and 142 Recommendations had been adopted by the ILO. Each of them is a stimulus, as well as a model, for national legislation and for practical application in member countries.

A second major task, which has steadily expanded for the past two decades, is that of technical cooperation to assist developing nations. More than half of ILO's resources are devoted to technical cooperation programs, carried out in close association with the United Nations Development Program and often with other UN specialized agencies. These activities are concentrated in four major areas: development of human resources, through vocational training and management development; employment planning and promotion; the development of social institutions in such fields as labor administration, labor relations, cooperatives, and rural development; conditions of work and life—for example, occupational safety and health, social security, remuneration, hours of work, welfare, etc.

Marking the beginning of its second half-century, the ILO has launched the World Employment Program, designed to help countries provide employment and training opportunities for their swelling populations. The World Employment Program will be the ILO's main contribution to the United Nations Second Development Decade.

There are some 900 ILO experts of fifty-five different nationalities at work on more than 300 technical cooperation projects in over 100 countries around the world.

Third, standard-setting and technical cooperation are bolstered by an extensive research, training, education, and publications program. The ILO is a major source of publications and documentation on labor and social matters. It has established two specialized educational institutions: the International Institute for Labor Studies in Geneva, and the International Center for Advanced Technical and Vocational Training in Turin, Italy.

Since its inception the ILO has had six directors-general: Albert Thomas (1919–1932) of France; Harold B. Butler (1932–1938) of the United Kingdom; John G. Winant (1938–1941) of the United States; Edward J. Phelan (1941–1948) of Ireland; David A. Morse (1948–1970) of the United States; Wilfred Jenks (1970–   ) of the United Kingdom.

Selected Bibliography

«Fifty Years in the Service of Social Progress, 1919–1969», *ILO Panorama*, 37 (July–August, 1969) 1–88.

The ILO in the Service of Social Progress: A Workers' Education Manual. Geneva, ILO, 1969.

Jenks, Wilfred, *Human Rights and International Labour Standards*. London, Stevens, 1960.

Jenks, Wilfred, *The International Protection of Trade Union Freedom*. London, Stevens, 1957.

Johnston, G. A., *The International Labour Organisation: Its Work for Social and Economic Progress*. London, Europa Publications, 1970.

Landy, Ernest A., *The Effectiveness of International Supervision: Thirty Years of ILO Experience*. London, Stevens, 1966.

Morse, David A., *The Origin and Evolution of the ILO and Its Role in the World Community*. Ithaca, N. Y., Cornell University, New York State School of Industrial and Labor Relations, 1969.

Phelan, Edward J., *Yes and Albert Thomas*. London, Cresset Press, 1936.

The Story of Fifty Years. Geneva, ILO, 1969.

Valticos, Nicolas, «Fifty Years of Standard-Setting Activities by the ILO», *International Labour Review*, 100 (September, 1969) 201–237.

Peace 1970

NORMAN ERNEST BORLAUG

Presentation

by Aase Lionaes*, Chairman of the Nobel Committee

In the will and testament drawn up by Alfred Bernhard Nobel on November 27, 1895, he laid down the conditions to be fulfilled by a recipient of the Nobel Prize. Paragraph One states, *inter alia*, that the award of the prize shall be made to the person «who, during the preceding year, shall have conferred the greatest benefit on mankind».

The Nobel Committee of the Norwegian Parliament must bear this criterion in mind in selecting the prizewinner from among the many candidates proposed.

What might be a «benefit» to humanity today? Many answers could be given, just as varied, as many-sided, and as interesting as man himself.

Does history not offer one signpost indicating and for all time identifying the basic needs of man which it would be a «benefit» to satisfy?

One of the great historical events in Europe during the course of our dramatic century, the Russian Revolution of 1917, had this inscription on its banner: «Bread and Peace». Bread and peace present a combination of the vital needs mankind has always set as a goal vital to the development of its potential.

Freedom from starvation was furthermore one of the freedoms our first global peace organization, the United Nations, recognized in 1945 as a basic human right to be secured for all people. On October 16, 1945, FAO–that is to say, the United Nations Organization for Food and Agriculture, the first of UNO's specialized agencies–was established.

In 1949 FAO's secretary-general, the nutrition expert Lord Boyd Orr, was awarded the Nobel Peace Prize.

This year the Nobel Committee of the Norwegian Parliament has awarded

---

* Mrs. Lionaes, president of the Lagting (a section of the Norwegian Parliament), delivered this speech on December 10, 1970, in the Auditorium of the University of Oslo. The laureate responded to her presentation of the prize with a brief speech of acceptance. This English translation of Mrs. Lionaes' speech is, with minor editorial changes made after comparison with a tape recording of the speech in Norwegian, that appearing in *Les Prix Nobel en 1970*.

Nobel's Peace Prize to a scientist, Dr. Norman Ernest Borlaug, because, more than any other single person of this age, he has helped to provide bread for a hungry world. We have made this choice in the hope that providing bread will also give the world peace.

Who is this scientist who, through his work in the laboratory and in the wheat fields, has helped to create a new food situation in the world and who has turned pessimism into optimism in the dramatic race between our population explosion and our production of food?

Norman Borlaug, a man of Norwegian descent, was born on March 25, 1914, on a small farm in Cresco, Iowa, in the United States, and originally studied forestry at the University of Minnesota. It was as an agriculturalist, however, that he was to make his greatest contribution.

In 1944 Borlaug was appointed to a post as a genetics expert with the Rockefeller Foundation. In 1942 this Foundation, in cooperation with the Mexican government, had launched an agricultural program in Mexico. This project was directed by two outstanding plant pathologists, Professors Stakman and J. George Harrar[1]. Its aim was research into and a better exploitation of agricultural know-how, with a view to developing Mexico's agriculture and in this way increasing and improving local food supplies. For the outstanding contribution to peace this agricultural program represented, the Rockefeller Foundation was proposed in 1962 as a candidate for Nobel's Peace Prize by ten members of the Swedish Parliament.

It is interesting to note that the Norwegian Academy of Sciences in Oslo, as far back as 1951, elected the leader of this project, Professor Stakman, a member of its Mathematical-Natural Science class.

Twenty years later, in 1970, his pupil, Dr. Norman E. Borlaug, was made an honorary doctor by the Norwegian Agricultural College at Ås. The rector of this institution, Professor Jul Låg, declared that this honor had been awarded for the following reason:

«The basis for the award of the honorary doctoral degree to Dr. Borlaug is the impressive result he has achieved in wheat improvement, and the organization of the exploitation of the results of this improvement in agriculture, particularly in the developing countries. The new breeds of grain evolved by Dr. Borlaug and his assistants have resulted in improvements in

1. Elvin C. Stakman (1885–   ), professor of plant pathology (1918–1953), now emeritus professor, University of Minnesota; special consultant to Rockefeller Foundation (1953–   ). J. George Harrar (1906–   ), formerly professor of plant pathology; president of Rockefeller Foundation (1961–   ).

harvest, quantitatively and qualitatively, that previously were considered hardly possible.»

This distinction is only one of a great many academic honors conferred on Dr. Borlaug by universities and similar institutions in the U.S.A., Pakistan, India, and Canada.

Dr. Borlaug went to the International Maize and Wheat Improvement Center in 1944. Today he is director of the Wheat Improvement Program in Mexico.

Ever since that day, twenty-five years ago, when Dr. Borlaug started his work on the improvement of grain, and right up to the present, he has devoted all his energy to achieving the historical result which today is referred to all over the world as the «green revolution». This revolution will make it possible to improve the living conditions of hundreds of millions of people in that part of the globe which today might be called «the non-affluent world».

Nations with ancient cultures, which right up to modern times have suffered the scourge of recurrent hunger crises, can now be self-supporting in wheat. A long and humiliating dependence on the so-called rich nations of the world for their daily bread will have been brought to an end.

Behind the outstanding results in the sphere of wheat research of which the dry statistics speak, we sense the presence of a dynamic, indomitable, and refreshingly unconventional research scientist.

Dr. Borlaug is not only a man of ideals but essentially a man of action. Reading his publications on the green revolution, one realizes that he is fighting not only weeds and rust fungus but just as much the deadly procrastination of the bureaucrats and the red tape that thwart quick action. The following warning reminds us of this: «Strangulation of the world by exploding, well-camouflaged bureaucracies is one of the great threats to mankind.»[1]

Dr. Borlaug cannot afford to wait: there is an important cause weighing on his mind, something that must be carried out and must be carried out *now*.

He puts it like this: «I am impatient and do not accept the need for slow change and evolution to improve the agriculture and food production of the emerging countries. I advocate instead a ‹yield kick-off› or ‹yield blast-off›. There is no time to be lost, considering the magnitude of the world food and population problem.»[2]

1. Norman E. Borlaug, *Wheat Breeding and Its Impact on World Food Supply*, p.24.
2. *Ibid.*, p.26.

Apart from his work as a scientist and as an outstanding organizer in exploiting the results of research, Dr. Borlaug has also been an inspiring leader for the many young scientists who have been trained at the Wheat Institute in Mexico.

Dr. Borlaug prefers to teach his pupils out in the fields. Many people, we are told, who ask him to lecture or write a paper, get the following reply: «What would you rather have – bread or paper?»

In 1944, when Dr. Borlaug started work on the Mexican agricultural project, there were not so many people concerned with the relationship between the trends in population growth and the increase in food production in the world.

After the war, when most colonial empires were gradually dismantled, and sixty to seventy developing areas emerged as independent national states, it was primarily the incredibly poor standard of health in these countries that appealed to our conscience.

Through its World Health Organization, the United Nations launched a formidable attack in the 1950's on the major national diseases in these new states. One of the results of the preventive medical measures set afoot was a drastic decrease in the mortality rate of the developing countries. And it was not until the 1960's that the prospects of a population explosion constituted a menace, not only to the developing countries but to the whole world.

The population explosion is being attacked essentially from two angles: by information on family planning and by an increased effort, first and foremost through research, to increase the agricultural yield.

When Borlaug and other scientists initiated their work at the Wheat Center in Mexico, the Mexican authorities had little faith in their country's potential as an agricultural country. It was assumed that the country had neither the climate nor the soil required for advanced agriculture. The country spent a great deal of its foreign currency importing the necessary wheat.

Wheat researchers attached to the Rockefeller Foundation's project were set the task of helping Mexico, in as short a time as possible, to help herself. The scientists were to play the role not of consultants entrenched behind their documents in their offices, but of active participants in the practical manual labor and toil in the fields.

For many young scientists this last principle may have entailed a somewhat unpalatable reassessment of their social status, but it was undoubtedly a wholesome maxim.

In his writings on the green revolution, Dr. Borlaug relates that the Mexican wheat program aimed to analyze all the factors that hampered production. Furthermore, the idea was to train young scientists in all scientific disciplines associated with production. The purpose of this research, Dr. Borlaug continues, was to endeavor to develop a variety of wheat with greater yields, with a great degree of resistance to diseases, and with qualities that rendered it suitable for use in connection with improved agronomic methods, that is to say, the use of artificial fertilizers, improved soil culture, and mechanization.

The result of the concerted attack launched by the team of scientists on all these problems was the new Mexican breeds of wheat, which are now generally known, which produce astonishingly large yields, which are resistant to disease, and which facilitate intensive use of fertilizers. Unlike previously known breeds of wheat, the new types can be transferred to remote parts of the world that differ in climate.

The most important event in the Mexican Wheat Improvement Program was the development of the so-called «dwarf varieties». After years of research on the part of Dr. Borlaug and his collaborators to develop, by crossing and selection, the so-called Japanese breed of wheat, they evolved the now world-famous «dwarf variety».

These are breeds of wheat which, unlike previously known long-bladed varieties, have short blades. The long-bladed varieties of wheat, on which work was done in the 1950's, gave increased yields but snapped when they were given more than a certain amount of artificial fertilizer. The new dwarf varieties were able to stand two or three times more artificial fertilizer and to provide an increase of yield per decare from the previous maximum of 450 kilos to as much as 800 kilos per decare. These varieties can be used in various parts of the world because they are not affected by varying lengths of daylight. They are better than all other kinds in both fertilized and non-fertilized soil, and with and without artificial irrigation. In addition they are highly resistant to the worst enemy of wheat, rust fungus or oromyces.

Thanks to these high-yield breeds of wheat, Mexico was self-supporting in this grain in 1956, and in recent years this country has exported several hundred thousand tons annually.

At the invitation of FAO, Dr. Borlaug visited Pakistan in 1959. He was instrumental in having a number of Pakistani wheat experts sent to Mexico to study the wheat research center there. After striving hard to convince Pakistani authorities and other foreign experts, Dr. Borlaug persuaded the

political leaders of Pakistan to recognize the advantages of introducing the
new Mexican breeds of wheat into their country. At that time the agriculture
of West Pakistan was producing a steady annual deficit in relation to national
needs. Wheat yields were low, approximately 100 kilos per decare on an
average. Farming methods were primitive, the soil had been overcropped,
and artificial fertilizer was a rarity.

After a successful struggle to overcome bureaucracy, prejudice, and even
rumors to the effect that Dr. Borlaug's variety of wheat would produce
sterility and impotence among the population, it was finally decided that
Pakistan should import a certain quantity of Mexican seed corn of the new
breed. Once the seed corn had been introduced and had yielded superb
results in the form of increased crops, the triumphal march of the green
revolution was ushered in. Pakistan's present-day wheat production amounts
to seven million tons, and the country is self-supporting in wheat. That this
could be achieved in the course of three or four years was due in no small
measure to the fact that the President of Pakistan had personally supported
the program very strongly, and to the fact that the results achieved in Mexico could be used as a basis, thus saving the country a great many years of
research and experiment.

Dr. Borlaug was in India in 1963 in order to find out whether the breed of
wheat he had developed in Mexico could be used in this country too, and
history repeated itself. The highest results in the history of India were
achieved in 1968 with a crop of seventeen million tons. This event was
celebrated in India with the issue of a new postage stamp bearing the inscription «The Indian Wheat Revolution 1968».

After the successful results achieved in Mexico, India, and Pakistan, the
new varieties of wheat were introduced into certain parts of Turkey, Afghanistan, Iran, Iraq, Tunisia, Morocco, and the Lebanon. The Soviet Union,
too, is now interested in establishing contacts with the International Maize
and Wheat Research Center in Mexico.

This occasion is neither the time nor the place to give a detailed account of
Dr. Borlaug's great results in wheat research during the last twenty-five
years. But it has been established beyond doubt that his efforts have made
possible an unequaled increase in wheat production and an improvement in
quality that have postponed a crisis that a great many scientists have predicted would be the result of the growing gap between the population
explosion and food production.

An assessment of the effects of Dr. Borlaug's great contribution makes obvious the fact that a whole series of factors is involved, affecting not only economic, social, cultural, and political affairs – and these not solely in the various developing countries – but also affecting international relations. Problems of major importance such as the aid given by the industrialized countries to the developing countries must also be basically reassessed. It is obvious that we can no longer count on the export of grain to the developing countries. Loans for the purchase of industrial equipment and technical know-how must be given greater priority.

The new variety of wheat will be able to effect a total transformation of the economic picture in the developing countries.

Society will be richer and industry will be more varied if the politicians at the same time pursue an economic policy which aims at general economic growth. The increased earnings of agriculture will ensure «ring-effects» in the form of growth impulses in all the activities created by more productive agriculture. It will be possible to increase employment: sowing, fertilizing, hoeing, harvesting, marketing will have to be carried out several times a year. Seasonal unemployment will be reduced: a balanced economic policy, correctly pursued, should make it possible to provide work for the large surplus of available manpower in the developing countries. It is maintained, for example, by Lester Brown in his book *Seeds of Change* that there might even be a *shortage* of labor on a local basis.

The new technology in agriculture could also stimulate such branches of the economy as industry, building, and construction work throughout the social economy. For instance, the increase in crop yields will require the building of artificial fertilizer factories, roads, irrigation works, railways, warehouses, silos, and mills. Outlying districts will be able to receive the economic pollination necessary for the building of schools and hospitals. From whatever angle we consider them, the effects of the green revolution will entail an increased total production that will make the developing countries economically better off and more independent of the aid provided by the affluent countries, as far as foodstuffs are concerned.

In an article published in *Foreign Affairs*, the agricultural expert Lester Brown states that the new breed of grain in our age will have the same impact on the agricultural revolution in Asia that the steam engine had on the Industrial Revolution in Europe in the eighteenth century[1]. Or, as Eugene Black puts it, the new grain varieties will be «engines of change»[2].

1. Lester R. Brown, «The Agricultural Revolution in Asia», p. 694.
2. P. vii of Foreword in Lester R. Brown's *Seeds of Change*.

Not least, these «engines of change» will transform the position of the peasant in the community and the peasant's attitude to his own situation in life. A new policy of income distribution, socially oriented, will enable the peasant to break out of the vicious circle of poverty and the apathy which is a natural consequence of penury that offers no future prospects. Many writers who have dealt with the peasant population of developing countries have maintained that the peasants are conservative, in the sense that they do not want change. But Dr. Borlaug – who is a great admirer of the peasant – maintains that when changes involve a rise in the standard of living, the Asiatic peasant, too, will accept change. To quote Dr. Borlaug, «Although the peasant farmer may be illiterate, he can figure.»[1]

The new varieties of grain and the capital input required will increase the peasants' demands on the authorities for education, transport, agricultural credits, and the like. The capital-hungry peasants could constitute a political pressure group which the authorities would have to take into consideration in framing their economic policy. There would thus be an increase in political activity.

Dr. Borlaug realizes, however, that even though the new varieties of grain will involve a considerable increase in the crop harvested by the peasants, the green revolution may also create social problems of a negative kind. Social injustices may well occur if politicians in the developing countries should fail to ensure the requisite conditions by means of equitable taxation, a system of agricultural credits at reasonable rates of interest, a properly adjusted price policy, and a defensible employment policy.

In his speech on August 20 of this year at the Agricultural College at Ås, Dr. Borlaug expressed his social views as follows: «I've worked with wheat, but wheat is merely a catalyst, a part of the picture. I'm interested in the total economic development in all countries. Only by attacking the whole problem can we raise the standard of living for all people in all communities, so that they will be able to live decent lives. This is something we wish for all people on this planet.»

But this will be the responsibility and challenge to be faced by the political authorities in the countries concerned. Through his scientific contribution and his tremendous talent for organization, Dr. Borlaug has introduced a dynamic factor into our assessment of the future and its potential. He has enlarged our perspective; he has given the economists, the social planners,

1. Borlaug, *op. cit.*, p. 28.

and the politicians a few decades in which to solve their problems, to introduce the family planning, the economic equalization, the social security, and
the political liberty we must have in order to ensure everybody–not least
the impoverished, undernourished and malnourished masses–their daily
bread and thus a peaceful future.

And this is precisely where Dr. Borlaug has made his great contribution
to peace. During the twenty-five years that have elapsed since the end of the
war, those of us who live in the affluent industrialized societies have debated
in almost panic-stricken terms the race between the world's population
explosion and the world's available food resources. Most experts who have
expressed an opinion on the issue of this race have been pessimistic.

The world has been oscillating between fears of two catastrophes–the
population explosion and the atom bomb. Both pose a mortal threat.

In this intolerable situation, with the menace of doomsday hanging over
us, Dr. Borlaug comes onto the stage and cuts the Gordian knot. He has
given us a well-founded hope, an alternative of peace and of life–the green
revolution.

NORMAN E. BORLAUG

The Green Revolution, Peace, and Humanity

Nobel Lecture*, December 11, 1970

Civilization as it is known today could not have evolved, nor can it survive, without an adequate food supply. Yet food is something that is taken for granted by most world leaders despite the fact that more than half of the population of the world is hungry. Man seems to insist on ignoring the lessons available from history.

Man's survival, from the time of Adam and Eve until the invention of agriculture, must have been precarious because of his inability to ensure his food supply. During the long, obscure, dimly defined prehistoric period when man lived as a wandering hunter and food gatherer, frequent food shortages must have prevented the development of village civilizations. Under these conditions the growth of human population was also automatically limited by the limitations of food supplies.

In the misty, hazy past, as the Mesolithic Age gave way to the Neolithic, there suddenly appeared in widely separated geographic areas the most highly successful group of inventors and revolutionaries that the world has ever known. This group of Neolithic men and women, and in all probability largely the latter, domesticated all the major cereals, legumes, and root crops, as well as all of the most important animals that to this day remain man's principal source of food. Apparently, nine thousand years ago, in the foot-hills of the Zagros Mountains[1], man had already become both agriculturist and animal husbandryman, which, in turn, soon led to the specialization of labor and the development of village life. Similar discoveries and develop-ments elsewhere soon laid the groundwork from which all modern agri-culture and animal industry and, indeed, all of the world's subsequent civilizations have evolved. Despite the tremendous value of their contri-butions, we know none of these benefactors of mankind by name. In fact, it has only been within the past century, and especially within the last

* The laureate delivered this lecture in the auditorium of the Nobel Institute. The text, which in actual delivery was considerably shortened, is taken from *Les Prix Nobel en 1970*.
1. In what is now West Iran.

fifteen years – since the development of the effective radio-carbon dating system – that we have begun even vaguely to understand the timing of these epochal events which have shaped the world's destiny.

The invention of agriculture, however, did not permanently emancipate man from the fear of food shortages, hunger, and famine. Even in prehistoric times population growth often must have threatened or exceeded man's ability to produce enough food. Then, when droughts or outbreaks of diseases and insect pests ravaged crops, famine resulted.

That such catastrophes occurred periodically in ancient times is amply clear from numerous biblical references. Thus, the Lord said: «I have smitten you with blasting and mildew.»[1] «The seed is rotten under their clods, the garners are laid desolate, the barns are broken down; for the corn is withered... The beasts of the field cry also unto thee: for the rivers of waters are dried up, and the fire hath devoured the pastures of the wilderness.»[2]

Plant diseases, drought, desolation, despair were recurrent catastrophes during the ages – and the ancient remedies: supplications to supernatural spirits or gods. And yet, the concept of the «ever-normal granary» appeared in elementary form, as is clear from Pharaoh's dreams and Joseph's interpretation of imminent famine and his preparation for it, as indicated by this quotation from Genesis: «... And the seven years of dearth began to come, according as Joseph had said: and the dearth was in all lands; but in all the land of Egypt there was bread...»[3] For his time, Joseph was wise, with the help of his God.

But today we should be far wiser; with the help of our Gods and our science, we must not only increase our food supplies but also insure them against biological and physical catastrophes by international efforts to provide international granaries of reserve food for use in case of need. And these food reserves must be made available to all who need them – and before famine strikes, not afterwards. Man can and must prevent the tragedy of famine in the future instead of merely trying with pious regret to salvage the human wreckage of the famine, as he has so often done in the past. We will be guilty of criminal negligence, without extenuation, if we permit future famines. Humanity cannot tolerate that guilt.

Alfred Nobel was also very conscious of the importance of food, for he once wrote: «I would rather take care of the stomachs of the living than the glory of the departed in the form of monuments.»

1. Amos 4:9.
2. Joel 1:17, 20.
3. Genesis 41:54.

The destiny of world civilization depends upon providing a decent standard of living for all mankind. The guiding principles of the recipient of the 1969 Nobel Peace Prize, the International Labor Organization, are expressed in its charter words, «Universal and lasting peace can be established only if it is based upon social justice. If you desire peace, cultivate justice.» This is magnificent; no one can disagree with this lofty principle.

Almost certainly, however, the first essential component of social justice is adequate food for all mankind. Food is the moral right of all who are born into this world. Yet today fifty percent of the world's population goes hungry. Without food, man can live at most but a few weeks; without it, all other components of social justice are meaningless. Therefore I feel that the aforementioned guiding principle must be modified to read: If you desire peace, cultivate justice, but at the same time cultivate the fields to produce more bread; otherwise there will be no peace.

The recognition that hunger and social strife are linked is not new, for it is evidenced by the Old Testament passage, «... and it shall come to pass, that when they shall be hungry, they shall fret themselves, and curse their King and their God...»[1]

Perhaps no one in recent times has more pungently expressed the interrelationship of food and peace than Nobel Laureate Lord John Boyd Orr[2], the great crusader against hunger and the first director-general of the Food and Agriculture Organization, with his famous words, «You can't build peace on empty stomachs.» These simple words of wisdom spoken twenty-one years ago are as valid today as when they were spoken. They will become even more meaningful in the future as world population skyrockets and as crowding, social pressures, and stresses increase. To ignore Lord Orr's admonition would result in worldwide disorders and social chaos, for it is a fundamental biological law that when the life of living organisms is threatened by shortage of food they tend to swarm and use violence to obtain their means of sustenance.

It is a sad fact that on this earth at this late date there are still two worlds, «the privileged world» and «the forgotten world». The privileged world consists of the affluent, developed nations, comprising twenty-five to thirty percent of the world population, in which most of the people live in a luxury never before experienced by man outside the Garden of Eden. The forgotten world is made up primarily of the developing nations, where most

1. Isaiah 8:21.
2. Lord John Boyd Orr (1880–1971), recipient of the Nobel Peace Prize for 1949.

of the people, comprising more than fifty percent of the total world population, live in poverty, with hunger as a constant companion and fear of famine a continual menace.

When the Nobel Peace Prize Committee designated me the recipient of the 1970 award for my contribution to the «green revolution», they were in effect, I believe, selecting an individual to symbolize the vital role of agriculture and food production in a world that is hungry, both for bread and for peace. I am but one member of a vast team made up of many organizations, officials, thousands of scientists, and millions of farmers–mostly small and humble–who for many years have been fighting a quiet, oftentimes losing war on the food production front.

During the past three years spectacular progress has been made in increasing wheat, rice, and maize production in several of the most populous developing countries of southern Asia, where widespread famine appeared inevitable only five years ago. Most of the increase in production has resulted from increased yields of grain per hectare, a particularly important development because there is little possibility of expanding the cultivated area in the densely populated areas of Asia.

The term «The Green Revolution» has been used by the popular press to describe the spectacular increase in cereal-grain production during the past three years. Perhaps the term «green revolution», as commonly used, is premature, too optimistic, or too broad in scope. Too often it seems to convey the impression of a general revolution in yields per hectare and in total production of all crops throughout vast areas comprising many countries. Sometimes it also implies that all farmers are uniformly benefited by the breakthrough in production.

These implications both oversimplify and distort the facts. The only crops which have been appreciably affected up to the present time are wheat, rice, and maize. Yields of other important cereals, such as sorghums, millets, and barley, have been only slightly affected; nor has there been any appreciable increase in yield or production of the pulse or legume crops, which are essential in the diets of cereal-consuming populations. Moreover, it must be emphasized that thus far the great increase in production has been in irrigated areas. Nor have all cereal farmers in the irrigated areas adopted and benefited from the use of the new seed and the new technology. Nevertheless, the number of farmers, small as well as large, who are adopting the new seeds and new technology is increasing very rapidly, and the increase in numbers during the past three years has been phenomenal. Cereal production in the rainfed areas still remains relatively unaffected by the impact of the green revolution, but significant change and progress are now becoming evident in several countries.

Despite these qualifications, however, tremendous progress has been made in increasing cereal production in India, Pakistan, and the Philippines during the past three years. Other countries that are beginning to show significant increases in production include Afghanistan, Ceylon, Indonesia, Iran, Kenya, Malaya, Morocco, Thailand, Tunisia, and Turkey.

Before attempting to evaluate the significance of the green revolution one must establish the point of view of the appraiser. The green revolution has an entirely different meaning to most people in the affluent nations of the privileged world than to those in the developing nations of the forgotten world. In the affluent, industrialized nations giant surpluses of wheat, maize, and sorghum are commonplace; cattle, swine, and poultry are fed and fattened on cereal grains; meat, milk, eggs, fruits, and vegetables are within the economic reach of most of the population; well-balanced diets are more or less automatically achieved, and cereal products constitute only a modest portion of the «daily bread». Consequently, most of the people in such societies have difficulty in comprehending and appreciating the vital significance of providing high-yielding strains of wheat, rice, maize, sorghum, and millet for the people of the developing nations. Understandably then, the majority of the urbanites in the industrialized nations have forgotten the significance of the words they learned as youngsters, «Give us this day our daily bread». They know that food comes from the supermarket, but only a few see beyond to the necessary investments, the toil, struggle, and frustrations on the farms and ranches that provide their daily bread. Since the urbanites have lost their contact with the soil, they take food for granted and fail to appreciate the tremendous efficiency of their farmers and ranchers, who, although constituting only five percent of the labor force in a country such as the United States, produce more than enough food for their nation.

Even worse, urbanites often vociferously criticize their government for attempting to bring into balance the agricultural production of its farmers with the domestic and foreign market demands for farm products, and attempting thereby to provide the consumer an abundant food supply at reasonable cost and also to assure a reasonable return to the farmer and rancher.

Contrasting sharply, in the developing countries represented by India, Pakistan, and most of the countries in Asia and Africa, seventy to eighty percent of the population is engaged in agriculture, mostly at the subsistence level. The land is tired, worn out, depleted of plant nutrients, and often eroded; crop yields have been low, near starvation level, and stagnant for centuries. Hunger prevails, and survival depends largely upon the annual success or failure of the cereal crops. In these nations both undernutrition and malnutrition are widespread and are a constant threat to survival and to the attainment of the genetic potential for mental and physical development. The diet consists primarily of cereals, which provide from seventy to eighty percent of the calories and sixty-five to seventy percent of the protein intake. Animal proteins are so scarce and expensive as to be beyond the economic reach of the vast majority of the population. Although many of these nations were self-sufficient and some were exporters of cereals before the Second World War, they are now net importers, victims of population growth's outrunning agricultural production. There is little possibility in these countries of expanding the cultivated area to cope with the growing demand. The situation worsens as crop yields remain stagnant while human numbers continue to increase at frightening rates.

For the underprivileged billions in the forgotten world, hunger has been a constant companion, and starvation has all too often lurked in the nearby shadows. To millions of these unfortunates, who have long lived in despair, the green revolution seems like a miracle that has generated new hope for the future.

The significance and magnitude of the impact of the so-called green revolution are best illustrated by changes in cereal production in India, Pakistan, and the Philippines. In both India and Pakistan the rapid increase in yields per hectare of wheat has been the major thrust of the green revolution. Increases in rice yield also have played a major role in West Pakistan, but hitherto only a minor role in India. Increases in maize production have played a modest but significant role in expanded cereal production in both India and Pakistan; and increases in rice yields and production have been largely responsible for the change in cereal production up to now in the Philippines, Ceylon, and Indonesia.

The green revolution in India and Pakistan, which is still largely the result of a breakthrough in wheat production, is neither a stroke of luck nor an accident of nature. Its success is based on sound research, the importance of which is not self-evident at first glance. For, behind the scenes, halfway around the world in Mexico, were two decades of aggressive research on wheat that not only enabled Mexico to become self-sufficient with respect to wheat production but also paved the way to rapid increase in its production in other countries. It was in Mexico that the high-yielding Mexican dwarf varieties were designed, bred, and developed. There, also, was developed the new production technology which permits these varieties, when properly cultivated, to express their high genetic grain-yield potential–in general, double or triple that of the best yielders among older, tall-strawed varieties.

There are no miracles in agricultural production. Nor is there such a thing as a miracle variety of wheat, rice, or maize which can serve as an elixir to cure all ills of a stagnant, traditional agriculture. Nevertheless, it is the Mexican dwarf wheat varieties, and their more recent Indian and Pakistani derivatives, that have been the principal catalyst in triggering off the green revolution. It is the unusual breadth of adaption combined with high genetic yield potential, short straw, a strong responsiveness and high efficiency in the use of heavy doses of fertilizers, and a broad spectrum of disease resistance that has made the Mexican dwarf varieties the powerful catalyst that they have become in launching the green revolution. They have caught the farmers' fancy, and during the 1969–1970 crop season, fifty-five percent of the six million hectares sown to wheat in Pakistan and thirty-five percent of the fourteen million hectares in India were sown to Mexican varieties or their derivatives. This rapid increase in wheat production was not based solely on the use of Mexican dwarf varieties; it involved the transfer from Mexico to Pakistan and India of a whole new production technology that enables these varieties to attain their high-yield potential. Perhaps seventy-five percent of the results of research done in Mexico in developing the package of recommended cultural practices, including fertilizer recommendations, were directly applicable in Pakistan and India. As concerns the remaining twenty-five percent, the excellent adaptive research done in India and Pakistan by Indian and Pakistani scientists while the imported seed was being multiplied, provided the necessary information for modifying the Mexican procedures to suit Pakistani and Indian conditions more precisely.

Equally as important as the transfer of the new seed and new technology from Mexico to India and Pakistan was the introduction from Mexico of a crop-production campaign strategy. This strategy harnessed the high grain-yield potential of the new seed and new technology to sound governmental economic policy which would assure the farmer a fair price for his grain, the availability of the necessary inputs–seed, fertilizers, insecticides, weed killers, and machinery – and the credit with which to buy them. Collectively these inputs and strategy became the base from which the green revolution evolved.

Never before in the history of agriculture has a transplantation of high-yielding varieties coupled with an entirely new technology and strategy been achieved on such a massive scale, in so short a period of time, and with such great success. The success of this transplantation is an event of both great scientific and social significance. Its success depended upon good organization of the production program combined with skillful execution by courageous and experienced scientific leaders.

Experimentation with dwarf Mexican varieties was initiated in both India and Pakistan in 1963 and continued in 1964. Results in both countries were highly promising. Consequently, in 1965, 350 and 250 tons of seed of the Mexican dwarf wheat varieties were imported into Pakistan and India, respectively, for wide-scale testing on farms. Again, the results were highly promising, and India reacted by importing eighteen thousand tons during 1966. A year later Pakistan imported forty-two thousand tons. With these importations, the revolution in wheat production got under way in both countries. It was the first time in history that such huge quantities of seed had been imported from distant lands and grown successfully in their new home. These importations saved from three to five years' time in reaping the benefits from the green revolution.

During the past three years, wheat production has risen spectacularly in both countries. Using as a base the pre-green revolution crop year 1964–1965, which produced an all-time record harvest in both countries, the production in Pakistan increased from the 1965 base figure of 4.6 million tons to 6.7, 7.2, and 8.4 millions of tons, respectively, in 1968, 1969, and 1970. West Pakistan became self-sufficient in wheat production for the first time in the 1968 harvest season, two years ahead of our predictions. Indian wheat production has risen from the 1964–1965 pre-green revolution record crop of 12.3 million tons to 16.5, 18.7, and 20.0 million tons during 1968, 1969, and 1970 harvests, respectively. India is approaching self-sufficiency and probably would have attained it by now if rice production had risen more rapidly, because, with a continuing shortage of rice, considerable wheat is being substituted for it.

The introduction into West Pakistan of the high-yielding dwarf rice variety IR 8, developed by the International Rice Research Institute (IRRI) in the Philippines, together with the new technology that makes it highly productive, has also resulted in phenomenal increases in yield and production during the past two years. Unfortunately, this variety has been less well adapted to climatic conditions in the monsoon areas of India and in East Pakistan, and therefore has had only a modest and occasional impact there. Newer varieties which are now being multiplied promise to correct this situation.

The revolution in wheat and rice production in India and Pakistan has not only greatly increased food production, but it also has had many indirect effects on both the farmer and the economy. It is estimated that Indian and Pakistani farmers who are cultivating the new Mexican dwarf wheat varieties under the recommended management practices have increased their net income from thirty-seven dollars per hectare with the local varieties to 162 dollars with the dwarf Mexican varieties. During the past three harvests, a total of 1.4 billion dollars and 640 million dollars have been added to the gross national product (G. N. P.) of India and Pakistan, respectively, from the increase in wheat production above the record 1965 base. The injection of this large increase in purchasing power into the economies has had many effects.

Large numbers of tubewells are being sunk by farmers in both India and Pakistan in order to expand the irrigated area and improve the control of irrigation water. It is estimated that a total of seventy thousand private tube-wells were sunk during the 1969–1970 crop season in India, which brings about 1.4 million hectares of additional land under controlled irrigation, thereby greatly expanding the food production potential. It is estimated that at present less than half of the irrigation potential of India has been developed.

If the high-yielding dwarf wheat and rice varieties are the catalysts that have ignited the green revolution, then chemical fertilizer is the fuel that has powered its forward thrust. The responsiveness of the high-yielding varieties has greatly increased fertilizer consumption. The new varieties not only respond to much heavier dosages of fertilizer than the old ones but are also much more efficient in its use. The old tall-strawed varieties would produce only ten kilos of additional grain for each kilo of nitrogen applied, while the new varieties can produce twenty to twenty-five kilos or more of additional grain per kilo of nitrogen applied. Consumption of nitrogen fertilizer in India has increased from fifty-eight thousand metric tons of nutrients in 1950–1951 to 538 thousand and 1.2 million metric tons in 1964–1965 and 1969–1970 crop cycles, respectively; and about sixty percent of this amount was produced domestically. Phosphate consumption is approximately half that of nitrogen. A large part of the fertilizer currently being used is for wheat. The targeted consumption and domestic production needs of nitrogen for 1973–1974 are three million and two and a half million metric tons, respectively, a fantastic threefold increase in consumption and a fivefold increase in production. These fertilizer targets must be attained if the targeted production of 129 million metric tons of cereal is to be realized.

Mechanization of agriculture is rapidly following the breakthrough in wheat production. Prior to the first big wheat crop in 1968, unsold tractors accumulated at the two factories then in production; at present, prospective purchasers must make written application for them and wait one or two years for delivery. Although five factories, with an output of eighteen thousand units per year, are now producing tractors, thirty-five thousand units were imported in 1969–1970.

The traditional method of threshing by treading out of the grain with bullocks, followed by winnowing, is now inadequate for threshing the increased volume of wheat before the onset of the monsoon rains. Consequently, hundreds of thousands of small threshing machines have been produced and sold by hundreds of small village machine shops during the past three years, thus avoiding the loss of much of the crop after harvest and also providing additional employment in many new small-village industries.

Moreover, mechanization has had another very important indirect effect on the intensification of cereal production. When small mechanical threshers replace bullocks for threshing, the bullocks are released for use in the timely preparation of the land for the next (summer) crop. This need for timely preparation of land is also one of the main reasons for the surge in demand for tractors. Before the adoption of the new wheat and rice varieties, in combination with heavy applications of chemical fertilizer, the time of sowing was relatively unimportant because yields were limited primarily by the low level of available plant nutrients. Most farmers would expect to harvest about one metric ton of wheat during the winter (rabi) season and about one and a half metric tons of rice during the summer (kharif) season, or a total of two and a half metric tons of grain per hectare per year. But by using the high-yielding varieties, fertilizing heavily, sowing at the right time, and managing the fields properly, the same farmer can now harvest five tons of wheat and seven tons of rice per hectare from the same land, a total of twelve metric tons of food grain per hectare per year, as contrasted with the two and a half tons which he obtained with the old varieties and methods. If plantings are not done at the optimum time, however, the yield of wheat may drop to three tons and that of rice to four tons per hectare, a total production of seven tons per year instead of the twelve tons when all operations are proper and timely. A few of the most progressive farmers now use triple cropping, involving wheat– mung beans– rice, or wheat– rice– potato, or three consecutive crops of rice during the same year. By increasing the intensity of cropping, both food production potential and employment are increased. Yields must then be calculated on the basis of kilos per hectare per year rather than on the basis of kilos per hectare per crop.

The increased mechanization in cereal production has tended thus far to increase rather than decrease the employment opportunities for labor, and above all it has helped to reduce drudgery and increase the efficiency of human energy, especially in India.

Millions of farmers who have successfully grown the new wheat, rice, and maize varieties have greatly increased their income. And this has stimulated the rapid growth of agro-industry by increasing the demand for fertilizers, pumps, machinery, and other materials and services.

Farmers in many villages are investing in better storage facilities. In some locations, brick houses are beginning to replace those made of rammed earth. More electricity is being used to light the houses and to drive the motors on the wells. There also has been a rapid increase in demand for consumer goods. The purchase of transistors and radios for use in the villages has increased rapidly, and thereby the government for the first time can effectively reach the remote villages with educational programs. Sewing machines, bicycles, motor scooters, and motorcycles are coming to the villages, and truck and bus service between villages is improving.

The green revolution has forced the Indian government to improve many of its public services. Although there was an extreme shortage of storage space for the first record-breaking wheat crop in 1968, the government improvised satisfactorily and very little grain was lost. During the past two years, stimulated in part by criticism by farmers and the press, warehouse capacity has been expanded greatly to provide adequate storage for the increasing grain production. The villages are demanding better roads, better public transportation, and better schools; and they are beginning to get them. Thus the divorce between intellect and labor, which the great Indian leader Mahatma Gandhi over forty years ago regarded as the bane of India's agriculture, is coming to an end.

The changes wrought by the green revolution, which I have illustrated by the vast improvement of wheat production in India, have had similar effects in West Pakistan, Ceylon, the Philippines, and Thailand, although the effects in different countries were produced by changes in different crops or combinations of crops.

Although the contributions of the green revolution to increased food production are considerable and highly significant, they are nonetheless modest in comparison with the magnitude of present global needs. The greatest obvious achievements are the rapid increase in cereal production during the past three years and the generation of a climate of confidence in the developing nations with regard to their capabilities of achieving food self-sufficiency. Perhaps even more significant, however, is the change in organizations and attitudes which has accompanied the increases in cereal production.

The All-India Coordinated Wheat Improvement Program, which is largely responsible for the wheat revolution in India, has developed one of the most extensive and widely diversified wheat research programs in the world. Its success has generated confidence, a sense of purpose, and determination. The current agronomic research on wheat in India equals the best in the world. The breeding program is huge, diversified, and aggressive; already it has produced several varieties which surpass those originally introduced from Mexico in 1965. The first group of new Indian varieties, already in extensive commercial production, were derived from selections made in India from partially selected materials received from Mexico. A second group of varieties, now being multiplied, are selections from crosses made in India between Indian and Mexican varieties. The rapidity of creation and distribution of these new varieties has already diversified the type of resistance to diseases and therefore minimizes the menace of destructive disease epidemics if and when changes occur in parasitic races of the pathogens.

Contrary to a widespread and erroneous opinion, the original dwarf wheats imported from Mexico definitely carried a wider spectrum of disease resistance than the local Indian types that they replaced. But the newer Indian varieties are even better in resistance and of a different genetic type than the original introductions. This greater diversity reduces the danger from disease epidemics but cannot completely eliminate the dangers of disease epidemics, as has become vividly evident from the unexpected and destructive epidemic of southern leaf blight of maize over vast areas of the U.S.A. during the summer of 1970. The only protection against such epidemics, in all countries, is through resistant varieties developed by an intelligent, persistent, and diversified breeding program, such as that being currently carried on in India, coupled with a broad disease-surveillance system and a sound plant pathology program to support the breeding program. From such a program a constant flow of new high-yielding disease-resistant varieties can be developed to checkmate any important changes in the pathogens. The Indian program is also developing competence in research on the biochemical, industrial, and nutritional properties of wheat.

Perhaps the most important contribution of all is that the methods and tactics used so successfully in making the production breakthrough in wheat, first in Mexico and now in India and Pakistan, can serve as a model for production programs with many other crops and in many other countries.

West Pakistan has already used the wheat model to revolutionize its rice production. Although the Indian rice program has not yet achieved a nationwide breakthrough in production, rapid progress is now being made in several areas, and it seems probable that the area sown to the new seed and technology will be large enough to produce a strong impact on national production within another year. Varieties and new technology are also available for launching effective campaigns to increase the production of sorghum, millet, barley, soybeans, and cotton in many developing countries of Asia, Africa, and Latin America. What is still needed is the will and commitment of governments to support national production campaigns, both politically and financially, and the services of a few competent and dedicated agricultural scientists as leaders.

The quality of scientific leadership is certainly a vital factor in the success of any production campaign. It is deplorable but true that many agricultural scientists in some advanced countries have renounced their allegiance to agriculture for reasons of expediency and presumed prestige. And some institutions have furnished them a curtain behind which to hide. Some educational and research institutions have even restricted the amount of basic research that can be done under the aegis of its agricultural departments, however basic these researches may be to progress in increasing and insuring food production. Let the individuals live with their own motivations; let them serve science and themselves if they wish. But the institutions have the moral obligation to serve agriculture and society also; and to discharge that obligation honorably, they must try to help educate scientists and scientific leaders whose primary motivation is to serve humanity.

I want to reiterate emphatically that there now are available materials and techniques of great potential value for expanding the green revolution into additional fields of agriculture. But to convert these potential values into actual values requires scientific and organizational leadership. Where are those leaders? Where are the leaders who have the necessary scientific competence, the vision, the common sense, the social consciousness, the qualities of leadership, and the persistent determination to convert the potential benefactions into real benefactions for mankind in general and for the hungry in particular? There are not enough of them now; therefore we must try to identify and develop them in our educational systems and we must utilize them in our campaigns for food production. We need them and need them badly, for it is tragic to let potential values languish for want of leadership in capitalizing the potential. This is not theory; this is reality, as illustrated by the fact that the leadership has been the determining factor in the relative success of parallel but different crop production programs within the same country.

But let no one think that we can relax our efforts in research. All successful action programs must be preceded and accompanied by research. It has been pointed out that the rapid change in wheat production in both India and Pakistan was in part made possible by two decades of research in Mexico. How did this come about?

In 1943, several years before the establishment of the Food and Agriculture Organization (FAO) of the United Nations, a cooperative agricultural research and training program was launched in Mexico. This was a pioneer cooperative project between the Mexican Ministry of Agriculture and the Rockefeller Foundation, initiated at the request of the Mexican government for assistance in increasing the production of maize, wheat, and beans.

At that time Mexico was importing more than fifty percent of the wheat that it consumed, as well as a considerable percentage of its maize. Wheat yields were low and static, with a national average yield of 750 kilos per hectare, even though most of the wheat was grown on irrigated land. This situation was very similar to that in India and Pakistan before the recent advent of the green revolution. Mexican soils were impoverished and chemical fertilizer virtually unknown.

Mexico's need was urgent, and so a simple research program was started to increase production. The philosophy of the Rockefeller Foundation was «to help Mexico to help itself» in solving its food production problems, and in the process work itself out of a job. I have had the privilege and good fortune to have been associated with the wheat program almost from the beginning, and have remained a part of it for the past twenty-six years.

From the outset all factors limiting wheat production were studied; consequently, there were interdisciplinary researches between genetics and plant breeding, agronomy, soil fertility, plant pathology, and entomology. Cereal chemistry and biochemistry were added later.

After preliminary work in 1943, plant breeders, soil scientists, plant pathologists, and entomologists working as a team, began a concentrated attack on the various aspects of wheat production in 1944.

An in-service (intern) training component was added to the research program to train a new generation of Mexican scientists while they were assisting with the development of the research program. Provision was also made for fellowships to enable the most promising of these young scientists to study abroad for advanced degrees, hopefully in preparation for positions of leadership in Mexican agriculture.

Research from the outset was production-oriented and restricted to that which was relevant to increasing wheat production. Researches in pursuit of irrelevant academic butterflies were discouraged, both because of the acute shortage of scientific manpower and because of the need to have data and materials available as soon as possible for use in the production program.

To accelerate progress in varietal development, two generations of all segregating materials were grown each year. One generation was sown close to sea level in Sonora at twenty-eight degrees north latitude in the fall when the days were progressively shorter; the second was sown near Toluca, at eighteen degrees latitude and 2,500 meters above sea level during the summer when days were progressively longer. Through the use of this technique, we developed high-yielding, day-length-insensitive varieties with a wide range of ecologic adaption and a broad spectrum of disease resistance – a new combination of uniquely valuable characters in wheat varieties.

These characters were valuable in increasing wheat production in Mexico and neighboring countries, but were to prove even more valuable twenty years later when the Mexican varieties were introduced into Pakistan and India. Without this combination of characters the successful transplantation of the Mexican varieties into Pakistan and India would have been impossible; and the advent of the green revolution would almost certainly have been delayed many years.

In Mexico, as soon as significant improvements were made by research, whether in varieties, fertilizer recommendations, or cultural practices, they were taken to farms and incorporated into the production programs. We never waited for perfection in varieties or methods but used the best available each year and modified them as further improvement came to hand. This simple principle is too often disregarded by scientific perfectionists who spend a lifetime searching for the unattainable in biological perfection, and consequently during a lifetime of frustration contribute nothing to increasing food production.

Farm demonstrations of new varieties and technology were made by the research scientists who had developed them. Indeed, the revolution in wheat production in Mexico was accomplished before the extension service came into being. This forced the research scientists themselves to consider the obstacles to production that confronted the farmers. The same philosophy and tactic were used effectively to bring researchers in contact with the farmers' problems in the early years of the wheat improvement programs in India and West Pakistan. Later, however, the extension services were brought into the production programs in both countries.

Mexican wheat yields began to climb by 1948 and have continued their upward trend to the present time. During the past twenty-six years, the national average has risen from 750 kilos per hectare to only slightly less than 3,000 kilos during the past harvest, approximately a fourfold increase. During the same period, total production has increased sevenfold. Mexico became self-sufficient in wheat production for the first time in 1956 and has remained self-sufficient since. This «quiet revolution» in wheat production in Mexico became the progenitor of the green revolution in India and Pakistan a decade later.

As the use of fertilizer increased and yields climbed to four and a half thousand kilos per hectare, lodging (falling over of the plant) began to limit further increases in yields. A search was therefore made among wheats from different areas of the world to locate a suitable source of genetic dwarfness to overcome this barrier. Norin 10, an extremely dwarf wheat from Japan, proved to be a suitable source. Through a series of crosses and recrosses begun in 1954, dwarfness was incorporated into the superior, new-combination Mexican types, finally giving rise to a group of so-called dwarf Mexican wheat varieties. With this new development, the potential yield of the new varieties, under ideal conditions, increased from the previous high of four and a half thousand kilos per hectare to nine thousand kilos per hectare. The dwarf Mexican wheats were first distributed in Mexico in 1961, and the best farmers began to harvest five, six, seven, and even eight tons more per hectare, and within seven years the national average yields doubled. It was these same dwarf Mexican wheats from the quiet revolution that served as catalysts to trigger off the green revolution in India and Pakistan.

From the outset the Mexican Agricultural Program was watched with interest by many other countries. As progress became evident, the Rockefeller Foundation was besieged by requests from many countries for assistance in agricultural improvement programs. The Cooperative Mexican Agricultural Program had become a model. The Cooperative Colombian Agricultural Program, devoted largely to maize, wheat, potatoes, forage, and livestock, was established in 1950. Similarly, the Cooperative Chilean Agricultural Program was established in 1955 to work on wheat and forage. The Cooperative Indian Agricultural Program was established in 1956 to improve maize, sorghum, and millet production and to assist in the development of postgraduate agricultural education. Each of these programs subsequently played an important role in improving agricultural production and education in different parts of the world.

Meanwhile, back in Mexico, the program that had originally been confined to maize, wheat, and beans, and soon thereafter potatoes, was expanded to include many other crops. Larger numbers of young Mexican scientists were added to the research and training programs. Progress in research was generally good, and the training program also bore fruit. Between the years 1943–1963, a total of 550 interns participated in the overall agricultural research and training programs, of whom about 200 received a Master of Science degree and about thirty the Doctor of Philosophy degree while on fellowships for study abroad. With this corps of trained scientists a new National Institute of Agricultural Research was born in 1961. The Rockefeller Foundation «had worked itself out of a job», which was one of its original objectives.

The Mexican experience indicated that one of the greatest obstacles to the improvement of agriculture in the developing countries is the scarcity of trained people. This experience indicated clearly that training is a slow process. Where no corps of trained scientists exists, as was the case in Mexico twenty-seven years ago and remains the case in many countries of Asia, Africa, and Latin America today, it requires eighteen to twenty-five years to develop enough competent research scientists and educators to meet a country's needs. So great is the urgency of the food shortage in many underdeveloped and emerging countries that there is not enough time to develop an adequate corps of scientists before attacking food production problems. A shortcut and organizational change had to be invented to meet the needs. And so was born the first truly international research and training institute, the International Rice Research Institute (IRRI) at Los Baños, the

Philippines, in 1960, to work exclusively on the regionally all-important but too-long-neglected rice crop. The institute was jointly financed by the Ford and Rockefeller Foundations in collaboration with the government of the Philippines.

The research activities on wheat, maize, and potatoes in Mexico were informally internationalized in 1959 and organized as a second international center in 1963. This International Center for Maize and Wheat Improvement (CIMMYT) is supported also by the Ford and Rockefeller Foundations in collaboration with the government of Mexico. More recently, additional financial support has been provided by the U.S. Agency for International Development (U.S.AID), United Nations Development Program (UNDP), and the Inter-American Development Bank (BID).

A third center, the International Center of Tropical Agriculture (CIAT) in Colombia, and the International Institute of Tropical Agriculture (IITA) in Nigeria, the most recent, have been established to study problems and stimulate production of certain tropical crops and animal species, as well as to help train scientific specialists. CIAT is financed by the Ford, Rockefeller, and W. K. Kellogg Foundations in cooperation with the government of Colombia. The Ford and Rockefeller Foundations and the Canadian International Development Agency (CIDA) are supporting IITA in collaboration with the government of Nigeria.

These four international institutes represent a significant but modest start toward the construction of a worldwide network of international, national, and local research and training centers. This network will help solve problems and disseminate the benefits of science to all mankind in the shortest possible time and at minimum cost.

The impact of such an integrated approach is already evident in the green revolution. New varieties and the new technologies that make them highly productive have been the thrust behind the green revolution. In the Philippines, Ceylon, Malaysia, and West Pakistan, it was IR8 rice, developed at the International Rice Research Institute. The dwarf Mexican wheats, partly produced by CIMMYT, have provided the thrust in India and Pakistan, and this is now spreading to Turkey, Afghanistan, Iran, Morocco, and Tunisia. Contributing equally, or perhaps even more, to the evolution of the green revolution was the talented supporting leadership that has been provided by the centers to the national programs through temporary assignments of mature scientists skilled in organizing crop production programs to assist in the development of the national production campaigns.

The international centers were developed to supplement national agricultural research, production, and training programs, not to replace them. The centers are but one link in the worldwide network of organizations attacking basic food-crop production problems on a worldwide, regional, national, and local level. The backbone of this network is now and must continue to be the national programs. These must be given greater financial support and strengthened staffwise to meet the challenge of rapidly expanding food needs for the future.

The international centers, however, are in a unique position to assist the national programs. They are independent, nonpolitical international organizations, which, although originally funded by private foundations, now receive support from many diverse sources. Their scientific staffs are also international and comprise outstanding scientists representing the various scientific disciplines affecting crop production. Included on their staffs are a number of crop production experts who have the scientific competence and broad experience to assist national agencies in organizing and launching crop production programs.

The centers collaborate not only with the national agencies from many different countries but also with other international organizations such as the Food and Agriculture Organization (FAO) of the United Nations, the United Nations Development Program (UNDP), and international development banks. Each year the centers have been collaborating with an increasing number of countries of all political spectra.

I am convinced that the international agricultural research institutes are developing a bond of understanding among nations, based upon the common need for increasing food production. We must all strive to strengthen this bond in the spirit of Alfred Nobel «to promote brotherhood among the nations».

The international centers are uniquely equipped to do fundamental, long-time researches of worldwide importance. For example, the opportunity for plant breeders, pathologists, and entomologists to operate on a worldwide basis permits them to develop well-conceived, diverse gene pools of the important crop species. The final crop varieties are not currently generally selected at the centers but sent to collaborators in national programs in many parts of the world, who in turn make the selections that best suit their needs; and many eventually become commercial varieties. Similarly, the centers prepare a series of international crop yield tests, which include representatives of the best commercial varieties from the world and a few of the most promising experimental lines from collaborators. These are sent to collaborators in thirty-five countries for growing at eighty locations. The data from collaborators are returned to CIMMYT for summarizing and for subsequent distribution to scientists in all parts of the world. The data obtained on yield, adaption, disease, and insect resistance in one year in such tests are often more meaningful and valuable to scientists engaged in crop research and production programs than data obtained by independent testing at one location for a period of ten or fifteen years.

The international centers also are in a unique position to contribute to practical or internship type of training in all of the scientific disciplines affecting crop production. This type of training is particularly valuable for young scientists from the developing countries because it prepares them for initiating research work upon return to their native country and will also be of value if they subsequently continue their education at the graduate level.

In summarizing the accomplishments of the green revolution during the past three years, I wish to restate that the increase in cereal production, rice, maize, and wheat, especially in wheat, has been spectacular and highly significant to the welfare of millions of human beings. It is still modest in terms of total needs. Recalling that fifty percent of the present world population is undernourished and that an even larger percentage, perhaps sixty-five percent, is malnourished, no room is left for complacency. It is not enough to prevent the currently bad situation from getting worse as population increases. Our aim must be to produce enough food to eradicate all present hunger while at the same time striving to correct malnutrition. To eliminate hunger now in the developing nations, we would need to expand world cereal production by thirty percent. If it were, however, as simple as increasing the total world production by thirty percent, regardless of where the production is to be expanded, it could be accomplished rather rapidly by expanding it in the United States, Canada, Australia, Argentina, and Russia. But this would not necessarily solve the hunger problem of the developing world because their weak economies will not permit them to expand their food imports by thirty percent. Worse still, even if present production could be expanded rapidly by thirty percent in the developing countries–which I believe is possible based on recent progress of the green revolution–so as theoretically to eliminate hunger, the hunger problem as it now exists still would not be solved. There remains the unsolved social-economic problem of finding effective ways to distribute the needed additional food to the vast underprivileged masses who have little or no purchasing power. This is still the great unsolved problem with which the economists, sociologists, and political leaders must now come to grips.

I am convinced that if all policymakers would take sufficient interest in population control and in aggressively employing and exploiting agricultural development as a potent instrument of agrarian prosperity and economic advancement, many of the social ills of the present day could soon become problems of the past. The tropics and subtropics have abundant sunlight and other great biological assets, and it will be criminal to delay further the conversion of these assets into wealth meaningful to the poor and hungry.

Some critics have said that the green revolution has created more problems than it has solved. This I cannot accept, for I believe it is far better for mankind to be struggling with new problems caused by abundance rather than with the old problem of famine. Certainly, loyalty to the status quo in food production–when being pressured by population growth–cannot break the chains that have bound the peasant to poverty and hunger. One must ask: Is it just to criticize the green revolution, with its recognized accomplishments, for failure to correct all the social-economic ills of the world that have accumulated from the days of Adam and Eve up to the present? Change we must, or we will perish as a species, just as did the dinosaurs in the late Cretaceous.

The green revolution is a change in the right direction, but it has not transformed the world into Utopia. None are more keenly aware of its limitations than those who started it and fought for its success. But there has been solid accomplishment, as I have already shown by concrete examples. I have also tried to indicate the various opportunities for capitalizing more fully on the new materials that were produced and the new methods that were devised. And, above all, I cannot emphasize too strongly the fact that further progress depends on intelligent, integrated, and persistent effort by government leaders, statesmen, tradesmen, scientists, educators, and communication agencies, including the press, radio, and television.

But progress is continuous, and we can and must make continuous progress. Better varieties of wheat and other cereals with not only higher yield potential but also with higher content of protein are already in the process of creation.

We need also to explore more fully the feasibility of producing new man-made cereal species with greater production potential and better nutritional quality than those now in existence. Triticale, a man-made species, derived from a cross between wheat and rye, now shows promise of becoming such a crop.

During the past six years, the International Corn and Wheat Center in Mexico, cooperating with the University of Manitoba, has developed a large breeding program to improve Triticale. Within the past three years we have developed highly fertile lines, and the results up to the present indicate the possibility of combining the desirable characteristics now present in different lines into a single line, thereby creating a new kind of cereal that is superior to wheat in productivity and nutritional quality.

The rapid progress achieved in Triticale improvement suggests the desirability of initiating basic studies to determine the feasibility of developing other cereal species from wide crosses between different existing species or their wild relatives. Recent improvements in individual cell, tissue and embryo-culture techniques, in the development of culture media with additions of hormones and nutrients that foster cell and tissue differentiations, in achieving hybridization between somatic cells, and in the methods of inducing polyploidy and mutations, offer many fascinating possibilities of achieving crosses between species that were formerly uncrossable. Even the possibility of using protoplasmic and cell hybridization, followed by manipulation to promote cell differentiation for plant improvement, appears to be nearer.

I propose therefore that a bold program of wide crosses be initiated to improve both cereals and legumes (pulses). It should include attempts to make numerous intergeneric crosses among cereals, employing all of the modern techniques to consummate fertilization, and propagate the hybrids. If a series of new combinations can be made and doubled, as, for example, between maize and sorghum, wheat and barley, or wheat and rice, it would open the door to the possibilities for vast subsequent improvement by conventional methods.

Unfortunately, all cereals are deficient in one or more of the essential amino acids, especially lysine, which is essential for normal body growth and for the maintenance of health. Protein malnutrition is widespread, especially among children, and many of its victims die or are maimed both physically and mentally for life.

Although food supplements can alleviate this situation, the development of high-yielding varieties of cereal grains that have high levels of protein and better amino acid balance would be the ideal solution, since this would not involve added expense or special educational efforts, and there are good possibilities of producing them. The now famous opaque-2 gene in maize doubles the production of the amino acid lysine which is essential to growth and health in man and many other animals. Similarly, an Ethiopian strain of barley, and some lines of Triticale have genes for extraordinary production of essential nutrient materials. Plant breeders are trying to combine such genes with the best genes now available for productivity and other desirable characters, thus increasing not only the tonnage of food, but also its essential nutrient quality. As we are now striving to emancipate ourselves from dependence on artificial food supplements, I have a dream that we can like-wise emancipate ourselves to some extent from our dependence on artificial nutrients for the cereal plants themselves, thus lightening the financial burden that now oppresses the small farmer and handicaps his efforts to participate fully in the new technologies.

In my dream I see green, vigorous, high-yielding fields of wheat, rice, maize, sorghums, and millets, which are obtaining, free of expense, 100 kilo-grams of nitrogen per hectare from nodule-forming, nitrogen-fixing bacteria. These mutant strains of *Rhizobium cerealis* were developed in 1990 by a massive mutation breeding program with strains of *Rhizobium* sp. obtained from roots of legumes and other nodule-bearing plants. This scientific discovery has revolutionized agricultural production for the hun-dreds of millions of humble farmers throughout the world; for they now receive much of the needed fertilizer for their crops directly from these little wondrous microbes that are taking nitrogen from the air and fixing it without cost in the roots of cereals, from which it is transformed into grain...

Then I wake up and become disillusioned to find that mutation genetics programs are still engaged mostly in such minutiae as putting beards on wheat plants and taking off the hairs.

If we are to capitalize fully on the past biological accomplishments and realize the prospective accomplishments, as exemplified in my dream, there must be far greater investments in research and education in the future than in the past.

Few investments, if any, can match the economic and social returns from the wheat research in Mexico. The investment from 1943 to 1964 was estimated to have yielded an annual return of 750 percent. This study was made prior to the full impact of dwarf wheats on the national production. If the benefits were calculated now, with the inclusion of the returns from the increased wheat production in Pakistan, India, and other Asian and African countries, they would be fantastically high.

Nevertheless, vast sums are now being spent in all countries, developed and developing, on armaments and new nuclear and other lethal weapons, while pitifully small sums are being spent on agricultural research and education designed to sustain and humanize life rather than to degrade and destroy it.

The green revolution has won a temporary success in man's war against hunger and deprivation; it has given man a breathing space. If fully implemented, the revolution can provide sufficient food for sustenance during the next three decades. But the frightening power of human reproduction must also be curbed; otherwise the success of the green revolution will be ephemeral only.

Most people still fail to comprehend the magnitude and menace of the «Population Monster». In the beginning there were but two, Adam and Eve. When they appeared on this earth is still questionable. By the time of Christ, world population had probably reached 250 million. But between then and now, population has grown to 3.5 billion. Growth has been especially fast since the advent of modern medicine. If it continues to increase at the estimated present rate of two percent a year, the world population will reach 6.5 billion by the year 2000. Currently, with each second, or tick of the clock, about 2.2 additional people are added to the world population. The rhythm of increase will accelerate to 2.7, 3.3, and 4.0 for each tick of the clock by 1980, 1990, and 2000, respectively, unless man becomes more realistic and preoccupied about this impending doom. The ticktock of the clock will continually grow louder and more menacing each decade. Where will it all end?

Malthus signaled the danger a century and a half ago. But he emphasized principally the danger that population would increase faster than food supplies. In his time he could not foresee the tremendous increase in man's food production potential. Nor could he have foreseen the disturbing and destructive physical and mental consequences of the grotesque concentration of human beings into the poisoned and clangorous environment of pathologically hypertrophied megalopoles. Can human beings endure the strain? Abnormal stresses and strains tend to accentuate man's animal instincts and provoke irrational and socially disruptive behavior among the less stable individuals in the maddening crowd.

We must recognize the fact that adequate food is only the first requisite for life. For a decent and humane life we must also provide an opportunity for good education, remunerative employment, comfortable housing, good clothing, and effective and compassionate medical care. Unless we can do this, man may degenerate sooner from environmental diseases than from hunger.

And yet, I am optimistic for the future of mankind, for in all biological populations there are innate devices to adjust population growth to the carrying capacity of the environment. Undoubtedly, some such device exists in man, presumably *Homo sapiens*, but so far it has not asserted itself to bring into balance population growth and the carrying capacity of the environment on a worldwide scale. It would be disastrous for the species to continue to increase our human numbers madly until such innate devices take over. It is a test of the validity of *sapiens* as a species epithet.

Since man is potentially a rational being, however, I am confident that within the next two decades he will recognize the self-destructive course he steers along the road of irresponsible population growth and will adjust the growth rate to levels which will permit a decent standard of living for all mankind. If man is wise enough to make this decision and if all nations abandon their idolatry of Ares, Mars, and Thor, then Mankind itself should be the recipient of a Nobel Peace Prize which is «to be awarded to the person who has done most to promote brotherhood among the nations».

Then, by developing and applying the scientific and technological skills of the twentieth century for «the well-being of mankind throughout the world», he may still see Isaiah's prophesies come true: «... And the desert shall rejoice, and blossom as the rose... And the parched ground shall become a pool, and the thirsty land springs of water...»[1]

And may these words come true!

1. Isaiah 35:1, 7.

Biography

A central figure in the «green revolution», Norman Ernest Borlaug (March 25, 1914–   ) was born on a farm near Cresco, Iowa, to Henry and Clara Borlaug. For the past twenty-seven years he has collaborated with Mexican scientists on problems of wheat improvement; for the last ten or so of those years he has also collaborated with scientists from other parts of the world, especially from India and Pakistan, in adapting the new wheats to new lands and in gaining acceptance for their production. An eclectic, pragmatic, goal-oriented scientist, he accepts and discards methods or results in a constant search for more fruitful and effective ones, while at the same time avoiding the pursuit of what he calls «academic butterflies». A vigorous man who can perform prodigies of manual labor in the fields, he brings to his work the body and competitive spirit of the trained athlete, which indeed he was in his high school and college days.

After completing his primary and secondary education in Cresco, Borlaug enrolled in the University of Minnesota where he studied forestry. Immediately before and immediately after receiving his Bachelor of Science degree in 1937, he worked for the U. S. Forestry Service at stations in Massachusetts and Idaho. Returning to the University of Minnesota to study plant pathology, he received the master's degree in 1939 and the doctorate in 1942.

From 1942 to 1944, he was a microbiologist on the staff of the du Pont de Nemours Foundation where he was in charge of research on industrial and agricultural bactericides, fungicides, and preservatives.

In 1944 he accepted an appointment as geneticist and plant pathologist assigned the task of organizing and directing the Cooperative Wheat Research and Production Program in Mexico. This program, a joint undertaking by the Mexican government and the Rockefeller Foundation, involved scientific research in genetics, plant breeding, plant pathology, entomology, agronomy, soil science, and cereal technology. Within twenty years he was spectacularly successful in finding a high-yielding short-strawed, disease-resistant wheat.

To his scientific goal he soon added that of the practical humanitarian:

arranging to put the new cereal strains into extensive production in order to feed the hungry people of the world–and thus providing, as he says, «a temporary success in man's war against hunger and deprivation», a breathing space in which to deal with the «Population Monster» and the subsequent environmental and social ills that too often lead to conflict between men and between nations. Statistics on the vast acreage planted with the new wheat and on the revolutionary yields harvested in Mexico, India, and Pakistan are given in the presentation speech by Mrs. Lionaes and in the Nobel lecture by Dr. Borlaug. Well advanced, also, is use of the new wheat in six Latin American countries, six in the Near and Middle East, several in Africa.

When the Rockefeller and Ford Foundations in cooperation with the Mexican government established the International Maize and Wheat Improvement Center (CIMMYT), an autonomous international research and training institute having an international board of trustees and staff, Borlaug was made director of its International Wheat Improvement Program. In this capacity he has been able to realize more fully a third objective, that of training young scientists in research and production methods. From his earliest days in Mexico he has, to be sure, carried on an intern program, but with the establishment of the Center, he has been able to reach out internationally. In the last seven years some 140 young scientists from sixteen or so countries (the figures constantly move upward) have studied and worked at the Center.

Dr. Borlaug is presently participating in extensive experimentation with Triticale, a man-made species of grain derived from a cross between wheat and rye that shows promise of being superior to either wheat or rye in productivity and nutritional quality.

In addition to the Nobel Peace Prize, Dr. Borlaug has received extensive recognition from universities and organizations in six countries: Canada, India, Mexico, Norway, Pakistan, the United States. In 1968 he received an especially satisfying tribute when the people of Ciudad Obregón, Sonora, Mexico, in whose area he did some of his first experimenting, named a street in his honor.

Selected Bibliography

Borlaug, Norman E., «The Impact of Agricultural Research on Mexican Wheat Production», *Transactions of the New York Academy of Science*, 20 (1958) 278–295.

Borlaug, Norman E., «Mexican Wheat Production and Its Role in the Epidemiology of Stem Rust in North America», *Phytopathology*, 44 (1954) 398–404.

Borlaug, Norman E., *Wheat Breeding and Its Impact on World Food Supply*. Public lecture at the Third International Wheat Genetics Symposium, August 5–9, 1968. Canberra, Australia, Australian Academy of Science, 1968.

Borlaug, Norman E., «Wheat, Rust, and People», *Phytopathology*, 55 (1965) 1088–1098.

Borlaug, Norman E., and others, «A Green Revolution Yields a Golden Harvest», *Columbia Journal of World Business*, 4 (September–October, 1969) 9–19.

Brown, Lester R., «The Agricultural Revolution in Asia», *Foreign Affairs*, 46 (July, 1968) 688–698.

Brown, Lester R., *Seeds of Change: The Green Revolution and Development in the 1970's*. New York, Praeger, 1970. Contains a bibliography.

Freeman, Orville, *World without Hunger*. New York, Praeger, 1968.

The Green Revolution: A Symposium on Science and Foreign Policy. Proceedings before the Subcommittee on National Security Policy and Scientific Developments of the Committee on Foreign Affairs, House of Representatives, 91st Congress, First Session, December 5, 1969 (#38-612). Washington, D.C., U.S. Government Printing Office, 1970.

Hardin, Clifford M., ed., *Overcoming World Hunger*. Englewood Cliffs, N.J., Prentice-Hall, 1969.

Johnson, D(avid) Gale, *The Struggle against World Hunger*. New York, Foreign Policy Association, 1967.

Ladejinsky, Wolf, «Ironies of India's Green Revolution», *Foreign Affairs*, 48 (July, 1970) 758–768.

Myrdal, Gunnar, *The Challenge of World Poverty: A World Anti-Poverty Program in Outline*, chap. 4, «Agriculture», pp. 78–138. New York, Pantheon Books, 1970.

Paarlberg, Don, *Norman Borlaug: Hunger Fighter*. Foreign Economic Development Service, U.S. Department of Agriculture, cooperating with the U.S. Agency for International Development (PA 969). Washington, D.C., U.S. Government Printing Office, 1970.

«Statement to the Press from Dr. J. George Harrar, President of the Rockefeller Foundation.» New York, The Rockefeller Foundation, October 21, 1970.

«U.S. Agronomist Gets Nobel Peace Prize», the *New York Times* (October 22, 1970) 1.

Wharton, Clifton R., Jr., «The Green Revolution: Cornucopia or Pandora's Box?» *Foreign Affairs*, 47 (April, 1969) 464–476.

Name Index

Index of Biographies

Appendix A

Awards and other annual actions by the Norwegian Nobel Committee (1901–1970)

1901   Jean Henri Dunant (1828–1910), *Switzerland*; and Frédéric Passy (1822–1912), *France*

1902   Élie Ducommun (1833–1906), *Switzerland*; and Charles Albert Gobat (1843–1914), *Switzerland*

1903   William Randal Cremer (1828–1908), *Great Britain*

1904   The Institute of International Law (1873–   )

1905   Bertha von Suttner (1843–1914), *Austria*

1906   Theodore Roosevelt (1858–1919), *United States*

1907   Ernesto Teodoro Moneta (1833–1918), *Italy*; and Louis Renault (1843–1918), *France*

1908   Klas Pontus Arnoldson (1844–1916), *Sweden*; and Fredrik Bajer (1837–1922), *Denmark*

1909   Auguste Marie François Beernaert (1829–1912), *Belgium*; and Paul Henri Benjamin Balluet, Baron d'Estournelles de Constant de Rebecque (1852–1924), *France*

1910   The Permanent International Peace Bureau (1891–   )

1911   Tobias Michael Carel Asser (1838–1913), *The Netherlands*; and Alfred Hermann Fried (1864–1921), *Austria*

1912   The Prize was reserved in that year and in 1913 was awarded to: Elihu Root (1845–1937), *United States*

1913   Henri Marie La Fontaine (1854–1943), *Belgium*

1914   The Prize was reserved in that year and in 1915 the prize money was allocated to the Special Funds of the Committee.

1915   The Prize was reserved in that year and in 1916 the prize money was allocated to the Special Funds of the Committee.

1916   The Prize was reserved in that year and in 1917 the prize money was allocated to the Special Funds of the Committee.

1917   The International Committee of the Red Cross (1863–   )

1918   The Prize was reserved in that year and in 1919 the prize money was allocated to the Special Funds of the Committee.

1919 The Prize was reserved in that year and in 1920 was awarded to: Thomas Woodrow Wilson (1856–1924), *United States*

1920 Léon Victor Auguste Bourgeois (1851–1925), *France*

1921 Karl Hjalmar Branting (1860–1925), *Sweden*; and Christian Lous Lange (1869–1938), *Norway*

1922 Fridtjof Nansen (1861–1930), *Norway*

1923 The Prize was reserved in that year and in 1924 the prize money was allocated to the Special Funds of the Committee.

1924 The Prize was reserved in that year and in 1925 the prize money was allocated to the Special Funds of the Committee.

1925 The Prize was reserved in that year and in 1926 was awarded to: Austen Joseph Chamberlain (1863–1937), *Great Britain*; and Charles Gates Dawes (1865–1951), *United States*

1926 Aristide Briand (1862–1932), *France*; and Gustav Stresemann (1878–1929), *Germany*

1927 Ferdinand Édouard Buisson (1841–1932), *France*; and Ludwig Quidde (1858–1941), *Germany*

1928 The Prize was reserved in that year and in 1929 the prize money was allocated to the Special Funds of the Committee.

1929 The Prize was reserved in that year and in 1930 was awarded to: Frank Billings Kellogg (1856–1937), *United States*

1930 Lars Olof Jonathan [Nathan] Söderblom (1866–1931), *Sweden*

1931 Jane Addams (1860–1935), *United States;* and Nicholas Murray Butler (1862–1947), *United States*

1932 The Prize was reserved in that year and in 1933 the prize money was allocated to the Special Funds of the Committee.

1933 The Prize was reserved in that year and in 1934 was awarded to: Norman Angell (1872–1967), *Great Britain*

1934 Arthur Henderson (1863–1935), *Great Britain*

1935 The Prize was reserved in that year and in 1936 was awarded to: Carl von Ossietzky (1889–1938), *Germany*

1936 Carlos Saavedra Lamas (1878–1959), *Argentina*

1937 Edgar Algernon Robert Cecil, Viscount Cecil of Chelwood (1864–1958), *Great Britain*

1938 The Nansen International Office for Refugees (1930–1938)

1939 The Prize was reserved in that year and again in 1940; in 1941 it was suspended and the prize money allocated to the Main Fund of the Nobel Foundation.

1940   The Prize was reserved in that year; in 1941 it was suspended and the prize money allocated to the Main Fund of the Nobel Foundation.

1941   The Prize was suspended in that year and the prize money allocated to the Main Fund of the Nobel Foundation.

1942   The Prize was suspended in that year and the prize money allocated to the Main Fund of the Nobel Foundation.

1943   The Prize was suspended in that year and two-thirds of the prize money allocated to the Special Funds of the Committee and one-third to the Main Fund of the Nobel Foundation.

1944   After the Norwegian Nobel Committee ceased to function in 1944, the Board of Directors of the Nobel Foundation reserved the prize for that year; in 1945 the reconstituted Committee awarded it to: The International Committee of the Red Cross (1863–   )

1945   Cordell Hull (1871–1955), *United States*

1946   Emily Greene Balch (1867–1961), *United States*; and John Raleigh Mott (1865–1955), *United States*

1947   The Friends Service Council (1927–   ), *Great Britain* and *Ireland*; and The American Friends Service Committee (1917–   ), *United States*

1948   The Prize was not awarded in that year; two-thirds of the prize money was allocated to the Special Funds of the Committee and one-third to the Main Fund of the Nobel Foundation.

1949   Lord John Boyd Orr of Brechin (1880–1971), *Great Britain*

1950   Ralph Johnson Bunche (1904–1971), *United States*

1951   Léon Jouhaux (1879–1954), *France*

1952   The Prize was reserved in that year and in 1953 was awarded to: Albert Schweitzer (1875–1965), *France*

1953   George Catlett Marshall (1880–1959), *United States*

1954   The Prize was reserved in that year and in 1955 was awarded to: The Office of the United Nations High Commissioner for Refugees (1951–   )

1955   The Prize was reserved in that year and in 1956 two-thirds of the prize money was allocated to the Special Funds of the Committee and one-third to the Main Fund of the Nobel Foundation.

1956   The Prize was reserved in that year and in 1957 two-thirds of the prize money was allocated to the Special Funds of the Committee and one-third to the Main Fund of the Nobel Foundation.

1957   Lester Bowles Pearson (1897–   ), *Canada*

1958   Georges Pire (1910–1969), *Belgium*

1959   Philip John Noel-Baker (1889–   ), *Great Britain*

1960   The Prize was reserved in that year and in 1961 was awarded to: Albert John Lutuli (1898?–1967), *Union of South Africa*

1961   Dag Hjalmar Agne Carl Hammarskjöld (1905–1961), *Sweden*

1962   The Prize was reserved in that year and in 1963 was awarded to: Linus Carl Pauling (1901–   ), *United States*

1963   The International Committee of the Red Cross (1863–   ); and The League of Red Cross Societies (1919–   )

1964   Martin Luther King, Jr. (1929–1968), *United States*

1965   The United Nations Children's Fund (1946–   )

1966   The Prize was reserved in that year and in 1967 two-thirds of the prize money was allocated to the Special Funds of the Committee and one-third to the Main Fund of the Nobel Foundation.

1967   The Prize was reserved in that year and in 1968 two-thirds of the prize money was allocated to the Special Funds of the Committee and one-third to the Main Fund of the Nobel Foundation.

1968   René-Samuel Cassin (1887–   ), *France*

1969   The International Labor Organization (1919–   )

1970   Norman Ernest Borlaug (1914–   ), *United States*

Appendix B

Summary of Awards (1901–1970):
Laureates by Nationality; Organizations Honored

Country	Name and Year	Number
Argentina	Saavedra Lamas (1936)	1
Austria	Suttner (1905), Fried (1911)	2
Belgium	Beernaert (1909), La Fontaine (1913), Pire (1958)	3
Canada	Pearson (1957)	1
Denmark	Bajer (1908)	1
France	Passy (1901), Renault (1907), d'Estournelles de Constant (1909), Bourgeois (1920), Briand (1926), Buisson (1927), Jouhaux (1951), Schweitzer (1952), Cassin (1968)	9
Germany	Stresemann (1926), Quidde (1927), Ossietzky (1935)	3
Great Britain	Cremer (1903), Chamberlain (1925), Angell (1933), Henderson (1934), Cecil (1937), Boyd Orr (1949), Noel-Baker (1959)	7
Italy	Moneta (1907)	1
The Netherlands	Asser (1911)	1
Norway	Lange (1921), Nansen (1922)	2
Sweden	Arnoldson (1908), Branting (1921), Söderblom (1930), Hammarskjöld (1961)	4
Switzerland	Dunant (1901), Ducommun (1902), Gobat (1902)	3
Union of South Africa	Lutuli (1960)	1
United States	Roosevelt (1906), Root (1912), Wilson (1919), Dawes (1925), Kellogg (1929), Addams (1931), Butler (1931), Hull (1945), Balch (1946), Mott (1946), Bunche (1950), Marshall (1953), Pauling (1962), King (1964), Borlaug (1970)	15

Total number of individual awards 54

Organizations Institute of International Law (1904), International Peace Bureau (1910), International Committee of the Red Cross (1917), Nansen International Office for Refugees (1938), International Committee of the Red Cross (1944), American Friends Service Committee (1947), Friends Service Council (1947), Office of the UN High Commissioner for Refugees (1954), International Committee of the Red Cross (1963), League of Red Cross Societies (1963), United Nations Children's Fund (1965), International Labor Organization (1969)

Total number of organizational awards 12
(Ten different organizations)

Grand total of awards (1910–1970) 66

Awards not made 1914, 1915, 1916, 1918, 1923, 1924, 1928, 1932, 1939, 1940, 1941, 1942, 1943, 1948, 1955, 1956, 1966, 1967 18